Competition, Monopoly and Corporate Governance

Competition, Monopoly and Corporate Governance

Essays in Honour of Keith Cowling

Edited by

Michael Waterson

Professor of Economics, University of Warwick, UK

Edward Elgar
Cheltenham, UK • Northampton, MA, USA

Published by
Edward Elgar Publishing Limited
Glensanda House
Montpellier Parade
Cheltenham
Glos GL50 1UA
UK

Edward Elgar Publishing, Inc.
136 West Street
Suite 202
Northampton
Massachusetts 01060
USA

A catalogue record for this book
is available from the British Library

Library of Congress Cataloguing in Publication Data

Competition, monopoly, and corporate governance : essays in honour of
Keith Cowling / edited by Michael Waterson.
 p. cm.
 1. International economic relations. 2. Globalization—Economic aspects.
3. Globalization—Social aspects. 4. Technological innovations—Economic
aspects. 5. Competition, International. I. Cowling, Keith II. Waterson,
Michael, 1950–

HF1359.C673 2003
337—dc22   2003049259

ISBN 1 84376 089 4

Printed and bound in Great Britain by MPG Books Ltd, Bodmin, Cornwall

Contents

v

PART III   CORPORATE GOVERNANCE, MERGERS AND THE EVOLUTION OF INDUSTRIAL STRUCTURE

Contributors

John Cable, University of Wales Aberystwyth
Alessandra Canepa, University of Warwick
Dan Coffey, University of Leeds
Martin J. Conyon, The Wharton School, University of Pennsylvania
Paul A. Geroski, London Business School and Competition Commission
Sourafel Girma, Nottingham University Business School
Tim Hazledine, University of Auckland
Dennis Leech, University of Warwick
M. Mazzucato, Open University
Claire Morris, Office of Fair Trading
Dennis C. Mueller, University of Vienna
Robin A. Naylor, University of Warwick
Michael Shattock, London Institute of Education
Paul Stoneman, University of Warwick
Roger Sugden, University of Birmingham
Steve Thompson, Nottingham University Business School
Philip R. Tomlinson, University of Bath
Michael Waterson, University of Warwick
Peter W. Wright, University of Nottingham

Introduction

Keith Cowling has undoubtedly had a very large influence on economics, and industrial economics in particular, over his long (and continuing) career as an academic researcher and teacher. The two principal vehicles through which his influence has been felt are his published writings and his PhD students, although it would be remiss not to mention for example his role in the development of the European Association for Research in Industrial Economics, the *International Journal of Industrial Organization* and, more recently, the European Union Network for Industrial Policy. These two major influences provide the framework for the present tribute volume, since the set of contributors invited was drawn from those who have co-written with Keith and those (sometimes the same individuals) who have been his PhD students. Here I must enter a caveat – so far as I am aware no complete listing of Keith's PhD students exists. Thus it is entirely possible that I have omitted to ask someone who would qualify and who would have wanted to make a contribution. If so, I apologise to these individuals. Also of course, there were people who would have contributed but were unable to do so within the time available. Nevertheless, it is pleasing how many people have engaged with the substantial amount of work involved and so contributed to a significant volume in honour of Keith.

The volume has three parts covering three broad themes, each associated with a particular strand of Keith's own writings and each represented by four chapters. First, there is internationalisation, trans-nationalism and technical change. Then there is monopoly, oligopoly and social welfare. The final part relates to corporate governance, mergers and the evolution of industrial structure. Naturally, there is some overlap between the themes. In addition, I felt it important to note Keith's long association with the University of Warwick, spanning more than 30 years, so I am very pleased that Michael Shattock, sometime Registrar of the University and an old colleague (and adversary!) of Keith's has contributed a chapter on this. Indeed, is interesting to note some parallels between this and Roger Sugden's chapter, which relate to Keith's views about what a university should be. Keith has also provided a listing of his academic papers.

I would like to thank Roger Sugden in particular for useful discussions regarding this project, also to thank Gill Pearce and Margaret Nash for their assistance in assembling the collection.

This book is dedicated, posthumously, to two of Keith's former PhD students who clearly could not contribute but who certainly would have been asked – Simon Domberger and Ian Molho.

Michael Waterson
University of Warwick

PART I

Internationalisation, trans-nationalism and technical change

1. Coordination and hierarchy in the Japanese firm: the strategic decision-making approach vs. Aoki

Dan Coffey and Philip R. Tomlinson

1. INTRODUCTION

Throughout his academic career, Keith Cowling has been concerned with the increasing concentration of economic power and, in particular, its implications for the wider public interest. This is perhaps best illustrated in his 1982 book, *Monopoly Capitalism*, in which he extends Baran and Sweezy's (1966) seminal contribution to argue that the increasing monopolisation of capitalist economies is likely to lead to greater economic instability and stagnation.[1] This framework was developed subsequently to encompass the activities of the transnational corporation, in close collaboration with Roger Sugden (see Cowling and Sugden, 1987), an undertaking which sparked a critical reappraisal of the orthodox (Coasian) theory of the firm. In this and subsequent work Keith Cowling has emphasised the problem posed by the hierarchical nature of the modern corporation, where strategic decisions are taken in the boardrooms of large firms by corporate elites, able and willing to override the objections of other affected parties. Strategic decisions in this sense are those that affect the broad direction of the firm and hence the determination of a series of economic variables, such as the level and intended location of investment, employment, and output. When corporate elites take strategic decisions that conflict with the broader interests of a society, the social 'optimum' is necessarily breached. With no available market mechanism to redress the balance, the outcome is one of 'strategic failure' from the viewpoint of affected interests as a whole (see Cowling and Sugden, 1987, 1994, 1998). One case in point is the Japanese economy, where the global activities of Japan's large transnational corporations have precipitated and exacerbated a 'hollowing out' of Japanese industry, leading to the spectre of strategic failure (see Cowling and Tomlinson, 2000, 2002, 2003).

The strategic decision-making approach to industrial organisation evolved from initial dissatisfaction over the Coasian view of the firm, expressed in a critique subsequently extended to include Williamson's (1975, 1985) framework (see Cowling and Sugden, 1987, 1998).[2] The Coasian perspective is that internal direction within the firm *replaces* the market mechanism as a means of coordinating production activities, at the point where the net savings from a reduction in the costs of transacting through markets makes this the economically preferred option. The firm is defined so that its boundaries are reached where market exchange begins, while the emphasis on net cost reductions naturally suggests a Pareto-efficient outcome. Williamson's development of the Coasian perspective draws a similar distinction between 'markets' and 'hierarchies', and he similarly emphasises economising upon transactions costs as integral to industrial organisation. For Cowling and Sugden, however, the boundaries of the firm are more properly regarded as being determined by the locus of its strategic decision making. For example, a large corporation can elect to subcontract some of its production activities, but it remains the strategic decision maker controlling those activities: the boundaries of this firm might thus be viewed as extending to include the activities of its sub-contractors.[3] This leads to a definition of the firm as 'the means of coordinating production from one centre of strategic decision making' (Cowling and Sugden, 1998, p. 67), a perspective in which economic power governs decisions on issues such as a firm's governance structure, rather than the pursuit and attainment of Pareto-efficient outcomes.

In the strategic decision-making approach, corporations are viewed as hierarchical entities. This seems an eminently reasonable position to take given the apparent dominance of large (often transnational) corporations in the modern world where control is often concentrated among corporate elites. In the course of their review of the literature pertaining to the firm, however, Cowling and Sugden (1998, pp. 78–9) note the attempts by Aoki (1990) (amongst others) to develop a model of the Japanese firm (the J-mode) in which the emphasis is placed upon a so-called non-hierarchical mode of production and coordination.[4] In a defence of their own position, Cowling and Sugden insist that the strategic decision-making approach retains its validity, since in the case of the J-mode, as expounded by Aoki, a firm's strategic decisions are still made by a corporate elite; at the same time, however, they nonetheless appear to accept Aoki's account of a new organisational paradigm.

While this may appear a reasonable response, our main objective in this chapter is to suggest that Aoki's position can and should be challenged at a more fundamental level. To do so we reappraise two of the core claims made about the historical novelty of Japanese organisational forms and achievements. First, we observe that a purported organisational break-through in the sphere of 'flexible' manufacture, which Aoki cites as both illustration and proof of the novelty of the J-mode, is not empirically grounded – it is based upon premises that are historically counterfactual. Second, we show that an application *of* the strategic decision-making framework *to* a reappraisal of the evidence on relationships between Japanese firms and their subcontractors suggests that activities are coordinated along lines which are at least as hierarchical as those in the West. Both sets of issues are appraised through an assessment of evidence for the car manufacture and assembly sector, which is both a source for many of Aoki's key illustrations, and an inspiration for much of the wider literature on Japanese firms upon which his work draws. Finally, since this part of the discussion raises points that are particularly relevant in the context of recent debate(s) on the current problems afflicting the Japanese economy, we consider some wider implications.

2. FLEXIBILITY AND THE J-MODE

Perhaps the most striking claim advanced by Aoki – and the most obviously problematic – concerns the issue of process 'flexibility' for manufacturing operations (see Coffey, 2001). The particular dimension with which we are concerned is the ability of an individual factory unit to process a large mix of differentiated products using the same equipment. According to Aoki, one characteristic of what he calls the J-mode of organisation is that it is characterised by production principles and methods that enhance the ability of the adopting firm to produce a 'wide-selection'[5] of different specifications of product using a single integrated set of production facilities. In the exemplary case of the car manufacture and assembly sector, for example, Aoki (1990, pp. 4–5) cites the ability of Toyota Motor Corporation to offer customers a substantive mix of model specifications as evidence of the emergence of a new paradigm in manufacturing. The explicit assumption Aoki makes both here and elsewhere (see, for example, Aoki, 1988, p. 20), is that the ability of car manufacturers to build many different specifications of car on a single assembly line constitutes a relatively recent phenomenon – led from Japan – which is indicative of an underlying shift in the organising principles of manufacturing. Conversely, he assumes that factories organised along 'traditional' Western lines, prior to the emergence of the J-mode, were essentially 'Fordist' in character, and were limited to volume replication of more or less homogeneous products. On this basis Aoki attempts to construct a model of information flows based on a descriptive account of Toyota's production system, which is formally modelled and critiqued in Coffey (2001). In this chapter, however, we are concerned with the basic empirical claim regarding product variety.

An analogous claim is advanced by Asanuma (1994), who suggests that, in the car manufacture and assembly sector, the 'flexibility' of production processes (in this sense) evolved as follows. Following the pioneering efforts of Henry Ford with the Ford Model T, the 'classical example of mass production of a single standardized product', the product diversification strategy of Alfred Sloan and General Motors led to the production of separately built and individually badged models – like the Chevrolet, Pontiac, or Buick – aimed at specific market segments (Asanuma, p. 121). Decades later, car assemblers, led by Japanese producers, and in particular Toyota, learned how to offer customers increasing diversity by offering 'orderable variations' within individual car lines. Offering 'orderable variations' in turn involves building a mix of model specifications on a single assembly line, differing in features like body, engine, colour, or various options. However, the generally agreed date at which Toyota launched its first 'full line' of cars, with a wide selection of specifications following local experimentation with consignment assemblers, is 1966 (see Shiomi, 1995). The accuracy of this schematic – as with Aoki's assumptions about the industry – therefore requires that the advent of 'flexible' assembly systems in the car manufacture and assembly sector be dated to the mid-1960s.

The obvious, and in fact decisive, objection on this point is that this is not so. For instance, consider the following comment from a history of the (American) car industry:

> The assembly of motor vehicles has come a long way since Henry Ford's pioneering days at Highland Park. The customer for the 1950s could choose among engines, body styles, colors for both exterior and interior, and even hubcaps. He could designate what he wanted in the way of accessories – radio, heater, air-conditioner, for instance – and the car combining his preferences would roll off the assembly line in company with others representing different assortment of choices. (Rae, 1965, p. 200)

This statement appears a year before Toyota's first ventures into flexible assembly. Clearly, the notion that assemblers had to wait until the mid-1960s before offering prospective customers a mix of specifications falls someway short of the mark. In fact 'orderable variations' within individual car lines began to play a major role in the marketing campaigns, and in the factory organisation, of American firms from the start of the post-World War II era, as abundantly evidenced in contemporaneous commentary:

> Last year a Yale University physicist calculated that since Chevy offered 46 models, 32 engines, 20 transmissions, 21 colors (plus nine two-tone combinations), and more than 400 accessories and options, the number of different cars that a Chevrolet customer conceivably could order was greater than the number of atoms in the universe. This seemingly would put General Motors one notch

higher than God in the chain of command. This year, even though the standard Chevrolet never accounts for less than two-thirds of Chevy's sales, Chevy is offering still more models (a total of 50), and options, indicating that while they may not be increasing their lead over Ford, they are pulling away from God. (White, 1971, p. 189)

The 'year' in which this calculation was supposedly made was again 1965: one year before Toyota's first launch of a 'full line' of cars. In this sphere, Toyota was a laggard, not a leader.

Much ink could be spent establishing this point but, pending serious argument with reasoned evidence to the contrary, we draw the obvious inference.[6] A key assumption underpinning and illustrating Aoki's thesis, namely that Japan evolved a J-mode of production in car manufacture and assembly that led the break from 'Fordist' mass production,[7] is invalid. The implications quite generally are considerable. It has been asserted, for example, that 'flexible' manufacture of the type Aoki attributes to the J-mode firm, will act as a limiting factor in curtailing the globalising propensities of large transnational corporations, on the creative grounds that the sort of complex supply logistics evolved in the age of 'Fordism' are less viable in the age of Toyota: this is the position taken in Dicken (1998, pp. 165–72), a standard text on the global geography of production. While a full study of how it is done might be illuminating, the fact of the matter is that the global supply networks of large Western firms, in car manufacture and assembly, evolved *precisely* in the context of 'flexible' assembly of a very large number of alternate product specifications.[8] We will return to this issue in Section 4.

3. VERTICAL RELATIONS AND THE J-MODE

We may further assess the relative merits of the 'J-mode' as a depiction of the 'Japanese' firm by considering the relations that exist in the management of vertical supply chains. Aoki contends that the supposed advantages in 'flexibility' accruing to Japanese firms like Toyota are a corollary to, or a reflex of, a less hierarchical mode of coordination. Aoki contends that this is demonstrated both externally, in the relationships between firms, and internally, in the relationships between managers and workers. For present purposes we will consider only the first of these sets of relationships, since by focusing upon perceptions of the form and function of the *subcontracting arrangements* that are a widespread feature of Japanese manufacturing, we can apply Cowling and Sugden's strategic decision-making approach in a very direct way to an assessment of the empirical support for Aoki's claims. We take as our example once more the car-assembly sector, which is (again) the most cited example of Japanese industrial organisation.

If the general picture of Japanese manufacture which informs most commentaries is that production is organised through *keiretsu* networks, with intermediate goods and services supplied through an extensive system of vertical sub-contracting, the Japanese automobile industry has the largest and widest number of *keiretsu* linkages. For example, Dodwell (1997, p. 6) reports more than 10000 materials producers and other subcontractors servicing approximately 1400 component suppliers, and 11 car assemblers, in a pyramidal structure.[9] The descriptive assumptions often made about this sector are that it has been vertically disintegrated to a degree that marks its development as qualitatively distinct from historical patterns in the West, and that in their dealings with suppliers the large Japanese car assemblers contrive to maintain more cooperative relationships, based upon 'trust' and characterised by a (relatively) 'free exchange' of information. What we wish to show is that by applying the strategic decision-making approach to the same evidence it is both possible and plausible to arrive at a quite different set of conclusions.

In the first instance, while statistics confirm the widespread use of subcontracting in the Japanese automobile industry, the measured degree of vertical integration is sensitive to the ownership thresholds chosen by the analyst making the calculation. The best exposition of this point remains the important study by Cusumano (1985). On a narrow definition of 'inhouse' manufacture, and based upon the ratio of internal manufacturing and other operating costs to net sales revenue, vertical integration at Toyota and Nissan for the period 1979–83 was on average 28 per cent and 26 per cent respectively, compared to 43 per cent for GM (for 1979), 36 per cent for Ford (for 1979), and 32 per cent for Chrysler (for the whole period), a clear, although not huge, difference. However, these were the results calculated for a 50 per cent minimum threshold for manufacturers' equity in a supplier: when this threshold was changed to 20 per cent, the degree of integration rose sharply for the Japanese firms, to 74 per cent for Toyota and 73 per cent for Nissan, on which basis these latter could be viewed as belonging to groups which were *more* vertically integrated than GM, Ford, or Chrysler (Cusumano, p. 190). The selection of a 20 per cent threshold in this regard may be particularly apt, since it represents the degree of shareholding argued by Berle and Means (1932) to indicate effective control.[10] This takes us to the second point: it is effective control which is central to Cowling and Sugden's framework, and on this basis the images sometimes conjured by the depiction of the Japanese firm as a 'vertically de-integrated entity' (Ruigrok and van Tulder, 1995, p. 39) are somewhat misleading. If what we are interested in is the degree of real control a car assembler has over the direct management of its suppliers' activities, then in addition to equity holdings in *keiretsu* partners, due account must also be taken of other control levers, as for example the placing of former senior employees in commanding positions throughout the supply chain. At the very least, the contrast is overdone.

A particularly vivid example of the consequences of studying the boundaries of the firm from the viewpoint of strategic decision making and control can be constructed through a reappraisal of the findings of Womack et al. (1990) on the Japanese supply chain. This very influential contribution (see Coffey, 2003)[11] is one of the surveys which Cowling and Sugden (1998, p. 79) identify and accept as providing support for Aoki's thesis on the J-mode, and it contrasts North American with Japanese modes of managing supply chains in a way which *appears* at first glance to be consistent with Aoki's suppositions about the H-mode firm (Western) and J-mode (Japanese).[12] American assemblers are depicted as having relied historically either upon vertical integration or arms-length, short-term contracts, focusing upon price, quality, and regularity of supply. Little is said about 'in-house' divisions; however, where components are 'bought out', American suppliers are said to have been typically excluded from the core design process for components, and selected through a competitive bidding process in which tendering is exclusively concerned with winning the contract to make and deliver items with already determined specifications: only at the prototype stage is the supplier involved with some 'fine-tuning' of design, and even afterwards there would still be the possibility that a rival could undercut to win the contract for final production. The supplier would typically shield information on production costs from the assembler, retaining sole responsibility for operations behind its own factory gates. Against this, Womack et al. describe the Japanese system as one where vertical integration is relied upon a great deal less extensively than in the West, and where assemblers involve their suppliers from the outset of the design process for components, while suppliers cooperate in providing information on production costs to the assembler. According to the authors, this is both qualitatively distinct and conducive to a more efficient outcome (see Womack et al. especially pp. 139–53).

Let us now assess the evidence presented by Womack et al. as it stands with respect to Aoki's thesis, but from a viewpoint that approaches assembler–supplier relations from the perspective of dominance in strategic decision making. We have already noted that the comparative degree of vertical integration depends upon the ownership threshold selected by the analyst. So far as close cooperation in component design with suppliers is concerned, the first point to note is that devolved responsibilities fall to *first-tier suppliers*, precisely those suppliers in which the assembler is likely (as highlighted in Cusumano and Dodwell above) to hold a significant ownership stake, supplemented by other control measures. Even so, Womack et al. acknowledge that cooperation in design activity with first-tier suppliers still does not extend to 'parts considered vital to the success of the car' (ibid., p. 147), such as engines, transmissions, major body panels, or electronic management systems. This last point is consistent with subsequent surveys of the Japanese auto industry, like Dodwell (1997), which confirms that assemblers prefer to retain control of the manufacture of strategic components of this type, notwithstanding their ownership of equity in first-tier suppliers. The involvement of Japanese first-tier suppliers in detail design activity is therefore concentrated in, and confined to, what Womack et al. (p. 143) elsewhere call 'commodity parts', rather than 'complex and technologically advanced' components. The transfer of responsibilities for some design activity to first-tier suppliers carefully avoids transfer of 'proprietary technologies' (p. 147).

This is the situation as it pertains to *design*, for 'non-vital' parts. So far as *manufacture* is concerned, Japanese assemblers, according to Womack et al., rely upon multiple-sourcing of production to a *far* greater extent than their North American competitors: they report that for Japan (their data is for 1990) just over 12 per cent of parts were single-sourced by assemblers, compared to almost 70 per cent in America (see ibid., p.157). It should again be emphasized that this refers to the situation for *first*-tier suppliers.[13] As noted above, one of the comments Womack et al. make about North American supply chain management is that a supplier involved in 'fine-tuning' design on a component part specification could still lose the final contract, although the suggestion is also that this would be an extreme case. Since in Japan, however, they find that some production is always given to first-tier suppliers with *no* prior involvement in design (via multiple-sourcing), it might well be the case that, on the basis of their data, production *solely* to given specification is a more prevalent phenomenon in Japan than in America, measured upon the volume of work. Moreover, the (principal) reason given for Japanese multiple-sourcing is one of crime and punishment: they observe, approvingly, that a marginal shift in the allocation of work between 'two or more' first-tier suppliers by a firm like Toyota can have a 'devastating effect' on profitability, thereby providing the assembler with a mechanism by which to inflict 'punishment' (Womak et al., p. 154). The reason for the efficacy of this method of discipline, they also explain, is that the assembler jointly plans the supplier's *production schedules* and *capacity* so that it just 'breaks even', with an agreed margin for profit, at the volume of work the assembler plans to give it (ibid., p. 154).

The conclusions that could be drawn from this, while consistent with Cowling and Sugden's strategic decision-making approach to the firm, are not consistent with Aoki's depiction of the J-mode as both qualitatively distinct and less hierarchical than 'Western' corporate forms. From a strategic decision-making perspective the *first*-tier suppliers might be regarded as an effective extension of the assembler's own production and design capacity: if we accept this for the sake of argument, then how different is the behaviour of the Japanese assembler from its Western counterpart? On the basis of the evidence gathered in Womack et al., the most obvious observation would be that the Japanese 'strategic decision maker' (assembler central office) treats its competing 'divisions' (first-tier suppliers) in a singularly 'top-down' way: withholding information on 'proprietary technologies', combined with multiple-sourcing of production, gives credibility to a permanent threat of 'termination' supplemented with occasional 'punishment' (Womack et al., p. 154). The direct involvement of the assembler in planning supplier capacity, an arrangement which is not reciprocated, leaves little doubt as to the locus of control, or the limited autonomy it allows.

In part, this is precisely what Womack et al. applaud. Although Cowling and Sugden do tend to treat contributions like Aoki (1990), Womack et al. (1990), or Leibenstein (1987), as variants on a theme, a careful scrutiny finds that despite similarities of interest and language, the underlying conceptual structures of the analyses are frequently disparate (see Coffey, 2003). For Womack et al., reference to 'cooperation' does not, for example, imply a situation involving 'trust' in the sense that the word engenders in Leibenstein's game-theoretic framework. For Leibenstein, a cooperative equilibrium implies a situation where two parties in a potentially conflictual arrangement each gains by 'trusting' the other not to 'cheat' on an existing set of mutual obligations and reciprocities: for Womack et al. (1990, p. 155) the whole point of the Japanese system of supply chain management is that the 'rules of the game' are so constructed as to make 'trust' unnecessary; the supplier has *no* rational alternative strategy.[14] There are similar divergences from Aoki: for example, Womack et al. (pp. 158–9) criticise American (and European) firms for leaving their businesses open to the threat of trade union activity by single-sourcing supplies, and they approve of multiple-sourcing in Japan because it mitigates this threat. This suspicion of the workers, as well as the description of assembler–supplier relationships, is not consistent with the view of the J-mode advanced by Aoki (non-hierarchical), but it is easily reconciled, and instantly recognisable as an underlying structure of relationships, regardless of surface form, from the viewpoint of the strategic decision-making framework advanced by Cowling and Sugden. On this last point it is worth noting that while Womack et al. contrast the 'short-term' contracts of American suppliers (actually 3 to 5 years) with the 'long-term' relationship between Japanese assemblers and first-tier suppliers, if like is compared with like (that is contracts with contracts and 'relationships' with 'relationships'), and if the 'in-house' supply divisions of American firms are accorded a similar status to the first-tier suppliers of Japanese firms, it is difficult to see any evidence of a 'longer view' in Japan.

4.   GLOBALISATION AND THE J-MODE

The preceding analysis is particularly relevant when considering the effects of globalisation upon the Japanese economy and, in particular, the genuine concerns about the 'hollowing out' of Japanese industry. In recent years, Japan's large transnational corporations have begun to integrate their production activities on a global scale through the development of their own transnational supply networks. Indeed, since the early 1980s, Japanese transnationals have, in the aggregate, invested approximately $500 billion in establishing such overseas affiliates (Cowling and Tomlinson, 2000, p. F370). According to Cowling and Tomlinson (2000, 2002 and 2003), the subsequent growth in the global outsourcing of production has been at the expense of domestic (Japanese) industry, thus precipitating and exacerbating a 'hollowing out' of Japan's industrial base; a clear case of 'strategic failure'.

Yet, as we mentioned in Section 2, the theory of 'flexible' production, which underpins Aoki's J-mode firm, implies that Japanese industry should have been predominantly immune to the globalising activities of the economy's large transnationals. The argument often proffered is that since, under 'Toyotism' (*vis-à-vis* 'Fordism'), customers are offered a wider selection of products, there is a requirement that production is 'highly localised' in content so as to facilitate the smooth 'flow' of inputs from upstream suppliers to their assemblers. In contrast, a global outsourcing strategy (as employed by Western assemblers) is only regarded as being viable when the overall quantity of units demanded is large relative to the number of varieties offered, because otherwise accurate delivery schedules for the parts to be supplied to the assembly plant cannot be drawn up in advance of demand.[15] The problem with this argument is twofold. First, as we noted earlier, the premise that the Japanese were innovators in the sphere of 'flexible' assembly and offer a wider variety of products than their Western rivals is itself an historical counterfactual. Western assemblers have long used their transnational supply chains to outsource components in conjunction with the flexible assembly of a large variety of models. Given the problems of de-industrialisation that has often been attributed to the activities of transnationals in the West (see, for instance, Cowling and Sugden, 1987), there is no logical reason to suggest that the forces of globalisation should affect Japanese industry any differently (see Coffey and Tomlinson, 2003; Coffey, 2001, 2003).

Secondly, and related to this latter point, Cowling and Tomlinson (2000, pp. F370–79) provide a substantive body of evidence to suggest that the 'hollowing out' of Japan is actually quite severe. Their evidence suggests that there has been a significant diversion of output, new investment and employment away from Japan's industrial regions in favour of overseas affiliates. As a result, Japan's domestic small firm sector – which employs over 80 per cent of Japanese workers – has become increasingly isolated and is now in a more vulnerable bargaining position *vis-à-vis* its main contractors. This latter fact is reflected in Japanese small firms experiencing a 33 per cent decline in procurement rates and approximately a 40 per cent fall in profits between 1985 and 1996, while small firm business failures and bankruptcy rates rose to 'unprecedented post-Second War levels' (Cowling and Tomlinson, pp. F373–5). In the aggregate, these trends have contributed to higher unemployment and economic stagnation in Japan.

The growth in Japanese global outsourcing appears to have been driven by a quest to acquire lower labour costs via control over an international division of labour.[16] Japan's transnationals have primarily achieved this through establishing transnational production networks – sometimes referred to as the *new keiretsu* – which consist of their own affiliates and those of acknowledged suppliers in various locations around the globe. This *new keiretsu* provides Japan's transnationals with greater transparency in comparing and monitoring their international production costs, while the increasing ease with which Japan's transnationals can switch production from one global site to another provides them with greater bargaining power in their relationship with an international labour force. In many cases, it is merely the credible threat of relocating production within the *new keiretsu* that is sufficient to reduce labour militancy and depress their international labour costs. Cowling and Sugden (1994) describe such a strategy as 'divide and rule'.[17]

The 'divide and rule' activities of Japan's transnational corporations are explored further in Tomlinson (2001). Through direct interviews and a questionnaire survey of Managing Directors of Japanese First Tier auto-suppliers based in the UK, Tomlinson investigated the nature of business relationships between these supplier affiliates and their main (Japanese) assemblers. On the issue of the pricing of the assemblers' input components, Tomlinson (2001) found that prices were predominantly determined by a policy of 'target pricing'. For a particular component, the UK affiliate was typically set a 'target' price by the assembler and/or its parent. This target price was based upon the lowest price attained by one of the supplier's affiliates within the transnational network – with some consideration in the target price being made for ancillary costs, such as for transportation. Although occasionally assemblers offered 'assistance' to supplier affiliates to reduce costs and meet target prices, the general principle was that a failure to the reach the stated target price resulted in a lost contract. The beneficiary of the lost contract was rarely a competitor supplier, but a rival affiliate within the assembler's transnational network. For Tomlinson (2001), the extent of intra-firm competition within these transnational networks was evidence that Japanese automotive transnationals had adopted and implemented the 'divide and rule' strategy.[18] This is materially similar to the situation described by Womack et al. (above) for Japan, where the 'punishment' inflicted by assemblers on erring first-tier suppliers (by a shift of work to competing first-tier suppliers) would be occasioned by a failure to adhere to agreed price, quality, or delivery.[19]

At the industry level, Tomlinson (2002) also finds that the pursuit of lower foreign wages – by Japan's transnationals – has had a real effect upon the behaviour of both investment and employment within Japan's domestic machinery sector; a sector dominated by Japanese transnationals. Using a standard neo-classical domestic production function – which is then augmented with relevant foreign wage variables to reflect the attractiveness of alternative sites of production *vis-à-vis* Japan – Tomlinson employs a simultaneous equations estimator to estimate a series of investment and employment equations for five machinery industry sub-sectors. In each case, he finds that the behaviour of both investment and employment in Japan are highly sensitive to changes in relative international wage costs. The results not only highlight the real effects of globalisation upon Japan's machinery sector, but they also indicate the extent to which (Japanese) transnationals have integrated their global production activities and the substitutability of international production. Moreover, Tomlinson's (2001, 2002) research results appear particularly pertinent in the light of our earlier discussion on the J-mode firm and the inference that the geography of production within Japanese industry is 'highly localised' in content. This latter premise does not appear empirically grounded.

5.   CONCLUDING COMMENTS

There can be little doubt that Keith Cowling has made several seminal contributions to the field of industrial economics. In particular, his research into the increasing concentration of economic power and concerns about the potential abuse thereof (with its adverse consequences for regional and national economies) have provided those economists who have become disaffected with the unrealistic assumptions and perceived (Pareto) outcomes of the competitive neoclassical model with an alternative framework by which to examine industry structures and make inferences about the direction of industrial policy. Over the past two decades this has been amply exemplified in the strategic decision-making approach to industrial organisation; a framework that Keith has developed jointly with Roger Sugden.

In this chapter, we have considered the strategic decision-making approach in the light of Aoki's (1990) account of Japanese firms, the so-called J-mode. There is an obvious dissonance between the strategic decision-making approach, with its emphasis upon the concentration of economic power within corporate hierarchies, and the predictions of Aoki's model, where J-mode firms are categorised as being non-hierarchical entities and quite distinct from their Western counterparts. However, a closer examination of the nature of Japanese industrial organisation suggests that such perceived differences in Western and Japanese organisational forms are superficial. For instance, the J-mode is underpinned by the assumption that Japanese manufacturers (specifically auto-manufacturers) were novel in attaining 'flexibility' in production processes. As we have shown, this claim is historically incorrect since, in the sphere of 'flexible' manufacture, the Japanese car industry – as typified by Toyota – was a laggard and not a leader. Similarly, when considering the nature of vertical relationships within the Japanese car industry, the evidence suggests that production is coordinated along highly hierarchical lines. Indeed, whether considering the degree of vertical integration or the lines of effective control in the Japanese car industry, it appears that the strategic decision-making approach retains its validity: control is exercised from one centre of strategic decision making. Consequently, we reject Aoki's position and argue that it cannot be relied upon as an accurate account of Japanese firms.

Our analysis strengthens the case for the application of the strategic decision-making approach developed by Cowling and Sugden to Japanese industrial organisation; from this perspective apparent differences in structure and conduct from Western modes of operation appear of secondary importance compared to the underlying similarities in motive and function. It is also particularly relevant in the context of the recent problems that have afflicted the Japanese economy, particularly those posed by the globalising activities of Japan's large transnationals. Whereas the implications of the J-mode model suggest that Japanese industry should be relatively unaffected by the forces of globalisation, the reality is that Japan's recent experiences suggest otherwise. As Cowling and Tomlinson (2000, 2002 and 2003) have argued, the growth in Japanese transnational production networks and the adoption of 'divide and rule' strategies by Japan's large transnationals have had an adverse effect upon Japan's recent economic performance. The subsequent 'hollowing out' of Japanese industry is a clear example of 'strategic failure' (Cowling and Tomlinson, 2000). Finally, this all leads, of course, to the question of how to address the problems of 'strategic failure' that seem to be endemic within modern capitalist economies, such as Japan. It is beyond the scope of this chapter to consider such possible policy proposals in further detail. However, it is no surprise to note that, in recent years, Keith Cowling has himself taken a leading role in considering and developing a range of policy directives, which include a new defined role for industrial policy and state strategic planning.

NOTES

1. The basic premise in *Monopoly Capitalism* (see Cowling, 1982) is that a rise in industrial concentration has fundamental implications for prices, distribution, and demand. As concentration grows in any given sector the (output-weighted) average mark-up of price over marginal cost will rise as a consequence of the increase (*per se*) in concentration, more effective collusion between firms, and any change in the elasticity of demand for the industry's product brought about as a consequence of the advertising expenditures of the industry's incumbent firms. At an aggregate level, this rise in the degree of monopoly has distributional consequences, as a growth in the size of the potential surplus which firms are able to generate is corollary to a reduction in the relative income share of workers. The result, however, may be economic crisis and a tendency towards stagnation as firms are unable to 'realise' this potential surplus through actual sales: this is a consequence of problems of effective demand created by the fall in the income share of workers, who constitute the principal consumer group. Among the many striking applications of this framework is the finding that an increase in the exposure of a national economy to foreign competition can actually serve to increase monopoly, and so to further reduce the relative income of workers.
2. Anticipations of the strategic-decision making approach can also be found in Cowling (1982), where the view is expressed that transnational corporations could progressively develop as organisations controlling key aspects of product design and ownership, and subcontracting everything else: this in turn might tend to mask the real degree of corporate monopoly if analysts relied on a conventional definition of the firm.
3. One of the examples offered is of production at Benetton and its subcontractors: these latter should be viewed as an extension of Benetton, since the former is the strategic decision maker for their activities.
4. Aoki distinguishes between non-hierarchical relations in production activities, and rank-hierarchies in the status and remuneration of employees. This chapter deals only with the former. Subsequent references to 'non-hierarchical' structures or outcomes should therefore be read with this in mind.
5. This term is from Shiomi (1995).
6. In an interesting commentary on the quality of the historical observations underpinning Womack et al. (1990), a contribution which we discuss in the next section, Lyddon (1996) provides some interesting examples of past 'flexibility' and 'variety' in this industry that make much the same point.
7. It is perhaps worth noting that in Aoki's analysis there is more than a suggestion that this 'break', and the emergence (as he sees it) of the J-mode, represents not only a paradigm shift for the manufacturer, but also something of a triumph for consumer sovereignty: a firm like Toyota can, through flexible assembly, better satisfy 'diverse consumers' tastes' which come 'to demand a variety of products' (1990, p. 4). As a response to this, and further confirmation of the weak historical underpinnings for Aoki's account, it should be observed that critics of Western car assemblers of the first decades of the post-World War II era were prone to attacking 'flexible' production of many specifications as a key weapon in the armoury of the giant corporation intent on bamboozling the customer: Bannock (1973, p. 239), for example, heaps commination on Ford Motor Company for its marketing campaigns in the 1960s emphasising 'millions

of custom-built specifications' arrived at through permutating 'engines and interior and exterior trim and accessories in thousands of versions'. What is remarkable, in the context of recent preoccupations with Japanese flexibility and product variety, is that no reference is ever made either to what was once a vocal strand of anti-corporate criticism in the West, or to the corporate marketing strategies that occasioned the protest.

8. Interestingly, Cowling (1982) makes the intriguing remark that flexible technologies might, in some industries, actually encourage transnational production by acting to broaden the pool of workers suitable for employment in the industry. This aside is, unfortunately, not expanded upon.

9. This data is best treated as an indicative estimate of relative numbers at a particular moment in time.

10. As Cowling and Sugden (1987, pp. 15–16) note, there is controversy over Berle and Means' choice of share ownership threshold from the viewpoint of providing an effective degree of control, although some plausible estimates (subject to provisos on assumed market structures) do fall *below* 20 per cent.

11. Coffey (2003) considers the assumptions made by Womack et al. about Japanese exceptionalism in the context of a detailed study of recent transnational activity in the UK car assembly sector, and policy responses by the Department of Trade and Industry (DTI).

12. Womack et al. do also in fact differentiate 'European' management of supply chains from 'American' in a way which actually emphasises similarities with, rather than differences from, the Japanese case.

13. It has generally been recognised that multiple-sourcing is a norm further down the pyramid.

14. In terms of the old cliché, 'co-operation' is used (consistently) by Womack et al. in the way that is analogous to the 'co-operation' of suspects to a crime with the police.

15. This can be rationalised by an appeal to the law of large numbers. If the number of end-product specifications for a product exceeds total expected demand, then meaningful forecasts are impossible for the obvious reason that even perfect knowledge of the underlying probability distribution of orders will not provide an effective guide to the relative frequencies with which specific orders are actually made. The error in this formulaton is that it confuses the range of *final*-assembly specifications with the number of varieties of individual component parts: even if the number of end-product specifications is very 'large', for individual components the number will be 'small' (see Coffey, 2001; see also Coffey and Tomlinson, 2003).

16. We would note that the attainment of relatively lower wage costs through outsourcing has been and remains the predominant feature of the competitive weaponry of the Japanese motor industry. Yet Womack et al. (1990, p. 285) claim that outsourcing provides Japanese assemblers with only negligible labour cost advantages compared to Western assemblers. In support of this claim, these authors argue that, by 1990, wage differentials between the Japanese assembly and its supply sector were very similar to those recorded in the USA (approximately 20 per cent). Even so, contemporary data presented by Williams et al. (1994, p. 232) for 1989, shows that in Japan, small firms employing less than 100 workers accounted for 26.5 per cent of total car industry employment, as compared to 7.9 per cent for the USA (US data for 1987). Consequently, this provides Japanese assemblers with a significant (international) cost advantage since wage rates paid in these small Japanese firms are 'little more than half those in the large assemblers' (Williams et al., p. 60).

17. The transnational's bargaining position is strengthened by the inability of its international labour force to coordinate a collective response to its threats of relocation. This weakness in the power of international labour can be attributed, among other things, to problems in organising and maintaining international trade unions.

18. There is also the recent case of Nissan Motor pursuing a 'divide and rule' strategy, through ultimatums to its smaller domestic *keiretsu* partners to reduce costs or lose future contracts to overseas affiliates (see *Nikkei Weekly*, 25/10/99 and also 21/5/2001).

19. As described by Womack et al., contracting arrangements in Japan are analogous to the RPI-X approach to utility pricing in the UK. Given planned production capacities and

volumes, each competing first-tier supplier is expected to reduce prices in real terms or face a punishing transfer of business to its 'rivals' in the group: the contract assumes, therefore, a time profile of future cost reductions. However, if costs fall faster than required by planned price reductions, the supplier is allowed to pocket the difference (to earn above agreed profits). While this may well be conducive to 'efficiency', as Womack et al. argue, it is not non-hierarchical.

REFERENCES

Aoki, M. (1988), *Information, Incentives, and Bargaining in the Japanese Economy*, Cambridge, UK: Cambridge University Press.

Aoki, M. (1990), 'Toward an economic model of the Japanese firm', *Journal of Economic Literature*, **28** (1), 1–27.

Asanuma, B. (1994), 'Co-ordination between Production and Distribution in a Globalizing Network of Firms: Assessing Flexibility Achieved in the Japanese Automobile Industry', in M. Aoki and R. Dore (eds), *The Japanese Firm: Sources of Competitive Strength*, Oxford: Oxford University Press, pp. 11–40.

Bannock, G. (1973), *The Juggernauts: The Age of the Big Corporation*, Harmondsworth: Penguin.

Baran, P.A. and P.M. Sweezy (1966), *Monopoly Capital*, Harmondsworth: Penguin.

Berle, A.A. and G.C. Means (1932), *The Modern Corporation and Private Property*, New York: Macmillan.

Coase, R.H. (1937), 'The nature of the firm', *Economica*, **4**, 386–405.

Coffey, D. (2001), 'Fordism, Flexibility, and Toyota: Paradigm Failure in the Theory of Lean Enterprise and J-form Production', Paper presented to the EUNIP Annual Conference, November 2001.

Coffey, D. (2003) 'Best Practice Manufacture as Industrial Policy: Monopoly Capitalism and Production Politics in the UK', in D. Coffey and C. Thornley (eds), *Industrial and Labour Market Policy and Performance*, London: Routledge, pp. 45–61.

Coffey, D. and P. Tomlinson (2003), 'Globalisation, vertical relations and the J-mode firm', *Journal of Post Keynesian Economics*, forthcoming.

Cowling, K. (1982), *Monopoly Capitalism*, London: The Macmillan Press Ltd.

Cowling, K. and R. Sugden (1987), *Transnational Monopoly Capitalism*, Brighton: Wheatsheaf.

Cowling, K. and R. Sugden (1994), *Beyond Capitalism, Towards a New World Order*, London: Pinter.

Cowling, K. and R. Sugden (1998), 'The Essence of the Modern Corporation: Markets, Strategic Decision-Making and the Theory of the Firm', *The Manchester School*, **66** (1), January, 59–86.

Cowling, K. and P.R. Tomlinson (2000), 'The Japanese crisis – a case of strategic failure?', *The Economic Journal*, **110** (464), F358–81.

Cowling, K. and P.R. Tomlinson (2002), 'Revisiting the roots of Japan's economic stagnation: the role of the Japanese corporation', *International Review of Applied Economics*, **16** (4), 373–90.

Cowling, K. and P.R. Tomlinson (2003), 'Industrial policy, transnational corporations and the problem of "hollowing out" in Japan', in D. Coffey and C. Thornley (eds), *Industrial and Labour Market Policy and Performance*, London: Routledge, pp. 62–82.

Cusumano, M.A. (1985), *The Japanese Automobile Industry: Technology and Management at Nissan and Toyota*, Cambridge MA and London: Harvard University Press.

Dicken, P. (1998), *Global Shift: Transforming the World Economy*, 3rd Edition, London: Paul Chapman Publishing Ltd.

Dodwell Marketing Consultants (1997), *The Structure of the Japanese Auto-Parts Industry*, Tokyo: Dodwell.

Leibenstein, H. (1987), *Inside the Firm*, Cambridge, MA: Harvard University Press.

Lyddon, D. (1996), 'The myth of mass production and the mass production of myth', *Historical Studies in Industrial Relations*, No.1, March.

Nikkei Weekly (25/10/99), *Can Ghosn steer Nissan along the Road to Recovery?*, New York: Nihon Keizai Shimbun Inc.

Nikkei Weekly (21/5/2001), *Nissan Stages Swift Comeback, but still Trails Front-runners*, New York: Nihon Keizai Shimbun Inc.

Rae, J.B. (1965), *The American Automobile: A Brief History*, Chicago and London: The University of Chicago Press.

Ruigrock, W. and R. Van Tulder (1995), *The Logic of International Restructuring*, London and New York: Routledge.

Shiomi, H. (1995), 'The Formation of Assembler Networks in the Automobile Industry: The Case of Toyota Motor Company (1955–80), in H. Shioma and K. Wada (eds), *Fordism Transformed: The Development of Production Methods in the Automobile Industry*, Oxford: Oxford University Press.

Tomlinson, P.R. (2001), *The Nature of the Japanese Transnational Corporation and the Real Effects of Transnational Activity Upon Japan's Machinery Industries*, Unpublished PhD thesis, University of Warwick, UK.

Tomlinson, P.R. (2002), 'The real effects of transnational activity upon investment and labour demand within Japan's machinery industries', *International Review of Applied Economics*, **16** (2), pp. 107–29.

White, L.J. (1971), *The Automobile Industry since 1945*, Cambridge, MA: Harvard University Press.

Williams, K., C. Haslam, S. Johal and J. Williams (1994), *Cars: Analysis, History, Cases*, Oxford: Berghahn Books.

Williamson, O.E. (1975), *Markets and Hierarchies: Analysis and Antitrust Implications*, New York: The Free Press.

Williamson, O.E. (1985), *The Economic Institutions of Capitalism: Firms, Markets, Relational Contracting*, New York: The Free Press.

Womack, P., D.T. Jones and D. Roos (1990), *The Machine That Changed the World*, London: Maxwell Macmillan International.

2. Multinationals and labour: evidence from the international acquisition of UK firms

Martin J. Conyon, Sourafel Girma, Steve Thompson and Peter W. Wright

1. INTRODUCTION

This chapter examines the effects of multinational enterprise (MNE) on labour outcomes, using firm ownership change as an experiment to isolate its impact. Specifically, our primary contribution is to evaluate both the wage and productivity effects of domestic and foreign acquisitions within a large panel of UK firms over the period 1989–94. Our intention is to explore an issue that has become something of a battleground for competing hypotheses. This is whether multinational firms raise or lower employee wages, and improve or impede firm performance levels, in the domestic economy. The general debate has been considered by Caves (1996), Cowling and Sugden (1987, 1998) *inter alia*. A second contribution that we make is in methodology. The longitudinal nature of our data, which allows us to track firms over time, including changes in their ownership, means that we can provide superior econometric tests of the wage and productivity effects of MNEs. In particular, the panel data allows us to purge the analysis of many of the industry, technology and plant vintage effects that typically plague comparative work on wages and productivity.

In taking this approach, it seems entirely appropriate that we are using one of Keith Cowling's enduring professional interests, namely merger activity,[1] to explore another, namely the impact of international capital on labour.[2] Indeed Cowling and Sugden (1987) have advanced perhaps the most pessimistic of the scholarly assessments of the consequences of the internationalisation of production for wages whilst repeatedly warning of the difficulties of making wage comparisons across firms. Caves (1996) provides a review of the alternative mainstream approaches.

In addition to the competing theoretical analyses of the relative effects of multinationals on productivity and wage levels, there are methodological differences concerning the appropriate basis for domestic versus MNE comparisons. The putative wage and productivity superiority of the MNE that emerges in cross-sectional studies appears less robust when panel data techniques are employed. The latter methodology allows a before and after comparison, akin to an 'experiment', and so provides stronger tests of our research hypotheses. This technique has indicated that compositional effects and omitted variables may be responsible for much of the apparent superiority of the MNEs. For example, capital vintage and plant and firm size effects are rarely controlled for in cross-sectional work but may generate significant performance differences that are not attributable to multinational ownership *per se*. Omitting variables such as capital vintage and so on (which may be thought of and modelled as a 'fixed effect') causes bias in estimating the impact of multinational status on corporate performance. More seriously, multinational entrants may be attracted to more productive and/or more profitable industries leading to simultaneity bias in the cross-sectional evidence (Tybout, 2000). While it is suspected that the inclusion of plant and industry controls would reduce, if not eliminate, the residual multinational effect, the specification of appropriate control variables is normally problematic (Griffith, 1999), generally requiring information not included in the standard data sets.

The research described in this chapter aims to circumvent many of these difficulties by examining the productivity and wage effects of the foreign acquisition of existing UK manufacturing firms. It assumes that foreign take-over leaves most industry and plant characteristics unchanged, at least for the medium term. Accordingly, by observing productivity and wages before and after the event of acquisition, the chapter seeks to isolate that component of performance that is solely due to a change in ownership status.

The chapter is organised as follows. Section 2 explores the alternative internalisation and distributional hypotheses for the existence of the multinational enterprise. It then outlines some advantages and disadvantages of using ownership changes to isolate the impact of the internationalisation of production on labour market outcomes. Section 3 describes the database used, presents some sample characteristics and then generates some preliminary analysis of the data. In Section 4 the econometric methodology is outlined and the results presented. Some extensions of the basic models are offered to explore the impact of different nationalities of acquirer, the possible effects of endogeneity and an investigation of total factor productivity effects. A brief conclusion follows.

2.   MULTINATIONAL FIRMS AND WAGES: EFFICIENCY VERSUS DISTRIBUTIONAL ISSUES

The literature on the domestic consequences of the internationalisation of business is both large and diverse (for example Kogut and Kulatilaka, 1994; Berry, 2001). However, it is possible to characterise two opposing analyses of the impact of the multinational enterprise on labour. The dominant 'internalisation' – or transactions cost – paradigm (Casson, 1995; Dunning, 1981, and so on) views the MNE as an efficient solution to the problems of using international resource markets. It advances an efficiency rationale for MNEs and generally predicts higher domestic wages as workers share the higher rents enjoyed by such firms. The alternative 'distributional' view of the MNE (Cowling and Sugden, 1987; Sugden, 1991) views international production as a means of lowering labour costs. This occurs not merely via the obvious route of locating labour-intensive activities in low wage countries, but through the reduction in the bargaining power of an internationally fragmented work force. These alternatives may be reviewed briefly.

The internalisation model of the MNE presents it as an efficient solution to the problems of transferring proprietary assets across market boundaries. Caves (1996, p. 162) describes the MNE's rationale as: 'the administered internalised deployment of its proprietary assets to evade the failure of certain arm's-length markets. Premier among those assets is the knowledge embodied in new products, processes, proprietary technology and the like.' Thus incoming MNEs are assumed to bring with them certain assets, often intangible and frequently knowledge-based such as technological know-how, brand name capital and organisational routines that more than offset any advantages of incumbency possessed by domestic firms.

Technological knowledge and brand name recognition/reputation are widely regarded as assets whose transfer across markets in general may be problematic. Knowledge markets experience multiple forms of failure (Geroski, 1997), whilst brand name licensing involves the shared use of an intangible asset (reputation) with obvious dangers of horizontal externalities. Multinationality does appear to be associated with each. The empirical evidence – which draws particularly on Japanese entry to the USA and is surveyed in Caves (1996) – suggests that multinationals cluster in industries with high R&D and advertising intensities. Similarly, it has been hypothesised that some multinationals enjoy a competitive advantage through superior organisational routines and practices, again assets whose intangibility makes their transfer across markets difficult. For example, Japanese manufacturers pioneered superior logistical systems ('just-in-time' inventory planning and so on) and work practices, including team working and task flexibility. These organisational developments might be expected to be useful in particular industries and Japanese multinationals are prevalent in industries, such as motor vehicles, with assembly line working (for example MacDuffie et al., 1996; Pil and MacDuffie, 1999).

Radical critics of the MNE, such as Cowling and Sugden (1987) and Sugden (1991), point out that institutions are not neutral in their impact on the relative bargaining power of employers and labour. They cite the parallel argument of Marglin (1974) that the factory system, at least in its infant form, was less an instrument to raise productivity and more a device to assert control over independent textile outworkers. In a similar vein they suggest that internationalising the firm permits it to use a 'divide and rule' strategy, in which sets of employees separated by distance, culture and perhaps language, face a unified employer.

> The basic idea is that a labour force may have a greater bargaining power over strategic decision makers if it is able to act collectively but that division of labour across countries undermines this ability. Hence strategic decision makers may opt for production in various countries to reduce labour costs, at the expense of labour well-being. (Cowling and Sugden, 1998, p. 76)

Interestingly, recent evidence by Harrison (2002) supports the proposition that globalisation has impacted on labour's share. Using a panel of over 100 countries she analyses trends in labour's share over the period 1960–97 and the role that globalisation plays in this. She finds that in poor countries labour's share fell, but in rich countries it rose. These changes in labour's share are driven by factors including metrics for globalisation such as trade shares, exchange rate crises, movements in foreign investment and capital controls.

From the perspective of the MNE, the existence of actual and potential alternative production facilities gives the multinational employer a credible threat to switch production in the event of a dispute or to shelve or switch expansion plans (see Huizinga, 1990). When surplus capacity is evident within the MNE, perhaps as a consequence of global shifts in manufacturing, separate national groups of employees may compete in their willingness to accept the lowest wage in order to preserve their particular facility. The net result, according to the radical view, is that international production weakens the employees' bargaining position, leaving them to settle for a lower share of the rents than would be expected in a purely domestic firm.

Since the internalisation and radical perspectives appear to give such contrasting predictions for wage and performance effects, it might be expected that a simple comparison of wages and productivity across domestic- and foreign-owned firms would reveal the merits of the two approaches. Where such comparisons have been undertaken (see Caves, 1996, pp. 126–7 for a survey) the results have generally, but not universally, supported the wage and productivity superiority of the foreign-owned firms.

However, as has been noted above, both theoretical and empirical evidence suggests that the multinational form will be differentially attracted to some industries. This suggests the need for precise industry controls. Similarly, the size and relatively recent origin of many multinational subsidiaries, and the frequency of *de novo* start-ups among these, suggests that firm and plant scale effects and plant vintage effects may be important. Taking account of these caveats has not proved easy and the studies which have attempted to do so have generated very different results. Davies and Lyons (1991), for example, report that foreign-owned firms in the UK enjoy a 30 per cent productivity advantage over their domestic-owned equivalents. Of this, 40 per cent arises from their having located in high-productivity industries and the remainder is attributable to intrinsic advantages. By contrast, a study of Argentine industry by Vendrell-Alda (1978) finds the entire productivity differential enjoyed by foreign-owned firms to be attributable to market structural characteristics, leaving no multinational residual effect. Wage comparisons suffer from similar ambiguities. For example, Feliciano and Lipsey (1999) report that wage differences for non-manufacturing establishments persist after controlling for establishment, state and industry characteristics. However, they also report a much more fragile relationship for manufacturing, with differences persisting in some years but not in others.

An exploration of the short- and medium-term productivity and wage effects of a change in ownership for an existing firm should circumvent many of these control problems. First, it is straightforward to determine whether the acquired firm changes industry. If not, it can be assumed that industry effects will not impact on the analysis. Second, since the firm will initially work with existing physical and human capital, it seems reasonable to assume no changes in factor quality, including major changes in capital vintage. Third, whilst there may be performance changes associated with a change in ownership *per se* (Brown and Medoff, 1988; Conyon et al., 2002a), a comparison of foreign and domestic acquisitions should reveal the existence and extent of any distinctive foreign ownership effect.

Of course, it is necessary to recognise that only a minority of MNE affiliates are created through acquisition and therefore that such firms may not be typical of MNEs as a whole. The precise proportion of acquisition-to-*de novo* MNE entries is unknown, but Yamawaki (1994) reports that approximately 26 per cent of Japanese MNE affiliates in Europe originate via acquisitions. Since the UK is perhaps the most accessible acquisitions market in the EU, it might be expected that acquired affiliates are more representative here than elsewhere. It is also possible that entrants by acquisition have a different risk–return profile to that of *de novo* entrants, with implications for their performance. Caves (1996) suggests that MNE entry uncertainty may be lowered by the acquisition of staff with local knowledge. Similarly, he argues that what has been acquired on the market can, in principle, be divested in the same way in the event of failure. He does not attempt to quantify these effects, but if they exist they might indicate a lower equilibrium return for acquired affiliates.

It is also necessary to recognise that an ownership change may impact on the relative bargaining power of employers and employees, irrespective of the identity of the new owners. Shleifer and Summers (1988) have suggested that acquisition, especially hostile acquisition, offers the opportunity for employers to renege on implicit elements of the labour contract, perhaps eliminating non-monetary benefits or imposing changes in the pay–effort relationship. New owners may find it easier to make such changes, either because of weaker obligations to the workforce or because acquisition increases the credibility of the closure threat. We allow for this possibility by including purely domestic acquisitions as a control.

Finally it is worth noting that acquisitions might have consequences for distribution other than on the wages of the employees. In a recent work Wulf (2002) has investigated whether target CEOs, via the negotiation of the sale of their firm, capture a private benefit from power in the post-merger organisation. Evidence is presented from a merger of equals in US firms (where the post-merger governance structure – namely board representation – is the same for targets and acquirers). Wulf (2002) concludes that the data support the hypotheses that target CEOs trade power for premium in shared governance transactions (that is the share premium for targets is lower compared with a matched sample). So, CEOs negotiate control rights in the merged firm in exchange for a lower premium. But, as Wulf acknowledges, this lower return may also be due to CEOs concern for other stakeholders in the firm rather than their own preferences.

3. DATABASE CONSTRUCTION AND SOME SAMPLE CHARACTERISTICS

This research considers the acquisition of ongoing firms by foreign and domestic companies in UK manufacturing industry for the period 1989–94. The source of information relating to acquisitions and other firm level variables is the *OneSource* database of private and public companies in the UK. *OneSource* gives a yearly subsidiary indicator in each firm's record. A firm is identified as being acquired at year *t* if its status changes from being independent to being a subsidiary of another firm. Firms with more than one ownership change between 1989 and 1994 are excluded from the analysis. To distinguish between foreign and domestic acquisitions, we use *OneSource*'s 'ownership status' variable that gives the nationality of the firm's ultimate holding company. It is worth noting that the firms we observe are acquisitions rather than more radical forms of organisational change such as true mergers.

Since our aim is to study the change of ownership on productivity and wages, we screen the data for the availability of employment, wages and output for at least five consecutive years. In this way we have at least two years of pre- and post-acquisition information for each acquired firm, so that the sample period stretches from 1987 to 1996. The final sample consists of 331 domestic and 129 foreign acquisitions, the yearly frequency distribution of which is given in Table 2.1.

Table 2.1   Frequency of ownership changes by year

Year	Domestic	Foreign
1989	64	27
1990	67	27
1991	54	19
1992	61	21
1993	47	19
1994	38	16
Total	331	129

Source: Conyon et al. (2002b).

The 129 foreign acquisitions consist of 36 by American multinationals, 64 by EU-based firms and 29 by acquirers from other countries, including Japan. An industry-stratified random control sample of 642 firms was drawn from the population of foreign and domestic subsidiaries which did not experience a change in ownership during the sample period and which satisfied the data screening criteria. The overall balance of the resulting panel is described in Table 2.2.

Of the domestic acquisitions, 139 were made within the same three-digit SIC industry and these were classified as *horizontal* acquisitions. It was not possible to separately distinguish vertical and diversifying acquisitions among the remainder, so all were classified as *non-horizontal* acquisitions. The most striking difference between these two groups is that *non-horizontal* acquirers are approximately five times larger than their *horizontal* counterparts, with average output (employment) of £162m (2265 employees) compared to £24m (411 employees).

Table 2.3 reports the means and standard errors of four-digit SIC industry-adjusted employment, wages and labour productivity in our sample. As found in most previous studies, foreign firms are generally larger

Table 2.2   Balance of the panel

Number of periods	Domestic acquirers	Foreign acquirers	Control
5	7	9	42
6	23	4	47
7	20	10	54
8	35	18	45
9	94	45	199
10	152	43	255
Total	331	129	642

Source: Conyon et al. (2002b).

Table 2.3   Sample characteristics of domestic and foreign-owned firms in UK manufacturing industry: average employment, wages, and labour productivity

Variables	1989		1994	
Domestic				
Employment	414	(1650)	327	(1369)
Wage rate	11.35	(3.87)	13.29	(4.31)
Labour productivity	72.45	(163.77)	74.48	(96.77)
Foreign				
Employment	549	(1641)	434	(1098)
Wage rate	12.71	(3.90)	15.22	(4.40)
Labour productivity	104.68	(137.67)	118.28	(154.24)

Notes:
(i)   Variables are given in real terms.
(ii)   Wage rate and labour productivity are in £'000s.
(iii) The wage rate is defined as the wage bill per worker.
(iv)   Labour productivity is sales per worker.
(v)   Standard deviations are given in parentheses

Source: Conyon et al. (2002b).

than domestic firms, pay a higher average wage (10.3 per cent) and exhibit greater levels of productivity (28.8 per cent). Table 2.4 looks at the characteristics of the acquired firms and also those of the control sample. It indicates that acquired firms are smaller than the industry average in terms of employment, and only those acquired by foreign firms seem to exhibit a growth in their *relative* sizes post acquisition. Firms acquired by foreign (domestic) firms pay wages that are higher (lower) than the industry average by a factor of 1.01 (0.98) and 1.03 (0.94) during the pre- and post-ownership

Table 2.4   Relative employment, wage rates and labour productivity of foreign and domestic firms before and after acquisition

Variable	Domestic		Foreign		Control group characteristics	
	Before	After	Before	After	Foreign	Domestic
Employment	0.58	0.57	0.60	0.70	0.90	0.75
	(0.86)	(0.70)	(0.87)	(0.84)	(1.18)	(0.92)
Wage rates	0.98	0.94	1.01	1.03	1.07	0.97
	(0.31)	(0.29)	(0.30)	(0.27)	(0.25)	(0.22)
Labour	1.14	1.02	1.02	1.16	1.34	1.04
productivity	(1.48)	(1.04)	(0.69)	(0.89)	(0.79)	(0.68)

Notes:
(i)   All of the variables are relative to the corresponding 4-digit SIC average values.
(ii) Labour productivity is measured as sales per employee.
(iii) Standard errors in brackets.
(iv) 'Before' and 'After' refer to the observed time periods before and after the ownership changes.

Source: Conyon et al. (2002b).

change periods respectively. This is an early indication that foreign ownership is associated with an increase in the level of *relative* employee remuneration. Whether this is due to the noticeable increase in productivity from a pre-acquisition level that was just above the industrial average (1.02) to an impressive looking 1.16, or due to other factors is impossible to say at this stage of the analysis. Finally, a somewhat surprising finding is that firms acquired by domestic firms appear to lose their productivity advantage *relative* to the average firm.

Table 2.5 examines the post-acquisition trajectories of productivity and wages and conducts tests for the equality of the pre-acquisition and post-acquisition values. Both domestic and foreign ownership changes are associated with a significant increase in real wages and productivity over this period. In the case of foreign acquisitions, for example, average real wages and labour productivity grew by 13 per cent and 20.2 per cent[3] respectively, in the four-year period between the year prior to ownership change and three years following the event. The post-acquisition firm-level employment figures do not significantly differ from the pre-acquisition values, which suggests that some of the apparent productivity improvement may have been brought about as a result of a more efficient use of labour rather than through downsizing. It would be inappropriate to conclude from Table 2.5 that ownership changes are associated with wage and labour pro-

Table 2.5 Post-ownership changes of employment, wage rates and labour productivity

Variables	$t+1$	$t+2$	$t+3$
Domestic			
Employment	3.7	3.7	6.1
	(1.23)	(1.10)	(1.59)
Wage rate	1.0	3.7	8.8
	(0.42)	(2.42)	(5.59)
Labour productivity	−1.8	5.3	10.2
	(−0.83)	(2.64)	(4.46)
Foreign			
Employment	4.5	4.4	2.2
	(1.51)	(1.17)	(0.53)
Wage rate	3.9	6.4	13.0
	(2.11)	(3.41)	(5.98)
Labour productivity	11.8	13.5	20.2
	(3.50)	(3.99)	(5.27)

Notes:
(i) Column $t+s$ shows the percentage change in the relevant variables following ownership change s years after the event. The pre-ownership change year (that is $t-1$) is used as the base. Thus the fact that employment gains of 4.5 per cent are reported for employment in year $t+1$ means that between $t-1$ and $t+1$ employment grew by 2.25 per cent per annum.
(ii) Paired t-tests for equality to the base year are shown in parentheses.

Source: Conyon et al. (2002b).

ductivity increases, however. The simple t-tests presented do not control for other factors – for example technological progress – that may have impacted on wages and productivity over the period.

4. ECONOMETRIC METHODOLOGY

In order to estimate the *ceteris paribus* impact of ownership change on the level of labour productivity the following equation was estimated:

$$(q-l)_{it} = \alpha'_t + \beta'(k-l)_{it} + f'_i + \delta'_1 D_{it} + \delta'_2 F_{it} + \varepsilon_{it} \tag{2.1}$$

where i and t index firms and time periods respectively, $(q-l)$ is the logarithm of output per worker and $(k-l)$ is capital intensity.[4] In addition, year dummies (α'_t) are included to control for aggregate shocks, and firm-specific fixed effects (f') for permanent differences across firms. Finally, we allow for the possibility that domestic and foreign acquisitions may affect productivity in different ways by constructing separate dummies for take-overs by foreign (F) and domestic (D) companies.

Similarly, we estimate an equation of the following form for wages:

$$w_{it} = \alpha_t'' + \beta'' X_{it} + f_i'' + \delta_1'' D_{it} + \delta_2'' F_{it} + \varepsilon_{it}. \qquad (2.2)$$

Where w_{it} is log(wages) in firm i at time t; X is a vector that controls for observable changes that are correlated with wage rates such as firm size,[5] four-digit industry average wages and productivity.

(i)   Productivity Results

Table 2.6 reports the results of a fixed effect panel estimator for productivity. Controlling for capital intensity, fixed assets, firm fixed effects and autonomous technical changes (via time dummies), we find a 14 per cent labour productivity improvement due to foreign acquisition (Column A).

The evidence for an efficiency inducing effect of foreign acquisitions is supported by an estimate of a derived labour demand equation in column D of Table 2.6. This column shows, *conditional* on the level of output and wages, the decrease in wages that results from ownership change. It indicates that labour demand of the typical firm decreased by 6.2 per cent during the years following acquisition by a foreign company. That is, there was a substantial increase in the technical efficiency with which labour is used.

(ii)   Wage Results

Table 2.7 presents the results for wage outcomes. Column A gives the wage differentials after controlling for fixed firm and industry effects and aggregate time shocks only. It can be seen that a 3.44 per cent premium is paid to workers in foreign acquired firms, whilst wages fall by 2.11 per cent in domestically acquired companies. In column B, firm size and industry wages are controlled for, but the wage differentials observed previously appear to persist. However when productivity is added in the vector of control variables (column C), the wage premium due to foreign acquisitions disappears. Combining this result with our earlier evidence of no significant downsizing by acquired firms, it is justifiable to conclude that the impact of foreign acquisitions on wages is entirely driven by productivity growth. Indeed combining the information of the quasi-rents splitting parameter (0.30) on productivity with the productivity increase observed earlier, this translates into a 4.2 per cent increase in wages as a result of foreign ownership. This is of comparable magnitude to the crude 3.4 per

Table 2.6 The impact of ownership change on labour productivity

	Level of productivity		Endogeneity corrected productivity levels	Labour demand
	A	B	C	D
Capital intensity	0.05	0.05	0.054	
	(8.59)**	(8.59)**	(4.05)**	
Output				0.73
				(126.76)**
Wage rate				−0.70
				(47.83)**
Domestic acquisition	0.00			−0.01
	(1.27)			(0.09)
Foreign acquisition	14.10			−6.17
	(8.31)**			(4.70)**
Horizontal		2.00	3.45	
		(1.27)	(0.84)	
Non-horizontal		0.00	1.38	
		(0.34)	(0.64)	
USA		15.30	16.44	
		(5.23)**	(2.42)*	
EU		14.10	11.92	
		(6.25)**	(2.34)*	
Others		13.00	12.33	
		(3.88)**	(2.51)*	

Notes:
(i)   All estimations are based on 9648 observations corresponding to 1102 firms. Year effects are included.
(ii)   Absolute values of *t*-statistics are given in parentheses. * Significant at 5 per cent; ** significant at 1 per cent.
(iii)   Capital intensity is measured as fixed assets per worker.
(iv)   Coefficients on acquisition dummies in the level and growth equations are percentage and percentage point differentials respectively.
(v)   In column C the probability of acquisition in each year is used as an instrument for the acquisition dummies.

Source: Conyon et al. (2002b).

cent wage premium estimated in column B of Table 2.7. This result is robust to the inclusion of employment as an additional regressor to control for possible composition effects.

The experience of firms acquired by domestic firms is markedly different. Table 2.7, column C indicates that the reduction in wages due to domestic acquisition is unaffected by the introduction of productivity in

Table 2.7 The impact of ownership changes on wage rates by type of acquisition

	Wage levels			Endogeneity corrected wage levels			
	A	B	C	D	E	F	G
Industry wage		0.09	0.05	0.09	0.05	0.111	0.065
		(7.92)**	(4.93)**	(8.11)**	(5.03)**	(4.37)**	(3.77)**
Fixed assets		0.004	0.01	0.03	0.01	0.031	0.019
		(1.84)	(3.75)**	(8.12)**	(3.91)**	(5.39)**	(3.37)**
Domestic	−2.11	−2.10	−2.17				
	(3.16)**	(3.13)**	(3.79)**				
Foreign	3.44	3.38	0.00				
	(3.46)**	(3.42)**	(0.00)				
USA				4.70	0.00	6.60	1.60
				(2.78)**	(0.00)	(2.14)*	(0.52)
EU				3.90	−1.50	3.69	−1.28
				(2.56)*	(1.18)	(1.43)	(0.51)
Other foreign				3.20	0.10	3.91	1.60
				(2.56)*	(0.51)	(2.22)*	(1.05)
Horizontal				−3.12	−3.50	−2.69	−3.20
				(3.45)**	(4.48)**	(1.25)	(1.83)

	(1)	(2)	(3)	(4)
Non-horizontal	0.00	−0.80	1.0	0.40
	(0.00)	(1.29)	(0.69)	(0.32)
Labour productivity	0.30	0.29		0.29
	(5.42)**	(52.30)**		(11.44)**
Employment	−0.07	−0.019	−0.074	−0.020
	(12.94)**	(3.96)**	(5.88)**	(1.58)

Notes:
(i)   All estimations are based on 9648 observations corresponding to 1102 firms. Year effects are included.
(ii) The coefficient on acquisition dummies gives the percentage change in wage rates following ownership change.
(iii) Absolute values of *t*-statistics are given in parentheses. * Significant at 5 per cent; ** significant at 1 per cent.
(iv) In columns F and G the probability of acquisition in each year is used as an instrument for the acquisition dummies.

Source: Conyon et al. (2002b).

the control vector. Read in conjunction with Table 2.6, which shows that there are no positive or negative impacts on efficiency from domestic acquisitions, some support is found for the hypothesis of wealth-transfer away from workers to shareholders. This may reflect Shleifer and Summers (1988) reductions in extra-marginal wage payments.

(iii)   The Nationality of the Acquiring Firm

As was noted in Section 3, the internalisation theory of FDI suggests that a multinational firm is capable of transferring a range of intangible proprietary assets. Since multinationals from some countries are more strongly associated with the transfer of work practices than others, this suggests that it may be important to distinguish the acquisition by the acquirer's country of origin.

The results of this exercise are given in Tables 2.6 and 2.7 for productivity and wages respectively, where we compare the impact of acquisition by firms from the USA, EU and other foreign countries.[6] In both tables the structural coefficients are again well determined, though suggest some heterogeneity of merger outcomes. The increase in productivity is observed across all types of foreign acquisition (Table 2.6, column B), with the greatest increase observed for US firms. Some heterogeneity is also observed in wage changes. Workers in US-acquired firms experience a 4.7 per cent wage increase which, although insignificantly greater than the EU acquisitions case (3.9 per cent) is significantly greater than that for other foreign acquisitions (3.2 per cent). However, this largely reflects the productivity differences. Once labour productivity is included amongst the regressors, the wage effects of acquisition are again reduced to insignificance (Table 2.7, Column D). This again suggests that the impact of ownership change on wages occurs primarily via productivity effects and not because of internal redistributions of income.

Since Conyon et al. (2002a) suggest that horizontal acquisitions may impact differentially on performance to vertical or diversifying acquisitions, the tables also contain results where we split domestic acquisitions into horizontal and non-horizontal cases. We find that horizontal mergers are followed by a significant *ceteris paribus* pay cut, an effect that survives controlling for productivity, whereas non-horizontal mergers have a neutral impact.

(iv)   Total Factor Productivity Gains

In order to further investigate the productivity enhancing impact of foreign acquisition, we also estimated a total factor productivity (TFP) equation of the following form:

$$q_{it} = \alpha_t''' + \beta_1''' k_{it} + \beta_2''' l_{it} + \beta_3''' m_{it} + f_i''' + \delta_1''' D_{it} + \delta_2''' F_{it} + \varepsilon_{it} \qquad (2.3)$$

Where i and t index firms and time periods respectively, q,k,l,m, are the logarithm of output, capital, labour and intermediate inputs.[7] The results are reported in Table 2.8. Once again the beneficial impact of foreign acquisition is apparent. After controlling for firm fixed effects and autonomous technical changes (via time dummies), we find that firms subject to foreign acquisition experience an 8 per cent difference in total factor productivity.

This result survives (indeed is enhanced by) a number of robustness checks. In column B, we again allow for the possibility of endogeneity in the acquisitions process,[8] by using a fixed effects instrumental variables (IV) estimator. As in the labour productivity and wage equation results, this procedure generates instruments for acquisition using a multinomial logit model that predicts the probability of take-over. The results show that the 'standard' and IV fixed effect approaches yield remarkably similar estimates, confirming the finding that foreign take-overs lead to increases in total factor productivity.[9]

Column C suggests that foreign acquisition may have additional impacts. Here we allow foreign acquisition to affect the marginal productivity of the factors of production. The results indicate that the marginal productivity of capital has doubled in the post foreign acquisition period. This is in contrast to the impact of the marginal productivity of labour, which has if anything slightly decreased. Note that in this less constrained equation, the measured impact on total factor productivity is even larger (14 per cent).

Since it has been mooted that multinationals of some nationalities are more strongly associated with the transfer of work practices than others, Table 2.8 also distinguishes acquisitions by whether or not the foreign acquirer originates in the US. Column E indicates that although the increase in total factor productivity is observed across all types of foreign acquisition, the greatest increase is observed for US firms.

Columns C–E also distinguish domestic acquisitions by merger type and show that non-horizontal acquisitions appear to lead to productivity increases of 12 per cent, an improvement that is not matched by horizontal acquisitions.

(v) Endogeneity Corrections

As a final test of robustness for our results, we allow for the possible endogeneity of our acquisition indicators. If wages play some role in driving acquisitions, as is sometimes suggested, a stochastic dependence between the acquisitions dummies and the disturbances of the wage equation may bias our estimates.[10] Thus we estimate the probability of domestic and foreign acquisition in each year and use this as an instrument for the

Table 2.8   The impact of ownership on marginal factor and total factor productivity

	Fixed effect no interaction A	Fixed effect IV no interaction B	Fixed effect with interaction C	Fixed effect IV with interaction D	Fixed effect IV with interaction E
TFP effects					
Horizontal	0.011	0.024	0.113	0.165	0.147
	(0.80)	(1.64)	(1.37)	(1.85)	(1.63)
Non-horizontal	−0.026	−0.016	0.092	0.128	0.112
	(2.77)**	(1.63)	(1.94)	(2.52)*	(2.18)*
Foreign	0.082	0.086	0.140	0.146	
	(6.81)**	(6.28)**	(2.37)*	(2.11)*	
USA					0.148
					(4.75)**
Non-USA					0.065
					(4.09)**
Labour	0.511	0.510	0.516	0.517	0.515
	(59.72)**	(59.64)**	(58.99)**	(58.85)**	(40.70)**
Acquisition interactions					
Horizontal			−0.034	−0.042	−0.043
			(1.79)	(2.12)*	(2.17)*
Non-horizontal			−0.025	−0.042	−0.043
			(1.94)	(3.01)**	(3.05)**
Foreign			−0.050	−0.040	
			(2.77)**	(1.88)	
USA					0.072
					(0.43)

Non-USA					0.001 (0.00)
Capital	0.027 (5.69)**	0.027 (5.76)**	0.025 (5.03)**	0.025 (4.97)**	0.020 (3.36)**
Acquisition interactions					
Domestic			0.009 (0.64)	0.008 (0.53)	0.010 (0.69)
Non-horizontal			−0.001 (0.08)	0.006 (0.66)	0.008 (0.87)
Foreign			0.025 (2.21)*	0.017 (1.33)	
USA					0.10 (2.11)*
Non-USA					0.041 (0.55)
Intermediate inputs	0.383 (73.61)**	0.382 (73.51)**	0.382 (73.57)**	0.382 (73.47)**	0.384 (73.14)**
Hausman Test p-value		0.7402	0.76	0.6452	
R-squared	0.76	0.76			

Notes:
(i)   All estimations are based on 9648 observations corresponding to 1102 firms.
      Absolute values of *t*-statistics are given in parentheses. * Significant at 5 per cent; ** significant at 1 per cent.
(ii) Capital intensity is measured as fixed assets per worker.
(iii) Coefficients on acquisition dummies in the level and growth equations are percentage and percentage point differentials respectively.

Source: Conyon et al. (2002a).

acquisitions dummies.[11] The results of these panel IV estimates[12] are reported in Table 2.7, columns F and G. As far as foreign acquisitions are concerned, the impact of US acquired firms is more pronounced (6.6 per cent) and the significance of horizontal domestic acquisitions seems to disappear. Otherwise there were no noticeable differences compared with the 'uncorrected' results. Again, any wages gains from foreign acquisitions disappear when productivity is introduced, confirming our earlier results and interpretations. The results for productivity are also robust to corrections for endogeneity (Table 2.6, column C).

5.   CONCLUSION

The research described in this chapter has provided a systematic empirical analysis of the impact of foreign ownership on firm level productivity and wages in UK manufacturing industry for the period 1989–94. We have excluded from our analysis, but consider important for future research, employee reactions and responses to these changes in ownership structure (for example in the spirit of Freeman and Rogers, 1997, and Hunter et al., 2002).

Our chapter has identified a significant productivity gain (both labour productivity and TFP) following foreign acquisition that is *partly* translated into higher wage levels in foreign-owned companies. Therefore the results are broadly supportive of the internalisation efficiency-enhancing view of the MNE. At the same time the benefits to affected employees appear relatively modest. The *ceteris paribus* wage effect of foreign acquisition is under 3.5 per cent. Foreign acquisition appears to slow relative employment growth in affected firms such that *ceteris paribus* impact on labour demand exceeds *minus* 6 per cent.

If foreign acquisition appears, with the above caveats, to be relatively kind to labour, the same cannot be said of domestic acquisitions. The study finds that domestic acquisition activity – particularly horizontal merger activity – is followed by significant reductions in the wage rate. Moreover domestic acquisition produces no corresponding positive impact on labour productivity. Why this might be is uncertain without further study. It may reflect the managerial motives that have been widely hypothesised to drive merger activity. Likewise, the finding of a significant reduction in the post-acquisition wage is also consistent with the hypothesis that acquisitions are motivated by the opportunity that they offer to renege on implicit labour contracts and transfer surplus from the workforce. That result is suggestive of the importance of the distributional arguments, though it suggests these arise from changes in domestic control rather than from multinational acquisition.

NOTES

* Parts of the chapter draw on ideas and material first published in Girma et al. (2002) and Conyon et al. (2002a, 2002b). We are grateful to Mike Waterson for comments and suggestions. The authors would like to acknowledge the financial support of the Economic and Social Research Council under grant number R000221779 and the Leverhulme Trust (Programme Grant F114/BF), to whom the authors are indebted. Girma would also like to acknowledge support through the European Commission Fifth Framework Programme (Grant No. HPSE-CT-1999–00017).

1. Cowling et al. (1980) provided a path-breaking investigation of the impact of merger activity on firm costs and in so doing provided powerful evidence that many (perhaps most) large acquisitions failed to achieve their projected cost savings.
2. See for example Cowling and Sugden (1987) and Sugden (1991).
3. The average pre-acquisition output per worker is £69 000.
4. Capital (fixed assets) is defined as net (of depreciation) book value of equipment, plant and machinery, fixtures and fittings and vehicles.
5. Proxied by fixed assets.
6. This tricotomisation of foreign acquisitions was essentially driven by the preponderance of US and EU acquirers. Unfortunately, the number of acquirers from Japan, the country most obviously associated with distinctively different work practices, was too small for meaningful analysis.
7. Capital (fixed assets) is defined as net (of depreciation) book value of equipment, plant and machinery, fixtures and fittings and vehicles.
8. As before, excluded instruments used to predict probability of acquisitions were lagged (relative) wages and profits, sectoral concentration and foreign direct investment and firm size.
9. The Hausman tests find no systematic differences in the coefficient estimates between the standard and IV fixed effect models, and we find no evidence that foreign companies systematically acquire higher/lower total factor productivity firms.
10. A logit analysis of the determinants of the acquisition did give some support to this view. In particular, it suggested that the probability of being the subject of a domestic acquisition was negatively related to the (lagged) mean wage level (see Conyon et al., 2002b).
11. 'Excluded' instruments used to predict probability of acquisitions were lagged (relative) wages and profits, sectoral concentration and foreign direct investment and firm size.
12. Vella and Verbeek (1999) have recently shown that this type of instrumental variable approach generates estimates comparable to Heckman's (1978, 1979) endogeneity bias corrected OLS estimator.

REFERENCES

Berry, H. (2001), 'When does multinationality increase firm value? Evidence from US and Japanese firms, 1974–1997', Wharton School of Business Working Paper, September.

Brown, C. and J.L. Medoff (1988), 'The Impact of Firm Acquisition on Labor', in A.J. Auerbach (ed.), *Corporate Take-overs: Causes and Consequences*, London and Chicago: University of Chicago Press, pp. 9–25.

Casson M.C. (1995), *The Organization of International Business*, Cheltenham: Edward Elgar.

Caves, R.E. (1996), *Multinational Enterprise and Economic Analysis*, Cambridge: Cambridge University Press.

Conyon, M., S. Girma, S. Thompson and P. Wright (2002a), 'The impact of mergers and acquisitions on company employment', *European Economic Review*, **46**, 31–49.

Conyon, M., S. Girma, S. Thompson and P. Wright (2002b), 'Productivity and wage effects of foreign acquisition in the UK', *Journal of Industrial Economics*, **50**, 85–102.

Cowling, K. et al. (1980), *Mergers and Economic Performance*, Cambridge: Cambridge University Press.

Cowling, K. and R. Sugden (1987), *Trans-national Monopoly Capitalism*, Brighton: Wheatsheaf.

Cowling, K. and R. Sugden (1998), 'The essence of the modern corporation: markets, strategic decision-making and the theory of the firm', *Manchester School*, **66**, 59–86.

Davies, S.W. and B.R. Lyons (1991), 'Characterising relative performance: the productivity advantage of foreign owned firms in the UK', *Oxford Economic Papers*, **43**, 584–95.

Dunning, J.H. (1981), *International production and the multinational enterprise*, London: Allen and Unwin.

Feliciano, Z. and R. Lipsey (1999), 'Foreign ownership and wages in the United States, 1987–1992', NBER Working Paper no. 6923.

Freeman, R. and J. Rogers (1997), *What Workers Want*, Ithaca, New York: ILR Press, Cornell University Press.

Geroski P. (1997), 'Markets for technology: Knowledge, innovation and appropriability', Chapter 4 in P. Stoneman (ed.), *Handbook of the Economics of Innovation and Technological Change*, Oxford: Blackwell, pp. 90–131.

Girma, S., S. Thompson and P. Wright (2002), 'Why are productivity and wages higher in foreign firms?', *Economic and Social Review*, **33**, 93–100.

Griffith R. (1999), 'Using the ARD establishment level data to look at foreign ownership and productivity in the United Kingdom', *The Economic Journal*, **109** (456), 416–42.

Harrison, A. (2002), 'Has globalization eroded labor's share? Some cross country evidence', University of California Berkeley Working Paper (August).

Heckman, J.J. (1978), 'Dummy endogenous variables in a simultaneous equation system', *Econometrica*, **46**, 931–59.

Heckman, J.J. (1979), 'Sample selection bias as a specification error', *Econometrica*, **47**, 153–62.

Hunter, L.W., J.P. MacDuffie and L. Doucet (2002), 'What makes teams take? Employee reactions to work reforms', *Industrial & Labor Relations Review*, **55** (3), 448–72.

Huizinga, H. (1990), 'Unions, taxes and the structure of multinational enterprises', *Economic Letters*, **34**, 73–5.

Kogut, B. and N. Kulatilaka (1994), 'Operating flexibility, global manufacturing, and the option value of a multinational network', *Management Science*, **40** (1), 123–39.

Marglin, S. (1974), 'What do bosses do? The origins and functions of hierarchy in capitalist production', *Review of Radical Political Economy*, **6**, 60–112.

MacDuffie, J.P., K. Sethuraman and M.L. Fisher (1996), 'Product variety and manufacturing performance: Evidence from the International Automotive Assembly Plant Study', *Management Science*, **42** (3), 350–69.

Pil, F.K. and J.P. MacDuffie (1999), 'What makes transplants thrive: Managing the transfer of "best practice" at Japanese auto plants in North America', *Journal of World Business*, **34** (4), 372–91.

Shleifer, A. and L.H. Summers (1988), 'Breach of Trust in Hostile Take-overs', in A.J. Auerbach (ed.), *Corporate Takeovers: Causes and Consequences*, Chicago: NBER.

Sugden, R. (1991), 'The Importance of Distributional Considerations', in C.N. Pitelis and R. Sugden (eds), *The Nature of the Transnational Firm*, London: Routledge.

Tybout, J. (2000), 'Manufacturing firms in developing countries: How well do they do, and why?', *Journal of Economic Literature*, **38**, 11–44.

Vella, F. and M. Verbeek (1999), 'Estimating and interpreting models with endogenous treatment effects', *Journal of Business and Economic Statistics*, **17**, 473–8.

Vendrell-Alda, J.L.M. (1978), *Comparing Foreign Subsidiaries and Domestic Firms: A Research Methodology Applied To Argentine Industry*, New York: Garland.

Wulf, J. (2002), 'Do CEOs in mergers trade power for premium? Evidence from "mergers of equals"', The Wharton School, University of Pennsylvania, Working Paper 2002–03.

Yamawaki, H. (1994), 'Entry Patterns of Japanese Multinationals in US and European Manufacturing', in M. Mason and D. Encarnation (eds), *Does Ownership Matter?: Japanese Multinationals in Europe*, New York: Oxford University Press.

3.   Financial constraints on innovation: a European cross-country study

Alessandra Canepa and Paul Stoneman

1.   INTRODUCTION

If the subject of Keith Cowling's work is to be succinctly summarised, it would be that his prime concern has been the functioning of capitalist economies and the design of policies to improve their performance. His interests have centred in particular upon European economies and European policy. This chapter sits solidly within this area of interest. Its concerns are with the performance of capital markets and such markets are at the centre of the capitalist system. The orientation of the chapter is also very European. Although policy issues are not explicitly explored, there are implications.

The main aim of this chapter is to explore the impact of financial factors upon the innovative performance of European firms. Particular issues to be addressed are the relative importance of financial constraints versus other constraints upon innovation, and whether the importance of financial factors varies across firm sizes, industries and countries.

There has recently been extensive growth in the literature that looks at the impact of financial factors upon the investment of firms in both fixed capital and R&D (a common proxy for innovative performance). The empirical aspect to this literature largely relies upon the econometric exploration of firm or industry level panel data sets on investment and/or R&D and firm and market characteristics, with financial factors being represented by the inclusion of a cash flow variable as an indicator of potential financial constraints. Schiantarelli (1996) and Hubbard (1998) present reviews of this literature as regards investment in fixed capital. Hall (1992) and Himmelberg and Petersen (1994) argue that R&D and thus innovation might be expected to be even more sensitive to financial factors than physical investments because it is relatively more risky and generates less easily realisable assets in the case of bankruptcy.

In this chapter we rely upon quite different data. Our empirical research is based upon the responses of firms to questions in the Second Community

Innovation Survey (CISII) on the relative importance of different constraints upon innovative behaviour. The relative advantages and disadvantages of questionnaire data of this kind are well known. In the current circumstances the great advantage is that the data set encompasses all the EU countries (and EU-wide panel data sets suitable for the more common form of analysis are not available) and the questionnaire was standardised across those countries. It also provides direct information relating to firms' beliefs upon the importance of financial factors (although questionnaire data of this kind may of course produce biased responses) rather than requiring one to rely upon the use of a proxy (that is cash flow) as an indicator of financial constraints.

The chapter is organised as follows. In the next section we discuss why, theoretically, financial factors may play a role in innovation and why this role may differ across countries, firm sizes and industries. In Section 3 we discuss the data and in Section 4 present the econometric framework to be used in this chapter. In Section 5 we analyse CISII responses upon the relative importance of financial vs. other factors as a constraint upon innovation. In Section 6 we analyse the patterns of CISII responses upon the importance of financial factors by country and firm size and in Section 7 by country and industry. In Section 8 we discuss how the empirical findings relate to the theoretical predictions and draw conclusions.

2.   THEORETICAL FOUNDATIONS

The Modigliani and Miller (1958) theorem states that if there are perfect capital markets then the firm's financial structure is irrelevant to its investment (including innovation) decisions and, as such, investment and finance decisions are independent of each other. In a perfect capital market, therefore, financial factors would play no role in investment determination. However this result relies upon (at least) three basic assumptions holding: that there are (i) no possibilities of default on loans, (ii) no taxes and (iii) no transaction costs. As such conditions do not hold generally, investment and finance decisions are interdependent and thus the nature and functioning of capital markets may well impact upon investment and innovation undertaken.

Aspects of the nature and functioning of capital markets considered to be important in the investment and R&D literature (see Stoneman, 2001a) then encompass the following.

(i)   *Market completeness.* The completeness of a capital market concerns issues relating to the diversity of capital instruments available.

Debt and equity are the two main capital instruments, but other instruments such as derivatives, venture capital and convertible bonds may also be available. Not only might some less developed markets not offer all such capital instruments but it has been argued that even in the most sophisticated markets such as the UK and the US there are 'finance gaps' especially for small firms. If there are such gaps, firms may well be constrained in the achievement of their optimal finance arrangements and their investment and/or R&D spending may be affected.

(ii) *The number of buyers and sellers.* A perfectly functioning market requires a large number of buyers and sellers (large being defined to be sufficient to generate price-taking as opposed to price-setting behaviour). It may be that certain markets are very thin especially on the supply side and hence there are monopoly rents to be earned through higher finance charges. If so, then the higher costs of finance will either drive firms to use alternative, less suitable, financing and/or lead to less investment and/or R&D.

(iii) *Market inefficiency.* If markets are inefficient then security prices will not correctly reflect available information and the cost and availability of finance may not be that appropriate to the investment or R&D project being funded. If stock prices are not always strong-form efficient then at some time the firm's stock will be under-valued. Myers and Majiluf (1984) argue that in such a situation firms may be reluctant to finance an investment through the issue of new stock since the new shareholders will benefit from the ulti-mate revision of the value of the existing stock. In such cases the management may pass over profitable projects. Further, as firms may be reluctant to issue new equity, they would use either fixed interest debt or carry financial slack in the form of retained earn-ings. This model forms the basis of Myers' (1984) Pecking Order theory of finance in which firms rank sources of finance preferring to use internal funds first, then external debt and then finally new equity to finance new investments.

(iv) *Cost of capital.* When evaluating an investment project, the correct discount rate for the firm to use in the calculation of the net present value of the project is the opportunity cost of capital appropriate to the class of investments. For standard projects that are simply exten-sions or replications of existing assets this may be obtained from the CAPM or arbitrage pricing theory. If the investment is of a sort that has not been undertaken elsewhere before (an expected characteris-tic of innovation investments) then it may be particularly difficult to observe the systematic risk of similar projects in other firms

(Goodacre and Tonks, 1995) and thus difficult to determine the appropriate discount rate.

(v)   *Asymmetric information.* In general the manager or firm undertaking an R&D or investment project will have far better knowledge of the costs and payoffs of that project than the financier. This is asymmetric information. Goodacre and Tonks (1995) argue that because of the need for managers in such environments to provide signals to financiers as to the wisdom of their investment decisions, this may cause managers to undertake shorter-term rather than longer-term projects. In the presence of information asymmetries (or incomplete information) recent work (for example Winker, 1999, p. 170) argues that credit rationing may appear. Credit rationing is taken here to mean that banks (and others) deny loans to borrowers who are observationally indistinguishable from those who do receive loans. In such circumstances it is the availability of capital and not its cost that determines the level of investment. Even in the absence of credit rationing, asymmetric information may make external debt and equity more expensive than internally available funds.

(vi)   *Moral hazard.* If an entrepreneur sells equity claims to outside investors then s/he is no longer the sole owner of the project and may be better thought of as the manager employed by the outside investor. In such principal–agent relationships there is always a moral hazard problem in that the agent will try to maximise his/her own utility rather than that of the principal. In particular it could be that this problem is especially exacerbated for long-term firm decisions for the principal will then have to wait longer to see the outcome. In such circumstances the literature has discussed many varieties of contracts that will encourage the agent to pursue the desires of the principals. Goodacre and Tonks (1995) illustrate how these may discourage longer-term investments. There is also some evidence that with optimal incentive contracts there may be under-investment in risky projects by managers even when more attractive than a safe project.

(vii) *Taxes and subsidies.* Financing decisions will logically be based upon after-tax costs and returns. The tax environment will thus have considerable influence upon the extent of investment and the means of financing investment. As tax regimes may differ across countries one may expect to find inter country differences on preferred finance structures (e.g. the balance of debt and equity) and on after-tax costs of capital as a result.

(viii) *Bankruptcy costs.* If there are bankruptcy costs then the Modigliani–Miller theorem does not hold. In the context of R&D, bankruptcy costs may well arise from the inability of the owner of the R&D asset to receive a fair price for that asset in the event of insolvency because the assets are highly specific and difficult to resell. Given that with a risky project cash flows are uncertain, it is possible that early in the life of such a project the profits will be insufficient to cover any interest payments on a debt instrument used to finance the project. For a newly established firm this could mean liquidation. Potential debt holders may well also realise this. For new firms or single project firms, therefore, equity may be the preferred borrowing instrument. For existing firms, the possibility of cross financing from other projects alleviates the bankruptcy risk and costs and thus there is not the same bias towards equity and debt and equity finance may be equally likely.

For all the reasons discussed above, one may expect to find that to some degree at least, investment in plant and equipment or innovation may well be affected by financial factors. The importance of the several factors listed may, however, vary considerably across firm sizes, industries and countries. Treating each in turn we may argue as follows.

It is often considered that there are special finance-related issues in the context of SMEs. On the simplest level, firm size may of itself mean that the availability of internally generated funds for the financing of an innovation project of a given size may be more difficult for smaller firms than larger firms. In terms of raising outside finance, for smaller firms problems of information asymmetries may be more severe than for larger firms. Moreover, for smaller newer firms there may be no track record upon which to base a case for funding and/or there may be fewer realisable assets to use as collateral. The costs of search may mean also that the supply of finance to such firms (in the absence of government intervention) may be more severely limited, and in particular, unless venture capital markets are well developed, equity capital may not be available at all, that is there may well be finance gaps. SMEs may well thus either be unable to raise funding for innovation (be credit rationed) or only be able to raise funding at a higher cost. The European Commission (2000) reviewing the financial environment in which European SMEs operates, argues that SMEs do face specific problems in accessing finance and in particular that: early stage enterprises face the highest level of constraint; bank credit is the most common and for many enterprises the only external source of finance; apart from banks, friends, relatives and business angels are important sources of credit; small mature enterprises are least constrained by finance mainly relying on bank credit; highly innovative and expanding enterprises seem to have better access to credit than the average SME, mainly relying upon bank loans, but also having access to venture capital and business angels. The theory and such previous empirical findings would thus suggest that as firm size increases, financial factors might well be less important as a constraint upon innovation.

Differences across industries (for given firm size) may also exist. An obvious consideration is that in more profitable industries there is less need for external funding than in less profitable industries. In riskier industries it may be more difficult to raise funding from outside the firm purely because of the risk factor. In more high-tech sectors not only may risk itself be a factor but also the proportion of assets that are realisable may be lower. In high-tech industries innovation is more likely to be of a sort that has not been undertaken elsewhere before and it may be particularly diffi-cult to observe the systematic risk of similar projects in other firms (Goodacre and Tonks, 1995) and thus difficult to determine the appropri-ate discount rate to use in evaluating investment in the firm. All such argu-ments would suggest that in more traditional industries with extensive track records funding from internal and external sources will be easier. For more high-tech and newer industries funding is more likely to be a problem and thus impact more upon (constrain) innovative performance.

Differences across countries given firm size and industry are also likely to be apparent. These may relate to factors such as taxes and subsidy regimes, the completeness of markets for finance, the legal environment as regards bankruptcy, government intervention and so on. Such issues are part of the national systems of innovation literature (see Nelson, 1993). Part of the national system of innovation of particular interest here is the financial environment in different countries. European financial environ-ments are both heterogeneous and changing (see Stoneman, 2001b). On the one hand, in terms of the financial system per se there are bank-based systems as typified by the German situation, and on the other market-based systems as typified by the UK. Most continental European systems are largely bank-based although there are signs of some movement in certain countries (for example France) to a market-based system. Alongside these different systems there are different patterns of ownership of industry. The German system reflects greater private ownership, more concentrated ownership and more pyramid ownership. In the UK the pat-terns is for less concentrated holding, less private control and few intercor-porate holdings. The different patterns of ownership allied with different financial systems generate different emphases upon insider and outsider control in the management of corporations. In the UK-type system, although much of the equity may be owned by financial institutions, it is through the market itself, via the threat of take-over, that control is mainly exercised. In German-type systems there is greater emphasis upon direct intervention by banks and co-operation between banks and management. The financing of investment by firms also differs across systems. Although self-generated funds are the main finance source for firms (except SMEs) in all countries these are more important in the UK, with bank finance more important in bank-based systems.

It is argued that the different patterns observed in financial systems have important implications for the way firms behave. The argument is that bank-based systems with insider control are particularly favourable to longer-term steady development built upon the construction of trust-based relations, firm-specific investments and steady change, but may generate a higher cost of capital due to bank monopoly power and perhaps undue conservatism. On the other hand market-based systems with outsider control and more arms-length relationships between the financiers and the managers are seen as more favourable to major change and switches of strategic direction but encourage liquidation of investment in the event of dissatisfaction, with no obligation to take anything other than a short term view. It is not however being suggested that one system is better than another, it is more a matter of 'horses for courses'. Nevertheless, it would be a surprise if different national financial systems did not impact upon innovative behaviour. What is more difficult to predict is the direction and importance of that impact. A particular interest in the literature is the differences of impact between Anglo-American market-based systems and German–Japanese bank-based systems.

Bond et al. (1997) find that the sensitivity of investment to financial variables is quantitatively more significant in the UK than in France, Germany or Belgium 1978–89. This is interpreted as a particular failing of the market-orientated UK system. Mulkay et al. (2000) undertake a similar cross-country comparison, but this time for both R&D and investment and between the US and France. Again significant differences are found across the two countries with a greater importance of profit or cash flow as a determinant of investment in the US than in France, however any differences are much less obvious when it comes to R&D. Between 1982 and 1993, for investment, cash flow did not matter for French firms at all but significantly affected the investment of US firms. The authors argue that this is probably the result of real differences in the working of capital markets in the two countries. In particular they argue that US shareholders were somewhat more likely to sell their shares in adverse situations, hence providing greater market discipline and more rapid responsiveness of US firms to changes in their prospects. To the extent that US firms feel pressure to use internal funds to finance future spending, they will have a higher long-run response to surprises in profits (not accompanied by surprises in demands) than would otherwise be the case.

This review of the theoretical arguments and (some) empirical literature indicates that one might expect to find financial factors impinging upon innovative activity. One might also expect that this impact will be greater for small and medium-sized firms than for large firms. The impact will also differ across industries, with more risky, newer industries experiencing greater problems. There may also be differences across countries although theoretically it is difficult to predict the nature of the differences. Past empirical work suggests that market-based systems may experience the greatest problems. In the next section we consider the CISII data that we will be using to explore these issues further in the later sections.

3.   DATA DESCRIPTION

The data source used in this chapter is the Second Community Innovation Survey (CISII). This pan-European firm-level survey was conducted (largely by national statistical offices) under the auspices of the European Innovation Monitoring System (EIMS) and Eurostat in 1997, so that the reference year for the survey is 1996 for most of the sample countries (although Norway and Portugal refer to 1997).[1] The survey was designed on the basis of a harmonised questionnaire applied in each country, making the dataset suitable for cross-country comparison. The countries included in the survey are Belgium, Denmark, Germany, Spain, France, Ireland, Italy, Luxembourg, Netherlands, Austria, Portugal, Finland, Sweden, UK, and Norway with firms in each country classified by industry (11 manufacturing sectors, six service sectors) and by firm size class (small, medium and large, defined respectively as firms with 20–49 employees in the manufacturing sector (10–49 in the service sector), 50–249 employees and more than 250 employees). Unfortunately, to preserve firms' confidentiality, firm-level data was not available to us, the data used here is instead at the industry, country or firm class level of aggregation.

The section of the CISII questionnaire of most interest to us concerns the factors hampering innovation. The question asked is reproduced below.

The innovation activity of your company could be hampered by various factors which might prevent innovation projects or slow up or stop projects in progress

a)   Has at least one innovation project in 1994–1996 been

yes   no

– seriously delayed
– abolished
– not even started

*b) If yes on at least one question, tick the relevant factors in the respective
columns*
Hampering factors

	seriously delayed	abolished	not even started
1. Excessive perceived economic risks			
2. Innovation costs too high			
3. Lack of appropriate sources of finance			
4. Organisational rigidities			
5. Lack of qualified personnel			
6. Lack of information on technology			
7. Lack of information on markets			
8. Fulfilling regulations, standards			
9. Lack of customer responsiveness			

The data available to us on the responses to this question are the proportions (relative to the number of firms reporting some innovative activity in the sample) for each impact (delay, abolish, not start) by country and firm size class, and by country and industry (not by country, industry and firm size class). In the sections below we undertake two exercises with this data. In the first we are interested in how important are financial factors as opposed to other hampering factors as a constraint upon innovation in terms of their impact in leading to delay, abandonment or not starting innovation projects. In the second exercise we concentrate solely upon hampering factor three and explore more fully the nature of the financial constraints across firm size classes, industries and countries. In the next section we briefly summarise the econometric method to be used.

4.   THE ECONOMETRIC MODEL

The econometric method we used below is known as a generalised linear model (GLM). We refer the reader to McCullagh and Nelder (1989) for a detailed treatment of such models. The class of GLM can be considered as an extension of the classical linear model. In the classical linear regression model it is assumed that

$$Y_i = \beta' X_i + \varepsilon_i \tag{3.1}$$

where the elements of ε_i are assumed to be i.i.d. N $(0, \sigma^2)$, X_i is a matrix of non-correlated explanatory variables, and β is a vector of parameters.

Compared to this framework GLM allows two generalisations. First, the relationship between the response variable Y_i and the explanatory variables in X_i need not to be of the simple linear form incorporated in (3.1), but may be distributed as any monotonic differentiable function. Secondly, the Y_i does not need to have a normal distribution, but may come from an exponential family.

In our case we consider n independent random variables Y_i corresponding to the number of successes in the n different subgroups (for example different firm size class). Therefore, the dependent variable Y_i is a binary random variable assuming the value one with probability $Pr(Y=0) = \pi$ and value zero with probability[2] $Pr(Y=0) = 1 - \pi$. To model the probability π we need to specify the functional form of

$$g(\pi) = X'\beta$$

where $g(\cdot)$ is a monotonic differentiable function. Moreover, we need to ensure that π is bounded between zero and one. That is we need to choose a cumulative probability distribution such that

$$\pi = g^{-1}(X'\beta) = \int_{-\infty}^{x} f(z)dz$$

where $f(z) \geq 0$ and $\int_{-\infty}^{\infty} f(z)dz = 1$. Our choice of $f(z)$ is

$$\pi = \int_{-\infty}^{x} f(z)dz = \frac{\exp(X'\beta)}{1 + \exp(X'\beta)} \tag{3.2}$$

and taking the logit transformation we can write equation (3.2) as

$$g(\pi) = \left(\frac{\pi}{1 - \pi}\right) = X'\beta. \tag{3.3}$$

To estimate the model we use maximum likelihood, the log-likelihood function for (3.3) being given by

$$L(\pi, y_i) = \sum_{i=1}^{n} \left[y_i \log\left(\frac{\pi}{1 - \pi}\right) + n_i y_i (1 - \pi) + \log\binom{n}{y} \right].$$

Maximising this function with respect to the vector β and equating the resulting expressions to zero yields estimates of the unknown parameters. To measure the goodness of fit of the model we use the likelihood ratio test statistic given by

$$D = 2[l(\hat{\pi}_{max}; y)] - l(\hat{\pi}; y)$$

where $\hat{\pi}_{max}$ is the vector of maximum likelihood estimates corresponding to the maximal model and $\hat{\pi}$ is the vector of maximum likelihood estimates for our model. Another criterion of goodness of fit is given by the Pearson χ^2 statistic. This test statistic is derived by minimising the weighted sum of squares

$$S_w = \sum_{i=1}^{n} \frac{(y_i - n_i \hat{\pi}_i)^2}{n_i \hat{\pi}_i (1 - \hat{\pi}_i)}$$

since $E(Y_i) = n_i \pi_i$ and $\sigma^2(Y_i) = n_i \pi_i - (1 - \pi_i)$ which is asymptotically distributed as χ^2. Other measures of goodness of fit are the Akaike (1973) information criterion (AIC), and the Bayesian information criterion (BIC) (Raftery, 1996).

5.   THE IMPORTANCE OF FINANCIAL FACTORS

In this section we explore the importance in hampering innovation of financial and related cost and risk factors relative to the other hampering factors. The exercise is performed using data from 12 sample EU countries, it being necessary on the grounds of data deficiencies to drop Spain, Portugal and Luxembourg from the original sample of 15. The data allows a distinction between services and manufacturing and thus we also allow a two way industry split. The basic approach is to separately consider for each impact (delay, abandonment, not start), the proportion of sample firms in each of the two industry sectors in each country who report such an impact, and to relate that to the hampering factors reported. Defining i as representing impact ($i = 1,...,3$), j as the hampering factor ($j = 1,...,9$) and m as the industry ($m = 1,2$), the dependent variable, for each i (inn_out_{ijm}) is the proportion of firms in industry m in each country reporting hampering factor j as having impact i. For each i there are 216 observations upon ijm ($m \times j \times 12$ countries). The explanatory variables are the nine factors hampering innovating reported in the previous section. Therefore, the estimated equation for each i is

$$inn\_out_{ijm} = \alpha_0 + \beta_j \sum_{j=1}^{j-1} Fac_{j,i,m} + \varepsilon_{j,i,m}, \qquad (3.4)$$

where the right-hand side variables are dummy variables that take the value of unity when the data point relates to that factor and zero otherwise (in the estimates we keep factor 9 as a baseline). The estimated parameters, for each i, provide, in essence, an average across industries and countries of the

Table 3.1   *Estimated coefficients (project delayed), standard errors, Wald test, two-tailed p-values, odds ratios and 95 per cent confidence intervals*

	Coeff.	Std. Err.	Z	$P > |Z|$	Odds ratio	Odds ratio confidence int
Fac1	0.430	0.164	26.13	0.000	1.54	1.48–1.59
Fac2	0.491	0.163	30.07	0.000	1.63	1.58–1.69
Fac3	0.729	0.159	45.64	0.000	2.07	2.00–2.13
Fac4	1.205	0.154	78.18	0.000	3.33	3.24–3.44
Fac5	1.257	0.154	81.70	0.000	3.35	3.40–3.62
Fac6	0.337	0.166	20.24	0.000	1.40	1.36–1.45
Fac7	0.040	0.174	2.32	0.020	1.04	1.01–1.08
Fac8	0.307	0.167	18.36	0.000	1.35	1.32–1.40
Fac9	–	–	–	–	1	–
Cons	−1.75	0.124	−141.44	0.000	–	–

Note: $(1/df)$ Deviance: 108.67; $(1/df)$ Pearson: 108.68; AIC: 111.15; Log Likelihood: −12440.60.

relative importance of the nine different factors in hampering innovation. In the tables that immediately follow we report the estimated coefficients for equation (3.4), relating respectively to projects delayed (Table 3.1), abolished (Table 3.2), and not started (Table 3.3).

In terms of the goodness of fit, the Wald tests reported in Tables 3.1–3.3 indicate that the right-hand side variables are highly significant in each case, moreover the relative *p*-values are close to zero. However, the AIC criteria is lower for projects abolished as a dependent variable, implying that the model better fits the data on delayed and not started projects.

In the last two columns of Tables 3.1–3.3 we report the odds ratios and their relative confidence interval. The odds ratios are defined as

$$odds\ ratio = \exp(\hat{\beta}_i),$$

and the confidence intervals are calculated in the same way from the 95 per cent confidence interval of $\hat{\beta}_i$.

The main purpose of this exercise is to explore the relative importance of different factors in hampering innovation. In terms of the odds ratios we may observe that for projects not started and for projects abolished the dominant hampering factors are 1–3. These factors are still important in delaying projects but there factors 4 and 5 are relatively more important.

Table 3.2   Estimated coefficients (project abolished), standard errors, Wald test, two-tailed p-values, odds ratios and 95 per cent confidence intervals

	Coeff.	Std. Err.	Z	P>|Z|	Odds ratio	Odds ratio confidence int.
Fac1	0.444	0.019	22.94	0.000	1.56	1.50–1.61
Fac2	0.273	0.020	13.94	0.000	1.31	1.26–1.37
Fac3	−0.178	0.021	−8.62	0.000	0.83	0.80–0.87
Fac4	−0.627	0.022	−28.11	0.000	0.53	0.51–0.56
Fac5	−0.664	0.022	−29.53	0.000	0.51	0.49–0.54
Fac6	−0.828	0.023	−35.52	0.000	0.44	0.41–0.46
Fac7	−0.948	0.024	−39.52	0.000	0.39	0.37–0.40
Fac8	−0.914	0.024	−38.44	0.000	0.40	0.38–0.42
Fac9	–	–	–	–	1	–
Cons	−0.105	0.014	−73.84	0.000	–	–

Note: (1/*df*) Deviance: 46.61; (1/*df*) Pearson: 46.15; AIC: 50.57; Log Likelihood: −5655.2016.

Table 3.3   Estimated coefficients (project not started), standard errors, Wald test, two-tailed p-values, odds ratios and 95 per cent confidence intervals

	Coeff.	Std. Err.	Z	P>|Z|	Odds ratio	Odds ratio confidence int.
Fac1	1.550	0.018	85.89	0.000	4.75	4.55–4.93
Fac2	1.310	0.018	71.78	0.000	3.70	3.58–3.84
Fac3	1.477	0.181	81.25	0.000	4.38	4.23–4.54
Fac4	0.064	0.205	3.97	0.002	1.07	1.02–1.11
Fac5	0.405	0.019	20.75	0.000	1.50	1.44–1.56
Fac6	−0.325	0.022	−14.75	0.000	0.72	0.69–0.75
Fac7	0.128	0.020	6.32	0.000	1.14	1.09–1.18
Fac8	0.339	0.019	17.23	0.000	1.40	1.35–1.45
Fac9	–	–	–	–	1	–
Cons	−1.672	0.014	−114.02	0.000	–	–

Note: (1/*df*) Deviance: 77.94; (1/*df*) Pearson: 84.55; AIC: 80.92; Log Likelihood: −9095.08.

Factor 3, a lack of appropriate sources of finance, is a dominant factor in projects not started and an important factor in causing delay but is relatively less important in leading to projects being abolished. This would make some sense if one considers that firms will not start projects if financing is not likely to be available and thus abandonment on financial grounds will be uncommon (as might be delay). Thus there seems clear evidence (especially as regards not starting projects) that financial factors are relatively important. This result is further emphasised if we group the hampering factors into three sub-groups, the first covering factors 1–3 which we label finance, costs and risks (hereafter FCR), the second covering 4–7 (that is organisational rigidity, lack of qualified personnel, lack of information on technology, lack of information on markets) which we label internal factors and the third covering 8 and 9 (fulfilling regulations and standards, lack of customer responsiveness to new products) which we label external factors. In Appendix Table 3.1A we present the correlation matrix across the nine factors. The full impact of financial factors may well be better represented by the impact of the whole FCR group rather than just factor 3. We see for example that in terms of not starting projects, the FCR factors are 3–4 times as important as any other factor. In firms of abolishing projects, although factor 3 itself, a lack of appropriate finance, is not that important, the FCR factors in total are more important than other factors. In firms of delaying projects, the FCR factors are important but not as important as factors 4 and 5. The results lead us to conclude that a lack of appropriate sources of finance is a major hampering factor to innovation. The effect is most noticeable in terms of causing innovation projects to not be started. If financial factors are interpreted more widely to also encompass excessive risk and innovation costs too high then this result is further emphasised. As the sample is made up of firms that have actually recorded some innovative activity (non-innovators are not even included in the sample) our results may even underestimate, in an absolute sense, the impact of finance as a barrier to innovation.

6. FINANCIAL CONSTRAINTS BY FIRM SIZE AND COUNTRY

Having established the relative importance of financial constraints as a barrier to innovation, in this section we focus on the third hampering factor listed in the CISII questionnaire and reported in Section 2: this relates specifically to a lack of appropriate sources of finance (factor 3 hereafter). In particular, we consider, for the same sample of twelve EU Member States, whether the importance of factor 3 varies across countries and firm size. Defining i as before, as representing impact ($i = 1,...,3$), k ($k = 1,...,3$) as the size class (small, medium, large) and l as the country ($l = 1,...,12$), the dependent variable for this analysis (inn_out_{ikl}) is the proportion of firms (who record some innovative activity) in a country in a size class who report impact *i* from hampering factor 3. This provides a total of 108 data points. The right-hand side variables are 12 dummy variables for country, 3 for size class and 3 for impact that take values of one or zero to match the data point, plus a number of interactive dummies between countries and firm size to pick up different effects of size in different countries. In modelling this relationship we sought the most parsimonious model that still explained the data. The rationale for minimising the number of explanatory variables was to produce a more numerically stable model. It is well known (see for example Harrel et al., 1996 or Hosmer and Lemeshow, 2000) that the more variables are included in a model, the greater the estimated standard errors become, and the more dependent the model becomes on the observed data. The criterion followed for including or excluding a variable from the final model was based on the likelihood ratio.

The estimates were generated with large firms, projects delayed, and Germany incorporated in the base-line. Initial estimates using a likelihood ratio test and the Wald test statistic for each variable led us to drop several country dummies from our initial model.[3] The results of adding 21 interaction dummies (that is 3 firm classes times the remaining 7 country dummies with Germany in the base-line) one at a time to the model is shown in the Appendix (Table 3.2A). Our choices as to which of these remains in the final preferred estimates was based upon the likelihood ratio test

$$LR = -2\ln\left[\frac{likelihood\ main\ effects\ model}{likelihood\ of\ the\ model\ with\ the\ interaction\ variable\ j}\right]$$

for $j = 1,\ldots,21$ which is asymptotically distributed as a χ^2 with j degrees of freedom. We include in the final model only those interactions which are significant at the 5 per cent level or 10 per cent at most (see Table 3.2A in the Appendix). In Table 3.4a we present the estimated parameters and some goodness of t tests.

In Table 3.4b we present the odds ratios by country and firm size class that result from the estimates in Table 3.4a for projects delayed. They are calculated by taking the exponential of the sum of the size coefficient, the country coefficient and any coefficient on the cross product of country and size. The odds ratio for large firms in Germany is unity, with the odds ratios for Belgium, Denmark, Austria and the Netherlands not being significantly different from those for Germany.

From Table 3.4a we observe that the probability of delaying a project because of a lack of appropriate sources of finance (taking account of firm size and country specific effects) is greater than that of abandoning or not

Table 3.4a   Estimated coefficients, Standard errors, Wald Test, two-tailed
p-values, and 95 per cent confidence intervals

	Coeff.	Std. Err.	Z	P>|Z|	95% Conf. Int.
Small	0.094	0.050	1.84	0.065	(−0.005),(0.193)
Med	0.127	0.051	2.50	0.012	(0.028),(0.227)
PNS	−0.822	0.023	−35.95	0.000	(−0.867),(−0.777)
PAB	−0.274	0.020	−13.08	0.000	(−0.314),(−0.232)
France	0.275	0.041	6.75	0.000	(0.195),(0.355)
Ireland	0.432	0.088	4.87	0.000	(0.258),(0.606)
Italy	0.316	0.097	3.25	0.001	(0.125),(0.506)
Finland	−0.554	0.165	−3.35	0.001	(−0.878),(−0.229)
Sweden	0.780	0.135	5.80	0.000	(0.516),(1.044)
UK	0.860	0.063	13.63	0.000	(0.737),(0.984)
Norway	−0.432	0.148	−2.92	0.003	(−0.721),(−0.142)
S-France	−0.276	0.056	−4.89	0.000	(−0.387),(−0.165)
S-Italy	−1.201	0.101	−11.16	0.000	(−1.412),(−0.990)
S-Finland	−0.699	0.240	−2.54	0.011	(−1.080),(−0.138)
S-Sweden	−0.489	0.153	−3.18	0.001	(−0.791),(−0.187)
S-UK	−0.332	0.071	−4.68	0.000	(−0.472),(−0.193)
S-Norway	−0.650	0.221	−2.94	0.003	(−1.078),(−0.216)
M-Ireland	0.835	0.063	13.26	0.000	(0.712),(0.959)
M-Italy	−0.589	0.158	−3.72	0.000	(−0.899),(−0.278)
M-Sweden	−0.186	0.072	−2.59	0.009	(−0.327),(−0.045)
L-France	1.20	0.107	11.16	0.000	(0.990),(1.412)
L-Italy	0.869	0.260	3.34	0.001	(0.358),(1.380)
L-Finland	0.776	0.280	2.77	0.006	(0.226),(1.325)
L-Norway	1.03	0.260	3.99	0.000	(0.527),(1.549)
Const	−3.33	0.046	−72.15	0.000	(−3.420),(−3.239)

Notes:
(1/*df*) Deviance: 18.89; (1/*df*) Pearson: 19.21; AIC: 20.37; Log Likelihood: −1053.84.
* PAB, PNS; stand for project abolished and not started respectively. ** S-Country, M-Country, L-Country stand for the interaction between small, medium, large class and the relative country respectively.

starting a project (coefficients −0.822 and −0.274 respectively). This might be taken to contradict our finding in the previous section that factor 3 was relatively most important in causing non starts. However, that analysis was of relative importance within an impact and not across impacts as has been analysed here. Multiplying the parameters in Table 3.4b by the exponential of the coefficients from Table 3.4a would yield the odds ratios by country and firm size class for projects not started and projects abandoned.

The table of odds ratios by firm size indicates that for all countries the

Table 3.4b   Odds ratios by country and firm size class

	Odds ratio small	Odds ratio medium	Odds ratio large
France	1.10	1.49	4.37
Ireland	1.69	4.03	1.54
Italy	0.45	0.86	3.27
Finland	0.31	0.54	1.25
Sweden	1.47	2.48	2.18
UK	1.86	2.68	2.36
Norway	0.37	0.74	1.82
Germany and Others	1.10	1.13	1

probability of factor 3 constraining innovation is greater (up to a 100 per cent greater in some countries) for medium-sized firms than for small firms, that is medium-sized firms face greater financial constraints than small firms. This result is not as expected. There are two potential reasons for this result. The first is that many countries have introduced special measures to assist small firms and this may be reflected in these results. Secondly, the sample being used for this analysis is conditional upon firms actually doing some innovation. If the probability of doing some innovation was constrained by financial factors (for which we have some evidence even for innovating firms) and if small firms are more likely to face such financial constraints, only those small firms least constrained by financial constraints would be included in the estimation sample and that would bias the results towards lesser constraints for small firms.

Turning to comparisons of large firms to small and medium-sized firms, the data in Table 3.4b indicates that: in France, Italy, Finland, and Norway, large firms are more likely to experience financial constraints than small and medium-sized firms; in Sweden and the UK large firms are more likely to face financial constraints than small but not medium-sized firms; in Ireland large firms are less likely to face financial constraints than both small and medium-sized firms. The a priori expectation was that large firms would be least constrained and the data does not clearly support this view. Once again this could be because the sample is conditional upon firms actually undertaking some innovative activity and the presence of government assistance schemes to SMEs.

These results could also be reflecting different size compositions for firms in different industrial sectors. If, as we explore in the next section, firms in different sectors face different levels of financial constraints, and the average firm's size differs across sectors, then the results in Table 3.4b could be reflecting this. Unfortunately our data does not allow decomposition by country size and sector.

The analysis of the odds ratios in Table 3.4b by country reveals significant differences. For small firms, those in the UK have the highest probability of facing financial constraints, some 70 per cent greater than in Germany. Small firms in Ireland and Sweden also have high odds ratios. Small firms in other countries have odds ratios either the same as or less than German firms. For medium-sized firms, Irish firms stand out as having a particularly high odds ratio but Swedish and UK firms again have relatively high odds ratios. Italy, Finland and Norway show (internationally relatively) low odds ratios for medium-sized firms. For large firms, in France the odds ratio is 430 per cent higher than in Germany, and also high in Italy, the UK and Sweden. All other countries show odds ratios greater than or equal to Germany. Thus, as far as large firms are concerned, the German financial environment is particularly favourable.

One explanation for these results may be based on the distribution of the enterprises by technological sector. According to the CISII results Ireland, the UK and Sweden are the countries with the highest shares of enterprises in the high-tech sector, while Germany has a strong position in the medium–high and medium–low branches. In general the share of innovating firms in a sector is higher, the higher is the sector's level of technology. As we will see in the next section high-tech enterprises are the ones more likely to experience financial constraints. Therefore, to some extent, it seems reasonable to argue that the results in Table 3.4b are affected to some degree by the distribution of the enterprises according to the level of technology of the countries considered.

Having said this, however, in the theoretical section we argued that one might well expect financial constraints to have differing impacts in different countries, although it was difficult to predict a priori exactly in which countries the constraints would be most severe. However, it was suggested on the basis of previous empirical work that firms in countries with market-based systems as opposed to bank-based systems would experience more financial constraints and a comparison of the UK to Germany could be taken as an indicator of this. It is clear that for all three firm size classes, the odds ratios are greater in the UK than in Germany and this may be support for the view that market-based systems are more likely to constrain innovation. However only for small firms is the UK odds ratio the largest estimated. For medium-sized firms Ireland has a higher ratio and for large firms Italy and France have higher ratios. Given that many factors other than whether systems are market-based or bank-based is likely to affect these ratios one cannot be definitive, but as the UK odds ratios rank as numbers 1, 2 and 3 (out of 12) for small, medium and large firms respectively, the circumstantial evidence that there are particular financial constraints in the UK compared to all other European, largely bank-based, countries is strong. One might also note the empirical evidence quoted in Section 2 above compared the UK to France, Belgium and Germany suggesting that financial factors were more important in the UK as a constraint upon investment. Our findings corroborate this except for large firms in France.

7.   FINANCIAL CONSTRAINTS BY INDUSTRY

Having explored the relationship between financial constraints and firm size by country, in this final substantive section we explore inter-industry differences in the importance of financial constraints. Again we restrict ourselves to the importance of factor 3, a lack of appropriate source of finance. To see if our results are consistent with the ones in Section 6, we introduce as explanatory variables in the model not only industry dummies, but also country dummies. Defining i as representing impact ($i = 1,...,3$), l as the country ($l = 1,...,12$), and m as the industry, the dependent variable for this analysis (inn_out_{iml}) is the proportion of firms in a country in an industry who report impact i from hampering factor 3. Unfortunately, we are severely constrained by data availability and this has led us first to consider only two impacts, that is projects not started and projects delayed. We analyse these separately rather than together for reasons that will become apparent below. There are many gaps in the data at the industry level especially for the service sectors. Therefore, there is a trade-off between considering a larger number of countries but a smaller number of industries, or the opposite. Given the aim of the experiment, we have decided to reduce the number of countries considered in order to maximise the number of industries included in the model. Following this criteria our final data set contains 12 industries, and 9 countries for 'project delayed' (that is 108 data points), and 8 countries and 14 industries (102 data points) for 'project not started'.[4] The right-hand side variables in each regression are industry and country dummy variables that take the value of unity when the data point relates to that industry or country and zero elsewhere. The industry definitions are listed in Table 3.3A (see appendix).

In Tables 3.5a and 3.5b we report the estimated coefficients for projects delayed and projects not started, respectively.[5] The industry chosen as a base-line is 'Manufacture of basic metals and fabricated metal products', a rather traditional industry. As far as the country variables are concerned, to be consistent with the model in Section 6 we keep Germany as a baseline. From Tables 3.5a–b, we can see that the majority of the country odds ratios are less than one, meaning that the probability of having financial constraints for the countries analysed is less than the probability of having the same problem in Germany. The apparent inconsistency of this result with those reported in Table 3.4b can be explained by considering that, even though we do not know the characteristics of the firms in the industries, the proportion of the class 'small firm' in the sample is much bigger than the medium and large firm classes (the approximate sample composition is 60:30:10, small, medium, large). The sample is also unbalanced across countries with, for example, Italy being overrepresented. It is likely that the results we find reflect the composition of our sample and, as seen in Table 3.4b, the odds ratios for small firms are generally less than for large firms and often less than unity. The odds ratios in Table 3.5a are not inconsistent with those for small firms reported in Table 3.4b.

From Tables 3.5a and 3.5b it emerges that there are significant differences across industries in the importance of financial constraints and impacts on delay and non-starts are also different across industries. Our theoretical discussion suggested that firms in newer, riskier and less profitable industries

Table 3.5a   Estimated coefficients, standard errors, Wald test, two-tailed p-values, odds ratios and 95 per cent confidence intervals (project delayed)

	Coeff.	Std. Err.	Z	$P>|Z|$	Odds ratio	Odds ratio conf. int.
Food	−0.147	0.047	−3.11	0.002	0.86	0.78–0.94
Textiles	−0.189	0.051	−3.68	0.000	0.82	0.74–0.91
Wood	−0.133	0.057	−2.31	0.021	0.87	0.78–0.97
Rubber	0.086	0.045	−1.90	0.057	0.91	0.83–1.00
Office Machinery	0.159	0.036	4.39	0.001	1.17	1.09–1.25
Electrical Machinery	0.126	0.038	3.29	0.016	1.13	1.05–1.22
Transport Equipment	−1.67	0.069	−2.40	0.000	0.84	0.73–0.96
Computers	0.157	0.034	4.58	0.000	1.17	1.09–1.25
Engineering	0.648	0.031	20.69	0.000	1.91	1.79–2.03
Denmark	−0.292	0.062	−4.72	0.000	0.74	0.66–0.84
France	−0.139	0.106	−1.32	0.000	0.86	0.70–1.07
Italy	0.181	0.063	2.87	0.000	1.19	1.05–1.35
Netherlands	−0.797	0.070	−11.37	0.019	0.45	0.39–0.51
Finland	−0.608	0.123	−8.02	0.004	0.54	0.46–0.63
Sweden	−1.484	0.070	−12.01	0.000	0.22	0.17–0.28
UK	−0.435	0.085	−5.08	0.000	0.64	0.54–0.76
Norway	0.498	0.060	8.21	0.000	1.64	1.46–1.78
Germany	–	–	–	–	1	–
Cons	−2.347	0.059	−39.52	0.000	–	–

Note: (1/*df*) Deviance: 24.36; (1/*df*) Pearson: 31.18; AIC: 25.43; Likelihood: −1353.50.

Table 3.5b   *Estimated coefficients, standard errors, Wald test, two-tailed p-values, odds ratios and 95 per cent confidence intervals (project not started)*

	Coeff.	Std. Err.	Z	P > |Z|	Odds ratio	Odds ratio conf. int.
Food	0.241	0.047	4.91	0.000	1.27	1.15–1.40
Textiles	0.136	0.052	2.61	0.009	1.15	1.03–1.26
Wood	0.690	0.063	10.89	0.000	1.99	1.76–2.25
Chemicals	0.393	0.62	6.32	0.000	1.48	1.31–1.67
Office Machinery	0.406	0.040	10.02	0.000	1.50	1.38–1.62
Electrical Machinery	0.418	0.043	9.52	0.000	1.52	1.39–1.65
Transport Equipment	0.534	0.656	8.15	0.000	1.70	1.50–1.94
Telecommunications	0.720	0.083	8.66	0.000	2.05	1.74–2.41
Financial Intermediation	−0.406	0.061	−6.59	0.000	0.67	0.59–0.75
Computers	0.407	0.041	9.84	0.000	1.50	1.38–1.62
Engineering	1.603	0.041	48.07	0.000	4.97	4.65–5.30
France	−1.131	0.128	−8.80	0.000	0.32	0.25–0.41
Italy	−0.883	0.038	−23.03	0.000	0.41	0.38–0.44
Netherlands	−0.212	0.031	−6.77	0.000	0.80	0.76–0.85
Finland	−0.832	0.061	−13.52	0.000	0.43	0.38–0.49
Sweden	−2.097	0.119	−17.65	0.000	0.12	0.09–0.15
UK	−0.441	0.067	−6.50	0.000	0.64	0.56–0.73
Norway	−0.541	0.030	−17.73	0.000	0.58	0.55–0.61
Germany	–	–	–	–	1	–
Cons	−2.317	0.030	−77.02	0.000	–	–

Note: (1/*df*) Deviance: 35.29; (1/*df*) Pearson: 39.25; AIC: 34.51; Likelihood: −1896.70.

are likely to experience more financial constraints than in other industries. We observe that in 'Computers' and 'Engineering', which might be considered newer and riskier industries, the odds ratio is particularly high for both projects delayed and not started. In 'telecommunications', which again might be considered newer and higher-tech, firms are more than twice as likely to not start an innovating project as in 'Manufacture of basic metal'. In more traditional sectors such as Food, Textiles and Rubber the odds ratios are relatively small (although it is difficult to explain why Wood carries a high ratio in Table 3.5b). In Financial Intermediation which might be considered a more profitable industry, the probability of not starting an innovating project because of lack of financial resources at 0.67 is less than in the base industry.

To the extent that it is possible to draw conclusions from such patterns, therefore, it would appear that the findings are consistent with the view that high-tech and high risk imply greater financial constraints than low-tech, low risk, and also that high profitability means fewer financial constraints.

8. CONCLUSION

There is a growing literature on the extent to which financial factors constrain investment and innovation within firms. In this chapter we have explored questionnaire data taken from the second Community Innovation Survey to address the role of financial factors in the determination of innovative activity within Europe. The theoretical literature suggests that financial factors will constrain such activity, but the importance of such constraints will vary according to characteristics of national financial environments, firm sizes and industrial sectors.

Using a generalised linear econometric model we initially find that, of the several factors that could constrain innovative activity in Europe, financial factors, especially a lack of an appropriate source of finance, are the most important, generally outweighing the importance of other internal and external factors in causing projects to be delayed, abandoned or not started.

Exploring the role of a lack of appropriate sources of finance further we discovered significant differences between countries, firm size classes and industries in the extent to which the constraint binds. Theoretical predictions and past empirical work suggested that market-based financial systems are likely to generate more severe financial constraints than bank-based systems. Comparisons of the UK with other countries (especially Germany) confirmed this prediction. We also found evidence that higher risk, newer, less profitable industries are more likely to experience financial constraints. We found little evidence, however, that smaller firms are more financially constrained than larger firms, although there may be sample bias-based reasons for this.

In the next few months the results from the third Community Innovation Survey will be available. It is our intention to extend this work by exploring these issues in that data set, which will also provide a time dimension to this study.

APPENDIX

Table 3.1A   Correlation matrix for Fac1–Fac9

	Fac1	Fac2	Fac3	Fac4	Fac5	Fac6	Fac7	Fac8	Fac9
Fac1	1.000								
Fac2	0.925	1.000							
Fac3	0.616	0.808	1.000						
Fac4	0.258	0.391	0.533	1.000					
Fac5	0.286	0.416	0.587	0.925	1.000				
Fac6	0.378	0.466	0.583	0.635	0.821	1.000			
Fac7	0.862	0.866	0.747	0.524	0.648	0.750	1.000		
Fac8	0.808	0.870	0.744	0.721	0.750	0.670	0.878	1.000	
Fac9	0.799	0.812	0.742	0.461	0.578	0.716	0.916	0.818	1.000

Table 3.2A   Likelihood ratio test statistic, p-value for interactions of interest when added to the main effects model in Table 3.4a

Interaction	LR-test	p-value
Main effect model	–	
S-France	$\chi^2(1) = 12.61$	0.0004
S-Ireland	$\chi^2(1) = 7.19$	0.0073
S-Italy	$\chi^2(1) = 200.75$	0.0000
S-Finland	$\chi^2(1) = 9.14$	0.0025
S-Sweden	$\chi^2(1) = 4.76$	0.0291
S-UK	$\chi^2(1) = 6.57$	0.0104
S-Norway	$\chi^2(1) = 8.26$	0.0041
M-France	$\chi^2(1) = 0.000$	0.9998
M-Ireland	$\chi^2(1) = 8.46$	0.0036
M-Italy	$\chi^2(1) = 134.05$	0.0000
M-Finland	$\chi^2(1) = 0.09$	0.7626
M-Sweden	$\chi^2(1) = 10.72$	0.0011
M-UK	$\chi^2(1) = 2.48$	0.1155
M-Norway	$\chi^2(1) = 1.10$	0.2944
L-France	$\chi^2(1) = 29.61$	0.0000
L-Ireland	$\chi^2(1) = 0.10$	0.0000
L-Italy	$\chi^2(1) = 27.96$	0.0000
L-Finland	$\chi^2(1) = 12.62$	0.0004
L-Sweden	$\chi^2(1) = 2.45$	0.1176
L-UK	$\chi^2(1) = 2.21$	0.1370
L-Norway	$\chi^2(1) = 7.95$	0.0048

Table 3.3A Classification of the economic activities

Food	Manufacture of food products; beverages and tobacco.
Textiles	Manufacture of textiles and textile products; manufacture of leather and leather products.
Wood	Manufacture of wood products; manufacture of pulp, paper and paper products.
Rubber	Manufacture of rubber and plastic products; manufacture of other non-metallic mineral products.
Metals	Manufacture of basic metals, and fabricated metal products.
Chemicals	Manufacture of coke, refined petroleum products, and nuclear fuel; manufacture of chemicals.
Office Machinery	Manufacture of machinery and equipment n.e.c.
Electrical Machinery	Manufacture of electrical and optical equipment.
Transport Equipment	Manufacture of transport equipment.
Telecommunications	Telecommunications.
Financial Intermediation	Financial intermediation.
Transport	Land transport; transport via pipeline; water transport; air transport.
Electricity	Electricity; gas and water supply.
Computers	Computers and engineering activities, and related technical consultancy.
Engineering	Architectural and engineering activities, and related technical consultancy.

NOTES

1. A prior Community Innovation Survey (CISI) was undertaken in 1993. Unfortunately, it suffered from both country-specific problems (for example the response rate in some countries was so low that the results could not be published) and 'cross-country' problems (for example in some countries firms were selected according to the principle of random sampling, in other countries the census was used, while a third category of countries defined a sample of likely innovators). We thus elected to concentrate in this chapter on CISII.

2. Consider a random variable Y whose probability density function depends only on a single parameter θ. This distribution belong to the exponential family if it can be written in the form

$$f(y,\theta) = s(y)t(\theta)e^{a(y)b(\theta)},$$

where a, b, s and t are known functions. This equation can be rewritten in the form

$$\begin{aligned} f(y,\theta) &= \exp[\log s(y) + \log t(\theta) + a(y)b(\theta) \\ &= \exp[a(y)b(\theta) + c(\theta) + d(y)], \end{aligned}$$

where $s(y) = \exp d(y)$ and $t(\theta) = \exp c(\theta)$. The binomial distribution belongs to the exponential family since the distribution

$$f(y_i, \pi) = \binom{n}{y} \pi^y (1 - \pi)^{n-y}$$

where $i = 1, \dots, n$, can be written as

$$f(y_i, \pi) = \exp\left[y\log\pi - y\log(1 - \pi) + n\log(1 - \pi) + \log\binom{n}{y} \right]$$

which is the form above.

3. The country variables not significant are: Belgium (Wald test = 0.82 and p-value = 0.412, LR test: $\chi^2(1) = 1.62$ p-value = 0.4450); Denmark (Wald test = 1.26 and p-value = 0.206, LR test: $\chi^2(1) = 1.05$ p-value = 0.3047); Netherlands (Wald test = 0.59 and p-value = 0.557, LR test: $\chi^2(1) = 0.34$ p-value = 0.5580); Austria: (Wald test = 1.22 and p-value = 0.224, LR test: $\chi^2(1) = 1.56$ p-value = 0.2578).

4. The countries considered for 'project delayed' are Germany, France, Italy, Netherlands, Finland, Sweden, UK, Norway for the sectors described in Table 3.5a, while for 'project not started' we include Denmark but we do not include the following industries: 'electricity' and 'telecommunication'.

5. In Table 3.5a we do not include the following explanatory variables: 'Chemicals' (estimated parameter = 0.02, Wald test = 0.39 (p-value = 0.70)), 'Transport' (estimated parameter = −0.04, Wald test = −1.16 (p-value = 0.247)). For the restricted model the LR test gives: $\chi^2(2) = −2.32$; (p-value = 0.31): while in Table 3.5b we do not include: 'Rubber' (estimated parameter = 0.07, Wald test = 1.53 (p-value = 0.20)), 'Electricity' (estimated parameter = 0.19, Wald test = 1.01 (p-value = 0.31)). For the restricted model the LR test gives: $\chi^2(2) = 1.90$; (p-value = 0.38).

REFERENCES

Akaike, H. (1973). 'Information Theory and an Extension of the Maximum Likelihood Principle', in B.N. Petrov and F. Csaki (eds), *Second International Symposium on Information Theory*, Budapest: Akademei Kiado, pp. 267–81.

Bond, S., J. Elston, J. Mairesse and B. Mulkay (1997), 'Financial Factors and Investment in Belgium, France, Germany and the UK: A comparison using company panel data', NBER Working Paper no. 5900.

European Commission (2000), *The European Observatory for SMEs, Sixth Report*, Executive Summary, Enterprise Policy, Brussels.

Goodacre, A. and I. Tonks (1995), 'Finance and Technological Change', in P. Stoneman (ed.), *Handbook of the Economics of Innovation and Technological Change*, Oxford: Blackwells, pp. 298–341.

Harrel, F.E., K.L. Lee and D.B Mark (1996), 'Multivariate prognostic models: Issues in developing models, evaluating assumptions and measuring and reducing errors', *Statistics in Medicine*, **15**, 361–87.

Hall, B. (1992), 'Investment and Research and Development at the Firm Level: Does the Source of Finance Matter', NBER Working Paper, no. 4096.

Himmelberg, C. and B. Petersen (1994), 'R&D and internal finance: a panel study of small firms in high tech industries', *Review of Economics and Statistics*, **76** (1), 38–51.

Hosmer, D. and S. Lemeshow (2000), *Applied Logistic Regression*, Wiley series in Probability and Statistics, New York: John Wiley & Sons.

Hubbard, R.G. (1998), 'Capital market imperfections and investment', *Journal of Economic Literature*, **36**, 193–225.

McCullagh, P. and J.A. Nelder (1989), *Generalized Linear Models*, 2nd edn, London: Chapman & Hall.

Modigliani, F. and M.H. Miller (1958), 'The cost of capital, corporation finance and the theory of investment', *American Economic Review*, **48**, 261–97.

Mulkay, B., B. Hall and J. Mairesse (2000), 'Firm Level Investment and R&D in France and the US: a comparison', NBER Working Paper, no. 8038.

Myers, S.C. and N.S. Majiluf (1984), 'Corporate financing and investment decisions when firms have information that investors do not have', *Journal of Financial Economics*, **13**, 187–221.

Myers, S.C. (1984), 'The capital structure puzzle', *Journal of Finance*, **39**, 575–92.

Nelson, R. (ed.) (1993), *National Innovation Systems: a Comparative Analysis*, Oxford: Oxford University Press.

Raftery, G. (1996), 'Bayesian Model Selection in Social Research', in P.V. Marsden (ed.), *Sociological Methodology*, vol. 25, Oxford: Basil Blackwell, pp. 111–63.

Schiantarelli, F. (1996), 'Financial constraints in investment: methodological issues and international evidence', *Oxford Review of Economic Policy*, **12** (2), 70–89.

Stoneman, P. (2001a), 'Technological Diffusion and the Financial Environment', Working Paper, UN University, Maastricht, 2001.

Stoneman, P. (2001b), 'Heterogeneity and Change in European Financial Environments', Working Paper, UN University, Maastricht, 2001.

P. Winker (1999), 'Causes and effects of financing constraints at the firm level', *Small Business Economics*, **12**, 169–81.

4. Internationalism and economic development: transnational corporations, small firm networking and universities

Roger Sugden

1. INTRODUCTION

A frequently advocated policy for economic development relies on 'free markets' and emphasises a prominent role for large, typically transnational corporations. This approach leads to 'strategic failures', production governed in narrow self-interest with adverse consequences for societies. In contrast, an alternative suggests that strategic decision making in production be characterised by economic democracy, the prospect for which requires an analysis of certain sorts of clusters and networks. Underlying these alternatives is a choice between different forms of internationalism. One is based on economic activity characterised by a transverse structure, a mere crossing of nations without intending to meet the aims and objectives of the peoples of particular localities. The other is founded on a multinational perspective, a coming together based on and respecting different desires, experiences, histories, traditions, cultures and competencies.

This chapter illustrates these possibilities in the context of strategies for internationalisation in a particular sector – education, more specifically universities. Two models are considered. The first is based upon copying and serving large corporations. It is argued that adoption of this approach would imply significant failures in the educational process. In the extreme, it would result in a world with a small number of first-tier universities that fail to serve the interests of the communities and societies in which they operate. The second is a type of networking, a so-called multinational web. This draws on the behaviour of some small firms. It envisages research and learning that is inclusive, enhanced by widened experiences, understanding and options. Its emphasis is on democracy, positive freedom and multinationalism. This second model is explored in the chapter through a description of a specific case: the evolution of an ongoing experience in nurturing a multinational network of research and learning in industrial economics.

These topics are especially appropriate to this volume for a number of reasons. First, the nature and impact of large and in particular transnational corporations, market power and the governance of production are important issues in Keith Cowling's work. This chapter considers each of these, explicitly using aspects of his research. In doing so, it also draws on years of discussion on a relationship with him that shapes and influences all of my thinking on economics. Moreover, the chapter is about internationalism. It contemplates alternatives to the domination of transnational corporations without resorting to a narrow, nationalist perspective. Keith Cowling is an internationalist; an advocate of both the practice and ideals of co-operation and understanding between and across the peoples of different nations. Third, the chapter explores another of his passionate concerns: universities, their role and future. A university system that mimics and serves transnational corporations is not the type that Keith Cowling has sought and championed. And whilst he might not agree with all that the chapter suggests, its arguments are in line with his positive search for appropriate ways forward. Indeed, he has shaped and nurtured the experience described in the later part of this chapter; it would not exist without him, nor would it have its unique agenda and outputs.

The structure of the chapter is as follows. Section 2 characterises different forms of the research and learning process. Section 2.1 questions the alleged similarities between universities and large corporations, and examines internationalisation by analogy to the activities of transnationals. Section 2.2 then introduces the possibility of a model based on smaller firms. A specific suggestion is taken up in Section 3. A form of small firm networking is discussed in Section 3.1 and this is applied to the research and learning context in Section 3.2 Conclusions are drawn in Section 4.

2. THE RESEARCH AND LEARNING PROCESS

2.1 A Model Based on Transnational Corporations

Recent years have seen the emergence of a comparatively dominant set of market-based economic models throughout large parts of the world. For some, the end of the Cold War and transition in the old Soviet bloc marks the advent of hegemony for free market capitalism, for what Stiglitz (2002) calls 'market fundamentalism' (p. 221, for example). The entities that both drive and epitomise these forms of market economies are the large, transnational corporations, upheld by some as role models for all organisations and by others as at least a major determinant of future developments.

This influence is felt in the education sector. Dearing (1998), for example, suggests that 'higher education is nowadays big business, universities are major enterprises in their own right' (p. 4). Especially revealing is de Boer's (1999) analysis. He argues that some critics of universities have no trust in the academic community and instead 'advocate business models of management. They try to transform universities into organisations similar to ordinary commercial firms so that they can be assessed and managed in roughly similar ways' (p. 132). De Boer goes on to suggest that this approach may point towards a form of corporate hierarchy, with 'senior management teams and strategic plans, line managers and cost centres' (p. 132).

There is a danger with this approach: universities that copy such hierarchies will cause societies to suffer adverse outcomes. More specifically, the concentration of power in transnational corporations has significant implications for their impact and, by analogy, for the impact of their mimics in universities.

Free market systems founded on large, transnational corporations suffer from inherent deficiencies that prevent societies from attaining their objectives and constrain people's abilities, aims and aspirations (Cowling and Sugden, 1994, 1999). The starting point for this assessment is that corporations have market power (in line with Cowling's (1982) analysis of monopoly capitalism), that they are units of planning (as Coase, 1937, observes), and that this planning is undertaken by a subset of those with an interest in the corporation's performance (Cowling and Sugden, 1998a). By definition, to plan is to make the strategic decisions and the strategic decision makers are the controllers who determine the corporation's broad objectives (Zeitlin, 1974). Quite who these controllers are is a matter of controversy, but there is a consensus that they do not comprise everybody with an interest in the corporation's activities, for example control does not typically rest with the workforce. Add to this consensus the standard economists' assumption that decision makers act in their own self interest and the conditions are in place for an economy to suffer from inherent deficiencies. In part, problems arise because exclusive interests govern corporations in pursuit of their own objectives; they determine strategy, taking advantage of market imperfections, and do so despite the wishes of others. In part, there are deficiencies because the exclusion from decision making is itself a constraint on people's activities, hence welfare.

To illustrate, transnational corporations account for most of the world's international trade. Thus, a system of so-called free trade is essentially one where transnationals' strategic decision makers are free to trade in their own interests, governments simply being the guarantors of facilitating conditions such as property rights (Cowling and Sugden, 1998b). In line with Bailey (1999) and following the distinction made by Berlin (1969), the controllers of transnationals are negatively free to go about their business without interference from others. They are also positively free, meaning that they are free 'to be somebody, not nobody; a doer deciding, not being decided for' (Berlin, 1969, p. 131). However, the same cannot be said for those excluded from governance. For example, suppose a corporation opts for the strategic pursuit of profit. Free trade for this firm might mean that it dual-sources intermediate outputs and assembles its final product in different countries (Adam, 1975). It might thereby take advantage of economies of scale, of opportunities to 'divide and rule' labour as well as governments, and of chances to minimise tax liabilities through transfer pricing. Free trade would be central to this strategy. Of course the labour that has its bargaining power undermined by the divide and rule might prefer something different, as might the societies in which these corporations (do or do not) carry out their production and other activities. But in a system where transnationals are free to trade as their strategic decision-makers wish, it is not for the excluded to determine outcomes. They are nobodies, they are being decided for.

The fundamental problem that this illustrates is the strategic failure of a free market system, the presence in that system of a strategic decision-making process that prevents the attainment of socially desirable outcomes. If a university system were to mimic and simply serve transnational corporations, it would add to that failure.

This outcome follows because, first, serving transnational corporations would contribute to the socially undesirable outcomes resulting from those firms' activities. Second, because the direct effect of mimicking transnationals might be universities committed to socially unacceptable activities. As with transnationals undertaking free trade, problems would arise because emasculated interests without positive freedom would not have their concerns directly represented. For example, if a university was to exclude academics from strategic decision making, it might pursue a research and learning agenda that they and others would find unsuitable. See, for instance, the discussion in Craig et al. (1999) of corporate universities, organisations that provide extreme evidence on the connections between corporations and higher education. It is suggested that

> compatibility of corporate strategies and academic enquiry is contestable: in the corporate university one might well imagine conflict between what scholars consider ought to be enquired into, and what the corporate strategy dictates to be the current action plan. Consider, for example, the obvious conflicts between corporate strategies in the tobacco industry and the conduct of research into the health effects of smoking. (Craig et al., p. 513)

Other specific difficulties might include a university using a divide and rule strategy. Or a university might target a niche set of 'buyers' for its 'products', tailoring courses and charging fees to maximise net revenues. This might exclude those from relatively poor backgrounds. It might also bias student selection towards 'customers' from advantaged social or cultural groups. All of these possible outcomes might be considered undesirable by the society in which the university operates.

In addition, if universities were to mimic transnationals the world education system might reflect a corporate-type hierarchy. The internationalism of transnationals implies a spanning of nations in pursuit of corporate goals. This has been argued to lead to a world economy characterised by a core of development and wealth alongside a periphery of underdevelopment and poverty, a perspective seen in the suggestion by Hymer (1972) that economies dominated by transnationals will mirror the hierarchical form of those transnationals. He sees 'the highest offices of the [transnational] corporations concentrated in the world's major cities . . . These will be the major centres of high-level strategic planning. Lesser cities throughout the world will deal with the day-to-day operations of specific local problems. These in turn will be arranged in a hierarchical fashion' (p. 50). If universities were to follow the same logic, the implication would be a system of research and learning in which they establish branches in various countries, all designed to serve the aims and objectives of the parent. This would be likely to mean that certain of the world's 'leading' institutions would be able to capitalise on their expertise and image, similar to the way in which Dearing (1998) suggests 'prestigious universities' (p. 7) might be able to drive the introduction of new communications and information technology in 'transnational higher education' (p. 8). There would be a first tier of universities in the world made up of a handful of organisations headquartered in their 'home' nation but with facilities elsewhere.[1] These facilities would not be designed to serve the interests of the communities and societies in which they are located. An elite would govern the branches and local interests would be excluded.

2.2   A Model Based on Smaller Firms

To avoid the strategic failure of a university system that mimics and simply serves transnational corporations, alternative development paths would need to be introduced. One possibility is to learn from successful experiences amongst smaller firms.

Faced with the inherent problems of systems characterised by socially incomplete decision making, it has been argued in the case of transnational corporations generally that ways of democratising the strategic decision-making process are needed. It is necessary to search for ways of appropriately involving more and more people affected by strategic decisions in the process of making those decisions. As an aspect of this, it has been further argued that there might be potential in basing economic success on the activities of smaller firms (Cowling and Sugden, 1999). The intuition is that democracy in strategic decision making might be more feasible in an economy made up of smaller firms.

The appeal of this argument for universities is that, to a certain degree, academia can be realistically characterised as a production activity entailing many small-scale production units – the equivalent of small firms – inter-linked in a large-scale production process. The production activity is to provide and follow through research and learning opportunities. The small-scale production units are focused on the academics; scholars with more or less academic freedom and working in various institutional frameworks. Of course the analogy is not perfect but it builds on the strong (albeit threatened) tradition of many universities being federations of academics. This is a 'college of scholars' approach, and it might appear to be in line with the need for democracy in the research and learning process. A federation of academics implies a governance mechanism that empowers a significant number of university employees, although not all interest groups.[2] This structure contrasts with the complete, or near complete, exclusion of employees in the typical transnational corporation.

Also interesting is that a college is a network; the small-scale production units within it constitute a set of people connected with each other and working in some form of system or process. This argument is especially relevant because recent analyses of economic development have focused on certain types of networks amongst small firms, arguing that they have been very successful. The implication is that universities might draw on these analyses when looking for appropriate ways forward. More particularly, an understanding of internationalisation in research and learning and an alternative to the copying of transnationals might be found in the economic analysis of multinational webs. This is a certain type of network that has been proposed as a possible alternative to transnational corporations.

3. MULTINATIONAL WEBS

3.1 Webs in General

The concept of a web is a stylised possibility suggested by Sugden (1997) and by Cowling and Sugden (1999). It is a benchmark for analysing particular situations that is rooted in a response to the deficiencies of transnational corporations as models for internationalisation. This response implies an emphasis on democracy and positive freedom; webs are premised on the desirability of production governance that avoids concentration in the power to make strategic decisions, and on the need to emphasise freedom to act and to be.[3] Moreover, whereas the literature on networks typically adopts a blinkered approach to international linkages once it gets beyond international trade, the analysis of webs is different. Its emphasis is multinationalism, a coming together across nations to identify and pursue desirable ways forward, respecting and drawing on the different experiences, histories, traditions, cultures and competencies of localities. These differences are seen as a source of strength, providing opportunities for mutual benefit and being essential for the full development of ideas and imagination, therefore prerequisites for efficiency. This form of internationalism is in stark contrast to the activities of modern corporations; to be transnational is to have a transverse structure, to span nations for the advantage of specific interests without being rooted in the localities that make up those nations.

Further, the characteristics of multinational webs are drawn from the economics literature discussing various types of network – see, for example, Brusco (1982) on Italian industrial districts, Humphrey and Schmitz (1995) on clusters in 'developing countries', and Lundvall (1992) on systems of innovation – without being encumbered by the peculiar experiences associated with particular cases. A key feature is the capturing of economies of scale through large-scale production processes as against large-scale production units. A web would comprise many units which taken individually are relatively small but which taken as a group constitutes production on a large scale. The aim would be for each unit to be directly linked with others in a nexus of criss-crossing relationships. These relationships would neither be vertical chains of command, nor horizontal links for sharing information. They would be characterised by interdependence, not the dependence of networks centred on transnationals.[4] The units would also cooperate with each other by providing mutual support in a process that promotes the emergence of new and rival production units; without new units the network would be likely to wither and stagnate.

The process would be based on a culture emphasising that all people, individually and together, evolve, back and trust their ability to find successful ways forward. In part this refers to the potential of collective service provision but a deeper and wider set of concerns also comes into play. For example, especially interesting is the suggested importance of a munificent economic environment (Sweeney, 1997). Hence a web would not emphasise a constraining, stifling or prevention of others; it would stress the development of each and every person to realize his or her full potential. The intention would be to tackle head-on the problems that arise when there is a concentration of strategic decision making. As has been argued in the case of transnational corporations, such concentration channels people into particular roles, excluding the majority from governance. This is not to deny, of course, that in practice people and production units might see themselves as rivals and therefore look to constrain. Thus one of the necessary conditions for creating a successful web would be to design frameworks and processes which identify and highlight conflicts and tensions – they cannot be ignored – and which consequently develop means for resolving problems.

It is also important to recognise the mutual dependence of the social and the economic. For Bianchi (1993), 'the lesson derived from the Italian district analysis is that endogenous growth stems from the development of a local community, which is able to reinforce productive connections within a solid social context. Policy has to pay attention to both these elements' (pp. 26–7). It is vital to take this lesson on board, to see the fusion of the social and the economic into a single integrated process as a central issue. This entails a focus on the appropriate levels and mix of social, human and physical capitals (see also the wider literature on social capital, for example the collection in Dasgupta and Serageldin, 2000). Furthermore, it is important to appreciate that the fusion of the social and the economic in a web would only be born out of the particular histories, traditions, cultures and competencies of the components that make up the network. It is even insufficient to be rooted in such contexts.

Quite how a web might be created and nurtured is not unproblematic. However, what is clear is the necessity for learning as a way of confronting any problems. Hymer (1972) suggests that large corporations had to learn how to become transnational. Likewise, creating multinational webs would require that actual and potential participants have opportunities to learn for themselves how webs might be formed, evolved and developed. One aspect of this would be the provision of time, space and encouragement to look for and plan new ways forward.

This and other crucial features of such networking are summarised in Table 4.1.

3.2 Research and Learning; a Case in Industrial Economic Development and Public Policy

The conceptualisation of research and learning as a production activity in which small-scale production units are focused on individual scholars suggests that universities might deliberately and consciously create multinational networks by targeting the stylised characteristics highlighted in Table 4.1.

Table 4.1   Desirable characteristics for production networks?

- Democracy in strategic decision making
- Emphasis on positive freedom for each participant
- Multinationalism
- Small-scale production units
- Large-scale production processes
- Participants linked in a nexus of criss-crossing relationships
- Environment of mutual and cooperative support
- Encouragement for new production units
- Fusion of the social and the economic into one process
- Birth and growth from participants' histories, traditions and cultures
- Provision of continuous learning opportunities
- Development of each individual to realise his or her full potential
- Means to recognise, highlight and resolve conflicts and tensions

---

Creating a web would entail new practice and behaviour for universities. Although academics have often been isolated from each other – even within organisations there have been walls between departments and individuals have seen themselves as rivals with no basis for mutual support[5] – the magnitude of existing international links across universities is in one sense immense. For example, Seidel (1991), referring to programmes to send German students abroad and to bring foreign students into Germany, states that there are 1500 formal co-operation agreements for this purpose alone. Extend that to include informal arrangements as well as all countries, and there appears to be a lot of activity. And, of course, Seidel was writing at the start of the 1990s, since when there has been significant growth; see, for example, Dearing (1998) and Van Damme (2001) on European Commission ERASMUS and SOCRATES programmes. Nor is it in dispute that many academics attend conferences with colleagues from different nations, and that many are involved in joint research and learning projects.

Nevertheless, the multinationalism envisaged in Table 4.1 involves an alternative, long-run, continuous and dynamic process growing out of and bringing together the differences that are found amongst the people of different nations. It is not simply frequent attendance at international conferences, the equivalent of international trade in goods. It is not even a network based on a possibly expanding set of universities arranging for staff and student exchanges, joint research projects amongst those staff, and joint learning programmes; this is perhaps equivalent to a strategic alliance amongst corporations. It is certainly not the internationalism of a transnational-type university, as Section 2 makes clear. Rather, the aim is a joining across nations, a common development that builds from and respects differences so as to open new frontiers, a flexible and living process that reveals as yet unidentified possibilities.[6] The result of this multinationalism would be widened experiences, understanding and options, increased efficiency through an outward shift in the production possibility frontier. The benefit would be in unique research and learning outputs. It is not merely a case of given outputs achieved more cheaply – equivalent to the savings in transaction costs that Coase (1937), Williamson (1975) and others identify as the raison d'être of a corporation. Rather, it is a change in the type and form of transactions.

A web in research and learning would be rooted in the people involved. It would have an institutional framework that enables and facilitates those individuals, who would be drawn from a far wider set of organisations than are formally contracted into the framework. The driving force would be its individual members, linked in an environment of mutual co-operation and support. Across many universities throughout the world there are scholars working alone or in small groups yet all concerned with the same subject area; a multinational web envisages joining these individuals in an appropriate network. Not least, such an outcome would secure economies of scale as a result of individuals working together in the sorts of numbers that rarely if ever exist within one organisation, and economies of scope, due to co-operation between scholars with related yet differentiated interests.

Some of what would be entailed in establishing and nurturing a web can be illustrated from a particular case, a network of researchers based primarily in universities across Europe and the Americas, and concerned with policies for industrial development. This network has evolved since 1990. On foundations provided in particular by the activities of the European Network on Industrial Policy (EUNIP) and stimulated by L'institute (Institute for Industrial Development Policy), the network is now at the stage where creation of a multinational web is being explicitly discussed and pursued.

Table 4.1 emphasises learning as well as birth and growth from participants' histories, traditions and cultures. In the network on industrial economics and public policy, the creation of a multinational web is learning from, building on and developing out of EUNIP and other initiatives. The roots of EUNIP lie particularly in the two Summer Research Workshops jointly hosted by the Universities of Warwick and Birmingham in the early 1990s. These may be seen as constituting the first phase of a long-run, evolving programme. Despite wariness within Birmingham and Warwick about co-operation between two (geographically close) universities that saw themselves as 'competitors and rivals', the initiative was designed to yield mutual benefit. The aim was to provide a small yet expanding group of scholars – drawn from across Europe and to a more limited extent from the US – with the time and the space to discuss emerging issues in public policy. Learning from previous experience with Warwick Summer Research Workshops and unlike the typical conference, schedules were not filled with paper presentations; rather, space was given for interaction on a more informal basis, and the relevance of social activity as a catalyst to productivity was explicitly emphasised. This reflects the importance attached to the fusion of the social and the economic into one process, also seen in Table 4.1.

It was on these foundations that an approach was made to the European Commission for Human Capital and Mobility funding to take the project into its next phase. As a result, a partnership spanning nine universities across eight countries obtained support for a series of workshops and post-graduate research initiatives throughout 1994–7. EUNIP was formally created in the middle of this period. The Network quickly spanned many more than the nine core institutions and grew to encompass well over 200 individual scientists, mostly in Europe and the Americas. Unlike in a trans-national approach to research and learning, the aims and payoffs in the Network were neither designed nor realised exclusively for the advantage of the core partners. Moreover, the deliberate focus on postgraduate training and on young researchers reflected another of the characteristics in Table 4.1, the encouragement of new production units, in this case of new talent amongst those thinking about and analysing policies for industrial economic development. Also noteworthy is the way in which the Human Capital and Mobility initiative was explicitly tied into attempts to nurture a network in South America, and into an ACE project on foreign direct investment. The latter funded participation by scientists from Central and Eastern Europe in EUNIP Workshops. Although the Human Capital and Mobility and ACE projects had different co-ordinators, they created links amongst scientists in an emerging environment of mutual co-operation and support. The network was not seen as having a fixed boundary, and links across projects were ways of reaping economies of scale and scope.

There continued to be development building on these initiatives, although an early and ongoing difficulty was that participants typically looked for centralised authority. The structure of European Commission-funded projects and other experience has perhaps favoured approval seeking from a central co-ordinator, causing some participants to await action from the latter rather than being free to do things for themselves. Explicit encouragement of positive freedom and of democracy is con-stantly required. Despite this, the current and third phase has moved activ-ity into different dimensions.

Most notably, 1997 saw the inaugural EUNIP International Conference, hosted at Chatham House, London. This has since become an annual event, a means of further networking but also an important activity in its own right, providing benefits to researchers in linking internationally without depending on the success or failure of a multinational web.[7] Furthermore, based on the development of EUNIP, in 1997 L'institute was established.[8] It is now a joint venture between the Universities of Birmingham (England), Ferrara (Italy) and Wisconsin-Milwaukee (US). The aim is to provide an ongoing focal point for analysis and discussion of industrial development, to give a stimulus to dynamic networking that goes beyond the confines of (for example) Human Capital and Mobility projects by opening new possibilities. Moreover, by creating an organisation that sits firmly within established universities, vital roots are provided; they give networking a concrete presence, lifting it beyond short run initiatives and abstract theorising.

L'institute is not itself a multinational web, nor does it purport to be. Rather, one vision sees it as participating in and stimulating a range of activities that contribute to and catalyse a web. Not everyone within L'institute (or its partner universities) agrees with this view. Aims and objectives differ across individuals; whilst specific projects are seen by some as contributing to a multinational web, for others they have a different rationale. It is notable and problematic, for example, that the commitment to one of the fundamental characteristics seen in Table 4.1, democracy in strategic decision making, is not universally shared. The evolution of an appropriate democratic process is an issue demanding considerable, ongoing attention. On some occasions, democracy has been purportedly and apparently safeguarded by the exercise of distinctly undemocratic authority, and the long-run solutions to such dilemmas, contradictions and difficulties are yet to be worked out. Nevertheless, some within L'institute see it as a small-scale multinational enterprise participating in a large-scale production process, a web.

The idea of an expanding set of projects planned and undertaken by researchers identifying with each other in a multinational web is also an aim shared by some participants in EUNIP. The intention is to develop a nexus of criss-crossing relationships between those projects, as illustrated in simplified form in Figure 4.1. The most immediate inputs might be provided either by researchers working in a group or by a researcher working alone. Some projects might directly involve at their core researchers from different nations whilst others might be undertaken by essentially one person, nevertheless feeding into and from other activities that make up the web. In addition, each of the constituent projects is envisaged as independent – the 'property' of the individual or team undertaking the activity – yet based (in part) on recognition of mutual co-operation and support. Such recognition implies, for example, that each would explicitly identify its involvement in the web and look for opportunities to relate with others, thereby improving

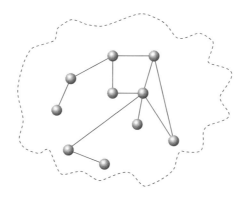

⬤   A specific research and/or learning project
───   An explicit relationship between projects
-----   The multinational web

Figure 4.1   A nexus of criss-crossing relationships

the quality and quantity of outputs from each project. This reflects the general importance of being conscious of the sorts of characteristics highlighted in Table 4.1; without awareness there would be very limited opportunities for participants to learn about and hence develop an appropriate networking process.

Among the specific projects that are central to developing the web is the attempt to nurture a set of Schools, motivated not least by the continued desire to encourage new production units. In 1998 the annual L'institute-Ferrara Graduate School in Industrial Development Policy was introduced. This is partly rooted in the Mediterranean Summer School on Industrial Organisation held in Corsica, hence related to the Ecole de Sophia Antipolis Sur la Firme et L'industrie (ESFI), both of which were inaugurated by one of the founders of EUNIP. The L'institute-Ferrara School is designed for approximately 20 students, deliberately small-scale to foster close relationships. It builds on the EUNIP experience with postgraduate training, significantly extending attempts to feed and involve new talent. It does so by circumventing the problems of different regulations for postgraduate research training across Europe, and by reaching a comparatively wide audience. In fact, the intention in L'institute is to develop a set of Schools in different parts of the world. A partnership has been formed with Nitlapán of the University of Central America, Nicaragua, for the Central American School in Industrial Development Policy; the third such School was held in July 2002. Overall, what is envisaged is Schools that are interrelated in terms of lecturers and students, and overlapping in subject matter. They will fuse emerging, young and established expertise, and will be developed in ways that feed into and off of the networking process. Especially important, each School will be explicit about the analysis underlying the creation and stimulation of webs.[9] Each will also be as clear as possible about its own role in the web process. It is for this reason that the Schools can provide the web with new production units while other, existing courses cannot meet that requirement.[11]

In nurturing the Schools, various characteristics highlighted in Table 4.1 are encouraged, not least the fusion of the social and the economic into one process; birth and growth from participants' histories, traditions and cultures; provision of continuous learning opportunities; and development of each individual to realise his or her full potential. Attaining these characteristics at the multinational level is especially problematic. For example, it has been argued that the 'cafe culture' has been influential in fusing the social and the economic in Italy's industrial districts (Brusco, 1990), yet such a culture is not readily available internationally. This absence represents a challenge but not one that is necessarily insurmountable. In particular, it seems that education can be especially influential and again Italian experience provides a revealing analogy.

Bologna's 'Packaging Valley' has been a successful industrial district producing packaging machines. Its development was closely connected to a vocational school – the Aldini-Valeriani Institute – established in 1844 by Bologna's city government and two professors at its University. The Institute has trained the majority of people involved in Packaging Valley and has undoubtedly been a key player in the locality's success. The common schooling that the Institute provided has been significant in part because it was crucial to people learning the 'rules of the game'; it helped to share and shape knowledge, experiences and normative structures.[11] Such experience points to the possibility of multinational networks in general being served by the creation of dedicated multinational schools. For research and learning in industrial economic development and public policy, it points to the importance of nurturing the set of Schools.[12]

The nurturing of the Schools also illustrates a particular difficulty with developing a web: the availability of suitable funding and the avoidance of funding that would fundamentally alter the nature of the activity. Access to financial support is a prominent issue throughout modern universities, not least due to the market forces discussed in Section 2 of this chapter. Indeed, it is typically highlighted as a key measure of success. In such an environment it is especially difficult, yet especially important, to reject funding possibilities that would be unsuitable. For example, the L'institute-Ferrara Graduate School has until now been supported by local municipalities and firms, a separate and new partnership having been created each year of its existence. This has been time consuming, and each year there has been uncertainty as to whether or not the School could be supported. Given this, a particular approach to the European Commission was contemplated, with the intention of core support covering the medium term. However, it emerged that the specific avenue under consideration would seemingly require either that the School grew enormously in size, or that it would be dominated by students from a small handful of universities. Both outcomes would alter its basic character. The concentration on a few institutions, for example, would imply a concentration of power, detracting from the idea of a democratic, open network.

Beyond the Schools, other specific projects that are relevant to developing the web include the extension of networking in North America by recreating the environment of the aforementioned Warwick-Birmingham Summer Research Workshops of the early 1990s; L'institute-Milwaukee Workshops were held in 2000 and 2001. Moreover, especially important are the identification of a common research agenda and the introduction of joint degree programmes. It is envisaged that the web will include a developing set of interlinked research projects encompassing its entire multinational ambit. The projects will be linked in terms of content, inputs and outputs. Taken as a whole they will comprise a large-scale production process but, in keeping with the concept of a web, they will each constitute a smaller-scale activity. They will be supported and, where necessary, funded from a range of sources, but the process of linking will help to realise that support and funding. For example, development of the web may help projects with which it is associated receive a sympathetic hearing from funding sources. In addition, by seeing the web as a specific entity, sources approached to support one activity can be shown related initiatives funded from elsewhere; hence requests will be made for matched rather than exclusive support, which will be likely to open up more opportunities. It should be possible to build up momentum in this regard, for success to breed success.

As for the introduction of joint degree programmes, this builds on the experience of EUNIP with postgraduate training. It is motivated in part by a desire to link into traditional learning activities, and to thereby overcome the shortcomings that result from being kept at the margin of educational activity. There are significant difficulties with co-ordinating across degree programmes in Europe, let alone more widely; differences and incompatibilities in regulations pose barriers, and frameworks for giving quality supervision to students are lacking. To address these problems, a 'virtual multinational faculty' providing Masters and PhD programmes in industrial economic development and public policy has been contemplated. This might be achieved via the establishment of suitable focal points for research and learning, using these focal points to evolve appropriate partnerships that are rooted in existing institutions. Associated with this prospect, the Universities of Birmingham and Ferrara have introduced a joint PhD programme in industrial economic development and public policy. Seen as an aspect of the activities of L'institute and incorporating the School held in Ferrara, the programme is explicitly conceived as a step towards including other partners throughout the world.

Like everything else in creating and stimulating a multinational web, time is a vital input in this process. Introduction of the new PhD comes as a simple step after a decade of experience and learning. It is impossible to form suitable relationships and to design appropriate instruments for further multinationalisation in an instant. Trust must be acquired, as well as knowledge of the heterogeneous behaviour, aims and objectives of people and institutions in various countries. There is also the significant problem of identifying new staff; in the experience of L'institute, the single most important constraint on the growth of a multinational web is the availability of scholars and administrators willing and able to cooperate in the spirit of the characteristics identified in Table 4.1. A necessary condition for overcoming this constraint is time, a requirement that compares with the frequent rush that Windham (1996) observes elsewhere: 'at present, there is no agreement on the answer of "why" a university or college should internationalize. Often, framing an answer to this question is skipped entirely in the enthusiasm to begin' (p. 11).[13] The need for time can be a drawback, because it tends to be linked to inertia and lack of dynamism, holding people back through inefficiency. Whilst enthusiasm might be beneficial, however, learning about distinguishing features across countries and drawing those differences together for mutual advantage cannot be a quick process. There is nothing efficient in rushing to an inferior endpoint, forever missing unique opportunities.

It should also be emphasised that the potential for new degree programmes might rise exponentially in the coming few years with the opportunities for distance learning suggested by new technologies. The same might be said for the activities of the multinational web more generally, although opinions vary on the significance of these changes. Following Dearing (1998), some argue that new technologies will prove a 'valuable supplement to time-proved practice, but no more' (p. 8), rather in the way that radio, television and the telephone, 'despite their potential to bring the world's best expositors or challenging lectures to every student, have caused no fundamental change to the process of learning throughout our universities or made higher education routinely transnational' (p. 7). Others suggest that the new technologies will transform practice, albeit leaving a place for traditional approaches, and others still that they will revolutionise higher education. Dearing observes that there has been no fundamental change up to now and, as part of the explanation, points to 'the reluctance of departments to use material not produced by them – the "not invented here" syndrome – coupled with the wish of academics to share their hard-won personal approach to their discipline and the fruits of their research, to give vitality to their teaching' (p. 80). If Dearing's comment on the wish of academics is correct, it points to the importance of developing new working practices based on trust and co-operation across international borders. The significance of this is that, in industrial districts and other groupings of smaller firms, issues of trust and co-operation are to the fore as determinants of productive success; it therefore follows that a model of internationalisation based on webs might offer an attractive way forward.

Although the potential with new technologies has to be recognised, however, it is pertinent to highlight observations by Halliday (1999). He suggests that 'information technology is not the solution to the problems of the modern university' (p. 111), and that 'no education can succeed without face-to-face discussion among students and between those students and their teachers' (p. 111). It is certainly the experience of L'institute that multinational linking requires that participants are sometimes in each other's presence; whilst electronic communication is an extremely important tool, it is only so in the context of periodic personal contact.[14]

4.   CONCLUSION

This chapter explores alternative approaches to economic development and a choice between different forms of internationalism; possibilities are illustrated in the context of strategies for universities.

If a university system were to mimic and simply serve transnational corporations it would add to the strategic failures inherent in free market economies. In the extreme, it would imply a world with a small number of first-tier universities headquartered in their 'home' nation but with facilities elsewhere. These would have branches that are not intended to serve the interests of the communities where they are located; an elite would govern the branches and local interests would be excluded. In contrast, a multinational web does not imply a transverse structure, a crossing of nations and localities that takes advantage of opportunities to satisfy sectional interests. Rather, it suggests a birth and growth from the particular histories, traditions and cultures in different localities and nations. Although there is no blueprint for the precise characteristics of a web – the stress on learning is consistent with a need for adaptation and modification over time – democracy, positive freedom and multinationalism are its essence. What is envisaged is a joining across nations, a mutual development based upon respect for differences. The result would be research and learning activities enhanced by widened experiences, understanding and options, the capturing of economies of scale and scope and an increase in efficiency through an outward shift in the production possibility frontier.

What the chapter identifies is a choice between two forms of internationalisation. However, in the case of education that choice is not in the hands of universities or of academics alone. If the future context in which universities operate is to be a pure form of free market capitalism characterised by the domination of transnational corporations, it seems certain that the transnational-type university will prevail. This would follow from the very idea of a transnational-type university as an organisation that mimics and serves the large, global corporations. Moreover, although such an organisation is not necessarily optimal for society, this does not imply that better alternatives can succeed in all market systems. As Keith Cowling has identified in other but related circumstances, purposive public policy is essential, enabling alternative forms of production activity to emerge and thrive.[15] In short, for universities and academics to develop multinational webs in research and learning, a facilitating context is necessary: a supportive society and an appropriately designed public policy.

ACKNOWLWEDGEMENTS

Thanks to J. Robert Branston, Maria Callejon, Keith Cowling and James R. Wilson for comments on earlier material incorporated in this paper. Some of that earlier material was presented at the L'institute-Milwaukee Workshop on *Enterprize Strategies and Regional Growth Policies in the New Global Economy*, University of Wisconsin-Milwaukee, July 2000. Thanks to participants at that event. Both the earlier material and the current chapter have also benefited from discussion with Marcela Valania. In addition, thanks to Michael Waterson for his observations on the first draft of the chapter. The opinions expressed are solely those of the author and, in particular, they do not necessarily represent the views of anybody else involved in L'institute or in the Universities of Birmingham, Ferrara or Wisconsin-Milwaukee. Any errors in the paper are of course the responsibility of the author.

NOTES

1. Compare the discussion of greater concentration of university activity in Colander (2000), considering changes in economics.

2. See Sugden (2002) for further discussion.
3. Whereas corporate governance refers to the control of a corporation, production governance refers to the control of an entire production process. The latter is a wider concept. For example, where production is based on a network of small firms, production governance includes the governance of that network, not merely governance in the individual production units.
4. Types of networks are discussed in Sacchetti and Sugden (2003).
5. See *The Economist*, 4 October 1997, on a survey regarding departmental independence.
6. Many academic staff and student researchers might see their current activities as implicitly in line with the features of a web, but this is not to say that the universities in which they are employed pursue strategies consistent with multinationalism.
7. For further information, see www.eunip.com.
8. More on the activities of L'institute can be found at www.linstitute.org.
9. Both what that analysis currently is, and how it needs to be further researched.
10. Related to this, if production generally was to be based on multinational webs, those webs would need an education system that meets the requirements of their businesses, including those that operate internationally. It follows from the discussion of Section 2 that this would not be provided by a model of universities based on transnational corporations. However, a model of education based on multinational webs might provide an appropriate process.
11. Further discussion of the Aldini-Valeriani Institute can be found in Miller and Sugden (1995).
12. As a web develops, it is vital not to follow a set pattern as regards form and content. For example, each School needs to be created in unique ways to serve unique purposes, yet linking and learning from each other. In all aspects of a web, no blueprint is advocated; rather, flexibility and imagination to achieve a purpose are crucial. It is also worth noting that in establishing a School attention needs to be given to location: fusing the social and economic to maximum effect depends on where the School is held and what venues it uses. For example, there was a conscious choice to host a School in Ferrara in part because, as compared to elsewhere, it was seen as a city with the sort of character that facilitates the type of networking L'institute is attempting to foster. It also provides access to venues with different facilities and unique atmospheres.
13. Williams (1994) suggests that international education is typically advocated 'as a means to a wider end: international understanding, or improved student learning, or increased trade, or a more productive world economy' (p. 115). A multinational web might contribute to each of these ends. However, what Windham (1996) refers to as 'economic and trade motivations' (p. 11) are also closely related to globalisation and transnational-type universities. See also Seidel (1991), who relates developments in universities to economic forces, for example trends in labour markets, and Mallea (1996), examining the views of 'stakeholders' in education in North America.
14. Sugden (2000) discusses the experience of L'institute as regards the Internet as a tool for linking.
15. He made the point as regards corporations in Cowling and Sugden (1998a).

REFERENCES

Adam, G. (1975), 'Multinational Corporations and World-wide Sourcing', in H. Radice (ed.), *International Firms and Modern Imperialism*, Harmondsworth: Penguin.
Bailey, David (1999), 'Japan's embrace of the "free market" – heightening the risks of strategic failure', *Kansai University Review of Business*, **1** (1), 49–62.
Berlin, I. (1969), *Four Essays on Liberty*, Oxford: Oxford University Press.

Bianchi, P. (1993), 'Industrial districts and industrial policy: the new European perspective', *Journal of Industrial Studies*, **1**, 16–29.

Brusco, S. (1982), 'The Emilian model: productive decentralisation and social integration', *Cambridge Journal of Economics*, **6**, 167–84.

Brusco, S. (1990), 'The Idea of the Industrial District: Its Genesis', in F. Pyke, G. Becattini and W. Sengenberger (eds), *Industrial Districts and Inter-Firm Cooperation in Italy*, Geneva: International Institute for Labour Studies.

Coase, R. H. (1937), 'The nature of the firm', *Economica*, **IV**, 386–405.

Colander, D. (2000), 'New millennium economics: how did it get this way, and what way is it?', *Journal of Economic Perspectives*, **14** (1), 121–32.

Cowling, K. (1982), *Monopoly Capitalism*, London: Macmillan.

Cowling, K. and R. Sugden (1994), *Beyond Capitalism. Towards a New World Economic Order*, London: Pinter.

Cowling, K. and R. Sugden (1998a), 'The essence of the modern corporation: markets, strategic decision-making and the theory of the firm', *The Manchester School*, **66** (1), 59–86.

Cowling, K. and R. Sugden (1998b), 'Strategic trade policy reconsidered: national rivalry vs free trade vs international cooperation', *Kyklos*, **51**, 339–57.

Cowling, K. and R. Sugden (1999), 'The wealth of localities, regions and nations; developing multinational economies', *New Political Economy*, **4** (3), 361–78.

Craig, R. J., F. L. Clark and J. H. Amernic (1999), 'Scholarship in university business schools. Cardinal Newman, creeping corporatism and farewell to the "disturber of the peace"?', *Accounting Auditing and Accountability Journal*, **12** (5), 510–24.

Dasgupta, P. and I. Serageldin (eds) (2000), *Social Capital. A Multifaceted Perspective*, Washington: World Bank.

Dearing, Lord, of Kingston-upon-Hull (1998), 'The Unauthorised Chapter of the Dearing Report', in Institute for Economic Affairs, *Higher Education After Dearing*, Oxford: Blackwell.

de Boer, H. F. (1999), 'Changes in Institutional Governance Structures: The Dutch Case', in J. Brennan, J. Fedrowitz, M. Huber and T. Shah (eds), *What Kind of University? International Perspectives on Knowledge, Participation and Governance*, Buckingham: SRHE and Open University Press.

Halliday, F. (1999), 'The chimera of the "international university"', *International Affairs*, **75** (1), 99–120.

Humphrey, J. and H. Schmitz (1995), *Principles for Promoting Clusters and Networks of SMEs*, UNIDO SME Programme Discussion Paper Number 1, Vienna: UNIDO.

Hymer, S. H. (1972), 'The Multinational Corporation and the Law of Uneven Development', in J.N. Bhagwati (ed.), *Economics and World Order*, London: Macmillan. Page numbers in the text refer to the reproduction in H. Radice (ed.) (1975), *International Firms and Modern Imperialism*, Harmondsworth: Penguin.

Lundvall, B.-Å. (ed.) (1992), *National Systems of Innovation: Towards a Theory of Innovation and Interactive Learning*, New York: St. Martin's Press.

Mallea, J. (1996), 'The Internationalisation of Higher Education: Stakeholder Views in North America', in OECD, *Internationalisation of Higher Education*, Paris: OECD.

Miller, L. and R. Sugden (1995), 'Small firm webs', *New Economy*, **2**, 85–8.

Sacchetti, S. and R. Sugden (2003), 'The governance of networks and economic power: the nature and impact of subcontracting relationships', *Journal of Economic Surveys*, forthcoming.

Seidel, H. (1991), 'Internationalisation: a new challenge for universities', *Higher Education*, **21**, 289–96.

Stiglitz, J. E. (2002), *Globalization and its Discontents*, New York: Norton.

Sweeney, G. (1997), 'Regional Economic Dynamism and a Munificent Environment', mimeo, Dublin: SICA.

Sugden, R. (1997), 'Economiás multinacionales y la ley del desarrollo sin equidad (Multinational economies and the law of uneven development)', *FACES, Revista de la Facultad de Ciencias Económicas y Sociales*, **3**, 87–109.

Sugden, R. (2000), 'The Internet as a tool for global linking', *Qualitative Market Research: An International Journal*, **3** (2), 107–9.

Sugden, R. (2002), 'A Small Firm Approach to the Internationalisation of Universities: A Multinational Perspective', mimeo, L'institute.

Van Damme, D. (2001), 'Quality issues in the internationalisation of higher education', *Higher Education*, **41**, 415–41.

Williams, G. (1994), 'Economic Issues in International Education', in A. Smith, U. Teichler and M. van der Wende (eds), *The International Dimension of Higher Education: Setting the Research Agenda*, Vienna: IFK.

Williamson, O. E. (1975), *Markets and Hierarchies: Analysis and Antitrust Implications*, New York: Free Press.

Windham, D. M. (1996), 'Overview and Main Conclusions of the Seminar', in OECD, *Internationalisation of Higher Education*, Paris: OECD.

Zeitlin, M. (1974), 'Corporate ownership and control: the large corporation and the capitalist class', *American Journal of Sociology*, **79** (5), 1073–19.

PART II

Monopoly, oligopoly and social welfare

5. 'Price–cost margins and market structure' revisited

Michael Waterson[1]

1. INTRODUCTION

In the summer of 1972, I forget whether for six or eight weeks, Keith Cowling employed me on a project examining oligopoly. His original idea, inspired by Means (1962), was that there was a link between oligopoly behaviour and the rate of inflation. However, upon developing the model, it became clear that the link in theory was between the *change* in the degree of oligopoly and the change in pricing. I recall, when I returned to my parental home, telling my mother what I had been doing over those weeks – developing a model – she thought it pretty poor value. In retrospect, I cannot agree; indeed I wish I had spent a few weeks so productively more often! Eventually, this translated itself, via my PhD and a lot of work by Keith, into our joint paper, 'Price–cost margins and market structure' (1976) which remains clearly the most-cited piece either of us have.

The model was one of the early elements to provide a rigorous theoretical underpinning for the cross-sectional structure–performance work so popular in industrial economics at that stage. It made two things clear, that the appropriate margin was a margin on revenue, not capital, and that an arguably appropriate measure of industry concentration was the Herfindahl. This latter finding led to a great deal of policy-driven work (for example Dansby and Willig, 1979; Farrell and Shapiro, 1990) and thus may have been one of the elements contributing to the use of the Herfindahl (or Hirschmann–Herfindahl, HHI) index in the landmark US Horizontal Merger guidelines, published in 1982 and revised 1984, 1992 and 1997.[2]

The empirical work was also somewhat innovative. We explicitly recognised (albeit to a lesser extent than is nowadays considered the case) that structure–performance studies were plagued by omitted variable problems, one of the most severe being the own price elasticity of demand. This we finessed by an approach, taking ratios of the formula across two years, which has echoes in the first-differencing that is used empirically these days to remove fixed effects.

Thus, both theoretically and empirically, the study drew attention rather widely and has been cited nearly 200 times. It also provided an element in the construction of what, in Keith's view, is his most important work, *Monopoly Capitalism* (1982).

Of course, things move on. The 'game theory revolution' has significantly impacted upon theoretical modelling in the area of oligopoly. Empirical studies of oligopoly behaviour still use in small part the basic framework (Genesove and Mullin, 1998). However, cross-sectional work has now gone rather out of style in favour of individual industry studies, in part for good reason. The policy pronouncements coming from cross-section studies were really rather heroic. The purpose of this short chapter is essentially to put these two areas, empirics and policy, into the context of modern work in Industrial Economics.

2.   EMPIRICAL ANALYSIS

The relationship Cowling–Waterson used related the profit (plus fixed cost) to revenue ratio, $(\Pi + F)/R$, to the Herfindahl index, H, and the elasticity of demand (written as a positive number), ε, as follows

$$\frac{\Pi + F}{R} = \frac{H\mu}{\varepsilon} \qquad (5.1)$$

Here μ is related to θ, the degree to which firms' actions are co-ordinated. Equation (5.1) was derived using a generalized Cournot-type model of fixed firm numbers, homogeneous products and constant marginal cost and is an intra-industry aggregation of the first order profit maximising condition for firm i

$$p = c_i - q_i.P'(Q).\theta_i \qquad (5.2)$$

where p is price, c_i is marginal cost, q_i is this firm's output and $P(Q)$ the inverse market demand curve. Under Bertrand behaviour, $\theta(\mu)$ is zero, under Cournot 1, whereas under joint profit maximisation, it is $Q/q_i(1/H)$.

It is clear in general that a series of cross-sectional observations on profits and on concentration along the lines of

$$\frac{\Pi + F}{R} = a + bH \qquad (5.3)$$

with the numerator of the left-hand side measured as revenue minus variable costs, will yield a poor and uncertain fit given this model (even assuming industries with products approximating to homogeneous can be found).[3]

As we (amongst others) recognised, the coefficient *b* will be influenced by variations in the elasticity of demand and the degree of co-ordination across industry. If instead we take a ratio of (5.3) at two points in time

$$\left(\frac{\Pi + F}{R}\right)_t \bigg/ \left(\frac{\Pi + F}{R}\right)_{t-1} = \frac{H_t \mu_t}{\varepsilon_t} \bigg/ \frac{H_{t-1} \mu_{t-1}}{\varepsilon_{t-1}}$$

then if the elasticity of demand does not change over the period (or if all elasticities change proportionately) and behaviour does not change, but concentration does significantly, then we may hope to identify the relationship more precisely. Probably, this is a big 'if', in particular as regards behaviour. But even if behaviour changes, but does so in a manner proportionate to the change in concentration, then we may hope to identify a relationship between changes in concentration and changes in the margin and to gain some insight into how powerful the relationship is. Thus, by taking the ratio, we eliminate some sources of unwanted variation across the sample.

More recently, concern has been expressed about the left-hand side of (5.3) and its meaning. The problems are related both to measurement and to interpretation. In terms of measurement, there is a difficulty over marginal costs and their relationship to variable costs. The upshot is that there is some unwillingness to view average variable cost as equal to marginal cost. As Bresnahan (1989, p. 1012), talking about the 'new empirical industrial organization' (NEIO) puts it 'Firms' price–cost margins are not taken to be observables . . .'. Thus costs are commonly estimated or approximated using output data and factor prices as explanatory variables. Porter's (1983) study of a railroad cartel is a classic example of this approach.

More significant for the prevailing climate is the feeling that 'Individual industries are taken to have important idiosyncrasies' (Bresnahan, 1989, p. 1012). Thus, cross- sectional studies are far too broad-brush in their approach. Individual industries, or small, connected groups of industries, have become the common focus of study. In this context, especially when intra-industry data are available,[4] conduct can be examined more directly.

Let us examine these arguments in a little more detail. The general relationship

$$p = c_i - q_i . P'(Q) . \theta_i \tag{5.2}$$

coming from a generalised Cournot homogeneous oligopoly model can be viewed as a form of supply relationship, dependent of course on demand through the term $P'(Q)$ and also on behaviour through θ. This suggests an approach of estimating demand in the industry jointly with the supply relationship. Estimation is ideally performed using data for individual firms, but can also be employed using time series data at industry level (for example Porter, 1983). In such approaches, marginal costs (c_i) are sometimes estimated as a function $c_i = c(w_i,...)$ of factor prices, rather than being assumed or gathered from recorded data.

In order to identify the supply relationship, it is necessary that there are factors which shift the demand curve. However, under at least some theories of oligopoly, the value of θ that is expected itself depends upon the state of demand. Therefore, in such cases, the conduct parameter is not independent of the instruments used to estimate it, resulting in a biased estimate. This is the essence of the Corts (1999) critique of the 'supply–demand'-type estimation procedure for obtaining an average conduct parameter. This issue is investigated by Genesove and Mullin (1998) in the context of the US sugar refining industry. They compare direct estimates of θ from (5.2) (at the industry level) using known cost information with indirect estimates, where cost is estimated as a function of the input price of raw sugar, and find that in the latter there is some underestimation of θ due to correlation between the margin and a demand instrument, High Season. However, they view their results as 'reassuring' so far as the NEIO approach is concerned since the effects are minor.

Furthermore, Genesove and Mullin investigate recovered estimates of cost where a particular value of the conduct parameter is assumed.[5] Clearly, from (5.2), if a more monopolistic form of conduct than is warranted by actual behaviour is assumed, estimated costs will be too low, and vice versa. Indeed, they find in their sample there is a significant bias to estimated costs as a result of inappropriate assumptions regarding conduct.

Of course, although there has traditionally been significant emphasis on structure–performance studies to provide an underlying rationale for competition policy by investigating the degree of market power present in industry, this has never been the only agenda for industrial economists. The newer techniques, such as the supply–demand or NEIO estimation methodology discussed above, are amenable to examining quite different issues. Interesting examples include Petrin's (2002) evaluation of the welfare impact of the introduction of the 'minivan' in the US, or Davis's (2001) study of provision of movie theatres relative to the optimum. In these cases, adoption of a specific demand structure in which differentiated products can be placed enables an explicit social welfare evaluation to be made.

But the fact that there are new and interesting questions does not eliminate older issues from consideration. Really, it seems to me, one of the reasons for the almost total abandonment of the broad cross-section study is a widespread lack of belief in the importance or immutability of structure.[6] This follows on from a game-theoretic revolution in which structure has been very much downplayed at the expense of the 'anything can happen' demonstrations of game theory. It is only really Sutton (for example 1990, 1991) who has taken a consistent line in promoting the idea of looking to establish broad-brush predictions valid for a wide variety of games rather than being concerned with the minutiae in modelling of individual cases. Thus Sutton (together with former students such as Symeonidis, 2002), keeps alive the broad cross-sectional study, although chooses to use it to examine the determinants of concentration, not its effect. Nevertheless, since the mirror of the distribution of concentration levels is the pricing structure of the industries concerned,[7] his work has implications for the relationship between structure and performance.

The other major and perhaps more significant reason for abandonment of the broad cross-sectional study is probably the recognition that Census industries are not good approximations to markets. This issue will be discussed in the section below.

3. POLICY-RELEVANCE

As Schmalensee (1988) points out in his survey of the field as a whole, 'Despite [their] problems, inter-industry studies have an important role to play. It is difficult to design broad public policies, such as antitrust and tariff policies, without a feel for the main economy-wide relations (structural or otherwise) among affected markets' (p. 649). This point is worth dwelling upon and is particularly true as regards the guidelines relating to competition policy, which are now a feature in many jurisdictions, having spread from the United States. However broad-brush the relationship when evaluated across industries, without the background of an overall cross-industry framework it is difficult to see how such a structure for policy could have been developed.

Unfortunately, in real life the occupants of industries are not symmetrically-sized firms. Thus, a summary statistic for the industry needs construction. Like any such summary measure, the Herfindahl index, used in the US merger guidelines, conceals as well as reveals information about industry structure. In particular, as Farrell and Shapiro (1990) point out, an increase in an industry's Herfindahl index is not equivalent to an increase in the monopoly welfare loss. This is essentially because improvements in efficiency can increase the Herfindahl index. Taking the simple example of the Cournot model, and measuring social welfare in the conventional manner, without regard to distribution, they show that the following relationship holds true

$$\text{sgn} dW = \text{sgn}[d \ln Q + 1/2 d \ln H] \tag{5.4}$$

Thus an increase in welfare is generated by an *increase* in the Herfindahl index, all other things equal, because in the Cournot model, a fall in costs for one firm causes it to gain share at the expense of the other players.

This itself leads to problems of interpretation of any cross-sectional aggregate relationship between (changes in) profitability and (changes in) concentration. The link may be from co-ordination to high profits for all, or it may be through superior efficiency on the part of some players in the market, leading to their domination of the industry. In the first case (where (5.4) is not the appropriate formula, although it illustrates the issues), an increase in the Herfindahl index is accompanied by a fall in industry output, whereas in the second case, this is not necessarily so.

Really, this is the focus of the Demsetz (1973) criticism of these cross-industry structure–performance estimations, although he did not put it into an explicitly welfare-theoretic framework. Without examining what happens *within* an industry, it is not possible in general to come to a conclusion regarding the social welfare impact of any relationship estimated. Demsetz did look at intra-industry relationships (large and small firm groups), but his results are not conclusive since he claimed that higher profits amongst large firms demonstrated they were more efficient, whereas in fact other explanations are equally plausible (Scherer, 1979). Thus his results are consistent with, but not determinative of, an efficiency explanation.

An at least partially successful attempt to use a cross-sectional approach alongside intra-industry data is provided by Clarke, Davies and Waterson (1984). They used Census size class distributions to provide intra-industry variation and combined this with a cross-sectional investigation of the results from the margin-size regressions, finding some evidence for a positive relationship between the degree of concentration and the level of apparent collusion. The approach was to take intra-industry size distribution information across a panel of years, with which to estimate the following relationship for each industry j

$$\left(\frac{p - AVC}{p}\right)_i = a + bs_i + cs_i^2 + u_i \tag{5.5}$$

where the i subscript now refers to the size group, rather than an individual firm. A simple rewriting of (5.2) suggests the following theoretical link

$$\left(\frac{p - c_i}{p}\right) = \frac{\alpha}{\varepsilon} + \frac{(1 - \alpha)s_i}{\varepsilon} \tag{5.6}$$

where α is the 'degree of implicit collusion', since a value of 1 corresponds to collusion, whereas a value of zero coincides with Cournot behaviour.

Thus estimates of α were retrieved from equation (5.5) and employed in a subsequent cross-sectional estimation relating α to the Herfindahl index (finding some evidence of a positive link).

Of course, this approach has a major weakness, namely that it takes as given that the Census SIC categories correspond to economically meaningful markets. Indeed, in their work, Clarke et al. (1984) find that only a minority of their industries are amenable to the second step (relating α to the Herfindahl index) of the above analysis. In many cases, the results of estimating equation (5.5) are not explainable either in terms of the theory underlying (5.6) or extensions of it to cover economies of scale and product differentiation. For example, in some industries it is the smallest firm sizes that have the largest margins. Therefore the implication is that in many cases either the industry does not operate at all along the lines of the generalised Cournot-type structure underpinning (5.2), or the Census industry is not coincident with a single 'real' market. This widespread view that Census industries have serious problems from the standpoint of meaningful markets is a major factor in the decline in popularity of Census-based cross-sectional work.

A more direct, but narrower, approach to competition issues is to estimate the degree of co-ordination in behaviour directly within a supply–demand relationship of the type (5.2) described earlier designed for a specific industry. In either case, the welfare interpretation is more straightforward than from Cowling–Waterson, since unambiguously the higher the degree of collusion the greater the welfare loss.

More recently, there has been a trend to estimate structural supply–demand relationships then simulate the social effects of a merger directly, commonly under the assumption of given behaviour. Assuming the demand relationship examined has an explicit interpretation in terms of consumer utility, meaningful welfare analysis can take place even for example in industries where products are differentiated (so concentration measures are ambiguous). A good example of this genre is Nevo (2000),[8] who having estimated the demand and supply relationships, simulates the impact of mergers in the US ready-to-eat breakfast cereal industry, some of which have taken place. To estimate demand, he uses data across most major (24) brands across 45 cities and 20 quarterly time periods, using the approach to differentiated products popularised by Berry, Levinsohn and Pakes (1995). He then recovers estimates of marginal costs from the supply relationship[9] and calculates the post-merger equilibrium following the simulated merger. It is then possible, for instance, to see how great a reduction in marginal cost would be required in order to offset the price rise caused by the merger. In principle at least, such an econometric investigation could take place over the period within which the decision by competition authorities regarding the merger takes place.

However, intriguing though they are, the question examined by such studies is fundamentally different from the agenda underlying Cowling and Waterson (1976), Clarke et al. (1984) and the many similar studies. The more recent writings are concerned with answering a question: Given that a particular merger is to be investigated, should it be allowed to take place? The earlier work was addressed to a much broader question: How might one decide *which if any* merger proposals to investigate further? This was the issue that concerned the authors of the landmark 1982 Merger Guidelines in the US (guidelines that have significantly influenced jurisdictions outside the US).[10] The key principles these enunciated come through in the following passage

> A merger is unlikely to create or enhance market power or to facilitate its exercise unless it significantly increases concentration and results in a concentrated market, properly defined and measured. (US DOJ/ FTC, 1997, at 1.0)

Thus market definitions, and a filter relating to market concentration, are at the heart of the guidelines. The early work was not very careful about the definition of market, but it was clearly addressed to the question of establishing if there was a broad link between concentration and performance. In that sense, given the continued importance of the Guidelines, it retains the significance of an underlying influence.

NOTES

1. I am grateful to Margaret Slade and Lawrence White for useful discussions on some of the issues presented here.
2. See for example Willig (1991) for a discussion of the intellectual antecedents and Muris (2002) for example regarding the impact of the guidelines. One clear influence on the guidelines was Stigler (1964).
3. Notice that we assumed the link was from structure to performance, despite the fact that (5.2) derives from an equilibrium relationship, with both sides endogenous.
4. This is true in by no means all examples of this genre.
5. This, in a more complex form, is one thing Berry, Levinsohn and Pakes (1995) do.
6. Another, less legitimate, reason might be that issues arising in particular antitrust cases in which they develop a consulting interest drive the agendas of key individuals.
7. A point exploited to great effect by Bresnahan and Reiss (for example 1987) and others in their inferences about structure derived from observations of distributions of outlets across markets.
8. See also Pinkse and Slade (2003) and Smith (2003), for example, for alternative approaches to the same issue.
9. This requires an assumption regarding behaviour, justified in this case on the basis of previous modelling.
10. The current Chairman of the FTC, Timothy Muris (2002), writes: 'The Justice Department's 1982 Merger Guidelines fundamentally changed the way we think about mergers and about how we should formulate competition policy. Not simply a matter of national significance, the analytical ripples of the 1982 Merger Guidelines have covered the globe.'

REFERENCES

Berry, S., J. Levinsohn and A. Pakes (1995), 'Automobile prices in market equilibrium' *Econometrica*, **63**, 841–90.

Bresnahan, T. (1989), 'Empirical Studies of Industries with Market Power', in R. Schmalensee and R. Willig (eds), *Handbook of Industrial Organization*, vol. 2, Amsterdam: North Holland.

Bresnahan, T. and P. Reiss (1987), 'Do entry conditions vary across markets?', *Brookings Papers on Economic Activity*, **3**, 833–71.

Clarke, R., S. Davies and M. Waterson (1984), 'The profitability–concentration relation: market power or efficiency?', *Journal of Industrial Economics*, **32**, 435–50.

Corts, K. (1999), 'Conduct parameters and the measurement of market power', *Journal of Econometrics*, **88**, 227–50.

Cowling, K. (1982), *Monopoly Capitalism*, London: Macmillan.

Cowling, K. and M. Waterson (1976), 'Price–cost margins and market structure', *Economica*, **43**, 267–74.

Dansby, R. and R. Willig (1979),'Industry performance gradient indices', *American Economic Review*, **69**, 249–60.

Davis, P. (2001), 'Spatial competition in retail markets: Movie theaters', mimeo, MIT Sloan, December.

Demsetz, H. (1973), 'Industry structure, market rivalry and public policy', *Journal of Law and Economics*, **16**, 1–9.

Farrell, J. and C. Shapiro (1990), 'Horizontal mergers: an equilibrium analysis', *American Economic Review*, **80**, 107–26.

Genesove, D. and W. Mullin (1998), 'Testing static oligopoly models: conduct and cost in the sugar industry, 1890–1914', *RAND Journal of Economics*, **29**, 355–77.

Means, G. (1962), *Corporate Revolution in America*, Sprinfield, OH: Crowell-Collier.

Muris, T. (2002), *Prepared Remarks* on the occasion of the celebration of the twentieth anniversary of the 1982 merger guidelines at http://www.ftc.gov/speeches/muris/1982mergerguidelines.htm

Nevo, A. (2000), 'Mergers with differentiated products: the case of the ready-to-eat cereal industry', *RAND Journal of Economics*, **31**, 395–421.

Petrin, A. (2002), 'Quantifying the benefits of new products: the case of the minivan', *Journal of Political Economy*, **110**, 705–29.

Pinkse, J. and M. Slade (2003), 'Mergers, brand competition, and the price of a pint', *European Economic Review*, forthcoming.

Porter, R. (1983), 'A study of cartel stability: the Joint Executive Committee, 1880–1886', *Bell Journal of Economics*, **14**, 301–14.

Scherer, F. (1979), 'The causes and consequences of rising industrial concentration', *Journal of Law and Economics*, **22**, 191–208.

Schmalensee, R. (1988), 'Industrial economics: an overview', *Economic Journal*, **98**, 643–81.

Smith, H. (2003), 'Supermarket choice and supermarket competition in market equilibrium', *Review of Economic Studies*, forthcoming.

Stigler, G. (1964), 'A theory of oligopoly', *Journal of Political Economy*, **72**, 55–9.

Sutton, J. (1990), 'Explaining everything, explaining nothing? Game theoretic models in industrial economics', *European Economic Review*, **34**, 505–12.

Sutton, J. (1991), *Sunk Costs and Market Structure*, Cambridge, MA: MIT Press.

Symeonidis, G. (2002), *The Effects of Competition*, Cambridge, MA: MIT Press
US Department of Justice/Federal Trade Commission (1997), *Horizontal Merger Guidelines*.
Willig, R. (1991), 'Merger analysis, industrial organization theory, and merger guidelines', *Brookings Papers on Economic Activity, Microeconomics*, 281–312.

6. Labour supply, efficient bargains and countervailing power

Robin A. Naylor

One of the many and profound lessons one learns even in casual conversation with Keith Cowling is the importance of challenging basic assumptions. This is at once liberating – as when the challenge is of the mainstream or orthodox – and intimidating – as when the questioning required is of oneself and one's own assumptions. In each case, engagement with Keith is stimulating, rewarding and always designed to be constructive. Keith's views on industrial and labour economics have influenced my own work in many respects. For example, Keith's view that oligopoly rather than perfect competition is the appropriate starting point for analysis is echoed in my focus on models of union-bargaining in contexts of oligopolistic product markets. From this, it is also natural to challenge the conventional wisdom that firms do not possess market power in their labour market.

In this chapter the concept of employer power in the labour market – virtually a heresy in the orthodoxy of mainstream competitive models – is a key feature of the labour supply model which we develop. Power is assumed to characterise firms in the labour market, enabling them to extract rent from workers. This leads to a non-orthodox view of labour supply and to corresponding implications for the desirability of labour market interventions such as minimum wage legislation. However, one implication of the model is that employers can respond to minimum wages by adjusting work hours upwards and hence undermining the benefits of wage protection to workers. To avoid this, labour market policies have to be strategically designed. A second implication of the model concerns the interpretation of union power. In mainstream economics, unions are seen as a distortionary imperfection in an otherwise efficient-functioning market place. Instead, in the model presented, unions are best perceived as exerting a countervailing influence against powerful firms. In the big picture, the overriding theme is one of a clash of interests: the competitive market outcome emerges merely as a very particular special case.

1. INTRODUCTION

In the canonical model of labour supply, utility-maximising workers are assumed to be free to choose their optimal hours of work at any given wage rate. This theoretical model not only underlies much macroeconomic analysis, but also provides the framework in which econometric evidence on labour supply is typically interpreted and on which tax and related microeconomic policy options – including welfare and labour market interventions – are then designed.

Dissatisfaction with this orthodox model has focussed on the observation that for most workers the length of the working week is chosen by the firm. Hence, only if there is a continuum of jobs will workers be able to equate a given market wage to their marginal rate of substitution between income and leisure. Against this, there is growing evidence of workers for whom the wage–hours combination lies off their labour supply curves. Section 2 of this chapter summarises some of this evidence.

In the current chapter, we develop a theoretical model of individual labour supply in which the canonical model emerges as a special case. More generally, we are able to characterise labour supply behaviour when, in the absence of a continuum of jobs, firms are able to push workers on to lower indifference curves than that corresponding to the tangency condition of orthodox theory: that is, push them to the right of the labour supply curve. The extent to which the firm is able to do this is shown to depend upon a number of factors, which include the state of the local labour market and the extent of any countervailing power available to the worker, such as insider power or trade union representation. Indeed, if the worker is sufficiently powerful it is possible that the wage will be pushed above the marginal value product of the worker's labour in which case hours worked will be to the left of the worker's labour supply curve: this can be thought of as equivalent to the case developed in Oswald and Walker (1993).

As with Oswald and Walker (1993), the model can generate a downward-sloping efficiency locus in wage–hours space. This can occur even if there is an underlying positively sloped labour supply curve characterising the worker's unconstrained optimal choice of hours for a given wage. Unlike Oswald and Walker (1993), the efficiency locus describes the wage–hours combinations for both unionised and non-unionised workers and can exist at wage rates below the level which would obtain in a perfectly competitive market and hence, it is shown, will lie to the right of the unconstrained labour supply curve for such wage levels. The existence of such a wage–hours locus has a number of further implications. First, it is consistent with empirical evidence showing workers' actual hours to exceed desired hours for given wage rates. Second, it has implications for the analyses both of monopsony power in the labour market and of the union/non-union wage differential. Third, it offers a possible re-interpretation of the stylised fact of a backward-bending labour supply curve.

In the traditional model of static monopsony, the individual firm is assumed to face a positively sloped labour supply curve and is able to push wages below the level which would obtain in a perfectly competitive labour market. As the wage falls, the number of workers offering to supply labour to the firm diminishes. Thus, the model typically ignores the possibility that individual workers continue to offer labour to the firm but adjust their optimal wage–hours bundle. In this chapter, in contrast, we allow not only for this possibility, but also for the case in which the firm is able to push the worker off his or her labour supply curve. The wage–hours combination then lies on a contract curve rather than on the supply curve. Accordingly, the model can be interpreted as an efficient bargaining model of monopsony.

In terms of policy implications, the model predicts that the imposition of maximum hours regulations – such as occurred in the UK with the implementation in 1998 of the EU Directive on Working Time – will be unlikely to improve the overall remuneration package of workers. This is because workers whose hours are likely to be affected by the legislation will face pressure from monopsony employers to reduce the hourly wage rate to compensate for the profit-damaging restriction on weekly hours. Similarly, minimum wage legislation – as passed in the UK in 1998 (see Metcalf (1999) for a discussion) – will induce low-paying firms to raise weekly hours if this is possible: again, affected workers will not benefit where employers are able to push them to a reservation utility level. Instead, a corollary of the model is that workers will gain only if *both* maximum hours and minimum wage legislation are introduced, as occurred in the UK in the late 1990s.

In the standard theoretical model of union–firm bargaining, the union is assumed to be bargaining for a wage in excess of the competitive wage which would obtain in the absence of unions. It is well known that the resulting wage gain, assumed to be positive, is not accurately measured by the union/non-union wage gap for the simple reason that in a partially unionised labour market the non-union wage need not correspond to the competitive wage of a non-unionised labour market. Nonetheless, econometric evidence of positive union/non-union wage differentials is typically interpreted as implying that union wages exceed the level which would prevail in a competitive labour market and that a reduction in union bargaining power would induce union wages to fall towards the competitive outcome. In this chapter, any union bargaining power is interpreted as a countervailing power enabling workers to resist the employer's attempt to push them to lower wage outcomes along a contract curve. In this context, it is clear that one can infer nothing about union wages relative to a bench-mark competitive wage, from empirical estimates of positive union/non-union wage differentials.

The rest of this chapter is organised as follows. In the next section of the chapter we summarise relevant empirical and econometric evidence. Section 3 outlines the theoretical model and Section 4 presents a comparative static analysis of the properties of the model together with a discussion of predictions and implications in the context of labour market policy interventions. Section 5 closes the chapter with a summary and suggestions for further work.

2. EVIDENCE

Conventional wisdom suggests that, over time, economic growth will be associated with a reduction in the length of the working week. This view is consistent with the idea of leisure as a normal good, demand for which is increasing with income. Indeed, international evidence supports the hypothesis for many countries and over a long sweep of time. For both the UK and the US, for example, there was a secular decline in average weekly hours throughout most of the twentieth century: average hours were about 55 per week in both countries in 1900 and about 40 per week by the latter part of the century.

In the UK, however, a very unusual picture was emerging in the latter years of the twentieth century. Average hours actually increased in the UK from the mid-1980s and diverged substantially from average hours in the rest of the EU. Table 6.1 shows hours usually worked per week for male employees working full-time in the EU for 1991. The UK is clearly an outlier with an average of 45.2 compared to an average of 40.2 in the rest of the EU. The UK is also seen to be an extreme case with over one-third of male full-time industrial employees working 46 hours or more, compared to an EU average of 10.7 per cent (and a non-UK EU average of less than 6 per cent). Indeed, only Greece and Ireland have a figure of more than 10 per cent. The figures for 1999 are very similar to those for 1991.

From these figures one can see why the EU Directive on Working Hours has been more contentious in the UK than elsewhere: the regulation of a 48-hour maximum required workweek is unlikely to be a binding constraint outside the UK. Indeed, a number of other EU states have national maxima considerably below the 48-hour limit in the Directive.

In addition to this evidence on the length of the workweek in the UK, there is also evidence that workers would prefer to work fewer hours *at their hourly wage rate*. Stewart and Swaffield (1995), for example, using informa-

Table 6.1   Hours usually worked per week, 1991 and 1999 (male employees working full time)

Country	Average hours 1991 (all workers)	% working 46 hours or more 1991 ('Industry' only)	Average hours 1999 (all workers)
Belgium	38.5	2.5	39.1
Denmark	38.9	3.8	39.6
France	40.4	6.2	40.2
Germany	40	4.8	40.5
Greece	41	12.4	41.7
Ireland	41.7	12.5	41.3
Italy	39.8	8.6	39.7
Luxembourg	40.4	3.1	40.5
Netherlands	39.1	1.2	39.2
Portugal	42.7	5.8	41.5
Spain	40.9	3.9	41.1
UK	45.2	34.8	45.2
Austria			40.3
Finland			40.1
Sweden			40.2
EU average	41.1	10.7	41.2

Sources: Stewart and Swaffield (1997) for 1991 data. See also Eurostat, 1993 and Eurostat, 2001 for 1999 data.

tion from the British Household Panel Survey (BHPS) (1991) find that about 44 per cent of male employees aged 21–64 indicated that their desired hours – at their current wage rate – were different from their actual hours, and hence that they are off their labour supply curve. Of these workers, the majority (36.3 per cent of the whole sample) indicated a preference to work fewer hours at the prevailing hourly wage rate. Table 6.2 shows both the hours preferences for 1991, taken from Stewart and Swaffield (1995) and the author's own calculations for 1992–99. The breakdown over time in hours preferences is quite stable.

Additionally, evidence from the British Social Attitudes Surveys (BSAS) is consistent with the view that workers are working more hours than they would freely choose. For example, in the BSAS for 1990, 30 per cent of workers indicated that they would prefer a job in which they worked fewer hours. Oswald (1995) has observed that the question in BSAS does not explicitly state that the wage rate would be constant if hours varied and noted that when workers are asked if they would still like to work fewer

Table 6.2   Hours preferences, BHPS, 1991–99 (male employees aged 21–64)

| Would prefer to work | | | | | | | | | |
| | 1991 | 1992 | 1993 | 1994 | 1995 | 1996 | 1997 | 1998 | 1999 |
	%	%	%	%	%	%	%	%	%
Fewer	36.2	34.2	35.6	36.3	37.9	36.7	35.5	36.7	38.6
More	7.4	8.5	7.9	7.9	7.7	7.4	7.5	7.4	6.7
Same	56.4	57.3	56.5	55.8	54.5	55.9	58	55.9	54.7
Total	2204	2062	1939	1962	1988	2089	2162	2443	3555

Source: BHPS, 1991–99.

hours even if it meant earning less money as a result, only 7 per cent of workers respond in the affirmative. The question structure seems less clear than in the BHPS. Further evidence comes from Eurostat (1991, 1996) figures on hours preferences across EU countries for 1989 and 1994 respectively. For the UK, only 48 per cent of workers were happy with their hours in 1994, while 39 per cent would have preferred to work fewer hours. Across the EU, 46 per cent of workers would have chosen the same hours (very similar to the UK figure) and 31 per cent would have chosen fewer hours (a smaller percentage than in the UK). Between 1989 and 1994, the percentage of workers happy with their hours fell from 51 per cent to 46 per cent.

Stewart and Swaffield (1995, 1997), using 1991 BHPS data, analyse the breakdown of workers' hours preferences by various characteristics. They show that workers are more likely to prefer shorter hours: (i) the longer are the hours they work; (ii) the greater is the level of unemployment in the local labour market; and (iii) if they are non-unionised. On the issue of unionisation, Oswald and Walker (1993) develop a contract model of labour supply in which unionised workers are off their labour supply curve. Analysing Family Expenditure Survey data, they find that the contract model is consistent with the data for the union sector.

In this chapter we develop a non-competitive labour supply model and focus on the extent to which the properties of the model are consistent with the evidence on labour supply and workers' hours preferences.

3.   THE THEORETICAL MODEL

In this section of the chapter we first provide an intuitive description of the model before subsequently developing the more formal analysis.

In the canonical model of labour supply each worker chooses optimal hours, h^*, for a given wage rate, w, and non-labour income, m, in order to maximise utility defined over income (or consumption), c, and leisure, l. For given w, if the worker is constrained to work a number of hours different from h^*, then utility will be sub-optimal. The optimising labour supply decision is normally represented in income–leisure space, but we can also represent the problem by the family of indifference curves plotted in (w, h) space, as shown in Figure 6.1. Higher indifference curves represent greater levels of utility.

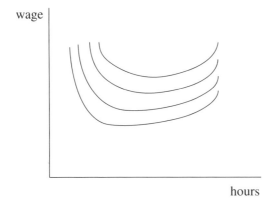

Figure 6.1   Indifference curves in (w, h) space

In terms of Figure 6.1, the labour supply curve of the canonical model is, of course, the locus of turning points of the indifference curves, showing the choice of hours associated with the highest obtainable indifference curve for any wage rate. In Figure 6.1, the underlying labour supply curve is implicitly positively-sloped, although in general this need not be the case.

The worker can be assumed to choose a job offering a wage–hours bundle which maximises the worker's utility. If, at any given wage, there is a continuum of jobs, then the worker will be able to select hours along the labour supply curve. Suppose initially that the representative worker is on the labour supply curve supplying h_1 hours to a particular firm at a wage rate w_1 and attaining indifference curve U_1, as shown in Figure 6.2. Suppose further that the wage, w_1, is just equal to the marginal product of the worker's labour at h_1. The marginal product of the worker's labour (m.p.h.) is assumed to be diminishing.

If the firm attempts to alter the wage–hours bundle in such a way that the worker's utility falls, for example by reducing the wage or increasing the workweek, and if other jobs with wage–hours bundles yielding U_1 utility are

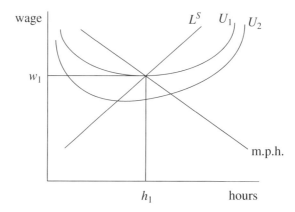

Figure 6.2   Indifference curves and marginal productivity

costlessly available to the worker, then the worker would quit this employment. But suppose that the utility level associated with the worker's next best
alternative activity is less than U_1, say U_2, for example. Then this gives the
firm some scope for offering the worker a wage–hours bundle which pushes
the worker off the labour supply curve. A profit-maximising employer would
select that bundle which maximised the firm's profit from this representative
worker, subject to satisfying the minimum worker–utility constraint. Such a
bundle would lie on an efficiency locus, *cc*, representing points of tangency
between the worker's indifference curves and the firm's iso-profit curves for
the representative worker. The efficiency locus is shown in Figure 6.3.

Along the contract curve, the individual worker is working more hours

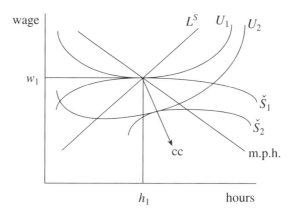

Figure 6.3   The efficiency locus

than would be optimally chosen for any wage rate. Similarly, the marginal product of the worker's labour exceeds the wage rate. This outcome occurs because the worker's next best alternative activity yields an alternative utility level below that associated with the competitive outcome. Hence, the employer is able to extract a rent from the worker. Such rent might have a number of sources. If workers are heterogeneous, then the marginal worker may have utility equal to reservation utility in the competitive equilibrium, but intra-marginal workers will experience some rent. Similarly, even in the presence of alternative job opportunities, firm-specific skills, search and mobility costs will enable firms to exercise a degree of monopsony power. Furthermore, if there is high unemployment in the local labour market with few alternative employment opportunities, then this too will give the firm potential to push the worker down the contract curve: exercising a degree of monopsony power. The alternative utility level sets the lower bound on the contract curve. The lower is the worker's outside utility, the further the firm is able to push the outcome down the contract curve.[1] If the worker has any countervailing bargaining power, for example through union representation or 'insider' status, then he or she might be able to resist being pushed to the lower bound of the contract curve.

Indeed, it is possible that the worker's bargaining power might outweigh that of the firm. In this case, it is possible that the contract curve will extend upward above the competitive benchmark with the wage exceeding the worker's marginal product. In such a case, as illustrated in Figure 6.4, the contract curve will be bounded by a minimum iso-profit curve reflecting the value of the worker's average product in this employment.

We turn now to examine the properties of this contract curve in a more formal representation of the model.

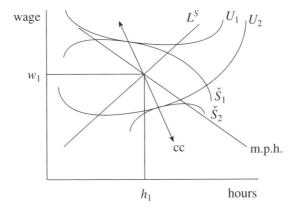

Figure 6.4   The general case of the contract curve

Formal Model

For simplicity, we examine the case of the linear labour supply function:

$$h = \alpha w + \beta m + \gamma, \tag{6.1}$$

where h is hours worked, w is the hourly wage rate and m is non-labour income. In this case, as is well known, if $\alpha \geq 0$ and $\beta \leq 0$, then $h \geq 0$ is sufficient for the Slutsky condition to be satisfied.

The direct utility function associated with the linear labour supply curve can be written as:

$$U(c,h) = \frac{1}{\beta^2}(\beta h - \alpha)\exp\left[\frac{\beta(h - \beta c - \gamma)}{\alpha - \beta h}\right], \tag{6.2}$$

where $c = wh + m$ is consumption. Substituting this expression for c into (6.2) yields:

$$U(c,h) = \frac{1}{\beta^2}(\beta h - \alpha)\exp\left[\frac{\beta(h - \beta wh - \beta m - \gamma)}{\alpha - \beta h}\right]. \tag{6.3}$$

Taking logs and re-arranging, (6.3) yields:

$$2\log\beta + \log U - \log(\beta h - \alpha) = \frac{\beta(h - \beta wh - \beta m - \gamma)}{\alpha - \beta h}, \tag{6.4}$$

which implies that:

$$w = \frac{1}{\beta h}\left[h - \beta m - \gamma - \left(\frac{\alpha - \beta h}{\beta}\right)[2\log\beta + \log U - \log(\beta h - \alpha)]\right]. \tag{6.5}$$

Equation (6.5) represents the expression for the indifference curve in (w, h) space. Differentiation of (6.5) with respect to h produces an expression for the slope of the indifference curve:

$$\frac{dw}{dh} = \frac{1}{\beta h}[2\log\beta + \log U - \log(\beta h - \alpha) - \beta w]. \tag{6.6}$$

Substituting (6.5) into (6.6) and re-arranging yields:

$$\frac{dw}{dh} = \frac{1}{h(\alpha - \beta h)}[h - \alpha w - \beta m - \gamma]. \tag{6.7}$$

From (6.7), it is readily checked that the indifference curve has zero slope at the point of intersection with the labour supply curve, $h = \alpha w + \beta m + \gamma$ and is positively (negatively) sloped to the right (left) of the supply curve.

In order to derive an expression for the contract curve depicted in Figure 6.4, it is necessary to specify the firm's profit as a function of the hours worked by the representative employee. This is given by equation (6.8):

$$\pi - R(h) - wh, \tag{6.8}$$

where π is profit associated with the representative worker and R is the value of the worker's product. It is assumed that $R'(h) > 0$ and $R''(h) < 0$. Rearranging:

$$w = \frac{R(h) - \pi}{h}. \tag{6.9}$$

For given π, differentiating (6.9) with respect to h gives an expression for the slope of the iso-profit curve:

$$\frac{dw}{dh} = \frac{R'(h) - w}{h}. \tag{6.10}$$

The contract curve is the locus of points of tangency between the iso-profit curves and the indifference curves of the representative worker. Hence, it follows from equations (6.7) and (6.10) that the contract curve is such that:

$$\frac{h - \alpha w - \beta m - \gamma}{(\alpha - h)h} = \frac{R'(h) - w}{h}. \tag{6.11}$$

Rearranging, we obtain

$$w = \frac{1}{\beta h}[h - \beta m - \gamma - (\alpha - \beta h)R'(h)], \tag{6.12}$$

as the equation of the contract curve.

We turn now to investigate the comparative static properties of the model.

4. PROPERTIES OF THE MODEL

From equation (6.12), we can derive the expression for the slope of the contract curve. This is given by

$$\frac{dw}{dh} = \frac{1}{\beta h}\{1 + \beta[R'(h) - w] - (\alpha - \beta h)R''(h)\} \tag{6.13}$$

Property 1

*At the competitive market outcome, where the contract curve passes through
the point of intersection of the marginal product and labour supply curves,
$R'(h) = w$ and hence, assuming leisure to be normal, the contract curve has a
negative slope.*

This follows because $(1/\beta h) < 0$, if leisure is normal, whilst the terms inside
the square brackets have a positive sum: $\beta[R'(h) - w]$ equals zero at the
competitive outcome, $R''(h)$ is negative under the assumption of a diminishing marginal product of hours, and $\alpha - \beta h$ is positive if the Slutsky condition is satisfied.

It follows from continuity, at least in the neighbourhood of the competitive outcome, that if the firm is able to push the representative worker
down the contract curve and onto a lower indifference curve, not only will
the worker's wage fall but also the hours worked will rise. This might occur
if either the relative bargaining power of the firm increases, for example
through legislative changes, or if the worker's alternative employment
opportunities, and hence outside utility, deteriorate. Thus, the model would
predict that, *ceteris paribus*, wage rates will be lower and hours worked will
be greater the higher is the level of unemployment in the local labour
market. Conversely, where workers have sufficient bargaining power to
negotiate wage rates above the competitive level, these bargains will be
associated with fewer hours worked than in the competitive case.

This property of the model explains evidence that workers are off their
labour supply curves – supplying more hours than they would choose at
their wage rates – as being a consequence of employer monopsony power.
The property of the model is also consistent with the finding of Stewart and
Swaffield (1997) that the probability of an individual working more hours
than he or she wishes is an increasing function of the local unemployment
rate.

A corollary of Property 1 – and, in particular, of the negative slope of
the contract curve – is that, at least in the neighbourhood of the competitive outcome, workers who are working longer hours will be those who are
off their labour supply curve *to the right*. Thus we would expect long hours
and a preference for short hours to be positively correlated, which is consistent with the evidence reported by Stewart and Swaffield (1997).

Property 2

*The contract curve is negatively-sloped when the worker's wage exceeds the
value of the marginal product.*

It follows from equation (6.13) that, under our assumptions, dw/dh is negative if $R'(h) < w$. This result is consistent with the analysis of Oswald and Walker (1993) who derive a negatively-sloped contract curve for unionised workers. The prediction that, *ceteris paribus*, union workers will be further up the contract curve working fewer hours for a higher wage rate compared to non-union workers is also consistent with the evidence. The existence of a union/non-union wage gap is well-established. With respect to hours worked, Stewart and Swaffield report from the 1991 BHPS that individuals covered by a trade union work 1.7 hours less per week than those not covered. This is consistent with the theoretical prediction.

Property 3

For any wage less than the competitive wage, hours worked exceed not only desired hours at that wage but also desired hours at the competitive wage.

This would be self-evident were we able to show that the contract curve is negatively-sloped for all $w > R'(h)$. It appears from (16.3), however, that there is no intuitively simple sufficiency condition for this. Instead, it can be shown that for solutions on the contract curve associated with wages below the competitive level, hours worked must be in excess of competitive hours. To show this, consider equation (6.12) rewritten as:

$$w = R'(h) + \frac{\alpha}{\beta h} \left[\frac{h - \beta m - \gamma}{\alpha} - R'(h) \right]. \tag{6.14}$$

Expressed in this form, it is apparent that the contract curve is given by the marginal product schedule minus a proportion of the difference between the labour supply and marginal product schedules, where the proportion is not fixed but varies with hours worked.

From (6.14), if $w < R'(h)$, it follows that $R'(h) < (h - \beta m - \gamma)/\alpha$ and hence that h is such that the labour supply curve lies above the marginal product curve. Thus it follows that h is greater than hours worked in the competitive equilibrium.

A corollary of this result is that below the competitive outcome, the contract curve lies everywhere to the right of the labour supply curve and hence that in this region of the contract curve the worker is working more hours than he or she would choose, given the wage rate. Workers are off their labour supply curves. This is also true for outcomes on the contract curve above the competitive equilibrium: in this case, however, workers are working fewer hours than they would choose given the wage rate. Outside the special case of the competitive equilibrium, the wage–hours outcome lies off both the labour demand and the labour supply curves. From this perspective, the competitive equilibrium can be seen as a special case of the more general contract curve model, occurring when any monopoly bargaining power on the part of the worker (deriving from, say, skill-specificity or union representation) just offsets any monopsony power on the part of the firm (deriving from limited employment opportunities in the local labour market, for example).

In general, it is likely that trade union representation will enhance the worker's bargaining strength. In the model of Oswald and Walker (1993), for example, union bargaining raises wage rates and reduces hours worked relative to the competitive equilibrium. In the Oswald and Walker model the contract curve exists only above the competitive outcome, in the presence of union bargaining power. In this chapter, the contract extends also below the competitive outcome in the presence of bargaining power by the firm, deriving from limited outside options of workers. In this more general framework, any union bargaining power can be seen as a countervailing power. If the worker's bargaining power only partially offsets the firm's bargaining strength, then unionised workers will receive wages which, though they may exceed the counterfactual non-union level, will nonetheless be below the benchmark competitive level.

Property 4

If wages are below the competitive level, then – by itself – maximum hours legislation will not succeed in raising worker utility. Similarly, on its own, minimum wage legislation will not raise worker utility.

Below the competitive equilibrium – where hours are longer and wages lower – the imposition of a maximum hours constraint will induce firms to optimise subject not only to the reservation utility level but also to the hours constraint. In this situation, the profit-maximising solution will no longer be on the contract curve but will be at that point on the reservation utility curve at the maximum hours level. As a consequence, workers do not gain from hours regulation. Essentially, monopsony firms adjust to the regulation by requiring workers to trade off the benefit of an hours reduction with the disutility of a wage cut.

Similarly, on its own, minimum wage legislation raising wages at levels below the competitive level does not induce a utility gain for workers. Instead, workers gain only if minimum wages and maximum hours are imposed *simultaneously*. By coincidence, this is what has happened in the UK in recent years and, therefore, the prospects for the legislation to have been of genuine benefit to low-paid workers have been enhanced.

5.   CONCLUDING REMARKS

In most jobs workers are not free to choose the number of hours they would like to work at the given wage rate. Thus, the conventional labour supply model, in which the worker's wage–hours combination corresponds to the tangency point at which the marginal wage rate equals the marginal disutility of hours, is valid only if workers face a continuum of jobs. In the absence of this, it is possible that workers will be employed in jobs with hours requirements pushing workers off their labour supply curves. If a worker has limited alternative employment opportunities outside the current employer, then there is the potential for the firm to offer the worker a wage–hours bundle yielding a utility as low as the worker's reservation utility level. This chapter develops the concept of a contract curve, which is a locus of wage–hours bundles extending downwards from the perfectly competitive outcome towards the reservation utility threshold. In the presence of alternative employment opportunities the contract curve will be bounded below by the utility level associated with the worker's next best job alternative.

The properties of the contract curve model have been analysed and particular implications drawn out. First, it has been shown that for outcomes which, to the worker, are inferior to the competitive outcome, not only are wages lower than competitive wages but, additionally, hours worked are longer. It follows that workers are to the right of their labour supply curves, working longer hours than they would choose at given wage rates. Second, where workers are able to bargain for contract curve outcomes which are superior to the competitive outcome, wages are greater than competitive wages and hours worked are less. This is consistent with the union-sector model developed in Oswald and Walker (1993). Third, the worse are the worker's alternative employment opportunities, the lower will be the alternative utility level and hence the further will the contract curve extend downwards away from the competitive outcome. Hence, we would expect that hours worked will be longer and wage rates will be lower the greater is the local unemployment rate. Fourth, we have indicated that hours are more likely to exceed desired hours the more hours are actually worked. We have argued that the empirical evidence and analysis presented by Stewart and Swaffield (1995, 1997), based on data from the BHPS of 1991 are consistent with a number of predictions from the model developed in the current paper.

It has recently been observed that not only are average male hours worked longer in the UK than in other EU countries, but also that only in the UK is it the case that average hours rose in the latter part of the last century – during a period of persistently high unemployment and decreasing union bargaining power. Within the framework of the model we have developed in this chapter, it is not surprising to find rising hours associated with deteriorating employment prospects for workers, coupled with a shift in bargaining power towards employers. That hours worked in the UK exceed those in other EU countries has puzzled labour economists. This chapter offers one possible insight into this: namely that the origin of long hours in the UK might lie in a high degree of monopsony power by employers, a higher unemployment risk for workers or less bargaining power by trade unions – or some combination of these.

Finally, we have noted the model predicts that only by implementing maximum hours and minimum wage regulations *simultaneously* is it likely that workers can benefit from these interventions. Thus, from a low-paid overworked worker's perspective, the policy combination of the minimum wage and the EU working time directive – both approved by the UK Parliament in 1998 – represents a happy coincidence.

NOTE

1. This analysis corresponds with an industrial relations literature linking diminished worker bargaining power with a process of intensification of the labour process (see, for example, Nolan and Marginson, 1990).

REFERENCES

Eurostat (1991), *Labour Force Survey Results, 1989*, Bruxelles.
Eurostat (1993), *Labour Force Survey Results, 1991*, Bruxelles.
Eurostat (1996), *Labour Force Survey Results, 1994*, Bruxelles.
Eurostat (2001), *Labour Force Survey Results, 1999*, Bruxelles.
Metcalf, D. (1999), 'The Low Pay Commission and the national minimum wage', *Economic Journal*, **109**, F46–66.
Nolan, P. and P. Marginson (1990), 'Skating on thin ice? David Metcalf on trade unions and productivity', *British Journal of Industrial Relations*, **28** (2), 227–47.
Oswald, A.J. (1995), personal communication.
Oswald, A.J. and I. Walker (1993), 'Labour supply, contract theory and unions', Working Paper, November, Institute for Fiscal Studies.
Stewart, M.B. and J.K. Swaffield (1995), 'Constraints on desired hours of work, trade unions and the length of the working week for British men', Working Paper, October, University of Warwick.
Stewart, M.B. and J.K. Swaffield (1997), 'Constraints on the desired hours of work of British men', *Economic Journal*, **107**, 520–35.

7. Market share instability and the competitive process*

John Cable and Claire Morris**

1. INTRODUCTION

The determinants of market share, and the interconnection between market share and market power, form major themes in Keith Cowling's early work, as is evident in his paper with Tony Rayner (Cowling and Rayner, 1970), the subsequent DTI sponsored analysis of advertising and economic behaviour (Cowling et al., 1975) and his more or less contemporaneous and highly influential piece with Michael Waterson (Cowling and Waterson, 1976). From an early stage, too, welfare (and distributional) considerations and policy implications have been at the forefront of his concerns, notably in his work on the social costs of monopoly with Dennis Mueller (Cowling and Mueller, 1978), in his re-examination of monopoly capitalism (Cowling, 1982), as well as in his later work on industrial policy and corporate governance.

This chapter revisits the terrain of market share behaviour, and related welfare and policy issues. Specifically, it focuses on how far the mobility or 'instability' of market shares can be pressed as a reliable and informative indicator of the degree of competitiveness in a market, whether in a positive or normative sense, and with a particular eye on antitrust policy applications. First, in the following section, we review the a priori arguments previously raised in the literature, adding some of our own. We then report a case study of the diagnostic and analytical power of mobility indices in the UK national daily newspaper market, relating observed variations in the degree of mobility to known events and to price and advertising behaviour by the incumbent firms. The newspaper market presents a promising case for analysis, having undergone significant technological, entry and ownership shocks that might be expected a priori to perturb the competitive process, as well as the outbreak of a price war towards the end of our data period. It also has the benefit of reliable, high-frequency market share data based on independently audited circulation figures. Section 3 describes the instability measure we employ. The case study itself occupies

Sections 4 and 5, and Section 6 concludes. Our general findings are that the ambiguous welfare implications of instability and the limited diagnostic power of instability indices make them unsuitable on their own for use as a barometer of the intensity of competition. However, we argue that, used in conjunction with other industry-specific information, data summarising the dynamic behaviour of market shares can add purchase to the analysis of competitive rivalry in a market.

2.   INSTABILITY AND WELFARE

Reporting on an exhaustive empirical study of market dynamics in Canada, Baldwin and Gorecki (1994) called for conventional seller concentration indices, which calibrate competition 'as a state of affairs', to be supplemented with mobility statistics reflecting 'the [Schumpeterian] competition that matters' in order 'to pinpoint those industries where competition problems arise' (p. 102). The idea that the transfer of market shares between firms in a market (or changes in their ranking by size) tell us something valuable about competition was by no means new, having entered the literature two generations earlier (Tucker, 1936). Progress on devising specific instability measures followed somewhat later, in early work on measures derived from transition probability matrices by Adelman (1958), Hart and Prais (1956) and others in the 1950s, and on alternative mobility indices by Joskow (1960), Hymer and Pashigian (1962), Gort (1963) and others in the early 1960s. And across the timespan of this literature Baldwin and Gorecki are by no means alone in treating instability itself as more or less synonymous with (a form of) competition in some beneficial sense (not always specified), others to have done so including both Hymer and Pashigian and also Gort, together with later contributors such as Heggestad and Rhoades (1976, 1978) and Das et al. (1993).

If Baldwin and Gorecki's Canadian data are not atypical, following their policy recommendation would certainly yield a different set of cases and priorities for investigation; of the 35 most highly concentrated manufacturing industries in their database, only between 48.6 per cent and 57.1 per cent were also in the set of the 35 with the most stable market shares (the precise figure within this range depending on the mobility measure employed). But what exactly would the additional, mobility criterion pick up? More generally, what can we really infer about competition from market share instability, and what if anything does it tell us that static concentration measures do not?

Writers other than those cited above have been more circumspect when interpreting instability in welfare or performance terms. In an early survey,

Ogur (1976) noted that share instability had in fact been treated in the literature as everything from an undesirable element of market structure to a favourable dimension of market power.[1] Recognising the diversity of its possible causes and consequences, Caves and Porter (1978) shortly after concluded: 'we can make no overall judgement about the desirability of market-share instability . . . It is not desirable per se, but can pay for itself socially if it reduces monopolistic distortions in settings where they are immune to the application of cost-effective tools of public policy.' More recently Davies, Geroski and Vlassopoulos (1990) nicely reflect the temptations and reservations that arise for potential users of mobility indices, observing that, on the one hand: 'If market concentration . . . is both high and relatively stable over time, but if the identity of the leading five firms or the distribution of shares between them changes continuously, then one would be inclined to argue that the market was fairly competitive regardless of its level of concentration,' yet at the same time, 'however tempting it is to use high turbulence in markets . . . as a sign of a vigorous competitive process . . . markets must in the end be judged by how well they perform and not merely how they are structured.'

Clearly the inference from instability to competition in a welfare sense is not straightforward. Undeniably, observed mobility in market shares must at minimum imply that incumbents' market positions are contestable, and mobility barriers not insuperable. To this extent, Davies et al.'s first point is clearly right. However, mobility indices are generally agnostic with respect to whether concentration is increasing or decreasing[2] – and monopolisation also entails transfer of market share as, arguably, does healthy competition. Thus, while disregard for the *level* of concentration may be defensible, disregard of its rate and direction of change is another matter. Further relevant points are, first, that instances of significant market fluctuations have been observed even in the presence of price-fixing agreements (Alemson, 1969); and, perhaps relatedly, while advertising and product differentiation may be desirable up to a point, beyond that point 'share instability can get inflated beyond a socially desirable level in an industry that maintains a high collusive price and finds its rivalry diverted toward an excessive level of non-price competition' (Caves and Porter, 1978). In addition, as the last authors also point out, by destabilising profits, mobility of shares can be a form of risk for the suppliers of capital, and it may also reduce the utilisation of the capacities of fixed factors. By way of final complication, one could add the theoretical possiblity of a market being held to a pitch of competitive performance by continuous rivalry *without* changes in the size distribution of sellers, in particular when competitive responses are (observationally) instantaneous – there are no lags. Moreover, this ideal state of affairs has the attraction of minimal transaction costs – both those associated with competitive failure and those arising from the displacement of one firm's output by another's.

Given these uncertainties, and notwithstanding those who equate instability with the benefits of competition, it would evidently be inappropriate to interpret market turbulence – in particular in the context of high concentration – as evidence of welfare-enhancing competition. As a corollary, it would not be appropriate to interpret high concentration and low instability of shares or market positions as indicating the most productive areas in which to focus policy enforcement; and on a priori arguments the virtue in, and consequences of, supplementing static with dynamics indices for screening purposes, as Baldwin and Gorecki propose, remains opaque. This apparently leaves us with Davies et al.'s second point that, ultimately, if welfare inferences are to be drawn, resort to direct performance indicators is unavoidable.

Unfortunately, however, performance data at the right level of aggregation are often hard to come by (the UK daily newspaper industry being a case in point). And, though not unambiguous or wholly conclusive in themselves, it is possible that time series data on market shares and their movement might nevertheless, for example, reveal discontinuities demarcating phases of active rivalry in a market from periods of quiescence, which in turn might be associated with otherwise hard-to-detect tacit or secret collusion.[3] If so, indices based on such data could provide useful service in antitrust contexts. It is also possible that the use of such indices in conjunction with other data could produce additional insights into the nature of the competitive process, and thus serve further ends as an analytic tool in the course of subsequent investigations.

Our analysis of the newspaper market proceeds in this spirit. In effect, we explore the information content of the mobility statistics in the case in question. We begin, for each of three distinct segments of the market, by inspecting the index for any obvious trends or discontinuities, which might or might not be associated with conspicuous events or other information of a kind likely to be available to antitrust agencies when screening cases. We then introduce systematic information on two key, observable dimensions of competition – price and advertising – in order to determine how sensitive the instability index is to variations in these underlying behavioural variables, and hence to what extent it might serve as a surrogate for more detailed information in the screening process, as Baldwin and Gorecki propose. Before embarking on the analysis, however, we first briefly review the particular measure of instability we employ, our data sources, and a preliminary but important issue concerning the frequency of observation.

3. INSTABILITY MEASURE

This study employs Hymer and Pashigian's 'instability index', the sum of absolute market share changes (Hymer and Pashigian, 1962), the most widely used measure in previous work. In other work with this data we obtained similar results using the absolute change in the coefficient of variation of the log of firm size (Morris, 1998) and the sum of squared market share changes (Cable, 1997).

As originally presented, the H–P index was in terms of asset shares, but the use of assets data poses problems in that values are insensitive to short-run fluctuations; measurement problems arise for example from accounting practice; and company assets are not generally available on a high frequency, industry basis (Ogur, 1976). In common with most other researchers, our indices are sales-based. Absolute values are taken because, by definition, market share changes otherwise sum to zero. Hymer and Pashigian defend their use of the sum rather than the average of market share changes on the grounds that the measure is not overly sensitive to differences in the number of firms n, because relatively small firms contribute little to the index and grow, on average, no faster than larger firms (op. cit., p. 86). In our case, however, significant market entry occurred in each of the three market segments, and we therefore work in terms of averages.[4] Thus our measure of instability takes the form:

$$I_t = \sum_{i=1}^{n} |s_{i,t}/S_t - s_{i,t-1}/S_{t-1}|/n$$

where s_{it} denotes the sales of the ith firm at time t, S is total (sub)market sales and n is the number of firms. Entry also creates large 'spikes' in the measure in the month in which it occurs, which are really no more than a purely numerical effect. To eliminate these spikes, we replace the value in the month of entry with the average of the instability measure in the preceding and the succeeding months.[5]

The raw data consisted of audited monthly circulation figures as published by the Audit Bureau of Circulation (ABC) for the eleven titles in the national daily market over the period investigated. The overall industry is conventionally partitioned by practitioners and observers alike into three distinct sub-markets: the 'quality' or 'highbrow' titles (the *Telegraph*, *Guardian*, *The Times*, *Financial Times* and, from 1986, the *Independent*); the 'midmarket' or 'middlebrow' titles (the *Express*, *Mail* and, from 1986, *Today*); and the 'tabloid' or 'popular' titles (the *Mirror*, *Sun* and, from 1978, the *Star* together with, until 1970, the *Sketch-Graphic*). These sub-divisions can be justified in terms of clustering of competitive behaviour (prices, advertising expenditure and content) and outcomes (circulation figures and readership profiles).[6] For the purposes of the present analysis, they are treated as separate markets.[7]

Being independently audited, the circulation data is of high quality and it is also high frequency. There were, however, problems of missing observations, predominantly for months early on in our period when production of different titles was sufficiently disrupted by industrial action for the ABC not to record a circulation figure. These gaps were filled by inserting the mean of the circulation figures immediately before and after the missing observations before the instability measures were generated.[8] As previously mentioned, linear interpolations were also substituted in the instability measures to eliminate the purely statistical impact of entry giving rise to 'spikes' in the month in which it occurs.

The question of the ideal frequency of instability data has received little attention in the literature, perhaps because researchers have rarely enjoyed the luxury of choice. Typically, annual data has been used, but in several cases the period spans several years. That indices will tend to record higher values when longer periods are considered is well established (Shorrocks, 1978), but the issue of whether indices fail to detect active competition when no firm is the winner over time has not been widely discussed. Arguably, the data frequency should be (just) higher than the shortest time period required to respond to a rival's strategy. In the case of price changes this may be quite short, whereas a new advertising campaign may take longer to prepare, and new product development or process innovation may require several years to complete. It is therefore possible that annual, or lower frequency, data may more effectively capture competition in terms of product quality and technological changes, while price and advertising competition is best revealed in higher frequency data.[9] In this work we use monthly data smoothed to take out excessive month-to-month fluctuations, in the form of thirteen-month moving averages.[10]

4.   INSTABILITY IN THE MARKET, 1963–94

Figure 7.1 depicts indices of the instability of market shares in the three sub-markets of the newspaper industry over the period 1963–94, and Table 7.1 the relevant means and standard deviations. As suggested by inspection, the series are quite dissimilar. They are not significantly correlated: correlation coefficients between the monthly series for the quality and midmarket, quality and popular, and midmarket and popular titles were 0.041, 0.056 and 0.079 respectively, with only the last being significant and that at only 10 per cent. Analysis of variance indicates, also, significant differences

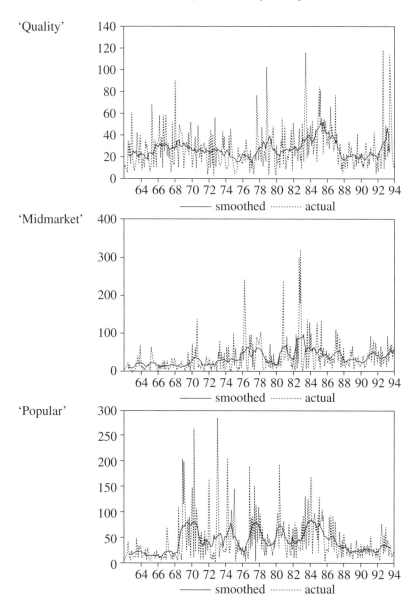

Figure 7.1   Average absolute market share change: actual and 13-month moving averages

Table 7.1   Mean market share volatility, 1963–94

	Quality	Midmarket	Popular
Monthly data ($n = 383$)			
Mean	26.86	33.85	40.10
Standard deviation	17.70	38.51	41.42
Smoothed data ($n = 371$)			
Mean	26.88	33.95	40.79
Standard deviation	7.60	17.78	20.99

between the submarket means, generating F statistics of 14.3 for the raw monthly data, and 65.9 in the case of the smoothed data. In passing, we note that this absence of correlation, and differences in means, provide further evidence of the distinctness of the market segments.

Using Baldwin (1995) and Baldwin and Gorecki's (1994) figures for the Canadian manufacturing industry as the most comprehensive available point of comparison, the degree of instability in the newspaper sub-markets appears low. On average across the 167 4-digit Canadian industries studied, 44 per cent of total sales changed ownership between 1970 and 1979 (calculated as half the sum of the absolute values of all individual share changes).[11] Over the period 1975–91 the corresponding figure for UK newspapers is 17.5 per cent for the market as a whole, and 13.25 per cent, 21.5 per cent and 15.0 per cent respectively for the quality, middle and popular segments. Converting to annualised rates to adjust for the different time periods yields a figure of 1.01 per cent for the UK newspaper market as a whole, and 0.78 per cent, 1.22 per cent and 0.88 per cent for the respective sub-markets. These figures are all very much towards the lower end of the Canadian inter-industry range of 0.65 to 6.2 per cent p.a. (with a mean of 3.48 per cent).

Comparisons such as these, however, and the values on which they are based, are likely to be sensitive to the choice of time period. As Figure 7.1 demonstrates, the striking feature of the instability series is that they are themselves unstable, in terms of both the raw month-to-month fluctuations and also the smoothed series. Thus in all three sub-markets it is possible to find periods of both increasing, decreasing and more or less constant instability at different times within the same market. Moreover, even when observed over relatively long periods of time, the degree and even the direction of change can depend critically on the choice of start- and end-dates, and this clearly creates a hazard if instability is to be employed as an indicator of the intensity of competition, whether for antitrust or for any other purposes.

The time path for the quality sub-market is particularly complex, with up to six or seven discernible phases. An initial period of relatively mild fluctuation at low levels to end 1965 preceded a sharp increase in 1966 and 1967, which was followed by a long period of gentle decline, with mild cycles, to early 1978. Thereafter we observe a very steeply increasing trend to an all time peak in 1986, with an earlier subsidiary peak in 1980, followed by a very sharp decline from the 1986 peak to a historically low level at the end of 1988. There was then a period of marked quiescence until the end of 1992, and finally a putative resumption of competition in 1993 and 1994.

Distinct phases are perhaps less easy to discern in the middle-market sector, though with a possible suggestion of quiescent phases, from early 1967 to mid 1970 in particular, and perhaps also over shorter periods in 1972/73 and 1979/80. The data also suggest a structural break in trend in 1983, with a rising trend and oscillations of increasing amplitude prior to the peak in that year, and a more level, or gently declining trend thereafter, though with instability on average distinctly higher than in the latter 1960s and early 1970s.

The series for the popular sub-market suggests three or possibly four main phases. Thus, a marked period of relative quiescence, with mild oscillation, up to mid 1969 switches to an apparently much more active competitive regime for a long period to end 1985, with very much higher average instability, and severe fluctuations of roughly equal amplitude but some variation in periodicity. After 1985 the market apparently subsides again into a relatively quiescent phase, particularly after end 1989, before re-awakening in 1993.

Table 7.2 reports means and standard deviations by sub-period for each of the three market segments. Analysis of variance confirms that the sub-period means are significantly different (at the 1 per cent level), yielding F-scores of 6.3, 6.1 and 16.9 for the quality, midmarket and popular segments respectively in terms of the raw monthly data, and 47.3, 41.7 and 113.2 in the case of the smoothed series. Of course, this confirms only that significantly different sub-periods exist, and not necessarily that the particular phases identified have been in any sense optimally demarcated.

On inspection, these patterns observed in the instability data correspond only loosely to, and remain largely unexplained by, the pattern of major events in the industry over the period, as might be known to an observer screening for antitrust purposes. On the positive side, the data do seem to pick up the price wars initiated by the Murdoch titles, *The Times* and the *Sun* respectively, in the quality and popular markets in 1993, after periods of quiescence in both cases. The abrupt switch to a regime of much higher volatility of shares in the popular market in 1969 also coincides with Rupert Murdoch's purchase of the *Sun*, which sparked a radical transformation of

Table 7.2   Mean market share volatility by sub-period

(a) Quality

Period	Obs.	Monthly Mean	St. Dev.	Obs.	Smoothed Mean	St. Dev.
63.02–65.12	35	20.59	13.04	29	21.45	1.88
66.01–67.12	24	28.68	17.12	24	29.04	4.61
68.01–77.12	120	24.72	14.22	120	24.66	4.54
78.01–85.12	96	28.62	19.07	96	29.24	6.44
86.01–88.12	36	38.91	19.75	36	37.73	10.14
89.01–92.12	48	19.76	8.55	48	19.62	1.56
93.01–94.12	24	34.04	29.64	18	32.72	8.41

(b) Midmarket

Period	Obs.	Monthly Mean	St. Dev.	Obs.	Smoothed Mean	St. Dev.
63.02–66.12	47	16.52	15.83	41	17.24	5.30
67.01–69.12	36	13.44	9.87	36	13.46	2.15
69.01–71.12	24	26.61	32.41	24	25.87	8.86
72.01–73.12	24	15.82	10.31	24	18.82	3.63
74.01–78.12	60	40.37	39.50	60	39.60	12.96
79.01–80.12	24	30.33	30.14	24	30.27	13.66
81.01–83.12	36	59.78	80.33	36	54.67	22.20
84.01–94.12	132	40.65	29.37	126	41.76	13.59

(c) Popular

Period	Obs.	Monthly Mean	St. Dev.	Obs.	Smoothed Mean	St. Dev.
63.02–69.06	78	15.11	12.11	72	16.05	3.94
69.07–85.12	198	53.72	49.38	198	53.56	17.19
86.01–89.12	48	43.35	32.52	48	42.58	16.30
90.01–92.12	36	22.08	10.28	36	21.97	2.33
93.01–94.12	24	28.47	21.11	18	30.71	5.74

the paper, with a move to tabloid format, the introduction of salacious stories and page three girls and a shift to the right (until May 1997) in the political allegiance of the paper.[12]

Other changes in ownership, however, do not produce readily discernible effects.[13] In particular, there is no clear evidence that, the takeover of the *Sun* by News International apart, changes in ownership exerted a destabilising effect on competition. There is some tendency for rises in instability to occur around the time of, or just after, purchase, but there are no clear patterns of 'before' and 'after' behaviour.

Moreover, and contrary to expectations, we do not detect discernible, competition-increasing impacts of the three cases of successful, large-scale entry into the markets: the *Star* in the popular market in 1978, and *Today* and the *Independent* in the mid- and quality markets in 1986.[14] On the contrary, entry appears to be followed by periods of decreasing instability. In the case of the *Star*, instability is at a peak in 1978, but as we have seen this is only one of a number of similar peaks between the breakpoints of 1969 and end-1985 in the popular market. Moreover instability falls sharply after the *Star*'s entry and remains low until late 1980. In the midmarket case, instability is not particularly high at the time of the entry of *Today* in 1986, and well below the peak level of 1983. Again, however, there is a fall in instability in the year after entry, as the market continues on a downward trend until late 1990 and, though there is a peak in 1988, this is two years post-entry. Finally, instability in the quality market also peaks in 1986, when the *Independent* entered, but as we have seen this marked the end of a long phase of increasing instability from about 1978. Moreover, instability yet again falls steeply, in this case for two years post-entry, before stabilising (perhaps suspiciously) at a low level for a further four years.

5. INSTABILITY, PRICE AND ADVERTISING

We next examine the relationship between the degree of competitiveness, as captured by the instability index, with other indicators of rivalry, in particular the more readily quantifiable dimensions of advertising and price competition. To this end, Figure 7.2 superimposes thirteen-month moving averages of total advertising expenditure and price, both deflated by the retail price index, on the smoothed instability series for the three submarkets.[15] The period covered by the analysis is now from 1975 to 1994, for which price and advertising data were available.

In the case of advertising, inspection suggests a definite relationship of some kind with instability in all three markets, but the dynamic structure of the relationship appears highly unstable. Not only are response lags of varying length, but also the identity of the lead variable itself changes, at least twice in the quality sector and once in the popular market – possibly indicating switches between offensive and defensive advertising at these points. In addition, the instability-advertising relationship in the midmarket sector appears to undergo a sea change in the mid 1980s. These intricacies merit closer investigation.

In the quality market, advertising is initially at a very low level and

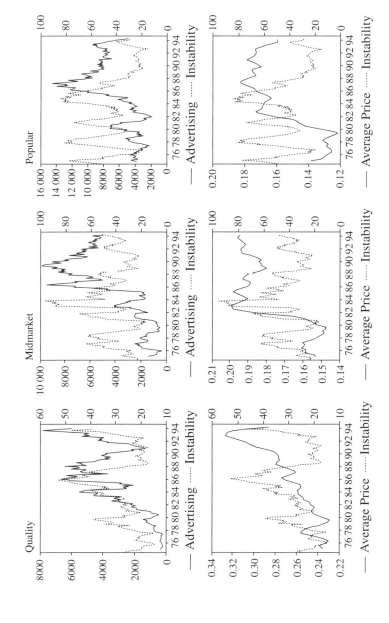

Figure 7.2   Market share instability, advertising expenditure and prices

apparently unrelated to the competitive process as captured by instability (which it may be recalled was at the time towards the end of a ten year period of gently declining trend with mild cycles). From 1978 onwards, however, advertising increases steeply and in sympathy with the instability series to the peak of 1986, both variables exhibiting subsidiary, contemporaneous peaks in 1980 and 1984, and to a lesser extent 1982 and 1983. Thus the main phase of increasing competitiveness we observe in this market appears to be closely related to advertising behaviour. The relationship between the series is broadly contemporaneous, and the series track one another particularly closely in the middle period from about 1982 to 1984. Prior to this, the amplitude of fluctuation in instability is much greater than in advertising, while later, in 1985, instability dips very much less than advertising. A possible interpretation here might be that initially, the market responded vigorously to a relatively novel form of competition to which it was hitherto unaccustomed. Later on, the apparent downward rigidity in, and lesser responsiveness to, advertising might reflect a higher level of habit-buying due to more firmly established consumer preferences based on the 'goodwill stock' built up by the advertising in the previous period.

After the peak in 1986 and particularly in 1988, advertising then at first remains at high, albeit fluctuating, levels while instability falls sharply, before following the decline in instability in 1989 at about a two year lag, extending to three years after a hesitation in its downward movement in late 1989 and 1990. Bearing in mind that 1986 was the year of successful entry by the *Independent*, this could possibly be interpreted as a switch to defensive advertising strategies in the context of uncertainty created by market entry, until a period of relative calm, as reflected in the instability statistics, had been observed in 1989 and 1990. Then, however, and interestingly, it appears there may have been a reversion to offensive advertising, which in any event takes off once more in mid 1991, and the price war of 1993 appears to have been preceded by an advertising war starting eighteen months or so earlier, though with only a modest impact on share mobility until the price war itself started.

From around 1976 to 1985 the midmarket sector also exhibits a fairly close correspondence between the instability and advertising series, though with some tendency for advertising to lead, and with fairly consistently greater amplitude of fluctuation in instability than in advertising. This pattern, however, breaks down entirely in 1986, which again is the year of moderately successful market entry by *Today*. The remarkable feature is not so much that advertising rises more than fourfold in the year, albeit from trough to peak in a rising series, but that thereafter advertising not only remains at very high, if fluctuating, levels, but if anything now moves in contrary motion, rather than in sympathy with, the instability series.

Like the quality and midmarket sectors, the popular market also saw a fairly spectacular increase in advertising, in this case especially from the low in 1982 to a peak in 1987, in part due to the adoption of more active advertising competition by the *Mirror*, against the *Star*, which followed a high advertising strategy from launch, and the *Sun*, which over the period of our data at least had also always advertised intensively. Also as in the other two markets, there is a distinct similarity between the instability and advertising time series, though again with an unstable dynamic structure to the relationship. Thus advertising appears to lead instability in 1980 but lag it in 1978 as well as, especially, consistently from around 1985 up to the outbreak of the price war in 1993. Once again the speculation might be that this instability in the dynamics reflects alternation between offensive and defensive advertising, though the events precipitating any such changes are less obvious in this case.

What is striking is that, whereas the instability statistics by themselves had indicated no discernible impact of entry, when instability and advertising are taken together we see that entry of the *Independent* and *Today*, into the quality and midmarket sectors respectively, apparently did impact on the competitive process by disrupting a previous, established pattern of advertising competition. From a policy perspective, we also see that the competitive process does appear to be substantially driven by (or driving) advertising behaviour, and this is important given the ambiguity of competition, in welfare terms, when it takes this form. Finally, it emerges that during the putatively suspicious period of low instability in the quality market from late 1988 to early 1993, intensive advertising competition was in fact taking place, probably reactive in nature up to mid 1991 but proactive thereafter, which does not sit well with the idea of competition being in abeyance.[16]

Turning to the data on instability and prices, analysis leads to two main conclusions. First, it is hard to detect a systematic relationship of any kind between the instability and price series in each sub-market. Second, and consistently with this, the instability series fails to pick up significant variations in pricing behaviour, in part entry-related, of which there are echoes in the price series, and corroborating evidence is to be found in data on the sequence of price changes (Table 7.3).

On the first point, if price competition and instability are connected, we would expect an inverse relationship in their levels, or to observe instability rising when competition is causing real price to fall, and *vice versa*. Some individual instances of this may be discerned, for example in the quality sector from 1979 to 1981, and the popular market from 1981 to 1986, and it is true that in all three markets in the latter part of the period (at least prior to the price wars of 1993 in the quality and popular sectors) we

Table 7.3 Dates of cover price changes to levels shown by market segment*

(a) Quality Titles

Daily editions:

Cover price	Telegraph	The Times	Guardian	Independent	F.T.
12p	17.3.80				
15p	6.10.80				
17p					
18p	24.8.81		2.6.80		
20p	25.10.82	24.3.80	23.2.81		
23p	**18.2.85**	**18.2.85**	10.5.82		
25p	14.10.85	16.12.85	11.3.85	7.10.86	21.7.80
30p	15.2.88	15.12.88	20.6.88	22.2.88	17.8.81
32p	30.1.89				
35p	19.3.90	30.7.90	5.3.90	30.10.89	9.8.83
40p	**18.2.91**	29.4.91	**18.2.91**	29.10.90	2.12.85
45p	3.2.92	30.3.92		17.8.92	2.1.88
50p					27.11.89
55p					25.2.91
60p					3.2.92

Saturday editions:

Cover price	Telegraph	The Times	Guardian	Independent
35p	4.2.89			10.9.88
40p	24.3.90	3.11.90		8.4.89
45p	23.2.91	4.5.91	28.3.92	29.10.90
50p	8.2.92	4.4.92	24.10.92	5.10.91

(b) Midmarket Titles

Cover price	Express	Mail	Today
5p	**23.9.74**	**23.9.74**	
6p	17.2.75	17.3.75	
7p	9.2.76	22.3.76	
8p	24.1.77	21.2.77	
9p	2.10.78	2.5.79	
10p	30.7.79	17.9.79	
12p	31.3.80	2.6.80	
15p	**20.7.81**	**20.7.81**	
17p	1.3.82		
18p	**18.10.82**	**18.10.82**	4.3.86
20p	**12.11.84**	**12.11.84**	9.6.86

Table 7.3 (continued)

(b) Midmarket Titles (continued)

Cover price	Express	Mail	Today
22p	2.2.87	19.10.87	24.4.89
25p	**13.11.89**	**13.11.89**	6.8.90
28p	**28.1.91**	**28.1.91**	
30p	**7.10.91**	**7.10.91**	
32p	2.8.93	26.7.93	

(c) Popular titles

Cover price	Mirror	Sun	Star
5p	**7.10.74**	**7.10.74**	
6p	**14.1.76**	**14.1.76**	2.11.78
7p	**18.4.77**	**18.4.77**	
8p	**22.5.78**	**22.5.78**	23.7.79
9p	24.9.79	4.2.80	
10p	**14.4.80**	**14.4.80**	2.6.80
12p	**15.9.80**	**15.9.80**	29.6.81
14p	7.9.81	**1.2.82**	**1.2.82**
15p		12.7.82	
16p	28.6.82	27.2.84	21.11.83
17p	5.3.84	**17.9.84**	**17.9.84**
18p	**4.2.85**	**4.2.85**	11.2.85
20p	23.3.87	1.6.87	16.2.87
22p	**24.4.89**	**24.4.89**	1.5.89
25p	8.10.90	3.10.90	15.10.90
27p	20.7.92		
30p		12.7.93	
32p		22.8.94	

Note: *Simultaneous changes denoted by bold type, first incidence of a particular price level (FT excepted in the quality sector) by underlining.

Source: Monopolies and Mergers Commission, *The Supply of National Newspapers*, Cm 2422, p. 25.

observe extended phases where real prices are high and instability is low or falling. But, even allowing for varying lag lengths and possible switching from aggressive to catch-up pricing strategies, there is no consistent pattern as there was in the case of advertising.

On the question of pricing behaviour, and focusing to begin with on the midmarket sector, the dominant feature of the real price series is clearly the very steep increase beginning in 1980 (Figure 7.2). Now, as Table 7.3(b) reveals, this coincides with the establishment of a regime of simultaneous, identical price changes up to 1984 by the incumbent duopolists, the *Express* and *Mail*. The entry of *Today*, selling at a discount, in 1986, apparently disturbed this pattern at least temporarily, and the real price series registers a decline up to 1989 when, as Table 7.3 again shows, the parallel pricing pattern is re-established, and real prices resume an upward trend. Given that our overall interest is in what instability statistics tell us about competition, the significance of all this is that here we have evidence of important changes in competitive behaviour – and also further evidence of the impact of market entry – which is clear in other data but not captured by the instability index.

Something similar appears in the popular market. Again, the entry of the *Star*, also selling at a discount, in 1978, disrupts an even clearer pattern of simultaneous, identical price increases over the preceding four years by the incumbent duopolists, the *Mirror* and *Sun* (Table 7.3(c)). In this case, the pattern of parallel pricing, though briefly restored in 1980, seems to have been more permanently modified. Thereafter there are a number of simultaneous, matching changes by pairs of titles up to 1989, but none by all three rivals, and with varying identities in the pairs. The relevant price series in Figure 7.2 registers a pronounced fall after 1978, coinciding with entry, and also a very sharp increase in 1980, when the *Mirror* and *Sun* again act in concert. However, there is no substantial increase – and in fact a fall – in the pre-entry period before 1978, and while some later increases coincide with paired increases, in particular in 1982 and 1985, not all do so. Thus the changes in pricing behaviour are not so clearly mirrored in the real price series in this case but, again, the significant point is that there is no hint of them in the instability series.

No similar pattern is evident in the quality sector, where there was no pre-entry pattern of contemporaneous, matching price increases amongst, in this case, the *three* incumbents (excluding the specialist *Financial Times*, which by this time had gone its own way on pricing).[17] In this case the *Independent*, entering at the common price, merged seamlessly into a pattern of price rounds with varying leaders (Table 7.3(a)). Entry may nevertheless have exerted an impact on prices, the real price series showing a marked dip after 1986 in an otherwise upward trend – again conspicuously *not* matched by an appropriate corresponding registering in instability. Other noteworthy features of the quality price series are that the phase of more active competition, as measured by share instability, from 1978 was apparently initiated by two years of falling real prices from 1978 to 1980 (as well as increased advertising); and it may be no coincidence that real price was at a very high level, and much above trend, just prior to the Murdoch-inspired price war of 1993.

6.   CONCLUSIONS

The welfare implications of market share instability are too ambiguous a priori for it to stand alone as an index of the intensity of competition. Ultimately, to derive welfare conclusions, resort must be had to performance indicators, though evidence on the relationship between instability and performance in the extant empirical literature is particularly scant.

On the evidence of our case study of three sub-markets within the UK national daily newspaper industry, instability can itself be highly unstable over time, exhibiting periods of significant increase, decrease and relative stagnation, typically subject to oscillations in each case, over a longer interval within a given market. It follows that, when assessing the degree of instability in a particular market, observations based on time series of short duration should be treated with caution, and observations between end-dates over intervals of any duration may be misleading, and highly sensitive to the choice of start- and end-date.

When related to other observables, the performance of instability indices in capturing the competitive process in our three markets was at best mixed. On the one hand, the indices did pick up the outbreak of price wars in two cases, and one case of particularly significant change in ownership. There was also evidence of distinct relationships in all three markets between instability and advertising expenditure, though the dynamic structure of the relationships was complex and unstable, with the identity of the lead variable itself changing on occasion. On the other hand, the instability indices failed to register twelve other ownership changes; nor did they capture the impact of significant new market entry that occurred in each of the three markets, even though other evidence suggested that entry disrupted pre-existing patterns of advertising competition and price behaviour in two of the three markets in each case. In addition, we observed instances of high and even strongly increasing market share instability, presumably driven by advertising and product competition, at times when real prices were also rising sharply, apparently due to phases of collusive, or at least mutually accommodating, pricing behaviour – a finding which strongly underlines the earlier conclusion as to the ambiguity of instability in welfare terms.

We conclude that, regrettably from the point of view of infusing dynamic considerations into antitrust cases, market share instability appears unreliable not only as a proxy for performance and welfare, but also as a diagnostic in screening cases for possible priority in policy application. That said, data on the turnover of shares undeniably constitutes information about a market that cannot be simply ignored; and, in our experience in the present case, can contribute usefully in teasing out the intricacies of the competitive process. In particular, if the present case is not wholly atypical, it can be instructive in bringing out the essentially *episodic* nature of competition over time within the same market, whereas coming from orthodox, static theory, our predisposition and instinct may be to attempt to categorize markets as typified permanently by this kind of behaviour or that. This point applies equally to analyses carried out in antitrust cases as to academic research.

NOTES

*   We are extremely grateful to Paul Geroski for a substantial part of the data used in this study.
**   The views expressed are the authors' personal opinions and do not necessarily reflect the views of the Office of Fair Trading.
1.   For later surveys see Cable (1998) and Caves (1998).
2.   Cable and Morris (1994) propose the use of the change in the variance of the log of firm sizes. Strategies which attract sales from rival firms will either reduce the dispersion of firm sizes, leading to a negative value for this index, or increase it, generating a positive value. Morris (1998) notes, however, that this measure is very sensitive to changes in the mean firm size arising, for example, from new entry. This problem can be avoided by adopting a similar measure, the change in the coefficient of variation of the log of firm sizes. The absolute values of these measures can be taken to yield an index which is comparable to the sum of absolute changes in market shares.
3.   So far as we aware, the usefulness or otherwise of mobility indices in this way has not previously been examined, though Sandler (1988) and Fitzsimmons and Knudsen (1991) have reported interesting analyses using them to assess the impact of deregulation in the US airline and railroad industries respectively.
4.   Entry will cause a purely statistical impact on our measure which cannot be completely eliminated. In other work with this data Morris (1998) used three versions of the index; the sum of market share changes, the average market share change and the sum of market share changes where the market was defined as only the incumbent titles. The choice of measure was found to make little difference to the patterns of instability detected.
5.   Meisel (1981) adjusts his measure for entry using two alternative assumptions about how the sales of entrants are attracted from incumbent firms: in proportion to pre-entry shares, and equally from all brands. This is reasonable for markets where products are homogenous or where product differentiation is of the non-address variety, but unsuitable in the present case where product differentiation is of the address type (see Morris, 1998), and entrants accordingly impact only on their neighbours.
6.   See Cronshaw et al. (1990) and Morris (1998). See also Morris (1997) which applies Schmalensee's (1985) test of competitive localisation. This test rejected generalised competition for this market but was unable to detect patterns of localised competition.
7.   Sunday titles were quite distinct from the dailies, at least over the majority of our period, and arguably serve a rather different (leisure and/or political weekly) readership need. Despite the existence of ownership links in some cases they are therefore treated as a further, separate market here. Thompson (1989) stresses the joint-product nature of the newspaper industry in supplying not only news/features for readers but also an advertising medium to advertisers, but this aspect is not addressed here.
8.   The missing observations are as follows: the *Telegraph* in November 1973, January 1974, April 1977, March, April and October 1978, April and June 1979, May 1980, and June and November 1985; the *Times* from December 1978 to November 1979; the *Guardian* in

October and November 1979; the *Financial Times* in February 1971, August 1977, October and November 1979, June and July 1983 and September 1984; the *Mail* between January and June 1971; and the *Sun* between July and December 1964 and July to December 1969. The lengthy absences of *The Times*, the *Mail* and *Sun* are periods when no production occurred, whereas some production occurred during the other periods. The method of smoothing used was considered likely to minimise fluctuations due to missing observations and, where missing values are for two or more successive months, the instability indices will reflect only changes in the sales of those titles which were produced as normal.

9. Longer-term strategies may still register in high frequency data but this is less likely to occur if they produce gradual, 'diffused' effects over time in the data.
10. Morris (1998), chapter 8, examines the impact of data frequency on instability measures. This work suggests that measures generated using annual and quarterly data may fail to reveal instability that arises when sales fluctuate with no firm gaining a long term advantage.
11. Figures include entry and exit by acquisition and divestiture. The overall figure excluding entry and exit was 36 per cent.
12. These changes brought about a dramatic rise in sales. In 1968 the average circulation of the *Sun* was just 1.0m. By 1975 daily sales were averaging 3.4m
13. Purchases in the quality market include those of *The Times* by Thompson in 1966 and by News International in 1981, of a controlling interest in the *Telegraph* by Hollinger Inc. in 1985 and of the *Independent* by Mirror Group Newspapers in 1994. Midmarket changes were acquisition of the *Express* by Trafalgar House in 1977 and its subsequent divestment in 1982 and purchase by United Newspapers in 1985, and the purchases of *Today* by Lonrho in 1986 and News International in 1987. In the popular market the *Star* was bought by United Newspapers in 1985, and the *Mirror* was purchased by Robert Maxwell in 1984. The impact of these acquisitions on instability in the market is discussed in more detail in Morris (1998).
14. There was also an unsuccessful entrant in the daily market, the *Post* which lasted just 33 issues in 1988. The period also saw the entry of the *Sunday Sport*, which also introduced some weekday issues, but this title can be excluded from the market considered here due to its idiosyncratic editorial material. Other market segments also saw entry, both successful (for example the *Independent on Sunday* in 1990) and unsuccessful (for example the *Sunday Correspondent* in 1989 and the *London Daily News* in 1987).
15. The advertising data were drawn from various issues of *Trimedia Digest of Brands and Advertisers*, published by Register MEAL Ltd. The initial price data were compiled from various issues of *British Rates and Data*, published by Maclean Hunter Ltd. This was supplemented with data published in the Monopolies and Mergers Commission Report on *The Supply of National Newspapers* (Cm 2422, HMSO) and information supplied by the Newspaper Publishers Association.
16. Especially as there is no evidence over the period of simultaneous price changes or patterns of price leadership.
17. Here as elsewhere perhaps (including the counting ability of crows), two is 'few' and three (or more) is 'many'.

REFERENCES

Adelman, I.G. (1958), 'A stochastic analysis of the size distribution of firms', *American Statistical Association Journal*, **53**, 893–904.

Alemson, M. (1969), 'Demand and the game of conflict in oligopoly over time: recent Australian experience', *Oxford Economic Papers*, **21**, 220–47.

Baldwin, J.R. (1995), *The Dynamics of Industrial Competition: A North American Perspective*, Cambridge: Cambridge University Press.

Baldwin, J.R. and P.K. Gorecki (1994), 'Concentration and mobility statistics in Canada's manufacturing sector', *Journal of Industrial Economics*, **42**, 92–103.

Cable, J.R. (1997), 'Market share behaviour and mobility: an analysis and time-series application', *Review of Economics and Statistics*, **79**, 136–41.

Cable, J.R. (1998), 'Market Share Dynamics and Competition: A Survey of the Empirical Literature', Aberystwyth Economic Research Paper 98–7, December.

Cable, J.R. and C. Morris (1994), 'The impact of entry on dynamic competition in the UK newspaper industry', Aberystwyth Economic Research Papers 94–104.

Caves, R.E. (1998), 'Industrial organization and new findings on the turnover and mobility of firms', *Journal of Economic Literature*, **36**, 1947–82.

Caves, R.E. and M.E. Porter (1978) ,'Market structure, oligopoly, and stability of market shares', *Journal of Industrial Economics*, **26**, 289–313.

Cowling, K. (1982), *Monopoly Capitalism*, London and Basingstoke: Macmillan.

Cowling, K. and D. Mueller (1978), 'The social costs of monopoly power', *Economic Journal*, **88**, 727–48.

Cowling, K. and A.J. Rayner (1970), 'Price, quality and market share', *Journal of Political Economy*, **78**, 1292–309.

Cowling, K. and M. Waterson (1976), 'Price–cost margins and market structrure', *Economica*, **43**, 267–74.

Cowling, K., J. Cable, Kelly M. and T. McGuinness (1975), *Advertising and Economic Behaviour*, London and Basingstoke: Macmillan.

Cronshaw, M., J. Cubbin and E. Davis (1990), 'The importance of product positioning', *Business Strategy Review*, **1**, 53–73

Das, B.J., W.F. Chappell and W.F. Shughart (1993), 'Advertising, competition and market share instability', *Applied Economics*, **25**, 1409–12.

Davies, S., P. Geroski and A. Vlassopoulos (1990), 'The stability of market shares in UK manufacturing industry 1979–1986', *Business Strategy Review*, Autumn, 37–51.

Fitzsimmons, E. and J. Knudsen (1991), 'Market share instability among class I railroads and the impact of deregulation', *Quarterly Review of Economics and Business*, **31**, 66–77.

Gort, M. (1963), 'Analysis of stability and change in market shares', *Journal of Political Economy*, **71**, 51–63.

Hart, P.E. and S.J. Prais (1956), 'The analysis of business concentration: a statistical approach', *Journal of the Royal Statistical Society*, Series A Part II, **119**, 150–91.

Heggestad, A. and S.A. Rhoades (1976), 'Concentration and firm stability in commercial banking', *Review of Economics and Statistics*, **58**, 443–52.

Heggestad, A. and S.A. Rhoades (1976), 'Multimarket interdependence and local market competition in banking', *Review of Economics and Statistics*, **60**, 523–32.

Hymer, S. and P. Pashigian (1962), 'Turnover of firms as a measure of market behaviour', *Review of Economics and Statistics*, **44**, 82–7.

Joskow, J. (1960), 'Structural indicia: rank-shift analysis as a supplement to concentration ratios', *Review of Economics and Statistics*, **42**, 113–16.

Meisel, J.B. (1981), 'Entry, multiple brand firms and market share instability', *Journal of Industrial Economics*, **29**, 375–84.

Monopolies and Mergers Commission, *The Supply of National Newspapers*, Cm 2422, HMSO.

Morris, C.L. (1997), 'Econometric Diagnosis of Competitive Localisation: An Application to the UK National Daily Newspaper Market', Studies in Economics 97/12, Department of Economics, University of Kent at Canterbury.

Morris, C.L. (1998), 'Product Differentiation, Predation and Competition in the UK National Daily Newspaper Industry', Unpublished PhD Thesis, University of Wales, Aberystwyth.

Ogur, J.D. (1976), 'Competition and Market Share Instability', Federal Trade Commission Staff Report, Bureau of Economics, R-6-15-31, Government Printing Office, Washington, p. 60.

Sandler, R.D. (1988), 'Market share instability in commercial airline markets and the impact of deregulation', *Journal of Industrial Economics*, **36**, 327–35.

Schmalensee, R. (1985), 'Econometric diagnosis of competitive localisation', *International Journal of Industrial Organisation*, **3**, 57–70.

Shorrocks, A.F. (1978), 'The measurement of mobility', *Econometrica*, **46**, 1013–24.

Thompson, R.S. (1989), 'Circulation versus advertiser appeal in the newspaper industry: an empirical investigation', *Journal of Industrial Economics*, **37**, 259–71.

Tucker, R.S. (1936), 'Increasing concentration of business not supported by statistical evidence', *The Annalist*, July 31, 149.

8. Oligopoly and rent-seeking: Cowling and Mueller revisited

Tim Hazledine*

1. INTRODUCTION

Keith Cowling and Dennis Mueller's 1978 *Economic Journal* paper, 'The Social Costs of Monopoly Power', is a classic. It has been reprinted at least four times,[1] and in a current Industrial Organisation text is cited, along with Harberger (1954), as one of the 'two seminal articles on measuring economy-wide losses from market power' (Church and Ware, 2000, p. 43). Nevertheless, despite dealing boldly with very large numbers, Cowling–Mueller has not provoked much further analysis and criticism: the present chapter is a contribution in that cause.

To Harberger are attributed the eponymous triangles of allocative inefficiency due to 'monopoly' pushing price above marginal cost, so that consumer surplus greater than the resource cost of production is not generated. Perhaps most researchers when they discover something naturally want to make it out to be as big as possible, but Harberger was happy to claim that the triangles are really rather tiny, and so perhaps not worth worrying about, especially when doing anything about them through antitrust brings with it its own economic and political costs.

Then Oliver Williamson (1968), in what is certainly another classic, at least of the partial equilibrium literature, pushed the laissez-faire point further by juxtaposing those tiny triangles against possibly larger 'rectangles' of foregone scale economy cost savings, should misguided antitrust prevent mergers on monopoly power grounds.

Cowling–Mueller can be seen as a two-pronged counterattack on Harberger and Williamson: in essence, pumping up the triangles to a more impressive size, and reclaiming the rectangles for the activist antitrust cause. I will suggest that the triangle argument is sound in principle but probably misdirected in practice, leaving the rectangles to be further pursued in this chapter. Here Cowling–Mueller propose that observed (rectangles of) above-competitive profits are to be interpreted as prizes or rents, in the pursuit of which a similar value of resources will have been expended and thus wasted. They do not explicitly model this rent-dissipation process – such is the contribution of this chapter.

The Industrial Organisation (IO) literature provides clear signposts towards modelling private sector rent dissipation, with the idea that incumbent firms will protect their monopoly rents by retaining sufficient capacity to respond aggressively to any entrant who might compete away those rents. To the extent that such capacity is greater than production needs, resources will thereby be wasted. It turns out that under monopoly conditions rent-protecting resource costs could be quite substantial, though there is no close link between their size and the size of observed profits. In the oligopoly case (two or more incumbents) there may be no rent-protecting costs, because the capacity actually used by the incumbents to produce their current output can be sufficient to deter entry – that is, there may be no 'excess'.

The next section reviews Cowling–Mueller and the issues they raise. Then we consider in turn monopoly and oligopoly rent protection, before noting some qualifications to the analysis. A final section summarises and concludes the chapter.

2.   THE CONTRIBUTION OF COWLING AND MUELLER

Harberger (1954), in his pioneering contribution to the quantitative normative analysis, had assumed a value for the elasticity of demand ($e = -1$) in order to make his calculations of the allocative costs of monopoly power. Cowling–Mueller pointed out, correctly, that in general elasticity is endogenous to the monopolist's pricing decision, and would not be –1 unless marginal costs were zero. Indeed, the monopolist will price in the elastic portion of the demand curve, such that (under constant cost and linear demand conditions) its output would be only one half of the perfectly competitive output which is the efficiency benchmark. Then, the allocative inefficiency triangle would be rather large, equal in fact in area to one half of observed monopoly profits!

The problem with this, as Cowling and Mueller conceded in their rejoinder to Steven Littlechild's Comment (1981), is that under the more usual oligopoly market conditions the monopoly mark-up formula does not apply and output is more than one half of competitive levels. Indeed, I will argue below that even under monopoly conditions pricing will not necessarily be in the elastic region of the demand curve. In any case, the welfare costs calculated in this chapter will be based on the 'actual' reductions in output from competitive levels, as these come out of the monopoly or oligopoly model.

This leaves as the real focus of interest those 'rectangles' of resources wasted in profit-seeking. Cowling–Mueller take over from the political economy rent-seeking literature (Tullock, 1967; Posner, 1975) the ingenious proposition that if there is competition for a monopoly or market power position conferred by some authority, and if the process of competition incurs real resource costs, then it is conceivable that most or even all of the monopoly rent could be dissipated in the struggle to procure it. An apparent problem with applying this to the market sector is that we do (or think we do) observe profits being earned and pocketed. So Cowling–Mueller make the striking assumption that the prize of observed monopoly profits (after tax) must have been matched by an equal expenditure of resources elsewhere in the economy by those who tried and failed to win the prize. With this, and the assumption that advertising expenditures are rent-seeking waste, they generate estimates of monopoly welfare costs around 7 per cent and 13 per cent of 'Gross Corporate Product' in the UK and the US respectively – not tiny numbers at all!

Now, it is natural to ask just *how* this rent dissipation process would actually operate. This is indeed a question that has concerned contributors to the political economy rent-seeking literature, some of whom have queried the assumption that competition on the demand side would necessarily waste all the rents. Would not the dictator or agency owning the monopoly be able to come up with mechanisms for realising some at least of its value, rather than ending up with nothing to show for their privileges? It is easy to think of such schemes – lotteries, nepotism, auctions, for example – even if they might not always realise all the potential value (that is, identify the highest value user). If, as someone (probably Gordon Tullock) put it, the Sultan gives all the lucrative concessions to the husbands of his daughters, the rents will not thereby be dissipated, except perhaps partially in expenditures to become a son-in-law. That is, rent-seeking does not necessarily imply (full) rent dissipation.

And what about the case of non-competitive rent-seeking, as when, for example, there are just a few firms big enough to tender for a lucrative government commission? Hillman and Riley (1987) are cited by Linster (1993) as demonstrating how the Nash Equilibrium solution concept can be applied in the situation where the prize is divisible, with oligopolistic bidders choosing their level of rent-seeking activity, which increases their expected share of the prize, given the levels of their competitors. Still, the actual processes and mechanisms – what the money actually gets spent on – remains a 'black box' mystery.

Cowling–Mueller's concern was with rents that the private sector creates for itself, and this turns out to be interestingly different from the usual publicly provided rent situation, being in one respect harder and in another easier to analyse. What is hard – or, at least, non-trivial – is to specify just how the rents are generated in the first place; what is easier is to specify plausible – or, at least, familiar – mechanisms whereby the possession of the rents may be contested – that is, the rent-seeking or protecting process itself.

State monopolies are protected, in essence, by main force – the state can confer property rights and back this up with its police powers. But, except in mafia-riddled situations, this is not possible for a private operator. Even a private monopolist does not legally own its market (unless by patent or other state-granted privilege): the demand curve, basically, is just sitting there, apparently available for exploitation by other suppliers. Cowling–Mueller suggest, without much elaboration, that rents are first generated by 'excessive accumulation of advertising goodwill stocks, and excessive product differentiation through R&D' (p. 733): in essence, the creation or manipulation of demand curves.

The normative implications of product differentiation are – to say the least – problematic. I will touch on them again in Section 5 in relation to advertising, but will not attempt to confront them in the main body of this chapter. Instead, I will limit my analysis to firms producing, or potentially producing, similar products (that is sharing a demand curve), and will ask whether a small number of such firms already in an industry, earning profits or rents from their fewness through restrictions in output below perfectly competitive levels, could protect those rents from dissipation by entry of new competitors.

This is 'easier' than following the Byzantine trails of political rent-seeking because economists have well-articulated procedures for analysing behaviour in homogeneous product markets. The standard story, at least since Bain, is this: monopolists or oligopolists protect their rents by deterring entry, and they do this (as Cowling and Mueller note) by retaining the capacity to aggressively compete with any entering firm, such that the latter would wish it had gone somewhere else (and so, being 'rational', would not have entered in the first place).

The IO literature actually now makes this quite hard, by worrying about two things: whether the threat to retaliate is 'credible' and whether, in an oligopoly situation, there will be 'free-rider' problems in coordinating incumbents to supply what is a public good for them – deterred entry. I will argue that they worry too much; that so long as retaliation is feasible it will be credible, basically as an implication of the sense of legitimacy or 'ownership' that incumbents feel for their market or their customers, and that the free rider problem is also seriously overrated as a practical difficulty for oligopolists in a mature industry.

So what is there to do? We have our normative rent dissipation idea from Cowling and Mueller; we have (in another part of a textbook such as

Church and Ware) the tools for the positive analysis of resource-using entry deterrence; all we need to do is put them together. In this chapter I will ask what it would take to protect a privately-producing rent-yielding position, whether it would be profitable to do what it takes, what the resource costs would be of these activities, and how these relate to the observed profits used by Cowling–Mueller as a proxy for the size of rent-seeking activities.

3.   THE MONOPOLY CASE

We consider the situation of an incumbent monopolist and ask whether steps that firm might take to protect its monopoly position could have efficiency implications beyond the usual Harberger triangle of marginal misallocations due to pricing above competitive levels. We will treat two possible production technologies: constant returns and increasing returns. We will assume that the technology is freely available, but that incumbency does confer what might be called a moral advantage: the monopolist feels a sense of entitlement or ownership of its market – at least against claimants who bring no cost advantage to the industry – and will act aggressively to protect its position. Basically, as first mover, it will tell any aspiring entrant with nothing new to offer in the way of superior product or technology to push off and find their own monopoly somewhere else, and that if they don't, they will regret it. This threat must however be plausible, in that the monopolist must have easy access to resources sufficient to respond quickly to any entrant, such that the latter would find itself not making any profit (and therefore, if rational, would not enter in the first place).

Our modelling throughout will be linear, with the assumption of homogeneous output. It is based on two constraining equations:

$$C_i = f_i + c_i q_i \tag{8.1}$$

$$P = 1 - Q \tag{8.2}$$

Equation (8.1) gives total costs for firm i with fixed and constant marginal costs, equation (8.2) is the market demand curve with price dependent on total industry output, Q. We will consider two cases: constant returns and increasing returns

3.1   Constant Cost Case

If there are no fixed costs ($f_i = 0$ in (8.1)) and marginal costs are the same, c, for everyone, very small-scale entry will be possible, and it will be hard for an incumbent monopolist to prevent it. It will not, however, be hard for the incumbent to credibly threaten to act aggressively, since the stakes will be very high – basically if any entry is allowed, all will be lost – small firms will flood in and eliminate monopoly rents.

So what, if anything, could the incumbent do to preserve its monopoly? The answer turns out to depend on the relationship between marginal costs and demand – specifically, whether market demand at the competitive price ($P=c$) is inelastic or elastic. We look at each possibility.

(a) Mature industry (inelastic demand)

Consider the situation of a 'mature' industry, in which demand has expanded and/or costs been reduced sufficiently for marginal costs to intersect the demand curve in its inelastic region, as shown in Figure 8.1.[2] Absent any entry threat the monopolist will of course set price in the elastic region, at P^m. But suppose entry is possible. To deter this the incumbent must be able to quickly expand output to the competitive level, $1 - c$, which leaves no profitable opening for any new firm. Take the extreme case that this entails actually purchasing sufficient inputs to produce $1 - c$ – that is, all these variable costs must be sunk.

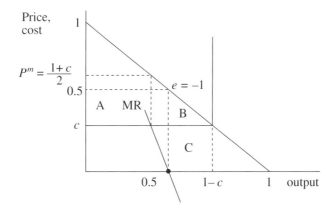

Figure 8.1   Monopoly rent protection

This will deter entry (so long as the threat to actually expand is believed, as I expect it generally would be), but at a cost. What is that cost? Note first that the monopolist will no longer wish to set price at P^m. Its marginal opportunity costs are now zero, and so it will optimally set $P=0.5$ – at the revenue-maximising point of unit elasticity on the demand curve.[3]

So, we have found some Cowling–Mueller rent-seeking costs in addition to the Harberger triangle. In Figure 8.1, the total social costs of (protecting) monopoly are areas $B+C$. How large will these be? In particular, how large are they relative to observed monopoly profits $A-C$? The formulae are:

$$\text{Area } A = 0.5[0.5-c]$$
$$\text{Area } B = 0.5[0.5-c]^2$$
$$\text{Area } C = c[0.5-c]$$

So, $A - C = [0.5-c]^2$ and, $B+C = [0.5-c][0.25+c/2]$.

We can calculate these for the range of possible values of c (Table 8.1). We see at once that observed monopoly profits would be no indicator of monopoly social costs, which may be larger or smaller. The higher are marginal production costs, the lower are social monopoly costs, because the closer is the competitive output to the revenue-maximising level, and thus the fewer are the inputs that need to be wastefully sunk to deter entry. As a percentage of observed market revenue, which is 0.25 ($=0.5\times0.5$), social costs are indeed quite high – rather more than the 'case of beer' that can emerge from allocative triangle calculations.

Table 8.1   Entry-deterring monopoly

Value of c:	0.0	0.1	0.2	0.3	0.4	0.5
Profits $= A - C$	0.25	0.16	0.09	0.04	0.01	0
Social Cost $= B+C$	0.125	0.12	0.105	0.08	0.045	0
Profits/ Social Cost	2	1.33	0.86	0.5	0.22	–
Social Cost/ Revenue	0.5	0.33	0.22	0.125	0.055	–

There are two qualifications to be considered. First, the incumbent may not need to sink all marginal costs, if some inputs are readily available on spot markets. For example, much of the entry deterrence literature assumes that only 'capacity' (capital stock) need be sunk, because both materials and labour are (it is supposed) freely available without prior commitment. This is good news because fewer resources need be wastefully tied up to protect the monopoly. But it is bad news because monopoly price will be higher – based on the optimal mark-up on the non-sunk marginal costs, which are no longer zero – and because the further restriction of output will mean some inputs sunk which were in production in the $q=0.5$ case.

The general formula for monopoly social costs can be shown to be:

$$\text{Social Costs} = \{[1-(c-s)]^2/2 - s^2\}/2 \tag{8.3}$$

where s is the part of c that is sunk. Part of (8.3) is increasing, part decreasing in s. The net effects are shown in Table 8.2, which reveals that monopoly with partially sunk costs is sometimes more costly and sometimes less so than the full sunk cost scenario.

Table 8.2   Monopoly social costs

s \ c	0.0	0.1	0.2	0.3	0.4	0.5
0	0.125	0.101	0.08	0.061	0.045	0.031
0.1		0.12	0.096	0.075	0.056	0.04
0.2			0.105	0.081	0.06	0.041
0.3				0.08	0.056	0.035
0.4					0.045	0.035
0.5						0

The second qualification is that some or all of the sunk inputs may be able to be deployed without commitment in some other value-creating activity – on maintenance work or in producing for a competitive spot market, for example. If so then equation (8.3) exaggerates the social costs of monopolies protecting their position from entry.

We should also note that the threat of entry does result in lower prices than the unconstrained monopolist would set, to the extent that the additional capacity is used. For relatively high-cost cases (closer to 0.5), the welfare outcome under entry deterrence will be preferable to having no entry threat at all.

(b)   Immature industry (elastic demand)

The case of an 'immature' industry, with marginal costs intersecting demand in the elastic zone, is quickly dealt with. Monopoly is not defensible, at least in the fully sunk cost case, because there is no price (>0.5) which would generate enough revenue to pay for entry-deterring sunk inputs (that is, the value of competitive costs and output exceeds the value of monopoly output). What we can expect to see in such industries is a succession of new entrants, most of whom in practice would be contributing to expanding the market and/or introducing new technologies.

3.2   Decreasing Cost Case

If fixed costs are positive, average costs decrease with output, and an incumbent is no longer faced with the prospect of very small-scale entry. The monopolist need only sink enough additional inputs to be able to expand output to the point[4] where the most profitable output choice by an entrant would still not yield sufficient revenue to cover (or more than just cover) its fixed costs.

If marginal costs are the same as before and are well below 0.5, so that the incumbent would continue to set price at 0.5,[5] then the results of a social cost of monopoly calculation are unequivocal. Compared with the counterfactual, protecting a monopoly is less wasteful than in the constant-cost case, for two reasons: first, fewer inputs are sunk, and, second, the counterfactual is less attractive than perfect competition – price must be higher to pay for the additional lump of fixed costs incurred by an entrant.[6]

4. OLIGOPOLY

The predominant industrial structure in most sectors of the economy appears to be oligopoly. Appearances are to an extent deceptive, as vertical and horizontal product differentiation carves out many monopoly niches in product and geographical space, to which the analysis of the previous section may be germane. But we must – as early commentators on Cowling–Mueller (1981, p. 723) were quick to point out – be able to deal analytically with the situation of small-number competition.

So might a group of incumbent oligopolists incur costs (excess capacity) in order to prevent new firms from entering and competing down their profits? To answer this, we will maintain from the monopoly analysis the assumption that incumbents will act to defend their market, though we will now check that it is actually profitable for them to do so. We will also assume, as justified below, that the potential free-rider problems of a group of inde-pendent agents providing what in essence is a public good (entry deterrence) are not in practice problematic. It is hard to explain how we could actually observe above-competitive profits in homogeneous industries unless the incumbents are indeed capable of successfully coordinated entry deterrence.

This leads to a series of three questions. The first is: does deterrence actu-ally require incumbents to commit to excess capacity? It turns out that in many cases no extra resources need be devoted to protecting incumbents' profits, because their Nash equilibrium output competing amongst them-selves actually exceeds the Bain–Sylos–Modigliani entry-deterring industry output.

The second question is: in those cases where additional capacity does have to be deployed to deter entry, will it actually be profitable to do so? It turns out that the answer is always yes. Then, we return to the question asked in Section 3 of the monopoly case: what are the social costs of such deterrence activities?

4.1   Modelling Issues

We will model oligopoly as Cournot–Nash, which is in line with much mainstream practice in applied IO analysis. Cournot conjectures are that each firm assumes its competitors will not change their outputs in response to changes in the firm's output. Such can be criticised as an 'irrational' expectation that competitors will not respond to actions, but I disagree. For firm j to hold its output 'constant' when firm i expands in fact requires quite vigorous reaction – reducing prices and/or increasing marketing activities. What Cournot really means, I suggest – and this is why it is attractive and plausible from a modelling perspective – is that incumbent firms feel a sense of ownership of their customers, and will fight to keep them. That is, the Cournot oligopoly conjecture is equivalent to the fighting-to-defend-the-market assumption made above in the monopoly case. A monopolist 'owns' its market; an oligopolist 'owns' its piece of the market; both will defend their 'property'. Such is, I believe, consistent with the experimental psychology evidence; in particular the quite general finding (Rabin, 1998) of 'loss aversion' – that agents will incur costs to hold on to what they already have over and above what is 'rational' (that is their willingness to pay *ab initio*, which is what an otherwise similar prospective entrant faces).

That tells us how to model competition between the incumbent oligopolists, and we know that the outcome (Cournot–Nash equilibrium) will be profits or rents earned by them. How then do we model the interaction between incumbents and potential entrants? I suggest that the prospective entrant will assume the incumbents will act to make entry unprofitable, unless the costs of so doing exceed the costs of accommodating another competitor on equal (Cournot) terms (which we will find they never do). This is the natural extension of the Cournot assumption to the asymmetrical incumbent/entrant situation: incumbents fight to defend their customers from each other and their industry from intruders.[7]

How will the fight be coordinated? The theoretical literature has often focused on free-rider problems, treating entry deterrence (correctly) as a public good and then (incorrectly, I believe) worrying that uncoordinated private provision of the public good will be troubled by shirking.

One reason this is not appropriate is that, as Bernheim (1984) pointed out, entry is a discrete event (not a marginal change),[8] so that uncoordinated entry deterrence can indeed be a Nash Equilibrium. If it takes x resources to deter entry, and if duopolist 1 puts up $0.5x$, then (unless x exceeds the gains from restricting entry) it is optimal for duopolist 2 to contribute the other half. That is, entry deterrence is not necessarily freighted with prisoners' dilemma problems, unlike competition between incumbents.

A second reason is that economic theorists, with their extraordinary fixation on achieving intertemporal 'consistency' do, I believe, vastly overrate the importance of free-rider problems. That cooperation turns out to be very hard to achieve in theory does not mean that it is beyond the capabilities of real firms in fact. It might be more useful if theorists developed a realistic sense of the 'rules of the game' and how these constrain actions in different ways in different situations.

Just as a squabbling couple will turn, united, on any third person attempting to intervene, so may a vigorously competitive duopoly act as one against entrants. Again, the burgeoning experimental psychology/ behavioural economics literature is strongly supportive of the ability of agents to make use of moral codes or rules to coordinate in their joint interests.[9] As an example of this, I offer from my own research the case of competition in the air travel market for trips between Australia and New Zealand (Haugh and Hazledine, 1999). This is a well-established duopoly 'owned' by the national carriers of the two countries, Air New Zealand and Qantas, who have 90 per cent of the market. Other major international airlines confine their presence to limited 'fringe' activities, but the airline business, being rather glamorous, is vulnerable to irrational entry, and such occurred in 1995 when a small charter operator, Kiwi International, began offering scheduled services from regional NZ cities to and from Sydney and Brisbane.

Before this the duopolists had been operating, we calculated, as non-cooperative Cournot rivals, competing very vigorously with each other for market share. But their response to the upstart entrant, though presumably not explicitly arranged (because such would be illegal) was well coordinated and brutal. First Air New Zealand set up a whole 'new' airline – Freedom Air – as a fighting brand operating only alongside Kiwi in its regional market and undercutting its prices. When that didn't succeed in forcing exit[10] Qantas took its turn by initiating an across-the-board price war (quickly matched by Air New Zealand), which soon made the hapless Kiwi extinct, just over a year after its entry into the market.

So my modelling strategy here will be to assume that any costs incurred by oligopolists to deter entry will be evenly shared between them, without fuss.

4.2 The Oligopoly Model

We use the demand and cost curves of equations (8.1) and (8.2), with industry output Q now the sum of the outputs of the firms in the industry. Write down the profit function for an oligopolist i:

$$\pi_i = q_i(P - c_i) - f_i = q_i(1 - q_i - q_j - c_i) - f_i \qquad (8.4)$$

where q_j is the total output of all other firms in the industry. Differentiating and solving for the optimal firm i output:

$$q_i = (1 - q_j - c_i)/2 \qquad (8.5)$$

For the symmetric $(c_i = c)$ case this 'reaction function' will be:

$$q = (1 - c)/(1 + n) \qquad (8.6)$$

and industry output is

$$Q = \frac{n}{1 + n}(1 - c) \qquad (8.7)$$

with price

$$P = (1 + nc)/(1 + n) \qquad (8.8)$$

and profits per firm

$$\pi - (1 - c)^2/(1 + n)^2 - F \qquad (8.9)$$

4.3   Is Entry Naturally Deterred?

With non-zero fixed costs we can use Bernheim's (1984) idea of a maximum feasible size of industry, with n firms, such that industry profits with n firms will just cover their fixed costs. I will call this a competitive n-firm oligopoly. Then we will ask if $(n-1)$-firm Cournot–Nash oligopoly would be naturally stable in the sense of being unattractive to any entrant. We repeat the question for all possible structures down to monopoly.

Noting from (8.6) that output per firm increases as n decreases, we can deduce immediately that $(n-1)$-firm oligopoly will be quite safe from entry, with no need to sink any resources into entry deterrence, *for any value of* N. This is because Q^{n-1} (the total output of an $(n-1)$-firm oligopoly) is greater than $Q^n[(n-1)/n]$, which is the output needed from these $(n-1)$ firms if they are to leave no profitable piece of the market for an entrant, given that Q^n only just yields enough profits to cover fixed costs. The $(n-1)$ firms need only defend their existing customer base to deter entry.

What about $(n-2)$-firm oligopoly? Output per firm will be higher still, but with the loss of another supplier, it is not necessarily true that total industry output, Q^{n-2}, will exceed $Q^n[(n-1)/n]$. From (8.7) we see that the answer clearly does not depend on the size of marginal costs, c: we show in Table 8.3 the industry output numbers for $c = 0.25$, with n ranging from 6 to 2.

Table 8.3   Oligopoly outputs; c $=0.25$

	Q^n	Entry barring output	Q^{n-1}	Q^{n-2}	Q^{n-3}	Q^{n-4}	Q^{n-5}
$n=6$	0.643	0.536	0.625	0.600	0.563	0.500	0.375
$n=5$	0.625	0.500	0.600	0.563	0.500	0.375	
$n=4$	0.600	0.450	0.563	0.500	0.375		
$n=3$	0.563	0.375	0.500	0.375			
$n=2$	0.500	0.250	0.375				

The results are quite interesting. In the competitive duopoly and triopoly cases ($n=2, 3$), monopoly would be secure with no investment in sunk costs. In the $n=4$ or 5 cases, duopoly (and of course less concentrated structures) are secure. If the maximum number of firms that could be supported in a Cournot–Nash oligopoly is 6, then a triopoly would be safe from entry without making any deterring investment.

4.4   Will Deterrence be Profitable?

This restricts to just a few cases the applicability of the question: would a monopolist or oligopolist *want* to deter entry? The answer in these cases is quite general: yes they would. We can prove this by backward induction. For any n, consider the situation of the m-firm oligopoly, where m is the largest number such that deterrence is not trivial – that is, such that those m firms will have to have access to some additional capacity so as to be able to feasibly threaten to increase output to the level $Q^n[(n-1)/n]$ which would leave no profitable output choice for an entrant. Suppose, for simplicity, that the $(m+1)$-firm oligopoly is like the duopoly in the $n=5$ case in Table 8.3, with just enough capacity in its normal Cournot–Nash outcome to deter entry. Then the total costs incurred by the m-firm group would at most (that is in the case when all costs must be sunk) equal those of an $(m+1)$ firm oligopoly, but the smaller group's revenues would be higher, because they would be competing less vigorously (price goes up as number of firms goes down). So, yes indeed, they would choose to defend their position.

But then consider the $(m-1)$-firm case. They too will at most have to incur the costs of the larger group, but will earn yet higher profits than m firms could manage. So they too would deter entry. And so on, right back to monopoly. That is, any extant structure will choose to protect its profits from entry by firms with no technology or product advantage.

4.5   Social Costs of Deterrence

It seems that in many oligopoly situations no resources will be wasted in defending above-competitive profits, and the social costs of imperfect competition will be just the Harberger triangle from marginal output reductions. Indeed, amongst all the cases shown in Table 8.3, there is only one non-monopoly example of excess capacity being needed to deter entry, which is the case of duopoly when the highest feasible number of firms would be 6 ($n=6$).

We can calculate the social costs of deterrence in this case. To do so we need to specify the amount, s, of marginal costs that need to be sunk. This gives us a complication – the *ex post* cost curves of the oligopolists will be backward-L shaped, becoming vertical at the entry-deterring output, which in this case for each firm is 0.268 ($=0.536/2$). We assume that if this capacity constraint is active, the firms will simply each produce 0.268. Then Table 8.4 shows the possibilities for a range of values of sunk costs:

Table 8.4   Entry deterrence by a duopoly when n $=6$; c $=0.25$

s	Ex post marginal cost	Entry-deterring output	Duopoly output	Costs of excess capacity
0	0.25	0.536	0.500	0.0
0.05	0.20	0.536	0.533	0.00015
0.10	0.15	0.536	0.536	0.0
0.15	0.10	0.536	0.536	0.0
0.20	0.05	0.536	0.536	0.0
0.25	0.0	0.536	0.536	0.0

If sunk costs are zero, then there are no social costs, because the duopolists do not actually have to carry any excess capacity – they can credibly threaten to expand instantly to 0.536 should entry occur. If sunk costs are 40 per cent of *ex ante* marginal costs or more ($s=0.10$ or larger), then there are no social costs because the duopolists will wish to use all the capacity in current production. Only in the $s=0.05$ case is there some unused sunk capacity, and the costs of this are just 0.00015 ($=0.003 \times 0.05$), which is a quite tiny fraction of the value of duopoly.

Overall, we can conclude that under conditions of oligopoly where scale economies place a limit on the number of firms that can profitably operate in an industry, it is quite hard to generate much concern about social costs from oligopolistic rent protection. Under many circumstances, the oligopoly Cournot–Nash equilibrium output will be sufficient to deter entry;

where it is not, costs will be incurred to the extent that the commitment to expand output to make entry unprofitable entails actually sinking variable costs in zero-revenue-yielding activities (or non-activities): over the whole business sector, the sum of such costs is likely to be small.

5.   FOUR QUALIFICATIONS

Here we quite briefly consider four qualifications to or elaborations of the analysis: the welfare implications of fixed costs; what to do about advertising; the possibility of internal (to the firm) rent-seeking, and the implications of non-Cournot behaviour.

5.1   Fixed Costs

The analysis of the previous section was driven by the assumption of small-number 'competitive' oligopoly, which we motivated using the cost equation (8.1) which has constant marginal costs plus a fixed component, so that only a certain number of firms can be profitably supported by a market. But if we take this literally, we should allow for a Williamson-rectangle of scale economy efficiency gains from entry deterrence, through the rationalisation of redundant fixed costs.

Such could be quite substantial. For example, in the $n = 5$ case shown in Table 8.3 (room for no more than five firms in a zero-marginal cost oligopoly), we can calculate that the implied value for fixed costs, f, in equation (8.1) is 1/64, so that the rationalisation of fixed costs achieved by a monopoly would be 4/64 or 0.0625, which is almost as large as the Harberger Triangle of allocative inefficiency due to monopolistic pricing (area = 0.070).

Rationalisation effects may indeed be sometimes important. They need to be considered in careful analysis of specific cases, as in weighing up an 'efficiencies defence' in a merger determination (Hazledine, 1998). My own view is that claims of rationalisation efficiencies – or 'synergies', as they are sometimes called – will not often survive such careful analysis, for at least two reasons. First, we have by now plenty of experience of *ex post* disappointment in the cost and even profit performance of merged firms (Cowling, 1982). Second, in many or perhaps most real market situations, variety has value; in terms of a homogeneous product model, we could represent this by shifting the market demand curve (the total surplus generated by the industry) with the number of firms.

This does not necessarily undermine the modelling approach adopted above, which basically depends on the notion of a minimum efficient scale, beyond which average cost curves could be flat, rather than the asymptotically declining curve implied by the simple cost function of equation (8.1).

5.2   Advertising Costs

Cowling–Mueller's treatment of advertising expenditures is brutal. They add 150 per cent of all advertising to their monopoly welfare loss – 50 per cent as the contribution to the welfare triangle allocative loss, and the other 100 per cent on the assumption that all advertising activity is pure monopoly rent-seeking. They do note that this will be an overstatement 'to the extent advertising provides useful information to consumers' (p. 733), but downplay this qualification in a footnote:

> Given the interests of the agent doing the advertising, there will always be an inherent bias in the information provided, so the argument for advertising as a provider of information should not be taken too seriously. (p. 733, n. 2)

I certainly would not go this far, and I wonder if Cowling and/or Mueller would still maintain such a hard-line position. As it is, their assumptions mean that advertising is actually the major contributor to their (very large) monopoly welfare loss numbers for the United States; rather less so for the UK.

In ignoring advertising (and R&D activities) in this chapter, we have limited ourselves to analysing the protection of (existing) monopoly or oligopoly rents, not their creation *ab initio*. This largely reflects a research strategy of searching for truth where the light shines brightest – that is, the light thrown by the existing body of IO analysis, which has a well-articulated theory of entry deterrence, but relatively little to say about the creation of consumer tastes and new technologies.

5.3   Internal Rent-seeking

All of the above has accepted the neoclassical fiction of the firm as frictionless profit-maximiser, rather than as a large bureaucratic organism with a life of its own. Such is surely not so, and the reality has potentially substantial implications for our rent-seeking estimates. Cowling–Mueller were well aware of this, and are worth quoting in full:

> Much of the competition for control over monopoly rents may take place within the firm itself among the factor owners. Such competition will lead to an understatement of actual monopoly rents both through the inflation of costs caused by wasteful competition among factor owners and through the inclusion of part of the winning factor owners' shares of monopoly rents as reported costs. A

large literature now exists on the variety of objectives managers have and the ways in which these objectives are satisfied through discretionary control over company revenues. (1978, p. 745)

What was plausible then and to Cowling (1982) is surely beyond any rational denial twenty years later, with the explosion of what I call 'surplus-stripping' at the higher levels of corporate management and amongst the banks and consultants providing financial 'services' to corporations. However, in the other direction, the last quarter of the twentieth century was also a period of the squeezing down of the costs of workers lower on the wage scale, under the pressures from increased global competition for markets, so that the net effect of these changes on monopoly and oligopoly welfare losses cannot be signed, a priori.

5.4 Non-Cournot Conjectures

I have worked with the Cournot–Nash solution concept for oligopoly, because I believe it makes a lot of sense, in particular for explaining how the behaviour of incumbents to each other may differ from their behaviour to entrants. If competition between incumbents was less competitive or more 'collusive' than Cournot, then the social costs of rent protection would tend to be bigger, because the shortfall between actual oligopoly output and entry-deterring capacity would be larger. We could redo the model and calculations easily enough to incorporate non-Cournot conjectures.

6. SUMMARY AND CONCLUSION

If a firm is in the position of earning some monopoly rent, it is plausible that this firm would be willing to devote some resources – to use up some of that rent – to protect itself from losing the rest of it to other, competing firms. This is the idea first proposed and quantified by Cowling and Mueller (1978), and explored analytically and numerically in this chapter.

My approach has been first to assume – or, rather, claim – that 'credibility' is not an issue for the incumbent rent receiver(s). That is, if it would pay the incumbent(s) to aggressively repel rent-seeking entry then it will be believed by potential entrants that such would occur, and entry will indeed be deterred. The question then becomes whether it will pay the incumbent(s) to protect their position, given that they may have to sink resources in excess capacity in order to make a fast, aggressive response feasible.

For the monopoly case, it turns out always to be profitable to deter perfectly competitive entry (and, *a fortiori*, to deter 'lumpy' entry when there is a minimum efficient scale of production), so long as demand is inelastic at the competitive price. The reason, in hindsight, is quite obvious: monopoly revenues will exceed total costs of producing competitive output, so that even if those costs have to be incurred in full to deter entry (all costs sunk), there will be a profit in so doing. An interesting 'wrinkle' on this is that monopoly will always set price where elasticity = −1 (revenue-maximising), because it in effect faces zero marginal variable costs. Thus, even though entry deterrence leads the monopolist into wasting some resources, it does have the beneficial side-effect of reducing monopoly price from where it would be (in the elastic zone of the demand curve, of course) in the complete absence of an entry threat.

The social costs of rent protection along with the traditional 'Harberger Triangle' of welfare loss due to monopolistic underproduction can be quite large, and may exceed observed monopoly profits. There is not, however, as Cowling and Mueller assumed, any direct relationship between profits and social costs – these depend on demand elasticity, the extent excess capacity needs to be sunk and the minimum scale of entry.

The competitive counterfactual is not the only possible alternative to monopoly: there is also oligopoly. Might a monopolist even prefer to share the market with one or two other firms, trading off the loss in trading profits with a shared burden of defending the industry from further entry? The answer turns out to be 'no', and again in hindsight it is obvious why. The point is that, whatever the number of incumbents, the total resources they will need to be able to deploy as a group to deter entry is the same: they must be able to quickly produce if necessary the Bain–Sylos–Modigliani level of output which leaves no profitable piece of the market for any entrant (given fixed costs or other sources of scale economies). Then, even in the absence, as I assume (or assert) of any 'free rider' problems of co-ordinating deterrence, any given n-firm oligopoly would never want to allow an expansion of numbers to $(n+1)$. This is because the n-firm oligopoly will, under Cournot–Nash rules, generate more total revenue to set against the fixed quantum of costs than would $(n+1)$ firms, and so *a fortiori* each one of the n firms will be better off without entry.

The interesting wrinkle here is that, because output per firm in n-firm oligopoly is a declining function of n, in many oligopolistic situations the incumbents will naturally have enough capacity to deter entry with no additional investments in capacity – that is, there will be no need for incurring costs of rent protection.

Overall, then, we should expect that, in an economy with a variety of mostly oligopolistic market structures, the extent of socially costly profit-protecting activities will not be large as a proportion of industry revenues or measured profits, especially to the extent that such profits are true rents from product or technical superiority, which are naturally protected from competition. On the other hand, we have not attempted to account for the costs of rent-seeking behaviour within firms, nor have we confronted the difficult question of how monopoly or oligopoly rents (that is, a favourable demand curve) are generated in the first place.

ACKNOWLEDGEMENTS

* The author is grateful to Michael Waterson and participants at the Warwick Industrial Economics Workshop for comments and suggestions.

NOTES

1. A search of *Econlit* throws up three reprints in books, but doesn't list Buchanan et al. (1980), which is the source of my own copy of the article.
2. My reading of the empirical literature is that, in mature markets (that is markets not growing much faster than GDP) it is very unusual to find evidence of the price elasticity of demand being larger than one, in absolute value, and that, probably, the modal demand elasticity is around -1. For example, in the passenger air travel market, Haugh and Hazledine (1999) survey the econometric demand literature and find that demand elasticities for leisure travellers are mostly about -1, whereas business travel demand is inelastic.
3. Note that revenue-maximising price setting is consistent with the elasticity of -1 used by Harberger and many others, and criticized by Cowling and Mueller.
4. This is the entry-barring level of output under the classic Bain–Sylos–Modigliani postulate that pre-entry incumbent output must be the same as post-entry. But we will not here assume that this is the level of output actually chosen, only that it could be chosen should threatened entry actually eventuate.
5. That is, fixed costs are not so large relative to marginal costs that the monopolist can get away with holding fewer inputs than would produce the revenue-maximising level of output.
6. But of course society would be better off (potential GDP larger) without fixed costs than with them, holding marginal costs equal.
7. Many theorists fret that such assumptions imply 'irrational' behaviour, lacking in 'subgame perfection', because if a firm did enter, it would be more profitable for the incumbents to pull back and 'accommodate' the newcomer. But it is still more profitable for the incumbents to deter entry from happening at all!
8. Appelbaum and Weber (1992) in effect marginalise entry by making it probabilistic.
9. See surveys of plays of the Ultimatum Game and other experimental games (Camerer and Thaler, 1995; Camerer, 1997; Hazledine, 2001).
10. Kiwi probably should have been driven out by Freedom Air – it transpired later that it had been operating for some time although technically insolvent, for which transgression its founder was eventually sent to prison.

REFERENCES

Appelbaum, E. and S. Weber (1992), 'A note on the free rider problem in oligopoly', *Economics Letters*, **40**, 473–80.

Bernheim, B.D. (1984), 'Strategic deterrence of sequential entry into an industry', *Rand Journal of Economics*, **15**, 1–11.

Buchanan, J.M., R.D. Tollison and G. Tullock (1980), *Towards a Theory of the Rent-seeking Society*, College Station, Texas: A&M University Press.

Camerer, C. (1997), 'Progress in behavioral game theory', *Journal of Economic Perspectives*, **11** (4), Fall, 167–88.

Camerer, C. and R.H. Thaler (1995), 'Anomalies: ultimatums, dictators and manners', *Journal of Economic Perspectives*, **9** (2), Spring, 209–20.

Church, J. and R. Ware (2000), *Industrial Organization: A Strategic Approach*, Boston, MA: Irwin McGraw-Hill.

Cowling, K. (1982), *Monopoly Capitalism*, London and Basingstoke: The Macmillan Press.

Cowling, K. and D.C. Mueller (1978), 'The social costs of monopoly power', *Economic Journal*, **88** (December), 727–48 (reprinted in Buchanan et al., 1980).

Cowling, K. and D.C. Mueller (1981), 'The social costs of monopoly power revisited', *Economic Journal*, **91** (September), 721–5.

Harberger, A. (1954), 'Monopoly and resource allocation', *American Economic Review*, **44** (May), 77–87.

Haugh, D. and T. Hazledine (1999), 'Oligopoly behaviour in the Trans-Tasman air travel market: the case of Kiwi International', *New Zealand Economic Papers*, **33** (1), 1–25.

Hazledine, T. (1998), 'Rationalism rebuffed? Lessons from modern Canadian and New Zealand competition policy', *The Review of Industrial Organisation*, **13**, 243–64.

Hazledine, T. (2001), 'Accepting the Ultimatum Game: The Moral Limits to the Wealth of Nations', presented to the Canadian Economic Association Annual Conference, Montreal, June 7, and to the NZ Economic Association Annual Conference, Christchurch, June 28.

Hillman, A. and J. Riley (1987), 'Politically contestable rents and transfers', paper presented at the World Bank Conference on Political Economy: Theory and Policy Implications, Washington, DC, June.

Linster, B. G. (1993), 'Stackelberg rent-seeking', *Public Choice*, **77**, 307–21.

Littlechild, S. (1981), 'Misleading calculations of the social costs of monopoly power', *Economic Journal*, **91** (June), 348–63.

Posner, R.A. (1975), 'The social costs of monopoly and regulation', *Journal of Political Economy*, **83** (August), 807–27.

Rabin, M. (1998), 'Psychology and economics', *Journal of Economic Literature*, **36** (1), December, 11–46.

Tullock, G. (1967), 'The welfare costs of tariffs, monopoly and theft', *Western Economic Journal*, **5** (June), 224–32 (reprinted in Buchanan et al., 1980).

Williamson, O.E. (1968), 'Economies as an antitrust defense: the welfare tradeoffs', *American Economic Review*, **56**, March.

PART III

Corporate governance, mergers and the evolution of industrial structure

9. The finance literature on mergers: a critical survey[1]

Dennis C. Mueller

Among the many important pieces of research by Keith Cowling is a co-authored book of case studies of UK mergers (Cowling et al., 1979). In that book Cowling and associates established that mergers and acquisitions (hereafter M&As)[2] can not only result in increases in efficiency and market power, they can also lead to less efficient enterprises. M&As that fall into the first two categories are consistent with the premise that managers maximise profits or shareholder wealth. M&As falling into the third category must be explained by theories that posit other managerial goals than profits, for example firm growth, or quasi-irrational behaviour as might occur because managers are overcome by hubris. From the point of view of the theory of the firm, the important question about M&As is whether they are best explained by a hypothesis from the third category, or by one that presumes profits maximisation. If *most* M&As are consistent with profits maximisation, then corporate governance structures can be assumed to align shareholder and managerial interests. If, on the other hand, a large fraction do not increase shareholder wealth, corporate governance structures must fail to bring about such an alignment.

To measure the social value of M&As, one must also distinguish between the first two sets of hypotheses. Only M&As that increase efficiency, broadly defined, have a positive impact on social welfare. To determine whether the thousands of M&As occurring every year increase social welfare, one might attempt to answer the following two questions: Do M&As increase shareholder wealth on average? What fraction of any wealth increases created through M&As are the result of increases in economic efficiency? If the answer to the first question is yes, and most M&As increase shareholder wealth by increasing efficiency, then one can readily conclude that M&As on average contribute positively to social welfare. If, on the other hand, the aggregate effect of M&As is to reduce shareholder wealth, then they must be judged harmful to social welfare, and any evidence that some M&As increase market power merely adds to one's estimate of the social losses from M&As.

Over the last three decades a huge number of empirical studies in corporate finance have examined the causes and consequences of M&As. From this vast literature one would hope to obtain answers to the questions posed above. This survey claims that this hope is in vain. Although the finance literature sheds light on many interesting questions about M&As, it fails to tell us whether they have resulted in a net increase in shareholder wealth and, at least for the M&As of the last 20 years, whether those increases in wealth that have occurred were the result of increases in market power or efficiency.

This interpretation of the finance literature on M&As will not be shared by many of those who have contributed to it, nor would one reach this conclusion by merely reading the 'bottom lines' of most finance studies of M&As. But I shall try and convince the reader that this interpretation is justified.

Given the amount of research on M&As, it is impossible to summarise the results of every study, and to discuss their methodological nuances and every slight difference in their findings. Instead, I shall concentrate on a set of studies whose findings either reveal a new and important aspect about M&As or typify the findings of numerous other studies.

The literature is divided into two parts: studies appearing up until 1983, and studies coming thereafter. This date is chosen as a breaking point, because it marks the publication of a special issue of *The Journal of Financial Economics* devoted to M&As, an issue which contained the influential literature survey of Jensen and Ruback (1983). Their survey reflects the consensus at that time among finance specialists as to the causes and consequences of mergers. Section 2 examines the literature that led to this consensus. In Section 3 this consensual view of M&As is called into question, and an alternative interpretation is offered. The post-1983 literature reviewed in Sections 4 and 5 reveals much less consensus over M&As, and over the best methodology for studying them. In Section 6, we return to the question of the motivation behind M&As. Event studies that have tried to determine whether mergers increase efficiency or market power are briefly discussed in Section 7. The article closes with some final thoughts on what we have and have not learned from the corporate finance literature on M&As. We begin, however, by briefly describing the event study methodology employed in this literature.

1. THE EVENT STUDY METHODOLOGY

Most early event studies calculate abnormal returns using either the market model or the capital asset pricing model (CAPM). Under the CAPM approach one first estimates the following equation for all listed firms

$$R_{it} = R_{ft} + \beta_i (R_{mt} - R_{ft}) \mu_{it} \tag{9.1}$$

where R_{it} is the return on a share of firm i in t, R_{ft} is the risk-free rate of return, and R_{mt} is the return on the market portfolio. The estimates of β_i are then used to estimate the parameters in the following equation

$$R_{it} = \gamma_t + \delta_t \beta_i + \mu_{it} \tag{9.2}$$

and these in turn are used to predict R_{it} during the event period. The difference between the actual and predicted returns in the event period is defined as the abnormal return.

Under the market-model approach the following equation is first estimated for some benchmark period

$$R_{it} = \alpha_i + \beta_i R_{mt} + \mu_{it} \tag{9.3}$$

The estimates of α_i and β_i are then used to predict R_{it} during the event period.[3] A third approach frequently employed in more recent work uses a portfolio of companies matched to firm i to predict its return in t. Under all three approaches, abnormal returns are calculated over a specific interval around the announcement date called the 'event window'. These event windows can range from a couple of days to several years. The importance of the differences among these methodologies and the choice of length for the event window is stressed below.

2. THE FINANCE LITERATURE ON M&As THROUGH 1983

One of the first investigations of the effects of M&As by scholars in finance was by Weston and Mansinghka (1971) (hereafter WM). They examined 63 manufacturing firms, which between 1958 and 1968 undertook a substantial number of diversification mergers, mergers that transformed them into 'conglomerates' – the hallmark of the late 1960s merger wave. WM found that these conglomerates went from having significantly lower profit rates than other industrial firms to having about the same profit levels at the end of the decade. They concluded that the M&As represented a successful 'defensive diversification' strategy by a group of large mature companies. A parallel study by Weston, Smith and Shrieves (1972) compared the conglomerates with mutual funds using performance measures based on the CAPM. The conglomerates outperformed the mutual funds, and Weston et al. concluded that the conglomerates' managers were not simply compiling

Corporate governance and mergers

portfolios of firms, but actively managed the acquired assets to increase their value.

Reid (1971) pointed out that the superior performance of WM's conglomerates came to a quick end, once the US economy went into recession. WM's data ended with 1968. Between the end of 1968 and the middle of 1970, the conglomerates' share prices fell by 56 per cent, while share prices for the industrials in the WM sample fell only 37 per cent. Melicher and Rush (1973, 1974) also reported a relative deterioration in performance for the WM conglomerates based on both accounting profits and various measures of share performance. The articles by Reid and Melicher and Rush suggested that an accurate picture of the effects of the 1960s conglomerate mergers could not be obtained merely by observing their performance during the stock market boom of the 1960s.

The application of the event study methodology to M&As was pioneered by Lev and Mandelker (1972), Halpern (1973) and Mandelker (1974).[4] Mandelker's (1974) findings illustrate a pattern that was to be repeated in numerous subsequent studies. The shareholders of the target companies earned a significant 12 per cent return, while the shareholders of the acquiring firms experienced virtually no change in wealth whatsoever.[5] Mandelker (1974, p. 321) surmised 'that for the stockholders of acquiring firms, "news" of an acquisition may not be worthwhile news'.

Two other patterns appeared in Mandelker's results that would reappear in future studies. Acquiring firms' shareholders earned an impressive 4.8 per cent return above the market portfolio over the 34 months leading up to the mergers, and lost a cumulative 1.5 per cent over 40 months beginning in month 7 following the mergers.[6] Both of these figures are much larger than the change in wealth for the acquirers' shareholders in the announcement month.

Several subsequent studies did not report cumulative returns before and after the mergers, but among those that did, the same four patterns Mandelker observed can often be found: (1) the acquired companies' shareholders enjoy large percentage increases in wealth from the time of mergers' announcements until they disappear; (2) acquiring companies' shareholders experience small and often statistically insignificant changes in wealth around the announcements; (3) they experience large and statistically significant increases in wealth over prolonged periods prior to the mergers; and (4) the losses in wealth of acquiring companies' shareholders extend over lengthy periods, and are sometimes large and statistically significant.

The pattern for the acquiring companies is illustrated in Figure 9.1, which has been constructed from data reported by Asquith (1983) and Dodd and Ruback (1977). Asquith's residuals are estimated using the CAPM and thus the null hypothesis is that the acquiring companies' shares

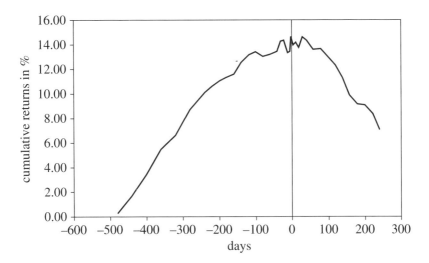

Source: Asquith (1983).

Figure 9.1a   Cumulative residuals for successful bidding firms

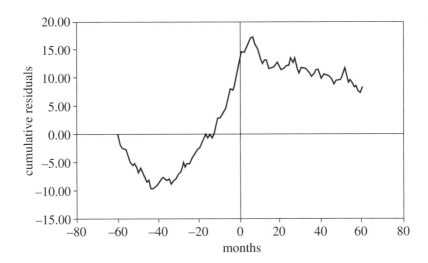

Source: Dodd and Ruback (1977).

Figure 9.1b   Cumulative residuals for successful bidding firms

would have performed as the market portfolio did for firms with comparable betas. Acquiring firms begin to earn positive abnormal returns roughly two years prior to the merger announcements. These cumulate to 14.3 per cent of the acquirers' market values by the day before the merger announcement. On that day, day 0, the bidders earn an average return of 0.2 per cent. Points to the right of day 0 represent observations following the consummation of the mergers. Thus, a gap of variable length averaging roughly 6 months occurs following day 0. Starting at the time that the mergers are completed, the acquirers' abnormal returns become negative and fall a cumulative 7.0 per cent. Thus, over about one year following the mergers, the acquirers' shareholders lost roughly half of the substantial gains that they experienced over the two years leading up to them.

The estimates of Dodd and Ruback are based on the market model. The importance of this choice *vis-à-vis* the CAPM is discussed below. Dodd and Ruback's cumulative abnormal returns look very similar to Asquith's, except that the upward trend begins almost four years before the announcements. The downward trend begins, as in Asquith's data, around the time when the average merger is completed. Note that in both studies the post-merger declines in returns continue until the data stop. Thus, the cumulative declines to the acquirers would quite likely have been greater than reported had longer post-event periods been chosen.

Table 9.1 reports the findings of eight representative studies. The criteria for inclusion in the table were: (1) that returns were measured in either days or months so that a short window around the announcements could be identified, and (2) abnormal returns were reported for at least 12 months prior to and after the announcements.

All eight studies report significant gains for the targets' shareholders (mean = 16.3 per cent). Six report positive abnormal returns to acquirers when the M&As are announced. But the gains are small and the mean over the eight studies is only 0.3 per cent. In stark contrast *all* eight studies report positive abnormal returns over the pre-event period, with the mean gain to acquirers being 11.3 per cent. Six of the eight report losses to the acquirers over post-merger intervals ranging roughly from one to six years. The mean cumulative loss to acquirers is −6.2 per cent.

What are we to make of these patterns of returns? The returns to the acquired companies are the simplest to explain. To induce a majority of the shareholders of a company to give up their shares, a premium over the pre-merger price usually needs to be paid. The gains to the acquired companies' shareholders reflect these premiums.

Interpreting the patterns of returns to the acquiring firms is less straightforward. The biggest gains for the acquirers come *before* the mergers are announced. Acquirers appear to begin to earn positive abnormal returns as much as 100 months prior to the mergers. Positive movements in share prices so far in advance of mergers obviously cannot have been *caused* by them. The post-merger declines, on the other hand, seem to be consistent with what Reid (1971) and Melicher and Rush (1973, 1974) observed for the 1960s conglomerates. From the point of view of the acquiring companies' shareholders the merger announcements are worse than just being not worthwhile news, as Mandelker put it. In fact, they should be treated as signals to sell.

This is, however, not the conclusion of the first wave of M&A studies. As already noted, several either ignored the post-merger performance of acquirers entirely or tracked it for only short intervals.[7] This choice reflected a strong belief in the efficiency of the capital market. The capital market was assumed to make an unbiased evaluation of a merger's effect on future profits at the time it was announced. The full long-run effects of the mergers could be measured by changes in share prices over short intervals around their announcements. As was true for several of the studies in Table 9.1, those that ignored the post-merger performance of acquiring companies tended to find small and often insignificant changes in acquirers' share prices around the announcements. The acquirers' shareholders were judged not to have lost as a result of the mergers, the acquired shareholders were clear winners, and thus the studies that ignored the post-merger performance of acquiring companies concluded that M&As increased total shareholder wealth.

Somewhat surprisingly, this was also the conclusion reached by several studies *that did report post-merger returns.* Of the eight cited in Table 9.1, only Firth and Malatesta concluded that the acquiring companies' shareholders had suffered significant losses. In Firth's case all losses occurred in the announcement month, in Malatesta's they occurred over the year following the mergers. Interestingly, Firth and Malatesta were among the very few first wave studies to add up the absolute wealth changes for both groups of shareholders. Both found that the aggregate losses to the acquiring companies' shareholders *exceeded* the gains in wealth of the targets. The remaining studies that reported post-merger losses for acquiring companies dismissed them as 'surprising' or 'puzzling', or simply ignored them.

Even if one ignores the post-merger losses for acquiring companies' shareholders, their small and often insignificant gains at the merger announcements seem inconsistent with the premise that their managers are maximising shareholder wealth. Although the managers of a target of a tender offer or of some other unwelcomed overture may be reluctant participants in the marriage of two companies, the acquirers' managers clearly are not. If the 'synergistic' gains that justify a merger are some form of scale or scope economy, or an increase in market power, then a straightforward

Table 9.1   Returns to acquiring and acquired companies' shareholders, first wave

Study	Time period (country)	Returns prior to merger announcement, acquiring firms	Returns in announcement day (d), month (m), acquiring firm	Post-merger returns in days (d), months (m) after merger, acquiring firms	Acquired firms' returns	Sample	Benchmarks
Mandelker (1974)	1941–63 (USA)	0.048[b] (m = −34, −1)	0.003[b] (m = 0, 6)	−0.015[b] (m = 7, 46)	0.120*	241 large mergers	CAPM[a]
Ellert (1976)	1950–72 (USA)	0.233* (m = −100, −1)[c]	−0.018[d]	−0.016 (m = 1, 48)		205 mergers challenged by Justice Dept. or FTC between 1950 and 1972	CAPM
Dodd and Ruback (1977)	1958–78 (USA)	0.117* (m = −60, −1)	0.028 (m = 0)	−0.05[b] (m = 1, 60)	0.206*	136 tender offers	Market model[a] (m = −72, −13) (m = +13, +72) (m = +13, +72)
Kummer and Hoffmeister (1978)	1956–74 (USA)	0.170[b] (m = −40, −1)	0.052[b] (m = 0)	0.006[b] (m = 1, 20)	0.187*	88 cash tender offers	CAPM
Langetieg (1978)	1929–69 (USA)	0.136* (m = −64, −1)	−0.028 (m = 0, 5)	−0.262 (m = 7, 78)	0.128*	149 mergers of all kinds	Market portfolio and industry index
Firth (1980)	1969–75 (UK)	0.014[b] (m = 48, −1)	−0.063 (m = 0)	0.001[b] (m = 1, 36)	0.363	434 mergers of all kinds	Market model (m = −48, −13) (m = +13, +36)

Study						Method
Asquith (1983) 1962–72 (USA)	0.143[b] (d = −480, −1)	0.002 (m = 0)	−0.072* (d = 1, 240)	0.133*	196 mergers of all kinds	CAPM
Malatesta (1983) 1969–74 (USA)	0.043* (m = −60, −1)	0.009 (m = 0)	−0.079* (m = 1, 12)	0.168*	256 mergers of all kinds	Market model (m = −62, −13) (m = 13, 60)

Notes:

Returns are measured as differences between merging companies' returns and control group returns in all cases. In those studies in which the data were centred around the date of final consummation, the series were displaced backwards by 6 months to allow for the fact that announcements generally precede mergers by 6 months.

* Statistically significant at the 0.05 level or better.

[a] CAPM implies the predicted performance given a firm's β if it performed as the market portfolio performs. Market model predicts firm *i*'s returns using the α and β from $R_{it} = \alpha_i + \beta_i \mu_{it}$ or some variant thereof. If only one time interval was used to estimate all residuals, only one is given. When three are given, the residuals prior to announcement are estimated from market model estimated over the first interval, the announcement residual from the second interval, and the post-announcement from the third.

[b] Reported data do not allow calculation of statistical significance.

[c] Month 0 in the Ellert study is the month in which a complaint is filed.

[d] Announcement of a merger in the Ellert study is measured as the period from judicial complaint through settlement.

169

application of Nash's (1950) bargaining theory would imply that the gains from the merger would be shared equally by the two companies. When one takes into account the size disparity between acquirers and targets, if anything one expects that a larger fraction of the gains from mergers go to the acquirers. How is it that the much smaller targets walk off with most, or all, or perhaps *even more than all* of the gains from M&As?

The answer given by most first-wave finance studies was that the gains from M&As come from replacing the targets' managers, as hypothesised in Manne's (1965) much-cited article about 'the market for corporate control'.[8] Once a company with poor management has been identified, bidding for it begins and continues until the premium paid reflects all potential gains from replacing its managers. Thus, all of the wealth gains go to the target's shareholders. Additional support for this interpretation was provided by those studies that found significant *below normal* returns for the targets in the months prior to their acquisition.[9]

After an exhaustive survey of the first generation finance literature on M&As, Jensen and Ruback (1983, p. 47) concluded that

> the evidence seems to indicate that corporate takeovers generate positive gains, that target firm shareholders benefit, and that bidding firm shareholders do not lose. Moreover, the gains by corporate takeovers do not appear to come from the creation of market power. Finally, it is difficult to find managerial actions related to corporate control that harm shareholders . . .

This statement succinctly summarises the consensus among nearly all contributors to the early literature as to the impact of M&As on shareholder wealth.[10]

3.   QUESTIONING THE CONSENSUS

The efficient capital market theory claims that at each point in time the market is capable of making an unbiased prediction of future share prices of firms. Yet, at stock market peaks, these predictions greatly overestimate future share prices. To understand *why* the stock market's implicit forecasts of corporate performance can be wide of the mark, one must relax or abandon the strong forms of rational behaviour assumptions that underlie the efficient capital market hypothesis. In periods like the late 1920s, 1960s and 1990s investors seem to be seized by 'irrational exuberance', to use Alan Greenspan's apt term, and stock prices reflect an overly optimistic view of future growth in corporate earnings.[11] Each share price increase reinforces the optimism that led to it, and in turn stimulates even more optimism and share purchases (Shiller, 2000, Ch. 3).

The optimism feeding stock market booms is often underpinned by various 'theories' advanced by market analysts as to why a given company's or sector's stocks are good value. The shares of these companies come into vogue and their prices are driven up even faster than the average share – as for example occurred at the end of the 1990s with the dramatic run-ups in share prices of the high-tech, new economy and dot-com companies.

The evidence that investors are overly optimistic about future earnings at stock market peaks is highly relevant for the use of event studies to determine the effects of mergers, since history shows that M&As come in waves, and that the crests of these waves coincide with stock market peaks.[12] Thus, a disproportionate fraction of any sample that includes a stock market peak consists of mergers that occurred when the market was seized by over-optimism. The possibility must be entertained that M&A announcements during stock market booms enjoy an overly optimistic market response, and thus that estimates of the *effects* of these mergers based upon share price movements at the announcements are biased upward.

This possibility is enhanced by the fact that 'theories' about why certain sorts of mergers produce large gains also abound during stock market booms. During the late 1960s, theories as to why conglomerate mergers would increase shareholder wealth appeared in great number, and the word 'synergy' first came into popular use to describe efficiency gains that did not fall under any of the conventional headings. The market's optimism about the conglomerates was reflected in their high price/earnings (P/E) ratios. Indeed, the conglomerates' high P/Es became the basis for yet another hypothesis about how they created wealth – they did it by 'P/E magic' (Mead, 1969). The market would reevaluate the earnings of a company with a P/E of 10 at 30 immediately upon its acquisition by a conglomerate with a P/E of 30. The investors' psychology that would support P/E magic is very similar to that which supports all forms of Ponzi schemes (Shiller, 2000, Ch. 3).

The arithmetic of P/E magic could justify premiums of 200 and 300 per cent, and thus made all companies with low P/Es look like bargains so long as the magic held. Even the premiums actually paid represented a great deal of optimism as to the effect of the mergers, however.[13] That the optimism prevailing in a booming stock market is not limited to gullible investors and fund managers driven by herd instinct is revealed by the fact that even John Lintner (1971), one of the developers of the CAPM, included P/E magic in his list of ways in which conglomerate mergers generate shareholder wealth.

In Table 9.1, the sample periods of five studies include the 1960s stock market boom. *All* report positive abnormal returns of more than 10 per cent for acquiring firms prior to the acquisitions.[14] Whether the share prices of these companies were driven up by announcements of unexpected increases in earnings and other sorts of good news, or by irrational exuberance, cannot be determined. If the acquiring companies' pre-merger share performance reflected real improvements in performance relative to other firms, then the post-merger performance of their shares implies that the acquirers suddenly shifted from outperforming other companies to underperforming them at the time of their acquisitions. If the acquiring companies' pre-merger share performance reflected merely overoptimism by the stock market, then their shares' post-merger declines in prices can be explained as the elimination of the market's overoptimism. In either case one obtains a false impression of the *effects* of the mergers by only examining the market's reaction at their announcements.

4.   THE FINANCE LITERATURE ON M&As SINCE 1983

Up until the mid-1980s, the finance literature on M&As exhibited a remarkable consensus about both the methodology for determining the causes and consequences of M&As, and what these causes and consequences were. In the mid-1980s, however, disagreements emerged about the motives of the managers who undertake M&As, about the effects of M&As, and about the proper methodology for measuring these effects. Each development is taken up in turn.

4.1   Hypotheses About Mergers that do not Presume that they Increase Shareholder Wealth

4.1.1   The managerial discretion hypothesis
The idea that the leaders of firms engage in 'empire building' has been around for a long time. In his treatise on economic development, first published in 1911, Schumpeter (1934, p. 93) placed 'the dream . . . to found a private kingdom' at the head of his list of entrepreneurial goals. In Robin Marris's (1963, 1964) theory of the 'managerial corporation', managers maximize the growth of their companies subject to the constraint of a possible takeover. Marris's model was the first formal treatment of the growth maximisation hypothesis.[15] I used Marris's growth maximisation hypothesis to explain conglomerate mergers (Mueller, 1969), and put forward a 'life-cycle' theory in which the divergence between managerial and shareholder interests was greatest for large, mature firms with limited internal growth opportunities and large cash flows.[16]

The first wave of finance studies either ignored the possibility that some mergers were driven by managerial motives toward growth, or claimed that their results rejected this hypothesis. WM (1971) were so vehement in their critique of Reid's (1968) characterisation of the conglomerates' managers as empire builders, that the *Journal of Finance* made the unusual decision of inviting Reid to respond to them in the same issue in which their article appeared. Although most authors were not as forceful as WM in rejecting managerial motives toward growth as an explanation for mergers, all studies which mentioned this motive rejected it with the exception of Firth (1980).

Then, in 1986, Michael Jensen published an article in which he argued that some managers use the 'free cash flows' at their disposal to undertake investments – like corporate mergers – that destroy shareholder value. Just as the development of the principal–agent model in the 1970s by scholars working within the neoclassical framework made it respectable for other neoclassical economists to address issues first raised by Berle and Means in 1932, the embracement of the hypothesis that managers have discretion to pursue their own goals and do so by engaging in empire building by one of the leading corporate finance scholars allowed others in the field to take up this hypothesis.[17] A stream of papers followed, which either used the free-cash-flow hypothesis to explain some otherwise puzzling phenomenon or tested it directly. We discuss some of these below, after first briefly discussing the hubris hypothesis.

4.1.2 The hubris hypothesis

Observers of merger activity throughout the last century often hypothesised that the speculative fever that grips investors during stock market booms also helps account for mergers. Jesse Markham (1955, p. 162), for example, noted in a survey that covered mergers over the first half of the twentieth century that

> The literature provides convincing evidence that the abnormally large volume of mergers formed in 1897–1900 stemmed from a wave of frenzied speculation in asset values. Several students of the early merger movement agree that excessive demand for securities was an impelling force in the mass promotion of mergers after 1896.

Students of the first two merger waves tended to focus on outsiders who profited from mergers during waves 'of frenzied speculation in asset values' as, for example, the investment banker J.P. Morgan.[18] During the 1960s merger wave, however, the prime movers were managers located inside the merging companies. In 1969 Michael Gort advanced a hypothesis to explain why merger activity increased during stock market booms. Gort argued that differences in expectations about the values of companies widened during these booms. Mergers occurred whenever the managers of one firm saw greater value in a second company than did its own managers or the capital market. Thus, Gort's theory was consistent with an image of the conglomerates' managers that was popular in the 1960s – they could spot value in other companies that no one else could see.

Gort's theory was consistent with mergers not generating any net wealth effects, but it was also consistent with the hypothesis that the acquirers' managers maximised their shareholders' wealth. If these managers could correctly spot firms that were underpriced, their shareholders would gain at the expense of the targets' owners who sold at too low a price. Richard Roll's (1986, 1988) hypothesis also relied on differences in expectations about mergers, but in addition offered an explanation for why acquiring companies' shareholders suffer losses. Roll assumed, as in the market-for-corporate-control hypothesis, that bidding for a target occurs, and that the bidding process is characterised by the 'winner's curse'. The company whose management has the highest expectations of the target's profit potential wins the bidding, but pays on average more than the target's true profit potential justifies.

Although the winner's curse can explain why acquiring companies' shareholders lose from M&As, it does not explain why managers, who seek to maximise the wealth of their shareholders, participate in a game when the 'winner' usually loses. Roll solved this riddle by suggesting that the managers suffer from 'hubris'. Each manager knows that the *average* acquirer loses, but believes that s/he is better at spotting value than the average acquirer.

4.2   Empirical Evidence Related to the Free-Cash-Flow and Hubris Hypotheses

4.2.1   Cash flow models of investment
Evidence linking cash flows to investment levels has existed for almost 50 years (Kuh and Meyer, 1957). Grabowski and Mueller (1972) were the first to test the managerial discretion hypothesis with a cash flow/investment model. They claimed that cash flow outperformed measures of the neoclassical cost of capital in explaining investment. Their article appeared, however, when Dale Jorgenson's neoclassical theory of investment was at its peak of popularity,[19] and for the next 15 years the investment literature was dominated by it and the equally neoclassical q-theory of investment.

At the end of the 1980s cash flow models of investment began to re-appear in great number. Most of these sought to test the hypothesis that asymmetric information about companies' investment opportunities leads to *under*investment by firms that are short of cash.[20] However, several papers also claimed support for an agency theory linking *over*investment to companies' cash flows or cash balances.[21]

Oil companies' acquisitions during the early 1980s fit perfectly with the managerial discretion hypothesis. Large, mature companies in a slow-growing industry used the huge increases in cash flows brought about by the OPEC-induced oil price increases to undertake diversifying acquisitions. Accordingly, several studies have examined the evidence regarding petro-leum company investments and their cash flows. Of these, Owen Lamont's (1997) is perhaps the most revealing. He focused on the investments of 26 major petroleum companies in 1985 and 1986. He found that petroleum companies tended to cross-subsidise investment in their non-oil business in 1985 when they were 'awash in cash', but ceased doing so in 1986 following the collapse of crude oil prices. Cash flows from oil operations were posi-tively related to investment in non-oil business in 1985, but not in 1986. Inefficient cross-subsidisation is thought to be a major reason why diver-sified firms underperform other companies, as documented below.[22]

4.2.2 Stock market evaluations of dividends

One of the implications of Modigliani and Miller's (1958) theory is that the stock market should evaluate a dollar of dividends and a dollar of retained earnings equivalently, *if the retained earnings are invested at a rate of return equal to the firm's cost of capital.* Numerous studies found, however, that for many firms and industries, a dollar of dividends had a much larger impact on a firm's share price than a reinvested dollar. This finding seemed to suggest a kind of 'myopia' on the part of the capital market that put its efficiency into question. A variety of explanations from bad econometrics to the tax treat-ment of dividends were offered to account for the puzzling finding.[23] The seemingly most obvious explanation – that managers were reinvesting their cash flows at returns less than their cost of capital – was ignored by students of corporate finance until the appearance of Jensen's (1986) article.[24]

Lang and Litzenberger (1989) were the first to test the implication of the free-cash-flow hypothesis for dividends policy. They used Tobin's q to iden-tify overinvesting firms. The stock market's reaction to announcements of dividend increases by firms with qs below one was much greater than for firms with high qs, as the hypothesis predicts. Additional evidence linking dividend policies to agency problems was presented by Agrawal and Jayaraman (1994) and Dewenter and Warther (1998).

4.2.3 Cash flow models of M&As

In contrast to the literature on investment, comparatively few studies try to explain M&As by either cash flows or cash balances. Harford (1999), however, found for M&As over the period 1950–94, that: (1) cash-rich companies are more likely to undertake acquisitions; (2) their acquisitions are more likely to be diversifying acquisitions; (3) the abnormal share price reaction of bidders is negative and lower than for bidders which are not cash rich; and (4) operating performance deteriorates after M&As by cash-rich companies. These results directly support a theory that links mergers to managerial discretion.[25]

4.2.4 Managerial discretion and the gains to acquirers

Doukas (1995) found that acquiring firms with high Tobin's q earned higher returns from overseas acquisitions than low q companies. He associated high qs with value maximising managements, and thus claimed support for an agency theory of mergers. Doukas also observed an inverse relationship between free cash flows and the M&As' returns. In further support of an agency theory of mergers, Hubbard and Palia (1995) reported that managers with small stakes in their companies 'tend to "overpay" when they acquire a target firm', causing their shareholders to lose money (p. 783).[26]

Studies which relate the acquirers' gains to the premiums paid for the targets, support this interpretation. *Every* study which has regressed the gains to the acquiring companies' shareholders onto the gains to the targets has found a negative relationship. The more acquirers pay, the more they lose.[27] This finding is *inconsistent* with both synergy hypotheses about mergers and the market-for-corporate-control hypothesis. If we interpret 'synergy' as meaning that the gains from a merger are specific to the two merging companies, as might arise in a vertical merger with considerable asset specificity on both sides, then one expects the synergistic gains from the merger to be shared by the two merging companies depending upon their relative bargaining strengths. A positive relationship between the acquirers' and targets' gains should be observed.

If, on the other hand, all gains from M&As come through the replacement of the targets' managements, as the market-for-corporate-control hypothesis assumes, bidding for targets could eliminate all gains for the acquirers so that mean acquirer gains are zero and uncorrelated with the gains to the targets. As noted above, this explanation was offered by several first-generation studies for the negligible gains to acquirers.

To obtain negative correlations between acquirers' 'gains' and targets' gains one must introduce either the hubris or the agency hypotheses. If managers undertake mergers where there are no synergistic effects, either for hubris or empire-building reasons, each dollar paid above the market value of the target should produce a dollar loss for the acquirer. Both hypotheses make the same predictions. Both are thus consistent with the evidence that acquirers' gains are inversely related to targets' gains.[28]

4.2.5 The discount for diversification

The early finance literature that tried to account for the wave of conglomerate mergers hypothesised the existence of synergistic gains from diversification, $2 + 2 = 5$.[29] Following the end of the stock market boom of the 1960s, the market's evaluation of the synergies from diversification seemed to reverse – two plus two became equal to three. Several studies have reported losses to acquirers' shareholders at the time diversification mergers are announced (Sicherman and Pettway, 1987; Morck, Shleifer and Vishny, 1990; Kaplan and Weisbach, 1992). Indexes of diversification have also been found to be negatively related to returns on shares (Comment and Jarrell, 1995), Tobin's q (Wernerfelt and Montgomery, 1988; Lang and Stulz, 1994; Servaes, 1996) and the market value of a given company (Berger and Ofek, 1995). Moreover, the discount for diversification is quite large. Berger and Ofek (1995), for example, estimate market values of diversified companies over the 1986–91 period some 13 to 15 per cent below the values that their assembled assets could realize as stand-alone companies. These studies imply that the creation of diversified companies – almost always through M&As – destroys wealth.

4.2.6 The gains from undiversifying

The process of diversification destroys wealth, reversing this process seems to create it. Spin-offs of previously acquired assets are greeted positively by the market, and the stock market gain is larger, the more negative the market's reaction was to the assets' acquisition (Allen et al., 1995). Assets remaining in a company after a spin-off or sale of unrelated assets perform better (John and Ofek, 1995). Diversified companies with low market value relative to their assets' book values are more likely to be taken over through a leveraged buyout, and experience the biggest sell-off of assets after the takeover (Berger and Ofek, 1995). Diversifying acquisitions are four times more likely to be spun-off later (Ravenscraft and Scherer, 1987, Ch. 6; Kaplan and Weisbach, 1992). Spin-offs between 1975 and 1991 that increased focus were greeted with larger increases in share prices than non-focus-increasing spin-offs, and were followed by improvements in the operating performance of the more focused company (Desai and Jain, 1999), and finally, spin-offs during the 1990s were also followed by share price increases (Mulherin and Boone, 2000).

4.2.7 Commentary

The early literature testing for the effects of managerial discretion combined with recent tests for the effects of free cash flow and managerial hubris yield a body of work dating back over 30 years that provides convincing evidence that many managers make investment decisions –

including M&As – reducing the wealth of their shareholders. This literature includes studies that find: (1) corporate investment to be sensitive to the levels of cash flows; (2) the likelihood of a firm making an acquisition to be sensitive to the level of its cash flows; (3) the size of the premiums paid for targets to be positively related to cash flows; (4) large mature companies earning returns on investment less than their costs of capital;[30] (5) the stock market valuing dividends more highly than reinvested cash flows; (6) the stock market reacting more positively to dividend announcements of low q firms; (7) the stock market reacting negatively to announcements of diversification mergers; (8) the stock market discounting the assets of diversified firms; and (9) the stock market reacting positively to announcements of spin-offs of assets unrelated to a firm's main line of business. Studies can also be found which question almost every one of these points. Nevertheless, enough evidence has certainly been accumulated suggesting that agency problems affect corporate investment decisions to warrant treating these problems as a *possible* factor explaining M&As.

To these studies one can add the large number that have found negligible or negative effects of mergers on profitability, internal growth and market shares.[31] Here, of course, there is also conflicting evidence and disagreement, but the number of studies finding negative effects of mergers on operating performance is again too large to dismiss.

Evidence that M&As destroy wealth can also be found in the event study literature, *if one examines the returns to the acquirers over a sustained period after the M&As occur.* As noted above, the literature up through 1983 overwhelmingly presumed that mergers were the consequences of the wealth maximising decisions of managers, and that capital markets were sufficiently efficient that the future effects of M&As could be unbiasedly estimated using short windows around the announcement dates. The papers by Jensen (1986) and Roll (1986) and the literature they precipitated call the first assumption into question, the work of Shiller and others calls the second assumption into question. Before one can safely conclude that M&As increase corporate wealth, one needs to consider why so many studies observe substantial and steady declines in the wealth of the acquirers' shareholders after the acquisitions take place.

5. THE LENGTH OF WINDOW AND PROPER BENCHMARK

5.1 Before versus After

As already mentioned, several first-wave studies reported negative abnormal returns for acquirers over prolonged periods after the mergers.

Although the early literature largely ignored these post-merger losses, more recently they have been the subject of a good deal of attention, as has the issue of the proper benchmark for measuring abnormal returns.

The benchmark used with the CAPM is the market portfolio, that is regardless of whether the merging firms were under- or overperforming the market portfolio prior to the merger announcements, they are assumed to perform as does the market portfolio starting with the announcements.

The market-model can give quite different results depending upon the benchmark period used to estimate its parameters. When, for example, estimates using the CAPM imply significant positive abnormal returns for acquirers before the merger announcements, as has been true for almost all studies, then the estimated αs for the market model (equation (9.3) above) will be large and positive. Residuals calculated with these estimates will be much smaller than if a benchmark is chosen when acquirers are earning normal returns.

The logical choice for a benchmark period is some interval *before* the merger announcements, since one wishes to measure the *changes* in performance as a result of the mergers. However, several studies, including that of Dodd and Ruback (1977) from which Figure 9.1b was constructed, estimated post-merger abnormal returns using a post-merger period to estimate equation (9.3). Because acquirers underperform the market portfolio following mergers, this choice of benchmarks significantly *understates* post-merger losses to acquirers relative to what they would be with a premerger benchmark. For example, using a benchmark period of from 36 to 3 months before the announcement month, Magenheim and Mueller (1988) calculated cumulative losses to acquirers of a significant 11.3 per cent over the first 12 months after the announcements. Using a post-announcement benchmark the losses were an insignificant 3.2 per cent.[32] Thus, studies that estimated the effects of mergers using the market model with a post-merger benchmark have *underestimated the change* in performance that occurred at the announcements.

Franks and Harris (1989), however, suggest that the use of the market model estimated over a pre-event period is inappropriate. With αs and βs estimated from before the announcements, they estimate a cumulative return to acquirers over the two years following the announcements of -12.6 per cent (see Table 9.2). They dismiss these negative returns, however, stating several possible alternative explanations for them including that 'bidders time mergers to take advantage of recent abnormal returns in their own stock prices . . . positive [pre-merger] αs, if unsustainable, would introduce a negative drift in abnormal returns, which could be interpreted as "too" high a control return rather than poor performance by bidders' (p. 246, footnote omitted). They do not discuss, however, why the acquirers

Table 9.2 *Returns to acquiring and acquired companies' shareholders with long post-merger windows*

Study	Time period (country)	Returns prior to merger announcement, acquiring firms	Returns in announcement day (d), month (m), acquiring firm	Post-merger returns in days (d), months (m) after merger, acquiring firms	Acquired firms' returns	Sample	Benchmarks
Magenheim and Mueller (1988)	1976–81 (USA)	0.127* 0.280** ($m = -24, -4$)	-0.004 0.014 -0.007 0.007 ($m = 0$)	-0.277** 0.089 -0.491** -0.273** ($m = -3, 36$)		51 mergers 26 tender offers 51 mergers 26 tender offers 51 mergers 26 tender offers	Market model ($m = -60, -25$) ($m = -60, -4$) ($m = -36, -4$)
Franks and Harris (1989)	1960–85 (UK)		0.010* ($m = 0$)	-0.126* 0.045* ($m = 1, 24$)	0.233* ($m = 0$)	1048 M&As	Market model ($m = -71, -12$) CAPM
Franks, Harris and Titman (1991)	1975–84 (USA)		-0.010 ($m = 0$)	-0.040[a] ($m = 1, 36$)	0.280* ($m = 0$)	399 M&As	Portfolio which controls for size, dividends and past returns
Agrawal, Jaffee and Mandelker (1992)	1955–87 1955–59 1960–69 1970–79			-0.103* -0.232* -0.151* 0.041		765 M&As 51 M&As 299 M&As 247 M&As	CAPM with adjustments for firm size

Study	Period (Country)				Sample	Method
	1980–87			−0.194*	168 M&As	Market model with adjustments for firm size ($t = 1, 1250$)
	1975–84 (USA)			−0.028 (m = 1, 60)	290 M&As	
Loderer and Martin (1992)	1966–86			0.075[b]	1298 M&As	
	1966–69			−0.612*[b]	261 M&As	
	1970–79			0.300[b]	598 M&As	
	1980–86 (USA)			0.175[b] (d = 1, 1250)	439 M&As	
Leeth and Borg (1994)	1905–30 (USA)	0.330* (m = −60, −4)	−0.001 (m = 0)	−0.238* (m = 1, 36)	191 M&As in mining and manufacturing	CAPM
Gregory (1997)	1984–92 (UK)		−0.005 (m = 0)	−0.125* (m = 0, 24)	408 M&As	CAPM with adjustments for firm size
Loughran and Vijh (1997)	1970–89 (USA)			−0.065	947 M&As	Firms matched by size and BV/MV[c]
				−0.242*	405 stock financed	
				0.185	314 cash financed	
				−0.096 (m = 1, 60)	228 stock/cash financed	
Higson and Elliott (1998)	1975–90 (UK)	0.315* (m = 0)	0.002 (m = 0)	0.008 (m = 1, 36)	830 M&As	Firms matched by size
					722 M&As	
	1975–80			−0.100* (m = 1, 24)	305 M&As	
	1981–84			0.263*	156 M&As	
	1985–90			−0.062*	315 M&As	

Table 9.2 *Returns to acquiring and acquired companies' shareholders with long post-merger windows* (continued)

Study	Time period (country)	Returns prior to merger announcement, acquiring firms	Returns in announcement day (d), month (m), acquiring firm	Post-merger returns in days (d), months (m) after merger, acquiring firms	Acquired firms' returns	Sample	Benchmarks
Rau and Vermaelen (1998)	1980–91 (USA)			−0.040*		2823 mergers	Returns of firms of similar size and BV/MV
				0.089*		316 tender offers	
				−0.173*		932 mergers, firms with low BV/MV	
				−0.042		105 tender offers with low BV/MV	
				0.076*		931 mergers, firms with high BV/MV	
				0.155* (m = ?, 36)		104 tender offers, firms with high BV/MV	
Andrade, Mitchell and Stafford (2001)	1961–93 (USA)	−0.038 ($t = −20$, c)[d]		−0.050* (m = 0, 36)	0.238 ($t = −20$, c)[d]	3688 mergers	(CAPM?)
						2068 mergers	
Conn, Cosh, Guest and Hughes (2001)	1984–2000 (UK)		0.012*	−0.057* (m = 0, 36)		3260 takeovers	Returns of firms in same industry matched by size and BV/MV

Notes:

* Indicates significant at 0.05 level or better.

[a] Franks, Harris and Titman, report only the α of the market model estimated over months +1 to +36. To make their results comparable to the others in the table, I have multiplied their estimate of α by 36.

[b] Loderer and Martin report only the α of the market model estimated over days +1 to +1250. To make their results comparable to the others in the table, I have multiplied their estimate of α by 1250. Only the negative estimate was statistically significant.

[c] BV/MV = (Book value)/(Market value).

[d] c = completion of merger.

183

in their sample outperformed the market portfolio by almost 1 per cent per month for a period of five years before the mergers, and why this extraordinarily good performance happened to come to an end at the time when the companies announced their acquisitions.

More fundamentally, however, their argument raises doubts about whether one can conclude anything about the effects of mergers on the operating performance of the merging firms from data on shareholder returns.[33] If we should not interpret declines in acquirers' abnormal returns following mergers as being *caused* by the mergers, should we not also question whether the gains to the targets' shareholders reflect real synergies caused by the mergers? As noted above, several studies reported that targets earned significant negative abnormal returns prior to being taken over. The usual explanation for this is that they were badly managed and that the takeovers occurred to replace their managers. But perhaps their shares were merely *undervalued* prior to the takeovers, just as the acquirers' shares might have been *overvalued*. The premiums paid may then not have reflected the creation of wealth through the replacement of bad managers or other synergies, but merely the return of the targets' market values to their unbiased levels just as, following Franks and Harris, the decline in returns to the acquirers was merely a return to normalcy. Should we not treat the two possibilities symmetrically? This methodological issue is taken up again below.

5.2   The Returns to Acquirers Over Long Post-Merger Windows

Most of the post-1983 studies, which have estimated abnormal returns to acquirers over long post-merger windows, have used either the CAPM or portfolios of companies of similar size, dividend payout ratios, book-to-market ratios, and so on. Twelve such studies are briefly summarised in Table 9.2. All but one cover M&As since World War II. Leeth and Borg (1994) examine mergers from 1905 to 1930 and show that large positive pre-merger abnormal returns and large negative post-merger returns are not a new phenomenon.

Of particular interest is the article by Agrawal, Jaffe and Mandelker (1992) (AJM). They estimate returns over five-year post-announcement periods. Over the 1955–87 period, the cumulative abnormal returns to acquirers is a significant −10 per cent. Significant negative post-merger returns were also estimated for the 1950s, 1960s and 1980s. Insignificantly positive abnormal returns were estimated, however, for the 1970s. This pattern is consistent with the hypothesis that merger waves are fuelled in part by stock market speculation and that acquiring companies undertake wealth-destroying M&As out of empire-building motives when their share prices and/or cash flows are high, or simply out of hubris fed by their companies' high share prices. The depressed share prices of the 1970s may have brought about a more sober approach to M&As.

Of interest, also, are AJM's results for the period 1975–84. This time period is identical to that used by Franks, Harris and Titman (1991) (FHT). FHT claimed that the significant negative returns reported in earlier studies were the result of inappropriate benchmark portfolios. Their preferred benchmark yielded an insignificant monthly abnormal return of −0.11 per cent. Half of FHT's sample period falls in the 1970s, however, where AJM observed slightly positive post-merger residuals. AJM also obtained small and insignificant negative post-merger abnormal returns for the time period used by FHT, but this finding was not representative of M&As over the entire 1955–87 period, or of three of the four subperiods as in the AJM data.

It is also worth noting that FHT's monthly abnormal return of −0.11 implies a cumulative loss to the acquirers after 36 months amounting to 4 per cent of their market values. Such a loss would offset the 28 per cent gains to the targets, if the acquirers were seven times larger than the targets, which was quite likely the case.[34] Thus, even using FHT's preferred benchmark might lead one to conclude that the net wealth gains from the M&As in their sample were insignificantly different from zero.

Estimates of returns by Loderer and Martin (1992) and Higson and Elliott (1998) are also sensitive to the time period in which the M&As occurred. Loderer and Martin obtained only one significant estimate of a post-announcement abnormal return – a negative return for M&As between 1966 and 1969.[35] This finding is, of course, consistent with the hypothesis that booming stock markets are associated with disproportionate numbers of ill-conceived M&As. Unlike AJM, Loderer and Martin did not estimate negative post-announcement returns for M&As during the 1980s, however.

The patterns of post-merger returns reported by Gregory (1997) and Higson and Elliott (1998) are quite interesting. Higson and Elliott find that mergers in the UK between 1975 and 1980, and again between 1985 and 1990 were followed by significant wealth losses to acquirers. Mergers between 1981 and 1984, on the other hand, were followed by significant positive abnormal returns. Gregory's data begin where Higson and Elliott's end. He estimates a significant −12.5 per cent abnormal return for acquirers for M&As between 1984 and 1992. Putting these two UK studies together, we see that M&As have been followed by negative abnormal returns to acquirers for every time period between 1975 and 1992, except for 1981–84.[36]

Finally, mention must be made of the study of Rau and Vermaelen (1998) (RV). They estimate significant post-announcement returns of −4 per cent for a sample of 2823 acquirers, and significant positive returns for

316 tender offers (time period 1980–91). They also provide considerable support for the hypothesis that high share prices fuelled by overoptimism are associated with wealth-destroying mergers. Acquirers with high market values relative to the book values of their assets earned a -17.3 per cent abnormal return over the three years following merger announcements. In contrast, companies with relatively low market values had positive post-announcement returns. RV conclude

> that these findings are consistent with the hypothesis that the market over-extrapolates the past performance of the bidder management when it assesses the benefits of an acquisition decision. As a result, the market, as well as the management, the board of directors and large shareholders overestimate the ability of the glamour bidder to manage other companies. (p. 251)[37]

5.3   Commentary

Anyone understanding the logic of event studies, but unfamiliar with their application to M&As, would undoubtedly, upon seeing Figure 9.1, conclude that the most important *events* affecting the acquiring companies in these two studies were those that led to the continual upward movements in the ac-quirers' abnormal returns over the two to four years prior to the acquisition announcements, and the steady and sizeable declines that began afterward. This person would certainly be surprised to learn that the preponderance of of M&A event studies have ignored both the pre-announcement run-ups in returns to acquirers and the post-merger declines, concentrating instead upon the tiny changes occurring around the announcements.

A few studies have tried to explain the post-merger losses to acquirers as the result of poor benchmark choices. Fama and French (1993), for example, criticised the use of the CAPM and market model to estimate gains to acquirers, because these models fail to account for the systematic effects of firm size and book-to-market ratios on company returns. They speculated that the acquirers' negative post-merger returns would disap-pear, once these characteristics were accounted for.[38] But the studies by AJM and others reviewed above indicate that the poor post-acquisition performance of the acquirers' shares does not disappear, even when these and other suggested changes in benchmarks are made. Substantial frac-tions of the M&As of the last half century have been followed by steady declines in the returns to the acquiring companies' shareholders over long time intervals.

There are two possible interpretations of these patterns. One is to assume that the positive abnormal returns preceding the merger announcements indicate that unexpected positive information about the current and future performance of prospective acquirers continually reached the market over periods of two, three or more years prior to the announcements. Conversely, the steady stream of negative abnormal returns commencing afterward indicates that unexpected negative information about the current and future performance of the acquiring companies continually reached the market over several years after the announcements. To assume that this dramatic change in the nature of the unexpected information about the acquirers' performance occurred around the time of the mergers and yet was totally independent of them seems hardly plausible.

The second possible interpretation of the pre- and post-announcement returns of acquirers allows the market's evaluation of shares to be subject to fads and over-optimism. The market begins mistakenly to bid up the share prices of some group of firms. These firms undertake mergers while their shares are overpriced. The post-merger declines in returns to acquirers are not *caused* by the mergers, but merely reflect the market's return to a more objective evaluation of these companies' prospects.

There is much in the evidence to support this latter interpretation. RV's findings that the acquisitions of low book-to-market 'glamour' firms had significantly lower post-merger returns than did high book-to-market firms is consistent with it. They also report that glamour acquirers more frequently issued stock to finance their mergers, suggesting perhaps that the managers thought that their stock was 'overvalued'. In further support of this interpretation are the findings of several studies that post-merger cumulative returns are much lower for M&As financed through exchanges of shares than for those financed out of cash.[39]

Further support for this interpretation is provided by analyses of the market's evaluation of diversification and conglomerate mergers during the 1960s. Servaes (1996) found that the market values of diversified companies were already significantly discounted in the late 1960s and early 1970s. Matsusaka (1993) reports, however, that announcements of conglomerate acquisitions at that time were coupled with *positive* and significant abnormal returns. Why would the market bid down the shares of companies which had already diversified, and simultaneously bid up the shares of companies announcing moves in that direction? An obvious answer is that conglomerate mergers were in vogue at the time. The conglomerates' managers were thought to be capable of adding value to any company they acquired. The price–earnings ratios of the conglomerates were bid up accordingly and each newly announced acquisition was greeted with still more enthusiasm. That this enthusiasm was unfounded is revealed in the significant negative post-merger returns for the mergers of the 1960s reported in most of the studies in Tables 9.1 and 9.2.

The possibility that the acquirers' shares are overvalued calls into question the interpretations of studies like those of Lang, Stulz and Walking

(1989) and Doukas (1995). Both found using very short event windows that firms with high Tobin's qs earned higher returns upon announcing M&As than low q acquirers. Both interpreted high qs as indicators of managerial talent and argued that acquisitions by companies with talented managers were more successful. Their index of managerial talent, a high q, is, however, very similar to RV's (1998) index of glamour – a low book-to-market ratio. RV's findings of poor *post-merger* performance of glamour firms' shares suggests that declaring the acquisitions of high q firms a success based on short event windows at their announcements is premature.

More fundamentally, the possibility that the pre-announcement positive abnormal returns reflect overoptimism and an overvaluation of acquirers' shares calls into question the common practice in event studies of measuring the effects of M&As using short windows. If the market can overvalue a group of companies' shares for a period of three to four years, it is possible that it continues to overvalue them for a few days or even a month or two around the announcements of acquisitions. Indeed, if the reason for the overvaluation of acquirers prior to the M&As' announcements is due to a mistaken acceptance of a 'theory' about the synergistic effects of mergers – as seems to have been true of the conglomerates – then the market's reaction to M&A announcements is certain to have an upward bias. Thus, explaining post-merger declines in acquirers' share prices by assuming their overvaluation prior to the announcements, casts a shadow of doubt over both the efficient capital market hypotheses and the event study literature that rests upon it.[40]

Before closing this discussion of long-run event windows I would like the reader to engage in the following *Gedankenexperiment*. Imagine that the pattern of returns observed in studies like that of Dodd and Ruback (1977), Langetieg (1978), Asquith (1983) and many others did not resemble those presented in Figure 9.1, but rather the reverse.[41] Instead of an inverse-U peaking around the time of the mergers, a normal-U with a trough near the time of the mergers was observed. Would the most plausible interpretation of such a pattern not be that the acquirers were continually releasing unexpected information of bad operating performance to the market over several years prior to the mergers? Such a pre-merger pattern *might* be expected, for example, from Weston and Mansinghka's (1971) defensive diversification hypothesis. Would it not also be natural to interpret the post-merger increases in returns to continually released unexpected information of improving operating performance after the mergers? Would it not be reasonable to conclude that the mergers had *caused* the turnaround in operating performance implied by the pattern of pre- and post-merger returns? Would the literature that evaluates the effects of mergers by looking at changes in returns on common shares not have taken into account the changes to the acquirers over a much longer timespan than have most of the contributions so far – if the long-run pattern of returns to acquirers had taken the form of a U instead of an inverted U?

5.4 The Effects of M&As with Short Windows

Although the post-1983 literature does contain several studies that estimate returns to acquirers over long post-event windows, much of the recent literature continues to estimate the effects of M&As over very short windows around the announcements. Table 9.3 summarizes the findings of 13 such studies. Five estimated zero or negative returns to at least some groups of acquirers, and concluded that agency problems and/or managerial hubris accounted for the mergers (Morck, Shleifer and Vishny, 1990; Houston and Ryngaert, 1994; Smith and Kim, 1994; Hubbard and Palia, 1995; and Doukas, 1995). The other nine studies claimed support for some form of synergy hypothesis – even when the acquirers' shareholders made non-positive returns – so long as the combined wealth changes around the announcements were positive. These studies can be seen as reconfirming the consensus view of M&As reached in the first wave of the literature.

6. THE MOTIVES OF MANAGERS ONCE AGAIN

In an early effort to explain how conglomerate mergers create synergy, John Lintner (1971) proposed as the test for synergy whether the market value of the combined company after the merger, V_C, was greater than the sum of the market values of the two merging companies, V_A and V_B. Although most of the finance literature has measured the effects of mergers by examining the percentage changes in returns to the two merging firms separately, the recent paper by Bhagat, Hirshleifer and Noah (1999) (BHN) has to some extent brought the literature on M&As full circle, for they judge the success of takeovers by seeing whether $V_C > V_A + V_B$. They find that it is on average for a sample of 510 takeovers spanning the years 1962 through 1997, and conclude that M&As as a whole increase corporate wealth.

BHN propose several modifications in the methods for measuring the market's reaction to a takeover, and make a convincing case that these improve the accuracy of the measures of market expectations around announcement dates. BHN do not report estimates for long post-merger windows, however. Thus, using their methodology, mergers between July, 1962 and June, 1968 increased the acquirers' market values by a significant 3.44 per cent. BHN, like numerous other studies, find that the market judges the mergers of the 1960s a success – at the time they were

Table 9.3   *Returns to acquiring and acquired companies' shareholders, short event windows*

Study	Time period (country)	Returns in announcement day (d), month (m), acquiring firm	Acquired firm's returns	Sample	Benchmarks
Dennis and McConnell (1986)	1962–80 (USA)	0.032*c (d=−6, +6)	0.137*c (d=−6, +6)	90 acquirers / 76 targets	CAPM
Bradley, Desai and Kim (1988)	1963–84 (USA)	0.001 (d=−5, +5)a	0.312*	236 tender offers	Market model (d=−300, −60)
Lang, Stulz and Walking (1989)	1968–86 (USA)	−0.049 / 0.002b / 0.102*b / −0.023b (d=−5, +5)a	0.320* / 0.418*b / 0.390*b / 0.466*b	87 tender offers / low q bidder/high q target / low q bidder/low q target / high q bidder/low q target / high q bidder/high q target	Market model (d=−300, −60)
Bhagat, Shleifer and Vishny (1990)	1984–86 (USA)	−0.009 (d=−3, +3)		32 hostile takeovers	Market model (d=−260, −60)
Kang (1993)	1975–88 (Japan, USA)	0.007 / 0.000 (d=−20, +20)	0.124* / 0.137* (d=−20, +20)	119 Japanese bidders +102 US targets / 119 US bidders + 102 US targets	Market model (d=−220, −20)
Houston and Ryngaert (1994)	1985–91 (USA)	−0.023* (d=−4, 0)d	0.144* (d=−4, 0)d	131 large bank mergers	Market model (d=−230, −31)
Smith and Kim (1994)	1980–86 (USA)	−0.016 / 0.017* (d=−5, +5)	0.328* / 0.286* (d=−5, +5)	56 high cash flow bidders / 57 low cash flow bidders	Market model (d=−100, −61)

Study	Period	Sample			CAPM
Hubbard and Palia (1995)	1985–91 (USA)	354 mergers	−0.004* (d = −4, +4)		CAPM
Doukas (1995)	1975–89 (US acquirers)	Foreign acquisitions by US firms 270 with $q>1$ 193 with $q<1$	0.004* −0.002 (d = −1, 0)		Market model (d = −220, −21)
Maquieira, Megginson and Nail (1998)	1963–96 (USA)	47 conglomerate mergers 55 nonconglomerate mergers all mergers stock-for-stock transactions	−0.048 0.061* (m = −2, +2)e	0.416* 0.381* (m = −2, +2)e	Market index for common stock
Eckbo and Thorburn (2000)	1964–82 (USA, Canada)	1261 Canadian bidders 390 US bidders 332 Canadian targets	0.013* −0.002 (m = 0)	0.036* (m = 0)	Market model (m = −60, −13)
Becher (2000)	1980–97 (USA)	558 bank mergers	−0.011* (d = −5, +5)	0.171* (d = −5, +5)	Market index
Bhagat, Hirshleifer and Noah (1999)	1962–97 (USA)	510 takeovers	0.006* (d = −5, +5)	0.293* (d = −5, +5)	Market model (d = −5, +5)

Notes:

a Window is from 5 days before first bid until 5 days after successful bid, so that window is longer than 11 days whenever more than one bid occurs.

b Estimates from a regression with low q bidder/low q target's returns as intercept and other returns estimated with dummy variables. Bidder's return for high q bidders/low q targets is the only one significantly different from the intercept; one cannot tell from the data whether it is significantly different from zero. High qs are qs are >1 over 3 years before the takeover.

c Returns are to common shareholders.

d Day −4 is four days before authors identify information about bidder (target) reaching market. Window is closed on day agreement announced. Window is 5 days when leakage and agreement dates are the same, larger otherwise.

e Window ends two months after effective data of merger.

announced.[42] Yet *every* study that has isolated the post-merger returns to acquirers from the mergers of the 1960s has found them to be negative and significant (see Tables 9.1 and 9.2).[43] Which findings are we to believe?

Even if we ignore the post-merger losses to acquirers, there is something awkward about the persistent findings of negligible returns to acquirers from the point of view of the theory of the firm. If the managers of the acquirers are trying to maximise the wealth of their shareholders, why do they continually undertake highly risky investments like M&As, which have near zero expected returns? If they are not trying to maximise shareholder wealth, is it legitimate to assume that they do so anyway?

The behaviour of the acquirers' managers becomes even more puzzling when it is contrasted with how they behave when they negotiate their compensation contracts. A standard result from the principal/agent literature is that the optimal compensation contract for managers trades off the advantages of aligning the interests of managers and shareholders by tying managerial compensation to changes in shareholder wealth against the utility losses suffered by risk-averse managers from such ties. The more risk-averse the manager is, the more his compensation contract resembles a fixed wage. The empirical literature on managerial compensation would seem to imply that managers are highly risk averse, since their compensation is very weakly tied to the wealth of their shareholders.[44] Why are managers so highly risk-averse when it comes to negotiating their compensation contracts, and then behave like river-boat gamblers when they become bidders in the market for corporate control? An obvious answer is that in one case it is their *own* income that is at issue, in the other it is someone else's.[45] This interpretation is buttressed by the finding of a significant relationship between the fraction of shares owned by an acquirers' managers and the returns to its shareholders from an acquisition (Hubbard and Palia, 1995). This finding in turn is consistent with both the managerial discretion and hubris hypotheses.

7.   THE EFFECTS OF M&As ON MARKET POWER

Have those M&As that increased shareholder wealth done so by increasing the market power of the merging firms or by increasing their efficiency? Those studies that have concluded that mergers increase shareholder wealth have implied that this increase comes from greater efficiency. But certainly, increases in market power could also qualify as 'synergies' that increase shareholder wealth. Have some of the wealth increases caused by mergers come from market power increases and, if so, to what degree?

A reason not to expect market power increases from mergers in the

United States is that the Justice Department (DoJ) and Federal Trade Commission (FTC) are charged with preventing such mergers. But it is unreasonable to assume that they succeed in blocking *all* anti-competitive mergers. If managers who are paid millions of dollars can make errors in predicting the effects of an acquisition, then one must assume that government economists and lawyers who earn tiny fractions of these sums also are vulnerable to mistakes.[46]

Two sorts of errors are possible: (1) mergers are blocked which would not have harmed competition, but would have increased efficiency, or (2) mergers are allowed that lead to increases in market power. A reasonable assumption would be that the antitrust authorities commit both types of errors. This is not the conclusion reached by most finance studies that have tested whether horizontal mergers have anti-competitive effects, however.

These tests consist of seeing whether a horizontal merger announcement that is subsequently challenged produces a significant positive abnormal return for the *rivals* of the merging companies. The rationale behind the tests is that a merger that increases market power and thereby prices benefits all firms in the industry, not just the merging companies. Some studies have not found an increase in rivals' returns when mergers are announced and subsequently challenged, and have concluded from this, that they did not have any anti-competitive effects (for example, Stillman, 1983). Other studies, which *have* observed significant increases in the returns of rivals when a horizontal merger is announced, have reached the same conclusion, however, arguing 'that the merger signals opportunities for efficiency gains available to the non-merging industry rivals as well'.[47]

This is a rather remarkable conclusion. Numerous models of oligopoly have derived a relationship between industry concentration or firm market shares and price–cost margins. Since *all* horizontal mergers increase industry concentration and one firm's market share, one expects that *some* horizontal mergers lead to price increases.

Particularly good data on prices, market shares and concentration are available for the airlines industry. They establish a strong link between airline market shares and market concentration and ticket prices.[48] Given this relationship, one expects mergers between competing airlines to lead to higher ticket prices – and so they have. Kim and Singal (1993) establish that airline mergers between 1985 and 1988 did lead to ticket price increases on the routes served by the merging airlines. Singal (1996) shows that the announcements of these mergers were accompanied by significant increases in the share prices of the merging airlines' rivals – exactly as the event study test for market power predicts.[49]

The event study literature, which tests whether mergers increase market power, has concentrated on mergers occurring in the 1960s and 1970s. Most students of antitrust would probably agree that during this period the anti-trust authorities are more likely to have blocked mergers that would have improved efficiency than to have allowed mergers that increased market power. The latter errors seem much more likely, however, during the period of lax antitrust enforcement that began in the early 1980s, when horizontal and vertical mergers were consummated on a scale that would never have been dreamed of during the 1960s and 1970s. Singal's (1996) application of the event study approach to the airlines industry suggests that it can identify anti-competitive mergers, and that they have occurred in at least one industry. Until event studies are conducted for horizontal mergers that occurred in other industries during the 1980s and 1990s, the most prudent conclusion to draw is that this literature is silent regarding the extent to which any wealth gains due to M&As over the last two decades were caused by increases in market power.

8.   FINAL THOUGHTS

Even if every manager's primary goal were to expand her company, or if every manager suffered from hubris, *some* mergers would increase efficiency or market power. A growth-maximising manager should never pass up an opportunity to increase profits, since any increase in profits provides more resources to pursue further growth. Thus, all mergers that would occur if all managers maximised shareholder wealth should also take place even if managers maximise growth or are vulnerable to hubris. The agency/hubris hypotheses lead one to expect additional mergers; however, mergers that may not increase shareholder wealth or even destroy it. The paramount questions for the theory of the firm are to determine how many mergers are wealth enhancing, how many merely redistribute corporate wealth between bidder and target shareholders, and how many destroy it. For those interested in the effects of mergers on social welfare, it is also necessary to determine whether any increases in wealth stemming from mergers are a result of efficiency or market power increases.

In 1983 Jensen and Ruback concluded that 'the scientific evidence' obtained from event studies proved that M&As increased shareholder wealth and that these wealth increases were solely due to efficiency gains. This conclusion could easily have been challenged on the basis of evidence available at that time (Mueller, 1977); it is untenable considering the evidence available today.

Although the finance literature has failed to answer the two basic questions posed in this survey, it does, of course, provide a wealth of information about mergers and the answers to many other questions. Moreover, some of this information can be used to begin to answer the more basic questions. For example, the studies of post-merger performance clearly suggest that mergers at some points of time are *not* followed by long declines in normalised returns to acquirers. The likelihood that these M&As increased wealth is much higher than for those that were followed by declines. Several studies found the returns to acquirers in tender offers and hostile takeovers to be larger than for friendly mergers. M&As financed by cash have higher returns than those financed by issuing shares, and so on. Of course, if the strong form of the efficient capital market does not hold, any differences in returns to acquirers observed at the announcements might just reflect differences in overoptimism among traders. Conglomerates were the fad of the 1960s, hostile takeovers the fad of the 1980s (Matsusaka, 1993, p. 377). When, however, positive abnormal returns at the announcements are sustained over long post-merger windows, as has been the case for tender offers in some studies,[50] one's confidence that the mergers have created wealth is enhanced.

Results like these both demonstrate that *some* acquisitions create wealth and suggest why they do so. The necessity of having to resort to a tender offer suggests that the targets' managers were not ready partners to the deal. This in turn calls to mind the market-for-corporate-control hypothesis and indicates why tender offers may create wealth. The fact that the targets of the tender offers were often diversified firms that had diversified through mergers also lends support to the agency theory of mergers, however, and calls into question the event studies that concluded that these mergers were successes based on the market's short-run reaction to their announcements. More generally, it emphasises the importance of determining the fractions of mergers which enhance wealth and the fraction that destroy it. Tender offers and hostile takeovers may on average be wealth creating, but they have been a fairly small fraction of all mergers and acquisitions. Bhagat, Shleifer and Vishny's (1990) were able to identify *only* 62 hostile takeovers from 1984 through 1986, for which the price paid for the target was at least $50 million. Rau and Vermaelen (1998) put together an exhaustive sample of mergers and tender offers between 1980 and 1991 and came up with 2823 mergers and 316 tender offers. Even if one feels confident that tender offers generate wealth by replacing bad managers, one is left with a lot of other mergers to account for both with respect to their effects on wealth and their underlying motivation.

The inconclusive findings regarding M&As in the event study literature highlights the need to supplement this work with studies that use profits, market shares and other indexes of performance, and it further highlights the value of careful case studies of individual mergers as conducted by Keith Cowling and associates (1979).

NOTES

1. I thank the Austrian National Bank for financial support under its Jubilaeums-fondsproject No. 8861.
2. I shall in general not distinguish between mergers and takeovers, but rather simply refer to all as M&As or mergers.
3. An alternative approach as in Malatesta (1983) is to estimate

$$R_{it} - R_{ft} = \alpha_i + \beta_i(R_{mt} - R_{ft}) + \mu_{it}$$

   for the benchmark period. If α_i were constrained to equal zero, this equation would be equivalent to the CAPM of equation (9.1). When α_i is unconstrained, however, the measures of abnormal returns obtained from (9.4) become sensitive to the estimates of α_i and the choice of benchmark period as with the market model, and so I have also categorised this approach as 'the market model',
4. This methodology is described and discussed below.
5. Cumulative residuals from the announcement month through 6 months afterward add to 0.3 per cent of the market value of the acquiring firms.
6. The statistical significance of these figures cannot be determined with the data reported.
7. For example, Halpern (1973), Franks, Broyles and Hecht (1977), Bradley (1980), Dodd (1980), Asquith, Bruner and Mullins (1983) and Bradley, Desai and Kim (1983).
8. Mandelker (1974), Dodd and Ruback (1977), Kummer and Hoffmeister (1978), Asquith (1983) and Bradley, Desai and Kim (1983) all conclude that their results support or at least are consistent with the market for corporate control hypothesis.
9. See Mandelker (1974), Smiley (1976), Asquith (1983) and Malatesta (1983). Not all studies found targets underperforming the market prior to being acquired, however (Dodd and Ruback, 1977; Kummer and Hoffmeister, 1978; and Langetieg, 1978). Targets in Ravenscraft and Scherer's (1987, Ch. 3) sample had significantly *higher* profit rates than their lines of business.
10. Of the studies cited so far, Firth (1980) would be the only exception, although Langetieg (1978) admitted the possibility of other motives.
11. See Shiller (1981, 1984, 1989, 2000), and De Bondt and Thaler (1985).
12. See, Nelson (1959, 1966), Melicher, Ledolter and D'Antonio (1983) and Geroski (1984). Although there has been some controversy over whether mergers actually come in waves, this issue seems to be resolved now. On this see Golbe and White (1993) and Linn and Zhu (1997).
13. Alberts and Varaiya (1989) determined, for example, that to justify the premiums paid in M&As in the 1970s and 1980s, the earnings growth rates of acquired companies would have to rise from being on average at the median of the distribution of growth rates to being in the top decile.
14. These are Ellert (1976), Dodd and Ruback (1977), Kummer and Hoffmeister (1978), Langetieg (1978) and Asquith (1983). For evidence consistent with P/E magic accounting for some conglomerate mergers, see Conn (1973).
15. Marris introduced the threat of takeover as the main constraint on managers, anticipating Henry Manne's (1965) market for corporate control hypothesis.
16. See Mueller (1972) and for an early test Grabowski and Mueller (1975).
17. All managerial discretion hypotheses assume that a manager's discretion arises from a separation between ownership and control *à la* Berle and Means (1932). Thus, those who claim that managers maximise profits or shareholder wealth have generally questioned the relevance of a separation between ownership and control.
18. See Nadler (1930), Thorp (1931) and Markham (1955).
19. Any reader of Jorgenson's survey, published in 1971, would certainly be led to the conclusion that the neoclassical investment theory had the most theoretical and empirical support.

20. See, for example, Fazzari, Hubbard and Petersen (1988) and Hoshi, Kashyap and Scharfstein (1991).
21. See Vogt (1994), Carpenter (1995), Kathuria and Mueller (1995), and Gugler, Mueller and Yurtoglu (forthcoming).
22. For further petroleum industry evidence consistent with both a cash flow model of investment and a managerial discretion interpretation of this model, see Griffin (1988) and Baltagi and Griffin (1989). See also Shin and Stulz (1998).
23. See Friend and Puckett (1964), which also contains references to many other studies.
24. A closer look at the early literature, however, would also reveal that the market's preference for dividends over retained earnings was most pronounced for firms in slow-growing industries or with low returns on investment. See, Mueller (1972) and Grabowski and Mueller (1975).
25. Corroborating evidence is provided by Hubbard and Palia (1995), conflicting evidence by Andrade and Stafford (1997).
26. See, also, Lewellen, Loderer and Rosenfeld (1985), and You et al. (1986). Mann and Sicherman (1991) also present evidence in support of the agency hypothesis. Amihud, Dodd and Weinstein (1986), however, interpret their evidence as consistent with the hypothesis that *both* managers and shareholders benefit from mergers.
27. See Gort and Hogarty (1970), Nielsen and Melicher (1973), Piper and Weiss (1974), Firth (1980), Travlos (1987), Varaiya and Ferris (1987), Berkovitch and Narayanan (1993) and Sirower (1997).
28. Although Berkovitch and Narayanan (1993) find an insignificant negative correlation between the gains to the two merging firms within their subsample with *positive* total wealth changes, within the subsample with *negative* total wealth changes this correlation is negative and significant. They thus conclude that hubris leads to overbidding even in those mergers that generate net wealth increases, and that agency problems and/or hubris account for the losses to acquirers in mergers that destroy wealth.
29. See Weston (1970), and Weston, Smith and Shrieves (1972).
30. Baumol et al. (1970) made the first contribution to this literature For more recent results and references, see Mueller and Reardon (1993) and Mueller and Yun (1998).
31. This literature is surveyed in Caves (1989), Scherer and Ross (1990, ch. 5), Mueller (1997) and for the UK; Hughes (1993).
32. Dodd and Ruback also used the post-merger period as the benchmark for calculating the returns to acquirers in the announcement month. They measured a statistically significant 2.8 per cent return to acquirers in this month and concluded that the acquisitions generated wealth for both acquirers and targets. Although the acquirers' shares underperform the market for several years after the mergers, they are deemed successful because the acquirers' shares did better in the announcement month than afterward.
33. An additional problem arises because the αs and βs for the market model appear to be unstable. See Conn and Connell (1990) and Coutts, Mills and Roberts (1997).
34. Franks and Harris (1989) report bidders being eight times larger than their targets, Higson and Elliott (1998) six times larger.
35. Loderer and Martin (1992), like FHT, report only estimates of α. Since they are made using daily observations, they are infinitesimally small. The figures in Table 9.2 are the daily estimates multiplied by 1250 to make them comparable to the others in the table. They seem too large in absolute value, however.
36. Franks and Harris's (1989) results also are consistent with these findings for the UK, if one uses the pre-merger estimates of the market model as a benchmark.
37. This is also the interpretation favoured by Agrawal and Jaffe (2000) in their survey of the 'post-merger puzzle', Philippatos and Baird (1996) compare *differences* between market and book values before mergers and post-merger performance and also find that relatively high pre-merger market values are associated with poorer post-merger share performance.
38. Fama and French (1993, pp. 45–55). See also, Franks and Harris (1989) and FHT (1991).
39. See in addition to RV, Travlos (1987), FHT, Gregory (1997) and Loughran and Vijh (1997).

40. Eugene Fama (1998) has recently taken up the challenge to the efficient capital market assumption posed by estimates of post-merger losses to acquirers and by other event studies using long windows. Fama concludes that these studies *do not* undermine the efficient capital market assumption. The downward drifts in post-merger returns to acquirers are the result of chance overreactions to the merger announcements, just as upward drifts often observed following announcements of dividend increases are chance underreactions. Space precludes our taking up Fama's arguments in detail. Suffice it to say that if he is correct, then the losses to the acquirers are real and are a *delayed* result of the M&As.

      Fama dismisses 'the negative post-merger abnormal returns to acquiring firms in mergers' as being 'economically small' (p. 303). This interpretation rests heavily on one's definition of 'small'. Several of the cumulative post-merger declines reported in Tables 9.1 and 9.2 exceed 10 per cent of the value of the acquiring companies. Once account is taken of the acquirers' being typically from 5 to 10 times larger than the targets, even one digit percentage losses to acquirers become *economically large* relative to the gains to the targets.
41. Many recent studies do not report returns for acquirers over lengthy pre-announcement periods, but some do report pre-event αs for the market model. These are typically positive implying positive pre-event abnormal returns. See, Franks and Harris (1989) and Gregory (1997).
42. These would include Weston, Smith and Shrieves (1972), Asquith (1983), Schipper and Thompson (1983) and Matsusaka (1993).
43. See Scherer (1988, pp. 71–2).
44. See, for example, Jensen and Murphy (1990) and the survey by Rosen (1992). As the stock market advanced by leaps and bounds during the 1990s, managerial compensation contracts shifted toward a greater alignment with shareholder interests. But the contracts that were in place when all but the most recent mergers took place are accurately characterised in the text.
45. Ravenscraft and Scherer (1987, p. 215) speculate that the conglomerates' managers may have been risk takers spurred on by a highly skewed distribution of returns to mergers. See also Gort and Hogarty (1970).
46. For examples of mergers that were or would have been real disasters, see Lys and Vincent (1995) on AT&T's acquisition of NCR; Kaplan, Mitchell and Wruck (1997) on acquisitions by Cooper Industries and Premark; and Bruner (1999) on Volvo's aborted merger with Renault.
47. The quotation is from Eckbo (1992, p. 1020). See also, Eckbo (1983) and Eckbo and Wier (1985).
48. See Evans and Kessides (1994) and Borenstein (1989).
49. See, also, Borenstein's (1990) case studies of the TWA–Ozark and Northwest–Republic mergers.
50. See Magenheim and Mueller (1988) and Rau and Vermaelen (1998).

REFERENCES

Agrawal, A. and J.F. Jaffe (2000), 'The Post-Merger Performance Puzzle', in C. Cooper and A. Gregary (eds), *Advances in Mergers and Acquisitions,* Vol. 1, New York: Elsevier Science, pp. 7–41.

Agrawal, A. and N. Jayaraman (1994), 'The dividend policies of all-equity firms: a direct test of the free cash flow hypothesis', *Managerial and Decision Economics,* **15**, March/April, 139–48.

Agrawal, A., J.F. Jaffe and G.N. Mandelker (1992), 'The post-merger performance of acquiring firms: a re-examination of an anomaly', *Journal of Finance,* **47**, September, 1605–21.

Alberts, W.W. and M.P. Varaiya (1989), 'Assessing the profitability of growth by acquisition: a "premium recapture" approach', *International Journal of Industrial Organization*, **7**, March, 133–49.

Allen, J.W., S.L. Lummer, J.J. McConnell and D.K. Reed (1995), 'Can takeover losses explain spin-off gains?', *Journal of Financial and Quantitative Analysis*, **30**, December, 465–85.

Amihud, Y., P. Dodd and M. Weinstein (1986), 'Conglomerate mergers, managerial motives and stockholder wealth', *Journal of Banking and Finance*, **10**, October, 401–10.

Andrade, G. and E. Stafford (1997), 'Investigating the Characteristics and Determinants of Mergers and Other Forms of Investment', mimeo, University of Chicago.

Andrade, G., M. Mitchell and E. Stafford (2001), 'New evidence and perspectives on mergers', *Journal of Economic Perspectives*, **15**, Spring, 103–20.

Asquith, P. (1983), 'Merger bids, uncertainty, and stockholder returns', *Journal of Financial Economics*, **11**, 51–83.

Asquith, P., R.F. Brunner and D.W. Mullings, Jr. (1983), 'The gains to bidding firms from merger', *Journal of Financial Economics*, **11**, 121–39.

Baltagi, B.H. and J.M. Griffin (1989), 'Alternative models of managerial behavior: empirical tests for the petroleum industry', *Review of Economics and Statistics*, **71**, November, 579–85.

Baumol, W. J., P. Heim, B.G. Malkiel and R.E. Quandt (1970), 'Earnings retention, new capital and the growth of the firm', *Review of Economics and Statistics*, **52**, November, 345–55.

Becher, D.A. (2000), 'The valuation effects of bank mergers', *Journal of Corporate Finance*, **6**, July, 189–214.

Berger, P.G. and E. Ofek (1995), 'Diversification's effect on firm value', *Journal of Financial Economics*, **37**, January, 39–65.

Berkovitch, E. and M.P. Narayanan (1993), 'Motives for takeovers: an empirical investigation', *Journal of Financial and Quantitative Analysis*, **28**, September, 347–62.

Berle, A.A. and G.C. Means (1932), *The Modern Corporation and Private Property*, New York: Commerce Clearing House; rev. edn, New York: Harcourt, Brace, Jovanovich, 1968.

Bhagat, S., D. Hirshleifer and R. Noah (1999), 'The Effects of Takeovers on Shareholder Value', mimeo, University of Colorado.

Bhagat, S., A. Shleifer and R.W. Vishny (1990), 'Hostile takeovers in the 1980s: the return to corporate specialization', *Brookings Papers on Economic Activity, Microeconomics*, 1–84.

Borenstein, S. (1989), 'Hubs and high fares: dominance and market power in the U.S. airline industry', *Rand Journal of Economics*, **20**, Autumn, 344–65.

Borenstein, S. (1990), 'Airline mergers, airport dominance, and market power', *American Economic Review*, **80**, May, 400–4.

Bradley, M. (1980), 'Interfirm tender offers and the market for corporate control', *Journal of Business*, **53**, 345–76.

Bradley, Michael, A. Desai and E.H. Kim (1983), 'The rationale behind interfirm tender offers: information or synergy?', *Journal of Financial Economics*, **11**, 183–206.

Bradley, M., A. Desai and E.H. Kim (1988), 'Synergistic gains from corporate acquisitions and their division between the stockholders of target and acquiring firms', *Journal of Financial Economics*, **21**, May, 3–40.

Bruner, R.F. (1999), 'An analysis of value destruction and recovery in the alliance and proposed merger of Volvo and Renault', *Journal of Financial Economics*, **31**, January, 125–66.

Carpenter, R.E. (1995), 'Finance constraints or free cash flow? A new look at the life cycle model of the firm', *Empirica*, **22** (3), 185–209.

Caves, R.E. (1989), 'Mergers, takeovers and economic efficiency: foresight vs. hindsight', *International Journal of Industrial Organization*, **7**, March, 151–74.

Comment, R. and G.A. Jarrell (1995), 'Corporate focus and stock returns', *Journal of Financial Economics*, **37**, Jan., 67–87.

Conn, C., A. Cosh, P. Guest and A. Hughes (2001), 'Long-run share performance of U.K. firms in cross-border acquisitions', ESRC Centre for Business Research, University of Cambridge Working Paper 214.

Conn, R.L. (1973), 'Performance of conglomerate firms: comment', *Journal of Finance*, **28**, June, 754–8.

Conn, R.L. and F. Connell (1990), 'International mergers: returns to U.S. and British firms', *Journal of Business Finance and Accounting*, **17**, Winter, 689–711.

Coutts, J.A., T.C. Mills and J. Roberts (1997), 'Time series and cross-section parameter stability in the market model: tests and time varying parameter estimation with UK data', *The Statistician,* Journal of the Royal Statistical Society, Series D, **46**, 57–70.

Cowling, K., P. Stoneman, J. Cubbin, J. Cable, G. Hall, S. Domberger and P. Dutton (1979), *Mergers and Economic Performance*, Cambridge: Cambridge University Press.

De Bondt, W. and R.H. Thaler (1985), 'Does the stock market overreact?', *Journal of Finance*, **40**, 793–805.

Dennis, D.K. and J.J. McConnell (1986), 'Corporate mergers and security returns', *Journal of Financial Economics*, **16**, June, 143–87.

Desai, H. and P.C. Jain (1999), 'Firm performance and focus: long-run market performance following spinoffs', *Journal of Financial Economics*, **54**, January, 75–101.

Dewenter, K.L. and V.A. Warther (1998), 'Dividends, asymmetric information, and agency conflicts: evidence from a comparison of the dividend policies of Japanese and U.S. firms', *Journal of Finance,* **53**, June, 879–904.

Dodd, P. (1980), 'Merger proposals, management discretion and stockholder wealth', *Journal of Financial Economics*, **8**, 105–38.

Dodd, P. and R. Ruback (1977), 'Tender offers and stockholder returns: an empirical analysis', *Journal of Financial Economics*, **5**, December, 351–74.

Doukas, J. (1995), 'Overinvestment, Tobin's *q* and gains from foreign acquisitions', *Journal of Banking and Finance*, **19**, October, 1185–303.

Eckbo, B.E. (1983), 'Horizontal mergers, collusion, and stockholder wealth', *Journal of Financial Economics*, **11**, April, 241–73.

Eckbo, B.E. (1992), 'Mergers and the value of antitrust deterrence', *Journal of Finance*, **47**, July, 1005–29.

Eckbo, B.E. and K.S. Thorburn (2000), 'Gains to bidder firms revisited: domestic and foreign acquisitions in Canada', *Journal of Financial and Quantitative Analysis*, **35**, March, 1–25.

Eckbo, E.B. and P. Wier (1985), 'Antimerger policy under the Hart–Scott–Rodino Act: a reexaminiation of the market power hypothesis', *Journal of Law and Economics*, **28** (1), April, 119–49.

Ellert, J.C. (1976), 'Mergers, antitrust law enforcement and stockholder returns', *Journal of Finance*, **31**, 715–32.

Evans, W.N. and I.N. Kessides (1994), 'Living by the "Golden Rule": multimarket contact in the U.S. airline industry', *Quarterly Journal of Economics*, **109** (2), May, 341–66.

Fama, E.F. (1998), 'Market efficiency, long-term returns, and behavioral finance', *Journal of Financial Economics*, **49**, September, 283–306.

Fama, E.F. and K.R. French (1993), 'Common risk factors in the returns on stocks and bonds', *Journal of Financial Economics*, **33**, 3–56.

Fazzari, S.M., R.G. Hubbard and B.C. Peterson (1988), 'Financing constraints and corporate investment', *Brookings Papers on Economic Activity*, **1**, 141–95.

Firth, M. (1980), 'Takeovers, shareholder returns, and the theory of the firm', *Quarterly Journal of Economics*, **94**, March, 315–47.

Franks, J.R., J.E. Broyles and M.J. Hecht (1977), 'An industry study of the profitability of mergers in the United Kingdom', *Journal of Finance*, **32**, December, 1513–25.

Franks, J.R. and R.S. Harris (1989), 'Shareholder wealth effects of corporate takeovers', *Journal of Financial Economics*, **23**, August, 225–49.

Franks, J., R. Harris and S. Titman (1991), 'The postmerger share-price performance of acquiring firms', *Journal of Financial Economics*, **29**, 81–96.

Friend, I. and M. Puckett (1964), 'Dividends and stock prices', *American Economic Review*, **54**, September, 656–82.

Geroski, Paul A. (1984), 'On the relationship between aggregate merger activity and the stock market', *European Economic Review*, **25**, 223–33.

Golbe, D.L. and L.J. White (1993), 'Catch a wave: the time series behavior of mergers', *Review of Economics and Statistics*, **75**, August, 493–9.

Gort, M. and T.F. Hogarty (1970), 'New evidence on mergers', *Journal of Law and Economics*, **13**, April, 167–84.

Grabowski, H.G. and D.C. Mueller (1972), 'Managerial and stockholder welfare models of firm expenditures', *Review of Economics and Statistics*, **54**, February, 9–24.

Grabowski, H.G., and D.C. Mueller (1975), 'Life-cycle effects on corporate returns on retentions', *Review of Economics and Statistics*, **57**, November, 400–409.

Gregory, A. (1997), 'An examination of the long run performance of UK acquiring firms', *Journal of Business Finance and Accounting*, **25**, September, 971–1002.

Griffin, J.M. (1988), 'A test of the free cash flow hypothesis: results from the petroleum industry', *Review of Economics and Statistics*, **70**, February, 76–82.

Gugler, K., D.C. Mueller and B.B. Yurtoglu (2003), 'Marginal q, Tobin's q, Cash Flow and Investment', *Southern Economic Journal*, forthcoming.

Halpern, P.J. (1973), 'Empirical estimates of the amount and distribution of gains to companies in mergers', *Journal of Business*, **46**, October, 554–75.

Harford, J. (1999), 'Corporate cash reserves and acquisitions', *Journal of Finance*, **54**, December, 1969–97.

Higson, C. and J. Elliott (1998), 'Post-takeover returns: the UK evidence', *Journal of Empirical Finance*, **5**, 27–46.

Hoshi, T., A. Kashyap and D. Scharfstein (1991), 'Corporate structure, liquidity, and investment: evidence from Japanese industrial groups', *Quarterly Journal of Economics*, **106** (1), February, 33–60.

Houston, J.F. and M.D. Ryngaert (1994), 'The overall gains from large bank mergers', *Journal of Banking and Finance*, **18**, 1155–76.

Hubbard, R.G. and D. Palia (1995), 'Benefits of control, managerial ownership, and the stock returns of acquiring firms', *Rand Journal of Economics*, **26**, Winter, 782–92.

Hughes, A. (1993), 'Mergers and Economic Performance in the UK: A Survey of the Empirical Evidence 1950–90', in M. Bishop and J. Kay (eds), *European Mergers and Merger Policy*, Oxford: Oxford University Press, p. 9–95.

Jensen, M.C. (1986), 'Agency costs of free cash flow, corporate finance and takeovers', *American Economic Review*, **76**, May, 323–29.

Jensen, M.C. and K.J. Murphy (1990), 'Performance pay and top-management incentives', *Journal of Political Economy*, **98** (2), April, 225–64.

Jensen, M.C. and R.S. Cuback, (1983), 'The market for corporate control', *Journal of Financial Economics*, **11**, April, 5–50.

John, K. and E. Ofek (1995), 'Asset sales and increase in focus', *Journal of Financial Economics*, **37**, 105–26.

Jorgenson, D.W. (1971), 'Econometric studies of investment behavior: a survey', *Journal of Economic Literature*, **9**, December, 1111–48.

Kang, J.-K. (1993), 'The international market for corporate control', *Journal of Financial Economics*, **34**, 345–71.

Kaplan, S.N. and M.S. Weisbach (1992), 'The success of acquisitions: evidence from divestitures', *Journal of Finance*, **47**, March, 107–38.

Kaplan, S.N., M.L. Mitchell and K.H. Wruck (1997), 'A clinical exploration of value creation and destruction in acquisitions: organizational design, incentives, and internal capital markets', mimeo, University of Chicago.

Kathuria, R. and D.C. Mueller (1995), 'Investment and cash flow: asymmetric information or managerial discretion', *Empirica*, **22** (3), 211–34.

Kim, E.H. and V. Singal (1993), 'Mergers and market power: evidence from the airline industry', *American Economic Review*, **83**, June, 549–69.

Kuh, E. and J.R. Meyer (1957), *The Investment Decision*, Cambridge, MA: Harvard University Press.

Kummer, D. and R. Hoffmeister (1978), 'Valuation consequences of cash tender offers', *Journal of Finance*, **33**, 505–16.

Lamont, O. (1997), 'Cash flow and investment: evidence from internal capital markets', *Journal of Finance*, **52**, March, 83–109.

Lang, L.H.P. and R.H. Litzenberger (1989), 'Dividend announcements', *Journal of Financial Economics*, **24**, 181–91.

Lang, L.H.P. and R.M. Stulz (1994), 'Tobin's q, corporate diversification and firm performance, *Journal of Political Economy*, **102**, 1248–80.

Lang, L.H.P., R.M. Stulz and R.A. Walking (1989), 'Managerial performance, Tobin's Q, and the gains from successful tender offers', *Journal of Financial Economics*, **24**, September, 137–54.

Langetieg, T. (1978), 'An application of a three-factor performance index to measure stockholders gains from merger', *Journal of Financial Economics*, **6**, 365–84.

Leeth, J.D. and J.R. Borg (1994), 'The impact of mergers on acquiring firm share-holder wealth: the 1905–1930 experience', *Empirica*, **21**, 221–44.

Lev, B. and G. Mandelker (1972), 'The microeconomic consequences of corporate mergers', *Journal of Business*, **45**, January, 85–104.

Lewellen, W., C. Loderer and A. Rosenfeld (1985), 'Merger decisions and executive stock ownership in acquiring firms', *Journal of Accounting and Economics*, **7** (1–3), April, 209–31.

Linn, S. and Z. Zhu (1997), 'Aggregate merger activity: new evidence on the wave hypothesis', *Southern Economic Journal*, **64**, July, 130–46.

Lintner, J. (1971), 'Expectations, mergers and equilibrium in purely competitive securities markets', *American Economic Review*, **61**, 1971, 101–11.

Loderer, C. and K. Martin (1992), 'Postacquisition performance of acquiring firms', *Financial Management*, **21**, Autumn, 69–91.

Loughran, T. and A.M. Vijh (1997), 'Do long-term shareholders benefit from corporate acquisitions?', *Journal of Finance*, **52**, December, 1765–90.

Lys, T. and L. Vincent (1995), 'An analysis of value destruction in AT&T's acquisition of NCR', *Journal of Financial Economics*, **39**, January, 353–78.

Magenheim, E. and D.C. Mueller (1988), 'On Measuring the Effect of Mergers on Acquiring Firm Shareholders', in J. Coffee, L. Lowenstein and S. Rose-Ackerman (eds), *Knights, Raiders and Targets*, Oxford: Oxford University Press, p. 171–93.

Malatesta, P.H. (1983), 'The wealth effect of merger activity and the objective functions of merging firms', *Journal of Financial Economics*, **11**, April, 155–81.

Mandelker, G. (1974), 'Risk and return: the case of merging firms', *Journal of Financial Economics*, **1**, December, 303–35.

Mann, S.V. and N.W. Sicherman (1991), 'The agency costs of free cash flow: acquisition activity and equity issues', *Journal of Business*, **64**, April, 213–27.

Manne, H.G. (1965), 'Mergers and the market for corporate control', *Journal of Political Economy*, **73**, April, 110–20.

Maquieira, C.P., W.P. Megginson and L. Nail (1998), 'Wealth creation versus wealth redistribution in pure stock-for-stock mergers', *Journal of Financial Economics*, **48**, April, 3–33.

Markham, J.W. (1955), 'Survey of the Evidence and Findings on Mergers', in *Business Concentration and Price Policy*, New York: National Bureau of Economic Research, pp.141–82.

Marris, R. (1963), 'A model of the "managerial" enterprise', *Quarterly Journal of Economics*, **77**, May, 185–209.

Marris, R. (1964), *The Economic Theory of Managerial Capitalism*, Glencoe, IL: Free Press.

Matsusaka, J.G. (1993), 'Takeover motives during the conglomerate merger wave', *Rand Journal of Economics*, **24**, Autumn, 357–79.

Mead, W.J. (1969), 'Instantaneous merger profit as conglomerate merger motive', *Western Economic Journal*, **7**, December, 295–306.

Melicher, R.W. and D.F. Rush (1973), 'The performance of conglomerate firms: recent risk and return experience', *Journal of Finance*, **28**, May, 381–8.

Melicher, R.W. and D.F. Rush (1974), 'Evidence on the acquisition-related performance of conglomerate firms', *Journal of Finance*, **29**, March, 141–9.

Melicher, R.W., J. Ledolter and L.J. D'Antonio (1983), 'A time series analysis of aggregate merger activity', *Review of Economics and Statistics*, **65**, August, 423–30.

Modigliani, F. and M.H. Miller (1958), 'The cost of capital, corporation finance and the theory of investment', *American Economic Review*, **48**, June, 261–97.

Morck, R., A. Shleifer and R.W. Vishny (1990), 'Do managerial objectives drive bad acquisitions?', *Journal of Finance*, **45**, March, 31–48.

Mueller, D.C. (1969), 'A theory of conglomerate mergers', *Quarterly Journal of Economics*, **83**, November, 643–59.

Mueller, D.C. (1972), 'A life cycle theory of the firm', *Journal of Industrial Economics*, **20**, July, 199–219.

Mueller, D.C. (1977), 'The effects of conglomerate mergers: a survey of the empirical evidence', *Journal of Banking and Finance*, **1**, December, 315–47.

Mueller, D.C. (1997), 'Merger policy in the United States: a reconsideration', *Review of Industrial Organization*, **12** (5–6), December, 655–85.

Mueller, D.C. and E. Reardon (1993), 'Rates of return on investment', *Southern Economic Journal*, **60**, October, 430–53.

Mueller, D.C. and L. Yun (1998), 'Rates of return over the firm's life cycle', *Industrial and Corporate Change*, **7**(2), 347–68.

Mulherin, J.H. and A.L. Boone (2000), 'Comparing acquisitions and divestitures', *Journal of Corporate Finance*, **6**, July, 117–39.

Nadler, M. (1930), *Corporate Consolidations and Reorganizations,* New York: Alexander Hamilton Institute.

Nash, J.F. (1950), 'The bargaining problem', *Econometrica*, **18**, April, 155–62.

Nelson, R.L. (1959), *Merger Movements in American Industry, 1895–1956*, Princeton: Princeton University Press.

Nelson, R.L. (1966), 'Business Cycle Factors in the Choice Between Internal and External Growth', in W. Alberts and J. Segall (eds), *The Corporate Merger*, Chicago: University of Chicago Press.

Nielsen, J.F. and R.W. Melicher (1973), 'A financial analysis of acquisition and merger premiums', *Journal of Financial and Quantitative Analysis*, **8** (2), March, 139–48.

Philippatos, G.C. and P.L. Baird, III (1996), 'Postmerger performance, managerial superiority and the market for corporate control', *Managerial and Decision Economics*, **17**, January/February, 45–55.

Piper, T.R. and S.J. Weiss (1974), 'The profitability of multibank holding company acquisitions', *Journal of Finance*, **29** (1), March, 163–74.

Rau, P.R. and T. Vermaelen (1998), 'Glamour, value and the post-acquisition performance of acquiring firms', *Journal of Financial Economics*, **49**, 223–53.

Ravenscraft, D.J. and F.M. Scherer (1987), *Mergers, Sell-Offs, and Economic Efficiency,* Washington, DC: Brookings Institution.

Reid, S.R. (1968), *Mergers, Managers and the Economy*, New York: McGraw-Hill.

Reid, S.R. (1971), 'A reply to the Weston/Mansinghka criticisms dealing with conglomerate mergers', *Journal of Finance*, **26**, September, 937–46.

Roll, R. (1986), 'The hubris hypothesis of corporate takeovers', *Journal of Business*, **59**, 197–216.

Roll, R. (1988), 'Empirical Evidence on Takeover Activity and Shareholder Wealth', in J.C. Coffee, Jr., L. Lowenstein and S. Rose-Ackerman (eds), *Takeovers and Contests for Corporate Control*, Oxford: Oxford University Press, pp. 241–52.

Rosen, S. (1992), 'Contracts and the Market for Executives', in L. Werin and H. Wijkander (eds), *Contract Economics*, Oxford: Basil Blackwell, pp. 181–211.

Scherer, F.M. (1988), 'Corporate takeovers: the efficiency arguments', *Journal of Economic Perspectives*, **2**, Winter, 69–82.

Scherer, F.M. and D. Ross (1990), *Industrial Market Structure and Economic Performance*, 3rd edn, Boston, MA: Houghton Mifflin.

Schipper, K. and R. Thompson (1983), 'Evidence on the capitalized value of merger activity for acquiring firms', *Journal of Financial Economics*, **11** (1–4), April, 85–119.

Schumpeter, J.A. (1934), *The Theory of Economic Development*, Cambridge, MA: Harvard University Press.

Servaes, H. (1996), 'The value of diversification during the conglomerate merger wave', *Journal of Finance*, **51**, September, 1201–25.

Shiller, R.J. (1981), 'Do stock prices move too much to be justified by subsequent movements in dividends', *American Economic Review*, **71**, 421–36.

Shiller, R.J. (1984), 'Stock prices and social dynamics', *Brookings Papers on Economic Activity*, December, 457–98.

Shiller, R.J. (1989), *Market Volatility*, Cambridge, MA: MIT Press.

Shiller, R.J. (2000), *Irrational Exuberance*, Princeton, NJ: Princeton University Press.

Shin, H.-H. and R.M. Stulz (1998), 'Are internal capital markets efficient?', *Quarterly Journal of Economics*, **112**, May, 531–52.

Sicherman, N.W. and R.H. Pettway (1987), 'Acquisition of divested assets and shareholder's wealth', *Journal of Finance*, **42** (5), 1261–73.

Singal, V. (1996), 'Airline mergers and competition: an integration of stock and product price effects', *Journal of Business*, **69**, April, 233–68.

Sirower, M. (1997), *The Synergy Trap*, New York: Free Press.

Smiley, R. (1976), 'Tender offers, transactions costs and the theory of the firm', *Review of Economics and Statistics*, **58**, February, 22–32.

Smith, R.L. and J.-H. Kim (1994), 'The combined effects of free cash flow and financial slack on bidder and target stock returns', *Journal of Business*, **67**, April, 281–310.

Stillman, R. (1983), 'Examining antitrust policy towards horizontal mergers', *Journal of Financial Economics*, **11**, 225–40.

Thorp, W.L. (1931), 'The persistence of the merger movement', *American Economic Review*, **21**, March, 77–89.

Travlos, N.G. (1987), 'Corporate takeover bids, methods of payment, and bidding firms' stock returns', *Journal of Finance*, **42**, September, 943–63.

Varaiya, N. and K.R. Ferris (1987), 'Overpaying in corporate takeovers: the winner's curse', *Financial Analysts's Journal*, May–June, 64–73.

Vogt, S.C. (1994), 'The role of internal financial sources in firm financing and investment decisions', *Review of Financial Economics*, **4** (1), Fall, 1–24.

Wernerfelt, B. and C. A. Montgomery (1988), 'Tobin's q and the importance of focus in firm performance', *American Economic Review*, **78** (1), March, 246–50.

Weston, J.F. (1970), 'The nature and significance of conglomerate firms', *St. John's Law Review*, 44, Spring, special edition, pp. 66–80.

Weston, J.F. and S.K. Mansinghka (1971), 'Tests of the efficiency performance of conglomerate firms', *Journal of Finance*, **26**, September, 919–36.

Weston, J.F., K.V. Smith and R.E. Shrieves (1972), 'Conglomerate performance using the capital asset pricing model', *Review of Economics and Statistics*, **54**, November, 357–63.

You, V., R. Caves, M. Smith and J. Henry (1986), 'Mergers and Bidders' Wealth: Managerial and Strategic Factors', in L.G. Thomas, III (ed.), *The Economics of Strategic Planning: Essays in Honor of Joel Dean*, Lexington, MA: D.C. Heath and Co., pp. 201–19.

10. Incentives to corporate governance activism

Dennis Leech

INTRODUCTION

Much recent discussion of policies to improve standards of corporate governance has increasingly focused on the role of shareholders: as the legal owners of a company they can be said to have the ultimate responsibility for all aspects of its conduct and performance and therefore are the group to whom management is accountable. This contrasts with the more traditional view in which investors are not supposed to become involved in the direction of their portfolio companies – simply buying or selling their shares according to whether they do well or badly – and relying on the market for corporate control to ensure high standards or performance through takeovers or threat of takeovers. As a form of market regulation this has been shown by many studies to be inadequate and there are strong arguments for the new approach based on corporate governance activism.[1] At the same time, and on the other hand, there is considerable evidence that investors have yet fully to embrace their new responsibilities and discharge their associated duties.[2]

Shareholder activism[3] or engagement derives from investors developing long-term face-to-face relationships with the companies in which they invest. Rather than their involvement being little more than that of anonymous speculators, trading their shares on the market, they become the owners with an interest in the company's progress, a knowledge of its business and personnel and a commitment to its long-term success; at the same time they have the capacity to influence the direction of the company through the voting rights that the shares carry.

The need for this changed relationship has come about in recent years because of the increased dominance of financial institutions as shareholders. The majority of shares on the London Stock Exchange are now held by British financial institutions: 51.9 per cent in 1999 (ONS, 1999). The growth in the size of pension funds and insurance companies means that increasingly, in many cases, institutional portfolios contain shares in a very large number of companies, if not every one listed on the market. At the same time relatively fewer shares are now held by individuals than in the past. This significantly restricts the opportunity for selling poorly performing shares without causing a substantial share price fall, and therefore limits the effectiveness of the market for corporate control as a discipline.

An activist shareholder engages with the company at the highest level. It[4] needs to be well informed about the company in order properly to be able to exercise its voting rights. It needs to engage in dialogue with the board of directors to understand its strategy and monitor its performance, especially when things are not going well, when it must take a view on the optimal action and if necessary intervene. An activist investor might increase its holding in a poorly performing company where it sees there is the potential for improvement after suitable changes have been made in its strategy or board membership. It needs to meet with the directors and management and use its influence to raise standards of performance on behalf of all the owners. That does not mean confrontation – cooperation is obviously much to be preferred – but the relationship is one where the owner has power over the directors based on the ultimate sanction that changes in board membership might be brought about by a vote at the annual general meeting.

It is often argued that the majority of shareholders cannot be expected to discharge the traditional duties of stewardship that stem from ownership because they lack the necessary financial incentives. This argument against investor activism arises where there is a liquid equity market like in Britain and the United States so that typically ownership stakes are small in percentage terms. While it might be true that the holder of a very large block shareholding (usually taken as above 20 per cent of the company's voting shares) has indeed a sufficient incentive to play the role of active owner – to monitor the company's performance, participate in decision making and to exercise the voting rights attached to the shares – nevertheless such large shareowners are few. Typically a company's largest shareholders each control only a few per cent of the equity, a small proportion both as a share of cash-flow rights and voting power. Therefore, on the one hand, they are seen as lacking the necessary private incentives: any benefit they may expect to gain from their activism in improved company performance is assumed likely to be less than the cost of doing so. On the other hand, a shareholder with only a small fraction of the votes is not in a very powerful position from which to challenge directors by voting against board recommendations at a company meeting.

This chapter examines this question by considering the private incentives faced by investors. It argues, in contrast to much of the theoretical literature, that the free-rider argument is frequently overstated and that very many shareholders, in fact, can be said to face the appropriate incentives attaching to their cash-flow rights. A typical shareholding held by an investor in a large company, although relatively small in percentage terms – the largest shareholder in a top 250 company not infrequently controls no more than 2 or 3 per cent – nevertheless is very large in absolute terms. Therefore the expected private returns to such a holding following an improvement in company performance are likely to be considerable. By contrast the likely costs that must be incurred in order to participate are of a different order, being related to such activities as research, analysis, attending meetings and voting. The issue of investor incentives to activism is a real one but it is empirical in that some investors will have strong incentives while most undoubtedly lack them. This chapter proposes an approach to this question based on a metric by which the returns to activism may be quantified. One of the main results I find is that it can be said that many leading investors in large companies have very large private incentives.

The approach adopted is a theoretical analysis applied to information on share ownership of real companies on the London Stock Exchange. The focus is on the question of whether the private incentives facing shareholders are such that it will pay them to behave socially responsibly by actively discharging the responsibilities of ownership. For a shareholder, being an activist means not only becoming informed about company performance and alternatives, becoming in a position to know what changes are needed to rectify weak performance; there is also the question of whether it has enough votes to be able to carry them out. I ignore this problem in this chapter by maintaining the reasonable fiction that the required changes will always be implemented. This is a reasonable assumption because there is also an incentive to share its information with the other shareholders in order to inform a vote that would bring this about. Competing shareholders have common interests in the outcome of such a vote.

The usual arguments against activism are considered before presenting the model and results for the UK. These typically run together a number of related issues that are better separated. I treat the free-rider arguments separately from those involving conflicts of interest, since their natures are fundamentally different. I address the question of whether the free-rider argument would be compelling by itself in the absence of conflicts of interest. I consider incentives formally abstracting from conflicts of interest.

The chapter is organized as follows. In Section 1 the free-rider argument is examined as a public goods problem but I show that the key issue here is whether there are private incentives to supply a public good; in the case where there are, the question becomes fundamentally different from that normally considered in the literature. Section 2 presents a conventional discussion of conflicts of interest that inhibit investors, and argues the need for rules to remove these. The model is presented in Section 3; this assumes a shareholder activist is also a passive portfolio investor: shares are held long term in the portfolio subject to the normal random fluctuations in returns, which are screened every year. Severe underperformance is taken as indicating a substantial problem with the management of the company and therefore likely returns to intervention. This is the basis of a measure of the expected returns to activism which can be compared with the associated costs. This model makes it possible to estimate the size of investment that would be large enough to carry private cash-flow incentives to activism. This is applied to two groups of British companies in Section 4, separate analyses for the Top 250 largest companies and a random sample taken from the whole market. I present results showing that there are in fact very strong incentives to corporate governance activism on shareholders of the largest companies but which are much more mixed for the market as a whole. Section 5 is the conclusion and discussion.

1. OBSTACLES TO ACTIVISM: THE FREE-RIDER ARGUMENT

Those who have advocated that shareholders should become more involved in the direction of their portfolio companies when they perform badly have argued, implicitly or explicitly, that such intervention is not only in the public interest but also in the investors' own best interests. The Cadbury Report, for example, described the voting rights attaching to ordinary shares as a valuable asset:

> Given the weight of their votes, the way in which institutional shareholders use their power to influence the standards of corporate governance is of fundamental importance. Their readiness to do this turns on the degree to which they see it as their responsibility as owners, and in the interest of those whose money they are investing, to bring about changes in companies when necessary, rather than selling their shares . . . Voting rights can be regarded as an asset, and the use or otherwise of those rights by institutional shareholders is a subject of legitimate interest to those on whose behalf they invest. (Cadbury, 1992)

This statement can be read as a plea to shareholders to use their votes collectively, as a service to the public, and slightly leaves open the question of whether there exist private incentives for individual institutional shareholders to use their votes.

The Myners Report, on the other hand, is explicit in suggesting that shareholder intervention in failing companies is in the shareholders' own interests:

In managing pension funds' assets, fund managers have also pursued only a limited range of strategies to deliver value to clients. In particular, the review found evidence of general reluctance to tackle corporate underperformance in investee companies, particularly pre-emptive action to prevent troubled companies developing serious problems. . . . The review was given a number of reasons for this, none of which it believes to be compelling. . . . If fund managers are truly to fulfil their duty of seeking to maximize value for their shareholders, then there will be times – certainly more than at present – when intervention is the right action to take. Of course there are many occasions when simply selling an entire holding is the appropriate response. But this is often difficult where holdings are large, where the share price is already depressed, or where a zero holding cannot be adopted for other reasons (such as constraints on departures from an index benchmark). . . . *The case for action does not rest on a public interest argument about shareholder responsibility but on the basic duty of the manager to do their best for the client.* Nor need (or should) it represent 'micro-management' by fund managers. (Myners, 2001, p. 10, emphasis added)

The review is not making a public interest argument about shareholder responsibility. *The most powerful argument for intervention in a company is financial self-interest, adding value for clients through improved corporate performance leading to improved investment performance. One would expect that for institutional investors with long-term liabilities, such an approach would appeal.* (Myners, p. 90, emphasis added)

Against this is the argument that shareholders typically lack suitable incentives to activism because that would, in effect, mean supplying what is a public good to the community of all shareholders. The following passage is typical of many:

Most public companies are held by many shareholders owning only small stakes . . . an active shareholder cannot capture all of the gain from becoming involved, studying the enterprise, or sitting on the board of directors, thereby taking the risks of enhanced liability. Such a shareholder would incur the costs but split the gains, causing most fragmented shareholders to rationally forgo involvement. In the language of modern economics, we have a collective action problem among shareholders – despite the potential gains to shareholders as a group, it's rational for each stockholder when acting alone to do nothing, because each would get only a fraction of the gain, which accrues to the firm and to all of the stockholders. This shareholder collective action problem is then layered on top of a principal–agent problem – agents, in this case the managers, sometimes don't do the principal's, in this case the stockholder's, bidding. (Roe, 1994)

Another example is:

[D]ispersed shareholders have little or no incentive to monitor management. The reason is that monitoring is a public good: if one shareholder's monitoring leads to improved company performance, all shareholders benefit. Given that monitoring is costly, each shareholder will free-ride in the hope that *other* shareholders will do the monitoring. Unfortunately, all shareholders think the same way and the net result is that no – or almost no – monitoring will take place. Sometimes this free-rider problem can be overcome by someone who acquires a large stake in the company and takes it over (or exerts control in some other way). (Hart, 1995).

This argument relies on the fact that the activist shareholder receives only a small fraction of the gain resulting from its actions. I wish to ague here that this comparison is inappropriate and that what actually matters as a basis for action is only whether the benefit exceeds the costs. An investor with a 1 per cent holding, for example, might nevertheless be substantially better off by being active than not, even though 99 per cent of the gains thereby generated benefit other shareholders. For there to be an appropriate incentive it is sufficient that the likely private benefit from an action exceeds the cost of taking it.[5]

There will always be a form of shareholder collective action problem but it is necessary to make a distinction between two different situations. The first case is where all shareholders have such small stakes that the benefits they might receive from activism never exceed the associated costs. This is the case described above, in the quotations from Roe and Hart, and which appears widely in the literature; this case gives rise to the 'rational abstention' of Downs (1957), and the 'logic of collective action' problem of Olson (1965). The coordination problem is decisive in this case and 'free-riding' behaviour by all shareholders is rational. This situation is obviously one where there is poor corporate governance.

The second case, however, is where the stakes of some shareholders are sufficiently large that the private benefits they can expect to receive as a result of successful intervention outweigh the costs they incur. This case is fundamentally different from the previous one because now the system of corporate governance can be based on companies being held accountable by active shareholders in possession of the right incentives; in this case the shareholders are economic actors with private incentives to supply a public good.

There remains a co-ordination problem in this case, however, because there is still an incentive to free ride. But a complete coordination failure, caused by all shareholders behaving in this way, that would result in the public good not being supplied, would be irrational and pathological.[6] An activist shareholder who is able to bring about an improvement in the company's performance is better off whatever the others decide to do in terms of activism. If others free ride by doing nothing in the knowledge that the public good will be supplied, then, *ceteris paribus*, the free riders will do better in relative terms. But that is irrelevant to an investor unless the investors are competing according to some common benchmark. It will be a problem in such cases – for example where they are fund management companies competing for business on the basis of relative performance. But the problem there is rather in the nature of a conflict of interests and will be discussed in the next section. If the shareholder is acting on its own account, as for example a pension fund which is managed in-house by its trustees, or a personal shareholding held by an individual then what matters is the return it receives on the shares, not the comparative position of different fund managers in the performance league tables.

The question of the dividing line between the first and second of these situations is essentially empirical. It is the thesis of this chapter that the second case does not give an empty group – far from it: that there are many shareholdings that can be shown to possess individual incentives to corporate governance activism. I will refer to them as 'significant shareholdings'.

I do not consider voting power in this chapter. In previous work I have investigated the relationship between the degree of dispersion of the share ownership and the voting power represented by the combined votes of a group of shareholders acting together (Leech, 1987, 2001; Leech and Leahy, 1991). A robust result to have emerged from this work is that in almost all companies of whatever size a few top shareholders – rarely more than seven – if they combined and voted together as a bloc, would have enough voting power for effective control (Leech, 2001).

In the current study I abstract from the question of voting power and make the assumption that an activist shareholder is always able to bring pressure to bear by having, as the ultimate sanction over recalcitrant management, the capacity to win votes in order to change the directors at company annual meetings. If an individual 'significant' shareholder, as a result of activism, is in a position to make proposals for changes in strategy or board membership that would improve results then it also has an incentive to make its information freely available to its rivals in order to induce them to support it in a vote. It is not unreasonable to make this assumption because all investors at this level of abstraction have a common interest in the matter and therefore the question of voting here is secondary to that of incentives. Obviously this is an unrealistic assumption to make in practice because there are many obstacles to coordinated shareholder action, some of which are detailed in the next section.

2.   OBSTACLES TO ACTIVISM: CONFLICTS OF INTEREST

Accepting that it is possible that shareholders may have the incentives described above, there remain major obstacles in the way of investor activism. I consider these conflicts of interest here before returning to the main theme in the next section. They may arise from several sources.[7]

First, the way in which financial institutions select and reward their fund managers creates perverse incentives. If fund managers are judged against performance criteria in terms of short-term, such as quarterly, figures they will have little motivation to press portfolio companies to adopt strategies that have a longer time scale, more relevant to institutional investors with long-term liabilities. This conflict of interest can perhaps be reduced by specifying a longer period over which performance should be judged.

Second, conflicts arise through fund managers having other interests because they may be part of a larger financial organisation. They will be keen to attract and keep other business, for example the company pension scheme, the investment banking or insurance business of the company and therefore will not risk losing this by activism. More generally a fund manager may not wish to risk losing similar business, or fail to attract new business, from other companies by being seen publicly, or get a reputation, as a 'troublemaker'. Such major disincentives can be reduced by effective 'Chinese walls' to ensure that the interests of their client funds are protected and not subordinated to their wider business interests.

Third, it is often said that investors do not seek to control the companies in their portfolio because that would entail them becoming part of management and might open them up to a charge of insider trading if they acted on the information they received. However where an investor, on the basis of a meeting with a company's management, decided not to sell a holding, but to hold it in the hope of being able to influence the company to adopt a better strategy that would benefit it in the long run, that would hardly lead to an accusation of insider trading, even though it might be acting on inside information.

Fourth, the most serious obstacle to activism might be the possibility, mentioned above, of other investors being able to free-ride off the efforts of the activist shareholder. If fund managers were competing against similar performance indicators there would be perverse incentives because the ones who did nothing – and avoided incurring the costs – would perform better in the league tables than the active one who intervened and did incur the costs. There would seem to be a simple remedy, however, in that the activist investor would be in a position of being able to trade on the information it possessed: the information that it had obtained both through its investment in activism (which need not be inside information) and also the fact that it was going to act on it to the benefit of the share price. Therefore it could gain by increasing its holding temporarily relative to its long-term portfolio level and then sell the overweight portion when the company performance returned to normal. In the absence of an agreement between investors the activist shareholder could recoup its additional costs by speculating on its own activism and need not lose out to free riders.

Such conflicts of interest as these are peripheral to the main issue of whether investors have pure private incentives to activism. I turn to this question in the next section.

3.   A MODEL OF THE INCENTIVES OF AN ACTIVIST SHAREHOLDER

In this section I propose a framework by which the financial incentives of institutional investors can be evaluated in terms of the costs and benefits of activism. The following assumptions are made. First, the conflicts of interest described above are ignored. Second, there are no practical obstacles in the way of shareholder activism being successful in achieving its aims of improved company performance. Both of these are very strong assumptions from a practical point of view but they are valid abstractions from the perspective of this chapter.

I assume that the key issue in corporate governance is the accountability of the company's management for its overall performance. The model of an activist investor presented in this section maintains the assumption that an activist investor is concerned with company performance *as a whole* rather than some aspect of strategy such as executive pay which may be incidental to it.

An activist investor is assumed to be a financial institution that consists essentially of two funds: (1) the main portfolio; and (2) an activist portfolio. The main portfolio comprises holdings in a wide range of companies' shares held on a long-term basis for income in the form of dividends. The main portfolio can be thought of as being managed according to a passive investment strategy that aims to track an index or benchmark. The activist fund consists of the shares of a small number of selected companies which have been chosen both because they have been underperforming and because there exist clearly identified remedies for this underperformance available within the company by changes at board level. The activist shareholder is a catalyst for change and looks for opportunities to bring about change to improve performance which it can exploit by bringing pressure to bear on the management. Companies are held in this portfolio for a limited time until their performance improves and then they are returned to the main portfolio.

A firm in the main portfolio is assumed to generate a return on its shares at rate r, a random variable. The expected rate of return is μ and risk (measured by the standard deviation) is σ. In what follows I assume r to be normally distributed for convenience. The relevant measure of risk is firm-specific risk.

3.1 The Private Benefits of Intervention

The investor screens the performance of all shares in the main portfolio. However, if the performance of a company is exceptionally bad its shares are considered for transfer to the activism fund.[8] Suppose the investor has a policy of transferring the worst-performing 100α per cent of companies in its main portfolio to the activism fund; equivalently the probability of intervention in a company is α.

Let the threshold rate of return below which the company's shares are transferred to the activism fund be r_α, defined by the condition,

$$P(r \cdot r_\alpha) = \alpha.$$

In the case where r is normally distributed, then

$$r_\alpha = \mu - Z_\alpha \sigma, \tag{10.1}$$

where Z is the standard normal deviate, and Z_α such that $Pr(Z < Z_\alpha) = \alpha$.
Therefore the minimum expected return to intervention is equal to:

$$\mu - r_\alpha = Z_\alpha \sigma \tag{10.2}$$

An investor holding a stake of £k of the shares of the company will expect to make an annual monetary return of $Z_\alpha \sigma\, k$ whose estimated capital value based on an expected rate of return of μ, will be

$$Z_\alpha \sigma\, k/\mu. \tag{10.3}$$

3.2 The Costs of Activism

It is assumed that the total additional direct costs of activism are equal to an amount £A. These costs include the additional management costs of holding the shares in the activism fund, the costs of research into the particular circumstances of the company that would lead to poor performance and remedies, the costs associated with meetings between senior personnel and top managers of the company, and the costs associated with shareholder voting and co-ordinated shareholder action to change company policy or directors. A major part of the costs of activism arise from the necessity that to be successful it be led by senior high calibre personnel, who are able to formulate and implement the intervention strategy including being able to deal with top company managers on equal terms.

The cost of activism is a one-off investment which must be compared with the present value of the expected returns it is expected to bring. Therefore the condition under which activism pays is,

$$Z_\alpha \sigma\, k/\mu \geq A \qquad\qquad (10.4)$$

3.3　Fiduciary Investors and Own Account Investors

The above analysis must be modified to allow for the case where the institution exercising control rights is different from the beneficial shareholder. Here the benefits received by the fund manager reflect the level of the management fee paid in the form of an *ad valorem* commission on the value of the fund. Let the shareholding of the institutional investor be £K and the rate of commission paid to the fund manager be c. Then the incentives which apply to the fund manager relate to a holding of cK rather than k, and this substitution must be made in (10.3) and (10.4) above. It is then possible to find the minimum size of shareholding which will be large enough that its manager would find activism profitable.

Writing $k = cK$ in (10.4) gives the condition

$$Z_\alpha \sigma\, cK/\mu \geq A \qquad\qquad (10.5)$$

and therefore,

$$K \geq A\mu/cZ_\alpha\sigma. \qquad\qquad (10.6)$$

Expression (10.6) is the basis for the definition of a significant shareholding.

3.4　Definition: A Significant Shareholding

A significant shareholding is one sufficiently large that there is a private incentive to the investor or fund manager who controls it to intervene to improve the performance of the company concerned. A significant shareholding, K_0, is the smallest value of K that satisfies inequality (10.6):

$$K_0 = A\mu/cZ_\alpha\sigma. \qquad\qquad (10.7)$$

The cost of capital for the company, μ, is estimated using the capital asset pricing model, by the relationship: $\mu = r_f + (r_m - r_f)\beta$, where r_f is the risk-free interest rate, r_m is the return on the market portfolio (both common to all companies), and β is the company's systematic risk.

4. SIGNIFICANT SHAREHOLDINGS IN BRITISH COMPANIES

Now I apply the model described in the previous section to evaluate significant shareholdings in UK companies and discuss their implications for corporate governance. The conclusion is that there is evidence of pervasive and very strong incentives for own-account investors, as might be expected, but also that strong private incentives exist also for fiduciaries managing holdings in very large companies.

4.1 The Data and Assumptions about Parameter Values

The data set consists of two groups of companies listed on the London Stock Exchange that were observed at the end of December 1999: (1) the largest 250; and (2) a 10 per cent random sample of all companies listed on the main exchange (166 companies). The share ownership data, which was purchased from a commercial financial company, comprises all shareholdings above a certain threshold. For the top 250 companies the threshold is 0.015 per cent of the issued ordinary share capital[9] which means that typically the largest 320 shareholdings representing about 85 per cent of the equity are observed.[10] For the smaller companies the threshold is 0.1 per cent[11] and for a typical company in this group this gives about 80 holdings with 86 per cent of the equity. The risk data comprising the market risk, beta, and the firm-specific risk, σ, was provided by the London Business School Risk Measurement Service.

The estimate of the costs of activism, A, that I have used is based on discussions with fund managers involved in the management of pension funds. The figure chosen is meant to be representative in that it is plausible to an order of magnitude in many cases rather than a precise estimate. I have taken a figure of £250 000 per year as the additional costs incurred by the investor, as a result of the company being the focus of activism and transferred to the activism fund, over the costs of its shares remaining in the main portfolio. I have assumed this figure to be independent of the size of company or the returns to activism. Experience reported by activist investors suggests that a successful intervention typically requires a minimum of two years to have the desired effect and restore the company's performance to normal. Therefore, I have used a ballpark estimate of $A = £500 000$ in the analysis, for all companies. This is, of course, a gross oversimplification and it is likely that these costs will increase with the size of the company. Many of the costs incurred by an investor who is active in the affairs of a large and complex company with many divisions might be expected far to exceed those for a smaller single product firm, for example. Moreover the costs of taking coordinated shareholder action might be expected to vary according to circumstances depending on many factors. Assuming a constant value for A is therefore a first approximation and much further empirical research into this area is needed.

I have conducted three different analyses assuming different levels of commission. The most important distinction here is between a shareholder who is an own-account investor, such as a private individual or a pension fund managed in-house, and a fiduciary fund manager who receives a fee in the form of commission. In an important sense (not least legally) this distinction should be irrelevant because fiduciaries have a moral and legal obligation to manage funds solely in the interests of their beneficiaries, so there should be no differences in behaviour. However the payment of fund managers by commission on an *ad valorem* basis gives rise to a possible principal–agent problem and a misalignment of incentives that is important from the point of this investigation.

For an own-account investor, all the gains from activism accrue to the investor and therefore I have assumed a value of $c = 1$ for this case. For the analysis of fiduciaries, I have taken two different levels of typical commission corresponding to different styles of fund management. Assuming an index tracker fund (corresponding to a 'passive' style of management), I have used a rate of commission of 19 basis points ($c = 0.0019$ or 0.19 per cent), a typical figure. Assuming a fund manager with an 'active' style of portfolio management, I have used the average fee for a £200M actively managed UK fund, reported in Brealey and Neuberger (2001), of 30 basis points, $c = 0.003$ or 0.3 per cent.

In calculating the cost of capital, I have taken the risk-free rate, r_f, equal to 5.5 per cent, and the equity premium, $r_m - r_f$, of 4.5 per cent. I have assumed the probability of a company being selected for the activism portfolio to be 1 per cent, $\alpha = 0.01$ ($Z_\alpha = 2.3263$); that is the investor is assumed to select the bottom-performing 1 per cent of the companies in the main portfolio for transfer to the activist portfolio. Therefore an investor whose main portfolio comprised all listed companies would expect to be actively involved in the governance of around 16 companies.

4.2 The Results

The results are presented in four ways in Tables 10.1 to 10.4. Tables 10.1 to 10.3 show descriptive statistics for both groups of companies and Table 10.4 gives results for the top 20 companies by name for illustration. Table 10.1 shows the distribution of estimates of significant shareholdings by size, Table 10.2 the numbers of significant shareholdings and Table 10.3 the voting rights controlled by significant shareholders. As well as the results of applying the model, Tables 10.2 and 10.3 also present analyses using other definitions of significant shareholdings that have been proposed by Charkham and Simpson (1999) and by Sykes (2000).

Significant shareholdings

The distribution of the estimates of significant shareholdings, K_0, obtained using expression (10.7) are shown in Table 10.1. As is to be expected there is a very large difference between the results for own account shareholders and those for fiduciaries.

Table 10.1   Estimated significant shareholding K_0 ($£M$)

	Top 250 companies			Random sample		
	Fiduciary		Own account	Fiduciary		Own account
	$c=19$bp	$c=30$bp	$(c=1)$	$c=19$bp	$c=30$bp	$(c=1)$
Minimum	7.9	5.0	0.01	2.5	1.6	0.005
Lower quartile	33.5	21.2	0.06	28.1	17.8	0.05
Median	44.3	28.0	0.08	34.7	22.0	0.07
Upper quartile	51.4	32.6	0.10	47.3	29.9	0.09
Maximum	245.6	155.5	0.47	226.3	143.3	0.43
Mean	47.8	30.3	0.09	41.8	26.5	0.08
Standard deviation	29.8	18.9	0.06	28.1	17.8	0.05

Own account investors   For own account investors virtually any shareholding is large enough to satisfy condition (10.6). In the top 250 group a significant shareholding held by an own-account investor ranges between a minimum of £10000 and a maximum of £470000 with a median £80000. In the random sample, it ranges around a median of £70000, between a minimum of £5000 and a maximum of £430000.

Fiduciary investors   For fiduciary investors significant shareholdings are very much larger. If $c=19$bp, corresponding to an index tracker, the median becomes £44.3 million among the top 250 and £34.7 million among the random sample. The range is between £7.9 million and £245.6 million among the top 250. The minimum is £2.5 million in the random sample. Higher levels of commission rates reduce the values of K_0 for both groups.

Numbers of significant shareholdings by company

Table 10.2 shows the distribution of the *numbers* of significant shareholdings per company, that is the number of holdings that are larger than K_0.

Table 10.2 Numbers of significant holdings by company

| | Top 250 companies | | | | | | Random sample | | | | | |
| | Fiduciary | | Own account | £25M | £10M | 0.50% | Fiduciary | | Own account | £25M | £10M | 0.50% |
	c = 19bp	c = 30bp					c = 19bp	c = 30bp				
Minimum	0	0	1	0	1	1	0	0	1	0	0	1
Lower Q	4.0	8.0	122.0	7	17	23	0.0	0.0	24.0	0	0	17
Median	8.5	13.0	165.5	14	28.5	29	0.0	0.0	44.0	0	1	22
Upper Q	17.8	24.0	227.8	26.8	46.8	33	0.0	1.0	80.0	1	5	30
Maximum	168	249	955	249	363	46	168	249	875	249	358	39
Mean	15.3	22.2	199.4	24.1	43.5	27.0	3.0	4.5	68.4	4.3	8.4	22.4
SD	21.9	29.5	131.5	33.9	51.6	8.7	14.7	21.3	87.8	21.3	31.4	8.7

These results are useful in giving one indication of the feasibility of improved corporate governance based on coordinated shareholder action.

The table also shows, for comparison, alternative numbers on different definitions of a significant shareholding that have been proposed in the literature. Charkham and Simpson (1999) proposed a slightly different definition of what they called 'significant ownership' from the one in this chapter. In order to improve corporate governance, they proposed placing formal obligations on large shareholders to act as guardians of companies and for the purpose suggested such significant ownership might be 0.5 per cent of the equity or, as an alternative in the case of a very large company where there might be few such shareholders, a cash sum of £25 million. I present results for both figures. A similar idea has been suggested by Sykes (2000) as part of his proposed programme for reform of corporate governance; one of his proposals is for institutional shareholders to be made 'accountable for exercising their voting rights in an informed and sensible manner above some sensibly determined minimum holding (e.g. £10m)'. I have taken this as the authority for an alternative definition of a significant shareholding, and presented numbers based on it also in Table 10.2.

Own account investors Table 10.2 shows somewhat different results for the two groups of companies. However, there are nearly always very many significant shareholders. Among the larger companies in the top 250 group, every company has at least one significant shareholder, the lower quartile is 122, the median 165.5, and the maximum 955. In the random sample, the median is 44 and three-quarters of companies have at least 24 significant shareholders. These figures suggest that most companies ought to have a substantial group of highly motivated shareholders.

Fiduciary investors Assuming investors are fiduciaries again leads to different conclusions for the two groups of companies. Among the top 250, most companies have a number of significant shareholdings, although there are some with none: assuming $c = 19$bp, the median is 8.5, the lower quartile 4 and the maximum 168 and there are thirteen with 0. However, among the random sample companies, the picture is different: for $c = 19$bp, 129 – more than three-quarters of the sample – companies have no significant shareholder. The higher level of commission, $c = 30$bp, gives slightly higher numbers, with a quarter of random sample having at least one significant shareholding.

Other definitions of significant shareholdings The numbers based on the fixed definitions of significant shareholding of Charkham and Simpson (£25M) and Sykes (£10M) are broadly similar: there is a substantial body of incentivised investors for almost all the top 250 companies but the random sample suggests this is not typical of the market as a whole. The numbers for the £25M definition of Charkham and Simpson are quite close to those assuming fiduciaries with $c = 30$bp. The 0.5 per cent definition of Charkham and Simpson gives many more significant shareholders in the random sample, there being always at least one, the lower quartile being 17 and the median 22.

Thus these results suggest that, for the market as a whole (in contrast to the largest companies such as the top 250), and on the assumptions made, a typical company is likely to have few significant shareholders with the necessary incentives to activism. This suggests the likelihood of a corporate governance failure due to financial institutions lacking incentives to activism among the smaller companies.

Voting rights of significant shareholders
Table 10.3 shows the percentage of the equity held by investors with significant holdings. For own account investors, these figures are nearly always very large suggesting the potential for voting control exists in the great majority of companies. For the other definitions, however, the results are, as before, different for large and smaller companies. For $c = 19$bp, in the top 250 group, the median is 40.2 per cent, and the lower quartile is 28 per cent, suggesting that most companies in this group could be controlled by a bloc of financial institutions, with the right incentives, acting together. In the random sample there is an absence of significant shareholdings on the definitions I have used; again, the figures for the £25M definition correspond fairly closely to those for $c = 30$bp. The 0.5 per cent group suggest there is no lack of significant shareholders.

5.   CONCLUSION

The argument often advanced against basing a policy of improving standards of corporate governance on investor activism – that there is a pervasive lack of incentives in a market-based system such as Britain where shares are widely held – has been shown to be untrue. What is important is whether the likely returns to be received by activist shareholders as a result of intervening to improve underperforming companies exceed the associated costs, a question that has scarcely been addressed by academic economists. The expected returns to activism depend strongly on the absolute size of shareholding while the costs are largely independent of it. The size of shareholding as a relative share of ownership is irrelevant to determining incentives to corporate governance activism. The incentives to activism

Table 10.3 Per cent equity held in significant holdings

| | Top 250 companies | | | | | | Random sample | | | | | |
| | Fiduciary | | Own account | £25M | £10M | 0.50% | Fiduciary | | Own account | £25M | £10M | 0.50% |
	c=19bp	c=30bp					c=19bp	c=30bp				
Minimum	0.0	0.0	3.4	0	2.9	2.9	0.0	0.0	3.0	0	0	3.3
Lower Q	28.0	38.6	63.6	38.2	51.5	48.2	0.0	0.0	68.4	0	0	61.0
Median	40.2	47.4	73.1	48.1	59.6	60.3	0.0	0.0	78.2	0	19.4	73.2
Upper Q	52.8	60.3	83.3	61.9	71.2	71.7	0.0	19.7	87.3	20.1	46.3	83.7
Maximum	100	100	100	100	100	100	100	100	100	100	100	100
Mean	40.2	47.8	72.2	49.3	60.2	59.8	9.5	13.6	74.3	13.1	24.5	69.2
SD	21.2	20.0	17.4	18.3	16.7	18.0	21.0	23.0	19.6	22.6	26.5	19.9

Table 10.4 Results for the top 20 companies

	c = 0.0019				c = 0.003				c = 1			
	(a) K_0^* £M	(b) $N > K_0$ #	(c) Equity £B	(d) Votes %	(a) K_0^* £M	(b) $N > K_0$ #	(c) Equity £B	(d) Votes %	(a) K_0^* £M	(b) $N > K_0$ #	(c) Equity £B	(d) Votes %
BP Amoco	55.3	153	66.4	54.8	35.0	211	68.9	56.8	0.105	955	73.7	60.8
British Telecom	46.9	127	53.7	54.6	29.7	163	55.1	55.9	0.089	530	57.6	58.5
Vodafone Airtouch	40.2	168	53.2	55.8	25.4	249	55.8	58.5	0.076	875	59.0	61.9
HSBC Holdings	71.3	72	28.7	39.4	45.2	94	30.0	41.2	0.136	599	33.9	46.5
Glaxo Wellcome	55.8	98	39.7	62.3	35.3	135	41.3	64.8	0.106	671	44.6	70.1
Shell T & T	58.9	78	26.9	52.6	37.3	106	28.2	55.2	0.112	473	30.5	59.7
AstraZeneca Group	47.8	82	32.5	71.2	30.3	106	33.4	73.2	0.091	481	35.3	77.3
SmithKline Beecham	51.0	85	34.8	78.5	32.3	120	36.2	81.6	0.097	706	39.3	88.8
Lloyds TSB Group	79.0	60	19.0	44.8	50.0	85	20.6	48.6	0.150	559	24.9	58.7
Marconi	50.0	59	16.3	54.5	31.7	75	16.9	56.7	0.095	394	19.1	64.0
Barclays Plc	59.2	49	15.5	58.5	37.5	67	16.3	61.8	0.113	504	19.0	71.9
Cable & Wireless	51.6	55	14.6	57.1	32.7	87	15.9	62.2	0.098	577	18.5	72.7
Prudential	55.0	59	13.0	54.8	34.8	85	14.1	59.3	0.104	499	16.8	70.6
NatWest Bank	53.4	60	14.9	67.2	33.8	80	15.7	71.0	0.101	396	17.3	78.0
COLT Telecom	20.6	67	13.5	65.1	13.0	84	13.8	66.5	0.039	235	14.4	69.2
BSkyB	33.2	11	11.8	68.4	21.0	15	11.9	68.9	0.063	193	12.3	71.7
DIAGEO	76.1	35	6.8	39.8	48.2	52	7.8	45.8	0.145	579	11.1	65.4
Anglo American	47.2	27	15.1	89.9	29.9	34	15.3	91.5	0.090	226	16.1	96.2
Rio Tinto	51.0	44	8.0	50.6	32.3	59	8.6	54.3	0.097	440	10.7	67.7
Halifax Group	36.4	31	10.4	67.5	23.0	43	10.8	69.8	0.069	215	11.3	73.2

Notes: The table shows (for each commission rate): (a) the significant shareholding (*£millions); (b) the number of investors with significant shareholdings; (c) the value of equity held by those investors (*£billions); (d) the percentage of the voting equity held by them.

possessed by individual shareholders are arguably more important than the voting power of their shares because all beneficial investors in a company have a collective interest in good performance and therefore activist shareholders rationally have a common interest in sharing costly information.

A model of the incentives faced by an activist investor has been proposed which provides a measure of the minimum expected returns to activism to compare with the associated costs. The model is based on the assumption that a company in the investor's main portfolio produces a return which is a random variable against whose distribution under-performance can be identified. The minimum expected returns to activism are defined using this distribution: activism is assumed to restore the company's performance to the expected rate of return and this provides the required measure.

The model has been applied to two samples of British companies, the largest 250 and a random sample of all listed companies, and for both own-account investors and fiduciary fund managers paid commission, assumed to be motivated solely by self interest. The results, which should be interpreted as representative orders of magnitude rather than exact estimates, indicate that, for fund managers, among the largest companies shareholder incentives to activism are powerful, while among the smaller companies they are mixed. The question of incentives should be seen as an empirical question with a lot of variation between companies. For the own-account investors incentives appear to be pervasive.

The approach used here is very preliminary and approximate; the results should be considered as no more than indicative of orders of magnitude and suggestive of directions for future research. In particular, the model of an activist shareholder is extremely stylised, the intention being to abstract from many real-world factors in order to focus on the pure private incentives. The model ignores conflicts of interest that affect many financial institutions to a substantial degree. It oversimplifies the nature of corporate governance activism by making the unreal assumption that it is always possible for a shareholder to turn round an underperforming company by making suitable changes in strategy or senior personnel, yet in practice a company's underperformance may reflect deeper, fundamentally intractable reasons. It sidesteps the whole question of voting power, which has been dealt with elsewhere; this would be justified if voting, and the formation of voting coalitions for control, were costless, since in determining incentives it would only be necessary to consider the shareholders' ideal points, and it would be irrelevant if they had a controlling holding or not. In practice, however, part of the cost of activism must be seen as due to the need to coordinate the votes of diverse shareholders. The assumptions made more generally about the costs of activism are extremely simplistic and crude, and further research is needed.

ACKNOWLEDGEMENTS

Many thanks for comments on earlier drafts from Jonathan Charkham, Jeremy Edwards, Ben Ferrett, Peter Law, Colin Mayer, Derek Morris, Dennis Mueller, Marianne Pitts, Aubrey Silberston, Mike Waterson. Previous versions have been presented at EARIE29 September 2002, Madrid, Spain and seminars at the Said Business School and Warwick University whose participants are thanked for their comments. Thanks are due to Robert Leech, Lorena Dominguez-Arocha, Emma Jacques and Erin Prather for research assistance. I am grateful for discussions with Tim Bush and Michelle Edkins of Hermes, and Stuart Bell and Paul Marsland of PIRC. The empirical research has been supported by grants from the Nuffield Foundation, the British Academy and the University of Warwick. Thanks are due to Thomson Financial for providing the share ownership data and for help in using it. All errors and opinions are the author's alone.

NOTES

1. See the Cadbury report (1992), Charkham and Simpson (1999), Monks and Minnow (2001).
2. Myners (2001). Discussions of corporate governance include Morris (1994), Shleifer and Vishny (1997), Tirole (2001).
3. It is important to note that the idea of activism embodied in the term shareholder – or sometimes shareowner – activism is fundamentally different from that implied in the term active portfolio management.
4. Shareholders are financial institutions and therefore it is appropriate to use the neuter gender for them.
5. This argument is also used by Stapledon (1996).
6. This is formally similar to a game of 'chicken' in game theory where the worst outcome is the one where all players defect.
7. The Myners report (Myners, 2001), provides a comprehensive description of conflicts of interest.
8. This depends not only on the share's performance but also on there being the potential for restoring it to normal profitability through activism. In the model it is assumed that this is always the case.
9. That is, all shareholdings larger than a fraction equal to 0.00015 of the equity.
10. Corresponding figures for the top 100 companies are 475 shareholdings and 85 per cent of the equity.
11. That is, all holdings bigger than 0.001 of the shares.

REFERENCES

Brealey, Richard A. and A. Neuberger (2001), *The Treatment of Investment Management Fees and Commission Payments: An Examination of the Recommendations Contained in the Myners Report*, London: Fund Managers' Association.

Cadbury, A. (Committee on the Financial Aspects of Corporate Governance), (1992), *Report*, London: Gee Publishing.

Charkham, J. and A. Simpson (1999), *Fair Shares: the Future of Shareholder Power and Responsibility*, Oxford: Oxford University Press.

Downs, A. (1957), *An Economic Theory of Democracy*, New York: Harper and Row.

Hart, O. (1995), *Firms, Contracts and Financial Structure*, Oxford: Clarendon Press.

Leech, D. (1987), 'Ownership concentration and the theory of the firm: a simple game theoretic approach', *Journal of Industrial Economics*, **XXXV** (3), 225–40.

Leech, D. (2001), 'Shareholder voting power and corporate governance: a study of large British companies', *Nordic Journal of Political Economy*, **27** (1), 33–54.

Leech, D. and J. Leahy (1991), 'Ownership structure, control type classifications, and the performance of large British companies', *Economic Journal*, **101** (6), 1418–37.

Monks, R. and N. Minnow (2001), *Corporate Governance*, 2nd Edition, Oxford: Blackwell.

Morris, D. (1994), 'The Stock Market and Problems of Corporate Control in the UK', in T. Buxton, P.G. Chapman and P. Temple (eds), *Britain's Economic Performance*, London: Routledge.

Myners, P. (2001), *Institutional Investment in the United Kingdom: a Review* (The Myners Report), HMSO.

Olson, M. (1965 and 1971), *The Logic of Collective Action*, Cambridge, MA: Harvard University Press.

ONS (1999), Office of National Statistics, *Share Ownership: A Report on the Ownership of Shares*, HMSO.

Roe, M. (1994), *Strong Managers, Weak Owners*, Princeton, NJ: Princeton University Press.

Shleifer, A. and R. Vishny (1997), 'A survey of corporate governance', *Journal of Finance*, **52**, 33–56.

Stapledon, Geoff (1996), *Institutional Shareholders and Corporate Governance*, Oxford: Clarendon Press.

Sykes, A. (2000), *Capitalism for Tomorrow: Reuniting Ownership and Control*, Oxford: Capstone.

Tirole, J. (2001), 'Corporate governance', *Econometrica*, **69**, 1–36.

11. Perspectives on the governance of executive compensation

Martin J. Conyon

1. INTRODUCTION

Corporate governance, broadly conceived, refers to the complementary mechanisms by which enterprises are owned, controlled and directed. As a result corporate governance is central to understanding the performance of firms and the wealth of nations. The primary areas of governance research focus on the role of the Board of Directors; the importance of executive compensation; the role of the market for corporate control and takeovers; and the importance of concentrated shareholdings and monitoring by financial institutions.[1] This chapter deals with the governance of executive compensation. Our objective is to explain some contemporary and dominant trends in executive pay. In addition, we discuss competing paradigms ('managerial power' versus 'optimal contracting') for understanding compensation outcomes at the apex of the modern corporation.[2]

The recent string of corporate scandals in the United States has catapulted corporate governance to the centre of business debate and raised fundamental questions about trust, integrity and the purpose of the corporation. The allegations of accounting fraud and irregularities at Enron, WorldCom and Global Crossing are by now well known. In addition, recent attention has focused on potentially egregious and avaricious self-dealing by corporate insiders. In June 2002, the Securities and Exchange Commission filed charges against the former CEO of ImClone Systems Inc. Samuel Waksal, for illegal insider trading.[3] In September 2002 a report by Tyco International Ltd said that it had uncovered tens of millions of dollars in fraudulent bonuses. Details from the company's internal investigation, contained in a 100 page filing with the US Securities and Exchange Commission, indicates that in year 2000, Dennis Kozlowski had Tyco authorise nearly $96 million in unapproved bonuses for 51 employees to offset relocation loans. Kozlowski and former Chief Financial Officer Mark Swartz are said to have received most of the money.[4] Even John F. Welch, former CEO of General Electric and regarded by some as the 'manager of the century', has not been immune to the lens of corporate governance scrutiny. The divorce proceedings between Mr Welch and his wife, Jane Welch, reveal significant insights into the retirement benefits provided to the former CEO. Mrs Welch contends that General Electric covered massive living costs for them while he was CEO of the company and will continue to do so for him for the rest of his life.[5]

Clearly, then, the institutions of enterprise governance and control remain highly contentious. Branston et al. (2001) recently argued that

> Although there is on-going controversy in debates about strategy and governance, there is a consensus that a corporation is typically governed by a subset of those having an interest in its activities. The existing literature places *de facto* control somewhere between an elite group of (large) shareholders and senior mangers/the company board. This concentration of power is one reason why issues of corporate governance continue to be controversial; those currently excluded from strategic decision making may prefer a corporation to pursue a different objective.

This chapter focuses on the governance of executive compensation since this is likely to heavily influence the decisions made by senior managers – the corporate elite.

The rest of this chapter is organised as follows. Section 2 provides a brief primer on the economics of executive compensation (that is data sources, stock options, measurement, and empirical trends). Section 3 deals with equity incentives (that is the relationship between pay and performance and the importance of options). Section 4 contrasts two views that seek to explain the level and structure of executive compensation (the 'optimal contracting' approach and the 'managerial power' hypothesis). Section 5 is a discussion and conclusion (it highlights recent policy changes that have occurred in the US).

2. EXECUTIVE COMPENSATION

2.1 Data

Murphy (1999) reviews the considerable research on executive compensation.[6] Our first issue is to identify US data sources in order to scrutinise the pay of CEOs. Enhanced federal reporting requirements for the fiscal years ending on or after December 15, 1992 significantly upgraded the amount of information US companies were required to disclose with respect to stock options granted to and held by their corporate directors.[7] Companies report compensation information and it is lodged with the Securities and

Exchange Commission in the Definitive Proxy form 14a (Referred to as DEF14A). Secondary data sources include the comprehensive Standard & Poors ExecuComp data, and somewhat the less-comprehensive surveys published by *Forbes*, *Business Week*, and the *Wall Street Journal* (Conyon and Murphy, 2000). In this chapter we use the data available in the ExecuComp data set.[8] We identified the CEO and collected information on common equity ownership, current and prior option grants, salaries, annual bonuses, benefits, and LTIP cash and restricted stock awards. Our data cover the period 1992 to 2001 inclusive. There are 917 separate CEOs in the S&P 500 industrials during this period.

2.2   Elements of Executive Pay

Executive compensation typically contains four basic elements (see Murphy, 1985; Murphy, 1999). CEOs receive an annual base salary. They are eligible to receive annual bonuses triggered by accounting performance. Importantly, CEOs receive stock options, which are rights to purchase company stock at a pre-specified 'exercise' price for a pre-specified term.[9] CEOs often participate in Long-Term Incentive Plans (LTIPs). They take two principal forms: (1) 'restricted stock' grants that vest with the passage of time (but not with performance criteria); and (2) multi-year bonus plans typically based on rolling-average three- or five-year cumulative accounting performance. Also, they may receive restricted stock grants.

2.3   Stock Option Valuation: Black–Scholes

Stock options are known to form an important part of an executive's compensation (Murphy, 1999). However, stock options are unlikely to be an effective governance instrument (that is resolving conflicts of interest between owners and managers) unless the option recipient understands how they are valued. Moreover, stock options will not work as an effective incentive device (that is alter managerial behaviour) unless the option recipient understands how changes in the option determinants impact upon option value. These are important issues in the economics of executive compensation which we now address.

The valuation of common stock (that is ordinary equity) is straightforward. It is the number of shares owned multiplied by the stock price at some point in time. Stock options, the right but not the obligation to purchase stock at a predetermined price in the future, are not as straightforward to value. The payoffs of the option contract are simple to articulate. When an option is exercised, if it is in the money, it has a payoff that increases by one dollar for each dollar that the stock price is above the exercise or strike price. If the stock price is below the exercise price when the option matures, then the option is left unexercised and its payoff is zero (Murphy, 1999; Cox and Rubenstein, 1985).

The future stock price is, of course, unknown at the date when the option is actually granted. In consequence, investors, compensation committees and the recipient of the options (the optionee) rely on a valuation model to determine the cost of granting an option. One common valuation methodology, to provide a present value estimate of an option grant, is the Black–Scholes (1973) approach. It gives, under precise assumptions, the expected cost to the firm of granting a stock option. The Black–Scholes approach is important and relevant since US firms typically use it when disclosing the value of compensation in their definitive proxy statements (that is DEF14A). Also, the Black–Scholes approach is very commonly used in executive compensation research by academics (Murphy, 1999).

The Black–Scholes value of a stock option is determined by six input variables: the stock price, the exercise price, the dividend yield, the volatility of returns, the time to maturity, and the interest rate. Each affects the value of the option in a systematic and predictable fashion. This can be illustrated with a numerical example that captures salient features of a standard executive compensation contract. The Black–Scholes (1973) pricing formula provides an estimate of the expected value of an option, subject to certain assumptions and available information. It calculates the value (c) of a single European call option (that is the right to buy a share at a pre-specified price at a date in the future) as:

$$c = Se^{-[\ln(1+q)]T} N(d_1) - Xe^{-[\ln(1+r)]T} N(d_2)$$

where $d_1 = \{ \ln(S/X) + [\ln(1+r) - \ln(1+q) + \sigma^2/2](T)\}/\{\sigma T^{1/2}\}$ and

$$d_2 = \{\ln(S/X) + (r - q - \sigma^2/2)(T)\} / \{\sigma T^{1/2}\}.$$

The six inputs to the function are: S the share price; X the exercise or strike price; T the time to maturity; q the annual dividend yield; r the annual risk-free rate of interest; σ the standard deviation of returns on the share; $N(.)$ the cumulative probability distribution function for a standardised normal variable. In general an executive stock option, granted with a fixed exercise price at the money, with characteristics not dissimilar to those described here, has an expected cost to the company of approximately 30 to 40 per cent of the prevailing stock price.[10]

The relationship between the Black–Scholes value function and the stock price is plotted in Figure 11.1. The figure illustrates that option value increases with the stock price. This has a strong intuitive element since the

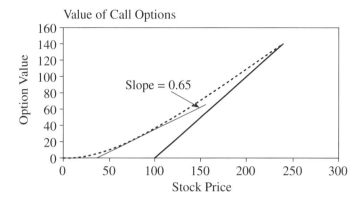

Note: Strike price, $X = \$100$; time to maturity, $T = 10$ years; dividend yield, $q = 2\frac{1}{2}$ per cent; volatility, $\sigma = 25$ per cent; risk free rate, $r = 7$ per cent. Dotted line is the Black–Scholes (1973) value function. The continuous line is the intrinsic value pay-offs.

Figure 11.1   The Relationship between Black–Scholes option value and the stock price

call option value increases with the underlying asset price and consequently furnishing executives with stock options appears to be a sensible way to align interests of owners and managers – which was a key issue during the 1980s and 1990s.[11] It is questionable, though, whether Black–Scholes is a reasonable approximation of the value that an executive places on the option. Hall and Murphy (2000, 2002) have argued that Black–Scholes overestimates the value of an option to a risk-averse executive based on simulations of various managerial utility functions.[12] In contrast, Lambert and Larcker (2001) find that middle level managers assign values to their stock options that exceeds the Black–Scholes value by between 50 per cent and 200 per cent indicating that managers' beliefs about the distribution of stock prices is different from the markets. Their evidence is based on studies of actual managers' responses to carefully constructed survey question-naires. Clearly, the paucity of existing evidence on how managers *actually* value their options, as opposed to how they are *assumed* to value them, sug-gests an urgent need for more research in this area.

Another important feature of the option contract is the convexity between asset value and stock price (see Figure 11.1): the value of the option increases at an increasing rate with the stock price.[13] This contrasts to the ownership of common equity where there is a simple linear relationship between change in share value and the stock price. Some authors have con-jectured that such linear pay-off structures potentially provide incentives for risk-averse managers to reduce firm risk or reject volatile but positive net present value projects (Smith and Stulz, 1985). Core et al. (2002) suggest that it may be optimal to add convexity to the manager's contract when there is a link between effort choice and variance. However, such convexity also means that option holders have incentives to take increasingly risky actions to increase the stock price since there are increasingly better payoffs to the option as the stock price steadily increases. The important point is that the convexity of the option contract has important consequences for managerial incentives which are deserving of further investigation.[14]

2.4 CEO compensation: evidence from 1992 to 2001

Empirically what has happened to CEO pay? We define total CEO compensation to include salaries, bonuses, stock options, restricted stock, payouts from long-term incentive plans, and other benefits. Stock options are valued in the Standard & Poors Execomp database using a modified Black–Scholes methodology.[15]

Figure 11.2 shows the median total compensation of chief executive officers in the S&P 500 industrials. The data covers the period 1992 through to the year 2001. The height of each bar depicts the median total compensation

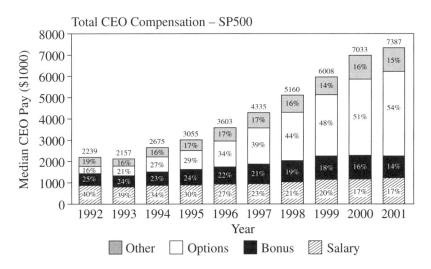

Note: Median executive compensation levels in 2001 constant dollars. Data is derived from Execucomp for the S&P 500 CEOs. Total compensation is given by the height of the bar. It is defined as the sum of salaries, bonuses, benefits, stock options (valued on the date of the grant using Execucomp modified Black–Scholes formula), stock grants and other compensation.

Figure 11.2   US CEO compensation S&P 500, 1992–2001

in CPI-adjusted constant 2001 dollars. There are four pertinent facts to draw from this figure. First, over this time period, the median total compensation has increased nearly threefold from about $2.2 million in 1992 to about $7.3 million in year 2001. Second, the figure also shows that the increase in CEO compensation in the S&P 500 Industrials reflects an explosion in the use of stock options, which are valued on the date of the grant. In 1992, option compensation, as a percentage of total pay, was approximately 16 per cent. By the year 2001 stock option compensation formed the majority of a CEO's pay package. Namely, using the Black–Scholes pricing methodology, options are worth about 54 per cent of total pay in year 2001. The growth in pay is largely attributed to the growth in stock options (Hall, 2000; Hall and Liebman, 1998). Third, the fraction of total pay that is comprised of a fixed component in the form of a salary has been falling over time. However the level of CEO salary in these firms has remained approximately constant. Finally, bonuses, as a fraction of total pay, have remained relatively constant over this time period.

3.   EQUITY INCENTIVES: PAY FOR PERFORMANCE

3.1   Equity Incentives[16]

Stock options, then, represent a significant and growing fraction of total CEO pay. The next issue to consider is how the value of an option varies as the underlying price of the asset changes within the Black–Scholes frame-work (see Hall, 2000). Executive compensation researchers refer to this general idea as 'pay-for-performance'. Stock options and other forms of equity pay provide a direct link between managerial wealth and firm value (Murphy, 1999). In the 1980s, when stock-based pay was less common, there were frequent calls for greater alignment between CEO pay and firm performance. Clearly, stock options and ordinary equity are important instruments in achieving this objective.

Ownership of common equity generates a clear one-for-one relationship between changes in equity value and asset prices. A one-dollar increase in the share price leads to a one-dollar increase in the value of the share. However, this is not the case for stock options. The derivative of the Black–Scholes call option value with respect to the share price is the option delta: $\partial c/\partial S = \delta$. For a European call option that pays dividends the delta is given as: $\delta = e^{-[\ln(1+q)]T} N(d_1)$. The value of the delta varies between zero and one; deep in the money options have deltas that are close to unity, whereas deep out of the money options have deltas close to zero (Cox and Rubenstein, 1985). The delta for a standard newly granted executive stock option is approximately 0.60. This means that a $1 increase in the stock price translates into an increase in the value of the option by $0.60.[17] The fact that the delta varies according to whether the option is in or out of the money can be seen in Figure 11.1. The slope of the Black–Scholes function for in the money options $(S > X)$ is greater than the slope of the line for out of the money options $(X > S)$.[18]

3.2 Measuring Executive Incentives

Two distinct incentive measures can be calibrated. The first metric is the dollar change in managerial wealth from a percentage increase in stock returns. This is the *portfolio equity incentive* measure (Core and Guay, 1999). The second pay-for-performance measure is the *Jensen–Murphy statistic* defined as the change in managerial wealth from a $1000 dollar change in shareholder wealth. The former metric defines managerial financial incentives as arising from a percentage change in performance whereas the latter uses a dollar change as the performance metric. Both measures treat executive financial incentives as the change in managerial rewards brought about by changes in shareholder wealth since holdings of any form of equity-based asset provide a direct linkage between managerial and shareholder wealth (Murphy, 1999; Jensen and Murphy, 1990a and b; Conyon and Murphy, 2000; Yermack, 1995).

Portfolio equity incentives, then, are calculated as the change in the dollar value of executive stock and option holdings for a 1 per cent change in the stock price. As previously established, the percentage change in the value of a stock option is less than the percentage change in the stock price and will depend upon the underlying factors in the option contact (Core and Guay, 1999; Cox and Rubenstein, 1985; Murphy, 1999). Accordingly, we have to weight the number of options held by the option delta to allow for the fact that there is a probability that the options will end up out of the money. Define portfolio equity incentives (that is the aggregate equity incentives) that arise from common equity claims and stock option holdings as:

$$\left(\frac{\text{Stock price}}{100}\right) \times \text{Shares Held} + \left(\frac{\text{Stock price}}{100}\right) \times \left(\frac{\text{Option}}{\text{Delta}}\right) \times \text{Options Held} \tag{11.1}$$

Equation (11.1) indicates the impact of a 1 per cent change in the stock price on the equity holdings of the CEO (agent) – for options it is weighted by the delta of the option.

The Jensen–Murphy metric treats a manager's equity incentives as proportional to the fraction of shares effectively owned by the manager. It is originally formulated in Jensen and Murphy (1990b)[19] and calculates the change in managerial equity brought about by a $1000 increase shareholder wealth. For common equity and stock options held by a CEO, the Jensen–Murphy statistic (or pay for performance sensitivity) can be calculated as:

$$\left(\frac{\text{Shares Held}}{\text{Common Equity}} \right) \times \$1000 + \left(\frac{\text{Options Held}}{\text{Common Equity}} \right) \times \left(\frac{\text{Option}}{\text{Delta}} \right) \times \$1000 \tag{11.2}$$

Equation (11.2) indicates that equity incentives increase with the percentage of common equity and stock options that the manager owns. Again, since there is a probability that stock options may end up out of the money, the percentage of options held is again weighted by the option delta. For instance, if the options were very deep in the money, and so the delta very close to one, then option equity incentives are high. If the options are deep out of the money, so the option delta is very close to zero, then option equity incentives are very low. Recently, there has been an important debate as to which measure best reflects executive financial incentives (Core et al., 2002). Baker and Hall (1998) argue that the choice of incentive measure is contingent on how CEOs action affects firm value. If actions affect the dollar returns (for example, perquisite consumption of a corporate jet) then the Jensen–Murphy statistic is appropriate. If they affect percentage returns (for example implementation of firm strategy) then the portfolio equity incentive is appropriate.[20]

3.3   CEO Equity Incentives: Evidence from 1992 to 2001

Empirically, what has happened to CEO equity incentives? We have calculated both the Jensen–Murphy statistic and the Portfolio Equity Incentive measure for CEOs in the Standard & Poors Execucomp dataset. Incentives from options are derived from the whole stock of stock options held, and not simply the current grant. However, US reporting means that the maturity term and the exercise price of previously granted stocks are not readily available. With respect to the stock of options held by directors at the financial year-end, US companies are required to report the total number of unexercised options held by each director (or top five executives) at the year-end. This does, however, have to be split between those that are currently exercisable and those that, at the year-end, still remained unexercisable. In addition, they must report the end of year intrinsic value of the two categories of the stock of options, calculated as the aggregate value of the difference between the exercise price of the options and the year-end stock price. Because of this valuation method, only options that are in the money are considered in determining the year-end value of the option stock.

However, to calculate the incentives from the stock of options a maturity term and exercise price must be calculated.[21] Given the lack of maturity term information, Murphy (1999) and Conyon and Murphy (2000) assume all outstanding options have a remaining life of seven years. The same authors then make an estimate of the average exercise price based on the intrinsic values and number of options disclosed, and an implicit assumption that all out of the money options have an exercise price equal to the year end stock price.[22] Conyon and Sadler (2001) show that recent estimates of US pay–performance sensitivities and total option values made using these reasonable assumptions for exercise prices and times to maturity will not have produced significant errors. This is done using a 'full information' sample of UK data and then imposing the 'incomplete' US reporting and showing that few statistical biases arise. However, the lack of any bias relies heavily on the proportion of executive options that are out of the money at any one time. A downturn in the US stock markets, or the increased use of premium options, would increase this proportion. The same reasonable assumptions would then lead to significant overestimates of option wealth and option incentives.

Figures 11.3 and 11.4 show the Jensen and Murphy statistic and the Portfolio Equity Incentive measure from 1992 to 2001. The Jensen–Murphy statistic has increased approximately threefold over the 1990s. For instance, in year 2000 a $1000 increase in shareholder wealth is associated with a $6 increase in CEO wealth. Over the course of the 1990s the share of any given increase in shareholder wealth that the CEO was able to extract increased. A similar pattern emerges with the portfolio Equity incentive measure. Over the course of the 1990s the dollar increase in CEO wealth for a percentage increase in shareholder returns increased markedly. Both of these measures are typically understood to reflect more alignment between CEOs and shareholders, since any given increase in the stock price is reflected more closely to changes in CEO Equity wealth. However, as the Jensen–Murphy statistic illustrates, this also means that the CEO captures a greater percentage of any given generated firm wealth.

Table 11.1 is from Conyon and Murphy (2002) and provides additional evidence on stock ownership and incentives of CEOs – both for the United States and the United Kingdom for the fiscal year 1997. The table illustrates that CEOs at UK firms hold an average of $11.4 million in own company shares. This is lower than the near $100 million average holdings among American CEOs. The ownership distribution is, of course, significantly skewed. The median holdings for UK and US executives are $700 000 and $5.3 million, respectively. The table shows that the value of shares held by

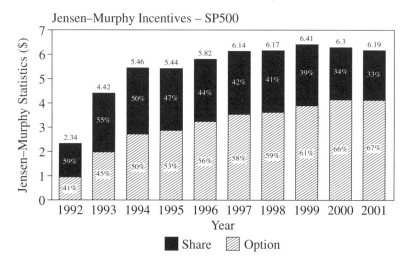

Note: The Jensen–Murphy statistic is defined as:

$$\left(\frac{\text{Shares Held}}{\text{Common Equity}}\right) \times \$1000 + \left(\frac{\text{Options Held}}{\text{Common Equity}}\right) \times \left(\frac{\text{Option}}{\text{Delta}}\right) \times \$1000$$

where $0 < \text{Option Delta} < 1$ is the slope of the Black–Scholes function at the year-end stock price at the fiscal year end. Options held are the CEOs aggregate options. Shares held include common equity-owned, restricted stock and LTIP shares. Data is for CEOs at the S&P 500 Industrials.

Figure 11.3   CEO Jensen–Murphy statistic

the CEO declines with company size in the UK but increases with company size in the US. In the largest firms, US CEOs hold on average shares worth $237 million (median $8.1 million). In contrast UK CEOs hold shares worth $5.5 million (median $500 000).

The CEO's share of ownership is an important metric of the seriousness of the agency problem. The average and median shareholdings for UK CEOs, expressed as a percentage of outstanding shares, are 2.13 per cent and 0.05 per cent, respectively. This is much smaller than the average and median holdings among US CEOs of 3.10 per cent and 0.29 per cent, respectively. In the largest firms, US CEOs hold on average 1.61 per cent of their company's shares (median 0.09 per cent), while UK CEOs hold only 0.21 per cent (median 0.01 per cent). So, whether measured in dollars or percentages, or at averages or medians, share ownership among US CEOs is substantially higher than ownership among UK CEOs for each size and industry group. Consequently, Conyon and Murphy (2000) conclude share ownership mitigates more of the agency problem in the US than in the UK.

Note: The Portfolio Equity Incentive statistic is defined as:

$$\left(\frac{\text{Stock price}}{100}\right) \times \text{Shares Held} + \left(\frac{\text{Stock price}}{100}\right) \times \left(\frac{\text{Option}}{\text{Delta}}\right) \times \text{Options Held}$$

where $0 < \text{Option Delta} < 1$ is the slope of the Black–Scholes function at the year-end stock price at the fiscal year end. Options held are the CEOs' aggregate options. Shares held include common equity-owned, restricted stock and LTIP shares. Data is for CEOs at the S&P 500 Industrials.

Figure 11.4   CEO portfolio equity incentives

Unexercised stock options also provide a direct link between CEO and shareholder wealth, because the value of the options held increases with increases in the share price. The table shows that the average US executive holds options to purchase 1.18 per cent of the company's outstanding shares (median 0.72 per cent), while the average UK executive holds options to purchase only 0.24 per cent (median 0.11 per cent) of his company's shares. Once again, like-for-like comparisons of the top and bottom panels reveal that holdings of previously granted (but as yet unexercised share options) are substantially higher in the US than in the UK for every size and industry group.

The final two columns of the table show the average and median pay–performance sensitivity for CEOs grouped by country, company size, and industry.[23] The average and median pay–performance sensitivities for US CEOs are 4.18 per cent and 1.48 per cent, respectively. This can be compared to UK CEOs where the average pay–performance sensitivity is 2.33 per cent and the median is 0.25 per cent. In the largest firms, a US CEO has

Table 11.1   Summary statistics for stock-based CEO incentives, by company size and industry

Group	Shareholdings ($ millions)		Shareholdings (% of Common)		Option holdings (% of Common)		Pay–performance sensitivity (%)	
	Average	Median	Average	Median	Average	Median	Average	Median
United Kingdom								
All companies	11.4	0.7	2.13	0.05	0.24	0.11	2.33	0.25
By firm sales (millions)								
Less than $125	16.1	2.3	4.38	0.63	0.38	0.21	4.72	1.09
$125 to $300	15.5	1.1	2.55	0.14	0.24	0.14	2.75	0.42
$300 to $920	7.4	0.2	0.76	0.02	0.19	0.12	0.91	0.16
Above $920	5.5	0.5	0.21	0.01	0.10	0.04	0.31	0.05
By industry								
Mining/manufacturing	9.8	0.4	1.91	0.04	0.24	0.14	2.11	0.23
Financial services	9.7	1.4	1.98	0.07	0.19	0.05	2.14	0.31
Utilities	0.3	0.2	0.01	0.00	0.03	0.02	0.05	0.02
Other	15.2	1.2	2.64	0.10	0.28	0.11	2.89	0.37
United States								
All companies	98.4	5.3	3.10	0.29	1.18	0.72	4.18	1.48
By firm sales (millions)								
Less than $125	27.1	3.4	5.32	0.96	1.84	1.37	6.98	3.65
$125 to $300	38.9	4.8	3.94	0.58	1.39	0.94	5.20	2.05
$300 to $920	52.6	4.3	2.36	0.25	1.12	0.70	3.43	1.26
Above $920	236.8	8.1	1.61	0.09	0.62	0.40	2.17	0.56

By industry

Mining/manufacturing	55.0	5.1	2.78	0.31	1.22	0.76	3.87	1.53
Financial services	207.8	12.4	2.25	0.31	0.98	0.52	3.17	1.01
Utilities	10.1	0.9	0.25	0.05	0.35	0.12	0.53	0.16
Other	148.9	6.9	4.63	0.38	1.40	0.95	5.96	2.01

Notes: Derived from Conyon and Murphy (2000, table 5) and published in Conyon and Murphy (2002). UK data from the largest companies in fiscal 1997, ranked by market capitalisation. US data include firms in the S&P 500, the S&P MidCap 400, the S&P SmallCap 600, and companies in S&P supplemental indices. Revenues for financial firms defined as net interest income (banks) and total income (insurance companies). UK pounds are converted to US dollars using the average 1997 exchange rate, 1.63£/$.
The pay–performance sensitivity is defined as:

$$\left(\begin{array}{c} \text{Shares Held as} \\ \text{\% of Firm Shares} \end{array} \right) + \left(\begin{array}{c} \text{Options Held as} \\ \text{\% of Firm Shares} \end{array} \right) \times \left(\begin{array}{c} \text{Option} \\ \text{Delta} \end{array} \right) + \left(\begin{array}{c} \text{LTIP Shares as} \\ \text{\% of Firm Shares} \end{array} \right) \times \left(\begin{array}{c} \text{LTIP} \\ \text{Delta} \end{array} \right)$$

where $0 < \text{Option Delta} < 1$ is the share-weighted-average slope of the Black–Scholes function at the year-end stock price, for options outstanding at the fiscal year end, and (LTIP Delta) = 1.

a median pay–performance sensitivity of 0.56 per cent, more than ten times the effective ownership of their British counterparts.

Recent work suggests the firms that use stock based pay more intensively perform better than otherwise similarly situated firms. Core and Larcker (2002) examine a set of firms that adopted 'target ownership plans' (that is managers are required to own a minimum amount of stock). They found that prior to the adoption of the ownership plan firms had both low equity ownership and low stock price performance. However, managerial equity ownership increased significantly in the subsequent two years. They found that excess accounting returns and stock returns were significantly higher after the plan was adopted. They concluded that the mandating increases in the level of managerial equity ownership yields superior firm performance.

4.   EXPLAINING CEO COMPENSATION

4.1   Optimal Contracting and Managerial Power

Understanding why executive pay contracts are structured as they are, and why pay levels and structures have changed over time is a complicated endeavour (Bebchuk et al., 2002; Core et al., 2002; Murphy, 1999, 2002). Bebchuk et al. (2002) offer a compelling and comprehensive review of the executive compensation literature. Their work is important because it distinguishes between the dominant approach to the study of executive compensation, which they refer to as the 'optimal contracting approach', and their own theory referred to as the 'managerial power approach'. Their review presents considerable evidence in support of the managerial power hypotheses. However, Murphy (2002) offers an alternative explanation of the empirical facts, in the sprit of optimal contracting, entitled 'the perceived cost view'.

4.2   Optimal Contracting

The optimal contracting approach can be characterised as one in which executive compensation contracts are designed to minimise agency costs between senior executives (the agent) and shareholders (the principal).[24] The corporate board, as the steward of shareholder interests, seeks to maximise shareholder value using compensation contracts that are designed to achieve this objective. Options are provided to senior executives to provide incentives and, as the evidence above indicates, options are certainly an increasingly important component of executive compensation. Financial economists have provided much theoretical and empirical evidence in favour of the optimal contracting approach (see Core et al., 2002). It is argued that a number of the salient factors, associated with agency costs or optimal contract design, determine equity-based incentives and so explain the structure of managerial contracts.[25]

Core et al. (2002) argue that firm size is expected to be positively associated with dollar equity incentives. This is because larger firms require more talented managers (Smith and Watts, 1992) who are expected to be relatively wealthy compared to managers in smaller firms (Baker and Hall, 1998). In addition, Core and Guay (1999) argue that owners find it more difficult to monitor managers in larger firms and so are more likely to use equity incentives as a substitute for monitoring. In contrast, Schaefer (1998) argues that incentives measured as a fraction of common equity owned are negatively correlated with firm size because the value of providing incentives for effort does not increase with size as fast as the cost of risk-bearing by the executive. Studies have tended to show that CEO portfolio incentives, measured as dollar value of equity incentives, increase at a decreasing rate with firm size (Core et al., 2002).

Second, Smith and Watts (1992) and Core and Guay (1999) argue that equity incentives and firm growth opportunities (or the firm's investment opportunity set) are positively correlated. The existence and prevalence of growth opportunities within the firm make it more difficult for owners to know what the correct value-maximising actions are for the CEO or, just as importantly, whether managers (agents) are selecting these right actions. Rather than bear higher monitoring costs, owners can substitute monitoring with higher equity incentives to motivate managers. Various studies have shown that equity incentives are positively correlated with a firm's growth opportunity.

Third, firms that operate in less predictable environments are expected to have more equity incentives. Demsetz and Lehn (1985) argue that risky environments increase monitoring costs for firm owners. Rather than tolerate these higher monitoring costs, owners use equity incentives as a substitute to motivate managers. In contrast, managerial risk aversion implies that fewer equity incentives should be used in risky environments. So the benefits from increased equity incentives in risky environments may increase at a decreasing rate (Zajac and Westphal, 1994; Core and Guay, 1999). Again, empirical evidence supports this hypothesis.

Finally, Core and Guay (1999) predict and find that firms use annual grants of options and other types of restricted stock to manage the optimal level of CEO equity incentives. They find that grants of new incentives from options and restricted stock are negatively related to the residuals from a model that purports to explain the optimal equity incentive levels for CEOs. They contend that their 'evidence suggests that firms set optimal equity incentive levels and grant new equity incentives in a manner that is consistent with economic theory'.

Overall, the comprehensive review of the economics, finance and accounting literature leads Core et al. (2002) to conclude that

> in contrast to the allegations of many media pundits (and some academics) who assert that incentive levels are random, arbitrary, or out of equilibrium, empirical evidence suggests that, on average, firms based equity incentives on systematic and theoretically sensible economic factors. Any research that assumes that incentives are systematically 'too high' or 'too low' is effectively assuming incentives are not in equilibrium.

4.3   Managerial Power

Bebchuk, Fried and Walker (2002) contrast the optimal contracting method with their managerial power hypothesis (see also Bebchuk and Jolls, 1999; Cowling, 1982, chapter 4). Their approach takes the perspective that executive insiders are able to influence their own compensation schemes. According to this approach, executive compensation contracts may deviate from optimal contracting because the Board of Directors can become captured by corporate management.[76] To the extent that the Board of Directors does become captured, subject to influence by insiders sympathetic to management, or indeed just ineffective in their oversight function, then deviations from optimal contracting can occur. Pay levels in excess of those that would be optimal for shareholders can then arise. This excess pay constitutes economic rents for the executive.

Bebcheck et al. (2002) introduce the idea of 'outrage costs' and 'camouflage' in building their managerial power theory. Even if executives can influence their pay contracts this does not imply that there are no constraints on their behaviour. Bebchuk et al. (2002, p. 756) state that 'Outrage can be costly to directors and managers by causing embarrassment or reputational harm. . . . The more outrage a compensation arrangement is expected to generate, the more reluctant directors will be to approve the arrangements, and the more hesitant managers will be to propose it in the first instance.' Outrage costs, then, limit managerial rent seeking. Nevertheless, the presence of 'outrage' generates an incentive for corporate insiders to obscure or legitimise their extraction of rents. Bebchuk et al. (2002) term this theoretical concept 'camouflage'. As an example they state (p. 756) 'Indeed, the extensive use of compensation consultants, which might be viewed as an attempt to optimize incentives under the optimal contracting approach, can itself be seen as a means of justifying and legitimizing pay under the managerial approach.'

Prior research from the management literature has focused on the issue of whether managers have power to influence the board and their own compensation (for example Main et al., 1993, and O'Reilly et al., 1988). Lambert, Larker and Weigelt (1993) consider a managerial power model of executive compensation. They extrapolate from Finkelstein's (1992) definition and define Power as the ability of the manager to influence or exert will on the remuneration decisions made by the board of directors or the compensation committee in particular. The sources of managerial power have different origins. For instance Useem (1984) and Hambrick and Mason (1984) propose an 'upper Echelon' theory where corporate CEOs tend to be part of an homogeneous and cohesive group of individuals who share common identities and purposes. In consequence, such elite groups occupy board positions at each others' firms and have a propensity to offer mutual support. Finkelstein and Hambrick (1989) argue that CEO power is derived from personal equity holdings and that this power will be relatively great if outsiders have small ownership stakes. Pfeffer (1981) argues that power can be achieved and enhanced by the nomination and election of 'loyal' individuals to the board of directors. For example, board members appointed by the CEO, or during the tenure of the CEO, or if they have business relationships to the firm, may be less likely to challenge an incumbent CEO.

Branston et al. (2001) too argue '*de facto* control of the corporation rests between an elite group of large shareholders and the company's senior managers/board. This is not to deny that countries differ in how the elites behave, because of variation in influence within the elites and/or because of constraints on the elites freedom for manoeuvre.' The implication of the analysis is that the elite, characterised as corporate insiders, have the power to determine, over a broad spectrum, their compensation and perquisites. Indeed, previous work by Cowling and Sugden (1998) develops a theory of the modern corporation centred precisely on strategic decision-making as the essence of the firm. In contrast to contemporary mainstream economic analysis Cowling and Sugden (1998, p. 64) emphasised the role of power within the firm: 'The power to make strategic decisions can be equated with power to control a firm, where controlling implies the ability to determine broad corporate objectives. Put another way, it may be argued that the power to make strategic decisions is the power to plan the overall direction of production in the firm. This includes the power broadly to determine a firm's geographical orientation, its relationship with rivals, with governments and with its labour force.' This approach sharply contrasts with the optimal contracting approach, and the agency theory of the firm, by placing the power of an elite as central to understanding the nature, direction, purpose and outcomes of the firm.

Earlier theoretical contributions by Cowling (1982) also stressed the importance of power and influence by senior managers and their ability to extract rents. His well-known pricing analysis investigates the dynamics of capitalism, and the development of Kalecki's 'degree of monopoly' theory of industrial pricing. Cowling argues that: 'Managerialism should therefore be identified with the adoption of profit maximizing rules with regard to short-run output-price determination, but also with the absorption of profits within various categories of overhead costs.' CEO compensation is a particular and important instance of an overhead cost. For Cowling (1982, p. 86), the various findings 'strongly suggests that management is able to siphon off a considerable proportion of the extra profits implicit in a higher degree of market control, so that at the limit we might observe firms in monopoly positions apparently being no more profitable than firms in more competitive markets'. This clear 'managerial power' perspective, then, is being developed in contemporary analyses of executive compensation.

Recent developments in the theory of the firm have also attempted to introduce the idea of 'power' by key actors to explain intra-firm organisational structures and outcomes (Cowling and Sugden, 1998). For example, Rajan and Zingales (1998) develop a theory of the firm in the property rights tradition. They argue that certain transactions take place in the firm rather than in the market because the firm offers power to agents who make such firm-specific investments. They suggest that prior research emphasises ownership allocation as the primary mechanism by which the firm does this. The access to critical resources however matters. 'Access can be better than ownership because (i) the power agents get from access is more contingent on their making the right investment and (ii) ownership has adverse effects on the incentive to specialize. The theory explains the importance of internal organization and third-party ownership.' Rajan and Zingales (2001a) develop these ideas. The governance of firms requires that 'entrepreneurs have to provide incentives for employees to protect, rather than steal, the source of organizational rents'. They suggest that: 'Large, steep hierarchies will predominate in physical-capital-intensive industries, and will have seniority-based promotion policies. By contrast, flat hierarchies will prevail in human-capital-intensive industries and will have up-or-out promotion systems.' Contemporary corporate governance theorising, then, aims to explain more how actor ability (traits) determine power within firms and organizational structure. See also Rajan and Zingales (2001b) and Zingales (2000).

Bebchuk et al. (2002) claim, however, that the managerial power and optimal contracting approaches to executive compensation are not mutually exclusive:

> One can take the view that compensation arrangements are shaped both by managerial power and by what would be optimal. The managerial power approach

merely implies that compensation practices cannot be adequately explained by optimal contracting alone. Rather, practices might be adopted that deviate significantly from those suggested by optimal contracting. Under the managerial approach, compensation practices can be fully understood only with careful attention to the role of managerial power.

Adopting this position actually raises many problems for empirical research in executive compensation. At face value, pay practices consistent with the optimal contracting approach might also be consistent with the managerial power approach. This makes statistical identification and hypothesis testing difficult. For example, suppose we observe a positive correlation between the presence of a compensation consultant and a high fraction of stock option pay for the CEO. This could be evidence of managerial power (that is reflecting a combination of 'outrage costs' coupled with 'camouflage') or simply optimal contracting (that is the Board of Directors garnering professional external advice about appropriate incentive structures). These, and other issues, will clearly be food for thought for future research.

Bebchuk et al. (2002) contend that a number of empirical facts regarding executive compensation contracts are actually inconsistent with the optimal contracting theory. These facts, they argue, are more easily explained by the managerial power hypotheses. First, they question why option exercise prices are set to grant date market prices and are not indexed to general market movements. The failure to filter out common stock price increases that are due largely to industry or general market movements, and are unrelated to managers' performance, are more consistent with the managerial power thesis they argue. Second, they question whether the nearly uniform use of at-the-money options is optimal. They contend that there are a multitude of factors which are likely to vary from executive to executive, and from company to company, and from time to time, that should yield a distribution of different exercise prices – which are not observed in practice (see also Core et al., 2002). Consequently, granting options at the money seems unlikely to be optimal. Third, they argue that an optimal contract should prohibit executives from unwinding the risk that is inherent in the option. However, they document a variety of routes that allows executives to hedge options or control the timing of stock sales. Fourth, the phenomena of repricing of options, or resetting when the market declines; or contracts that contain so-called 'reload' provisions they claim are inconsistent with optimal contracting.

Murphy (2002) concedes that the analysis by Bebchuk et al. (2002) is 'comprehensive and provocative, and their evidence that pay practices reflect more than optimal contracting concerns is compelling. Equally compelling is their evidence that most pay decisions are not made by truly independent boards in legitimate arm's-length transactions.' But Murphy is not wholly convinced. 'Ultimately, though, their managerial power view is both problematic as theoretical matter, and too simplistic to explain executive pay practices.' In contrast, Murphy offers evidence that is claimed to be inconsistent with the managerial power view but consistent with his alternative hypothesis termed 'the perceived cost view'.

The perceived cost approach is predicated upon two assumptions. First, because of accounting and cash flow considerations, companies incorrectly perceive the cost of granting options to be far below their economic cost. It is well known that United States accounting procedures mean that for fixed-price options there are no earnings implications for the use of options (Core et al., 2002). Second, risk-averse and non-diversified option holders correctly perceive that the value of options is below the companies' cost of granting options. Murphy shows that these two assumptions are consistent with the evidence put forward by Bebchuk (2002), including the lack of indexed options or relative performance evaluation. Again, this points to the difficulties of firmly testing these different hypotheses.

Murphy (2002, pp. 868–9) concludes there is a kind of observational equivalence between the perceived cost approach and the managerial power approach but that each has different policy implications.

> In particular, mitigating managerial power problems suggests revising corporate governance to require truly independent boards, without any real evidence that such changes would lead to improved corporate performance or more rational compensation decisions. In contrast, mitigating perceived cost problems suggests educating managers and boards on the true economic costs of stock options, imposing accounting charges for option grants, and eliminating the asymmetry between the accounting and tax treatment of executive and employee stock options.

5.   DISCUSSION AND CONCLUSIONS

5.1   Chapter Summary

Corporate governance is generally understood to refer to the complementary mechanisms by which enterprises are owned, controlled and directed. Branston et al. (2001, p. 28) assert that:

> concepts of strategy and governance are central to understanding modern corporations (and other organisations, private and public), their essence, their impact and the design of public policies that affect their activities. Corporations are centres of economic planning; to govern a Corporation is to plan its overall direction, to make its strategic decisions and therefore determine its broad impact.

Corporations are typically governed, *de facto*, by an elite group of share-holders, senior managers and the Board of Directors. A complete understanding of corporate governance should analyse the contributions and behaviour of these key actors. In this chapter I have focused on the topic of executive compensation since this is an important influence on executive behaviour.

We considered the level and structure of CEO compensation and showed that during the 1990s US CEOs saw tremendous growth in the level of their pay. Stock options are an important component of CEO compensation and we considered the important issue of how they should be valued. From the company's perspective a Black–Scholes valuation seems appropriate, but from the executive's perspective she may value these options much less (Hall and Murphy, 2002). We also considered the financial incentives arising from holding equity compensation such as stock options, restricted stock and so on. We analysed two measures of financial incentives that have arisen in the recent economics of executive compensation literature. These statistics are often referred to as the 'pay-for-performance' sensitivity. Our empirical results indicated that pay-for-performance sensitivity had increased markedly throughout the 1990s. Another way of thinking about this, especially from the perspective of the Jensen–Murphy statistic, is that the CEOs' share of any given increase in shareholder value had increased.

Next we highlighted two potentially competing explanations of executive compensation. The dominant approach in the mainstream economics literature is the 'optimal contracting' approach. This views executive compensation as the outcome of a contracting process whereby enterprise owners provide incentives to managers to select the correct shareholder-value maximising actions. In contrast the 'managerial power' hypothesis predicts that executive compensation outcomes are the result of the bargaining power of the CEO versus other actors in the organisation. According to this perspective, CEOs can extract rents suggesting that pay outcomes deviate from what would be considered optimal. These two paradigms provide a useful framework by which future executive compensation research may be conducted.

5.2 Policy Responses

This chapter was motivated by the recent spate of corporate scandals in the United States and so it seems worth briefly indicating some recent policy reactions. Large well-known publicly traded companies (such as Enron and WorldCom) have, it appears, engaged in accounting fraud and irregularities; the auditing community has failed adequately to account for the activities of firms by supplying accurate information to investors; and some senior executives have been involved in egregious and avaricious behavior.

The scandals have resulted in a sharp decline in public trust and confidence in the corporate governance system. The schisms in the corporate governance systems have already initiated reaction. President George W. Bush has signed the Sarbanes–Oxley Act (2002) which is designed to improve corporate accountability, financial disclosure and transparency.[27] It is too soon to judge the consequences of Sarbanes–Oxley – but it does reflect a new institutional framework within which corporations now act.

The Sarbanes–Oxley Act establishes a new independent regulatory body, the Public Company Accounting Oversight Board, to oversee the auditing of publicly-traded firms. This body will have the authority to establish and enforce auditing standards as well as to investigate and discipline accountants, or accounting firms, that violate standards. It requires auditors be hired by, and report to, the firm's audit committee, which sets compensation levels. The accounting firm would be prohibited from auditing corporations where the CEO or other high corporate officials previously worked for the auditor and participated in the companies awarded the previous year. In addition, the measures prohibit accounting firms from providing numerous non-audit services to the same publicly-traded company that they audit. Moreover, the agreement requires corporate CEOs to certify the accuracy of annual and quarterly financial reports, and if the company subsequently is forced to restate earnings, CEOs would have to pay back any bonuses or other compensation they received in the previous 12 months. Also, the measures prohibit companies from providing loans to directors or corporate executives, and it bans directors and executives from buying or selling company stock during the so-called blackout periods. The Act also substantially increases criminal penalties for corporate fraud, establishes new penalties for particular offences and extends the statute of limitations for investors to sue for alleged securities fraud. Overall, Sarbanes–Oxley can be viewed as a legislative response to public distrust of the corporate governance system as it was operating at the beginning of the new millennium.

Corporate governance and executive compensation have continued to be a contentious and important issue. Other formidable moves are afoot to restore confidence in the corporate governance system, the success of which is yet to be determined. The Conference Board recently established a Blue Ribbon commission on Public Trust and Private Enterprise. The 12 persons commission addressed the circumstances leading to recent corporate scandals and declining confidence in US capital markets. The commission's work involves three major areas: executive compensation, corporate governance and auditing and accounting issues. The findings and recommendations of part one (executive compensation) were published on September 17 2002.[28] In its report, Co-Chair John W. Snow said (referring to the malfeasance at Enron, WorldCom and others): 'these egregious failures evidence a clear breach of the basic contract that underlies corporate capitalism'. The commission has proposed various reforms including the expensing of stock options.[29] The pace of change in corporate governance regulatory arrangements is considerable, suggesting that even new academic contributions to governance debates may soon be outdated. However, an extremely useful corporate governance site, which monitors recent changes and provides policy and academic-related material, can be located at http://www.thecorporatelibrary.com/.

5.3 Closing Remarks

Executive compensation issues are at the centre of recent corporate governance deliberations. Recent public and policy debates seem to be informed by a perspective that suggests 'managerial power' (that is that compensation packages appear not to be determined optimally but are instead the result of senior managers engaging in rent-seeking behaviour). Although much of this chapter was concerned with the experience of the United States, the underlying theoretical constructs are applicable to other economies. For example, the rent extraction hypothesis may be also be applied to European or Asian economies but the degree to which rent appropriation is successful will depend upon institutional and other governance structures.

As the policy responses and public debate gather pace, and US stock markets continue to decline, the importance of corporate governance has moved centre-stage. The conclusions of Branston et al. (2001) seem apposite: 'public interest in corporate governance goes much deeper than laws and regulations'. Their perspective suggests that key issues of democracy and citizenship, together with identification of the true purpose and nature of the firm, are central to a complete and comprehensive understanding of corporate governance.

ACKNOWLEDGEMENTS

This chapter was prepared in honour of Professor Keith Cowling's Festschrift. I would like to thank Keith for his advice and encouragement over the years. I am grateful to Mike Waterson for the opportunity to contribute to this volume and for his comments on an earlier draft. I would also like to thank Peter Cappelli, Lerong He, Graham Sadler and Steve Thompson for their comments on this chapter. Lerong He generously assembled the data for me. Financial support from the Center for Human Resources, The Wharton School, is gratefully acknowledged.

NOTES

1. Contemporary reviews of corporate governance theory are provided by Tirole (2001), and Shleifer and Vishny (1997). Recent excellent texts on corporate governance include Vives (2000); Monks and Minow (2000) and McCahery et al. (2002).
2. Keith Cowling (1982, pp. 85–6) analyses the issue of executive compensation in relation to the growth of 'managerialism' and the ability of those at the top of the corporate hierarchy to extract profits. The topic of executive compensation has been superbly treated by Murphy (1999) and more recently by Bebchuk et al. (2002). Core et al. (2002) comprehensively survey the contemporary evidence on the provision of executive equity compensation and incentives. Given the immense set of issues raised within executive compensation literature this chapter will, of necessity, be somewhat partial and selective.
3. ImClone Systems Incorporated is a biopharmaceutical company. The Commission charged that in late December 2001, Waksal received adverse news that the United States Food and Drug Administration (FDA) would soon issue a decision rejecting for review ImClone's pending application to market its cancer treatment, Erbitux. Also, Waksal told this negative information to family members who sold ImClone stock before the news became public and then Waksal himself tried to sell shares of ImClone before the news became public. *Source:* http://www.sec.gov/litigation/litreleases/lr 17559.htm
4. The company also reported that it picked up the ticket for personal expenses including a $6000 shower curtain and a $2200 wastebasket for the indicted former Chairman Dennis Kozlowski's New York apartment. http://www.reuters.com/news_article.jhtml; jsessionid = ZK2BKL5ELZUCACRBAEOCFEY?type = businessnews&StoryID = 1459924
5. *The New York Times* (September 6 2002) reports that 'Along with access to corporate aircraft, mentioned previously in company footnotes, the documents filed by his wife, Jane, describe his use of a Manhattan apartment owned by G.E., floor-level seats to the New York Knicks, courtside seats at the U.S. Open, satellite TV at his four homes and all the costs associated with the New York apartment, from wine and food to laundry, toiletries and newspapers. The privileges, down to certain dining bills at the restaurant Jean Georges in the Manhattan apartment building where he lives, have continued even in retirement, the court papers indicate'. http://www.thecorporatelibrary.com/spotlight/scandals/welch_perks.html
6. In addition, there are several UK studies including Ezzamel and Watson (1998), Conyon and Leech (1994), Conyon and Murphy (2000), Conyon and Peck (1998), Conyon et al. (2000), Conyon et al. (1995), Cosh (1975), Cosh and Hughes (1987, 1997a,b), Main (1993), Main et al. (1996).
7. SEC Release numbers 33–6962, 34–31327 and IC-19032 pertaining to Regulation S-K. The new regulations were published in the Federal Register 57, No. 204 (1992): 48126–48159.
8. Other economies, too, are beginning to be more open about the pay packages received by the corporate elite. The UK has significant disclosure of (option) compensation of individual directors mandated by the London Stock Exchange rules which incorporate the recommendations of the Hampel Committee (1998). Detailed disclosure in Canada was authorised in 1993 by the Ontario Securities Regulation, and covers all publicly traded companies in the province of Ontario (including all companies on the Toronto Stock Exchange). Other countries (such as Germany and Japan) provide some but not complete information on board compensation.
9. US stock options vest with the passage of time. UK stock (or share) options also vest with time but typically have performance criteria attached as well (see Conyon and Murphy, 2000; Conyon et al., 2000). Also, as discussed in Conyon and Murphy (2000), UK option granting is typically governed much more by institutionalised considerations (such as the Association of British Insurers guidelines) relative to the US firms. For instance, UK firms used to grant options in terms of a multiple of base salary for UK executives – a procedure that is changing.

10.   Suppose we define a standard option where S the share price = $100; X the exercise or strike price = $100; T the time to maturity = 10 years; q the dividend yield = $2\frac{1}{2}$ per cent; r the risk-free rate of interest = 7 per cent; and σ the standard deviation of returns on the share = 25 per cent. These parameters correspond reasonably well to the characteristics of an executive stock option that is granted at the money (that is $S = X$) (Core et al., 2002; Murphy, 1999; Hall, 2000). This standard option has a Black–Scholes expected value of $36.12. In calculating these figures the risk-free and dividend variables are the annualised not the instantaneous rates.

11.   It is also worth stressing that (a) deep out of the money options ($X > S$) have low call values, (b) deep in the money options ($S > X$) have high call values that are near the intrinsic value of the asset ($S - X$), and (c) for an at the money option, that is in the region $S = X$, the option has little intrinsic value (equal to zero for at-the-money option) but positive option value. This refutes the common misconception that at the money options (or out of the money options) have no value since $S - X = 0$ (or $S < X$). Figure 11.1 illustrates that because there is a probability of the option ending up in the money, the option still has value even if the intrinsic value is zero.

12.   Hall and Murphy (2002) employ a certainty-equivalence framework to investigate the cost, value and pay-for-performance sensitivity of non-tradable options held by undiversified, risk-averse executives. They derive 'executive value' lines which are the risk-adjusted counterpart to the Black–Scholes function plotted in Figure 11.1. They distinguish between the value to the executive and the cost to the firm. The analysis provides insights into various issues including executive views about Black–Scholes values. The modelling builds upon the prior work of Lambert, Larcker and Verrecchia (1991).

13.   The standard agency model, whose solution results in the 'incentive intensity principle' (Milgrom and Roberts, 1992), solves a moral hazard model between the principal and agent by imposing a linear compensation contract structure. Explaining convexity, and importantly the optimal degree of convexity, in the pay contract is clearly an important issue.

14.   It is important to stress that the other inputs to the Black–Scholes function also give rise to systematic changes in the value of option that can help boards understand the incentives arising from options. Increasing the exercise price is equivalent to reducing the stock price. They both reduce the moneyness of the option. So, as the exercise price increases the value of the option decreases. Increasing the time to maturity increases the likelihood that the option will end up in the money. So, as the maturity term increases the call values increases. Paying dividends has the effect of reducing the stock appreciation (that is a $100 dollar share that may have risen to $105 but pays a dividend of $5 is still $100). Increasing the dividend yield reduces the expected stock price and hence reduces the value of the option. Accordingly, CEOs who hold options, and who care about stock appreciation, have incentives to lower the dividend rate as this increases option values. Increasing the volatility increases the likelihood that the option will end up in the money. So, the option value increases with volatility. Hall (2000) discusses these issues further in relation to executive pay. A general treatment is provided in Cox and Rubenstein (1985).

15.   This procedure uses an expected life of the option equal to 70 per cent of the actual term, and truncates unusually high or low volatilities and unusually high or low dividend yields.

16.   Incentives can be generated in a myriad of ways. Here we are concerned with equity incentives. But another important related area is dismissal incentives for poor performance. Such incentives may substitute for equity incentives since CEOs who do not select the correct actions face high dismissal probabilities. We do not cover this related work in this chapter. Murphy (1999) provides a review of central issues. Conyon and Florou (2003) provide recent evidence for the UK.

17.   For the standard option that we defined earlier the option delta is 0.64.

18.   One common misconception that sometimes arises is that common equity provides better incentives than options. It is based on the idea that since a dollar increase in the stock price leads to a dollar increase in the value of common equity, but a dollar increase in the stock price leads to a less than one-dollar increase in the value of an option,

common equity provides better incentives. This is wrong since it ignores the leverage effect of options (Hall, 2000). The leverage principle of stock options says that for the same money outlay, boards of directors can provide more options than common equity. Consider the cost to the company of granting one share. It is equal to the share price, which for our example is set at \$100. Define a standard call option with the following parameter inputs: $S = \$100$, $X = \$100$, $T = 10$, $q = 2.5$, $r = 7$ per cent, $\sigma = 25$ per cent. The cost to the company of granting one stock option (for the standard option issued at the money) is \$36.12 (that is the Black–Scholes value). For the same initial outlay the company could, however, have purchased 2.77 stock options (that is \$100/\$36.12). The aggregate incentive from holding the 2.77 stock options is therefore higher than holding common equity. It is equal to the option delta times the number of options purchased (that is $2.77 \times 0.65 = \$1.88$). So, for the same cost of \$100 to the company, executive incentives are either \$1 if the company chooses to grant ordinary stock or \$1.77 if the company allocates stock options. This illustrates that option leverage can yield greater incentives than the use of equity alone.

19. It has been used by Conyon and Murphy (2000), Demsetz and Lehn (1985), Jensen and Murphy (1990a, b), Yermack (1995).

20. Suppose there are two firms, A and B. The total number of shares (M) in firm A is 10000000 and in firm B it is 25000000. The stock price (S) in firm A is \$5 whereas the stock price in firm B is \$8. So total shareholder wealth ($W = S \times M$) is \$50000000 in firm A and \$200000000 in firm B. Suppose that the total number of options (N) held by the CEO in each firm is the same and equal to 1000000 and that the stock option delta (δ) is the same too and equal to 0.60. The Jensen–Murphy statistic [$\delta \times N \times (\$1000/M)$] for firm A is \$60 and it is \$24 in firm B. In contrast the Portfolio Equity Incentive measure [$\delta \times N \times (S/100)$] is \$30000 in firm A and \$48000 in firm B. The question then is which company is providing the better financial incentive? Both companies offer identical stock option compensation packages to their CEO. What differs is the size of the company measured by the market value/shareholder wealth. The answer depends on how CEOs are thought to affect firm value. If one believes it is just as easy for the CEO of Company A to raise the value of his or her company by \$1000 as it is for the CEO of Company B, then one needs to consider the incentive for doing just that, that is the Jensen and Murphy statistic. This may be a reasonable assumption since one could argue that to increase the firm value by \$1000, each company needs to take on a project with a net present value of positive \$1000 and both companies have an equal opportunity to do that. Clearly, then, Company A is providing the best option equity incentives from this perspective. It will reward the CEO \$60 for a \$1000 increase whereas the CEO of Company B gets only \$24. It could be argued that it is in fact easier for the CEO of Company B to raise the \$1000. Such a gain would represent an increase of only 0.0005 per cent in the value of Company B, whereas for Company A, the same \$1000 gain is an increase of 0.002 per cent. The belief about financial incentives in this context is that it is a lot easier for a large firm to increase its shareholder value by \$1000 than it is for a smaller firm. Thus, one might argue that a 'fairer' way to compare equity incentives is to determine what each CEO gets for increasing his or her firm value by the same percentage, say 1 per cent. This is what the percentage returns statistic does. Based on this, Company B now has the better financial incentive/payoff for its executive. If one is interested only in a single company then the Jensen–Murphy statistic is simply a transformation of the portfolio equity incentives measure. Specifically, the Jensen–Murphy statistic is equal to the portfolio equity incentive statistic divided by shareholder wealth multiplied by 10000.

21. Hall and Liebman (1998) attempted to overcome this problem by tracking CEOs' option holdings over time using consecutive year proxy statements to record all grants and exercises. However, because of the limited data on exercised options supplied by US companies, even this highly labour-intensive method still requires a number of assumptions to be made, resulting in errors in the estimates of the final stock of options held (see Hall and Liebman, 1998, p. 689). Similarly, Core and Guay (1999) use hand-collected data from up to 10 years of proxy statements to provide a more accurate estimate of the option portfolio's sensitivity to price. But once again the authors recognise that assump-

tions are required to determine which previously granted options have been exercised and which remain in the portfolio.

22. The intrinsic value (V) of the options is given as N times $\text{Max}\{(S-X),0\}$, where N is the total number of options held, S is the year-end share price and X is the average exercise price. Since S is known and both N and V are supplied, the average exercise price of the unexercised options can be calculated as $X = S = V/N$.
23. This is simply the Jensen–Murphy statistic expressed as a percentage rather than as a $1000 dollar change. Instead this represents fractional ownership. See Conyon and Murphy (2000).
24. The voluminous literature on optimal contracting cannot be adequately covered here. The important contributions used as underpinnings of the executive compensation literature are provided in Hallock and Murphy (1999). Important contributions include Mirrlees (1976, 1997, 1999), Holmstrom and Milgrom (1987), and Holmstrom (1982).
25. Demsetz and Villalonga (2001) argue that ownership structure and performance are endogenous. They find no statistically significant relationship between ownership structure and firm performance. This is consistent with a perspective that diffuse ownership, while it may cause some agency problems, also yields compensating advantages that generally offset such problems.
26. The authors assert that managerial power lies at the heart of the considerable amount of the public criticism that compensation levels and practices have attracted, but also note the managerial power approach generally has not really been sufficiently developed.
27. The Sarbanes–Oxley Act 2002 can be accessed at http://news.findlaw.com/hdocs/docs/gwbush/sarbanesoxley072302.pdf and is summarized at http://www.aicpa.org/info/sarbanes_oxley_summary.htm; or http://www.theiia.org/iia/guidance/issues/sarbanes-oxley.pdf. (visited 25 September, 2002).
28. The press release and report can be downloaded at: http://www.conference-board.org/utilities/pressDetail.cfm?press_ID=1473 (visited 25 September 2002).
29. See http://www.conference-board.org/utilities/pressDetail.cfm?press_ID=1473 (visited 25 September, 2002).

REFERENCES

Baker, G.P. and B.J. Hall (1998), 'CEO incentives and firm size', Harvard Business School Working Paper 99–060.
Bebchuk, L.A. and C. Jolls (1999), 'Managerial value diversion and shareholder wealth', *Journal of Law Economics and Organization*, **15**, 487–502.
Bebchuk, L.A., J.M. Fried and D.I. Walker (2002), 'Managerial power and rent extraction in the design of executive compensation', *University of Chicago Law Review*, **69**, 751–846.
Black, F. and M. Scholes (1973), 'The pricing of options and corporate liabilities', *Journal of Political Economy*, **81**, 637–54.
Branston, R.J., K. Cowling and R. Sugden (2001), 'Corporate Governance and the Public Interest', Warwick University Department of Economics Working Paper.
Conyon, M.J. and A. Florou (2003), 'Top executive dismissal, ownership and corporate performance', *Accounting and Business Research*, forthcoming.
Conyon, M.J. and D. Leech (1994), 'Top pay, company performance and corporate governance', *Oxford Bulletin of Economics and Statistics*, **56**, 229–47.
Conyon, M.J. and K.J. Murphy (2000), 'The prince and the pauper? CEO pay in the United States and United Kingdom', *Economic Journal*, **110**, F640–F671.
Conyon, M.J. and K.J. Murphy (2002), 'Stock-Based Compensation', in Joseph McCahery and Luc Renneboog (eds), *Convergence and Diversity in Corporate Governance Regimes and Capital Markets*, Oxford: Oxford University Press.

Conyon, M.J. and S.L. Peck (1998), 'Board control, remuneration committees, and top management compensation', *Academy of Management Journal*, **41**, 146–57.

Conyon, M.J. and G.V. Sadler (2001), 'CEO compensation, option incentives, and information disclosure', *Review of Financial Economics*, **33**, 251–77.

Conyon, M., P. Gregg and S. Machin (1995), 'Taking care of business – executive compensation in the United Kingdom', *Economic Journal*, **105**, 704–14.

Conyon, M.J., S.I. Peck, L.E. Read and G.V. Sadler (2000), 'The structure of executive compensation contracts: UK evidence', *Long Range Planning*, **33**, 478–503.

Core, J. and W. Guay (1999), 'The use of equity grants to manage optimal equity incentive levels', *Journal of Accounting and Economics*, **28**, 151–84.

Core, J.E. and D.F. Larcker (2002), 'Performance consequences of mandatory increases in executive stock ownership', *Journal of Financial Economics*, **64**, 317–40.

Core, J.E., W.R. Guay and D.F. Larcker (2002), 'Executive equity compensation and incentives: a survey', *Economic Policy Review*, forthcoming.

Cosh, A. (1975), 'Remuneration of chief executives in the United Kingdom', *Economic Journal*, **85**, 75–94.

Cosh, A.D. and A. Hughes (1987), 'The anatomy of corporate control – directors, shareholders and executive remuneration in giant United States and UK corporations', *Cambridge Journal of Economics*, **11**, 285–313.

Cosh, A. and A. Hughes (1997a), 'Executive remuneration, executive dismissal and institutional shareholdings', *International Journal of Industrial Organization*, **15**, 469–92.

Cosh, A. and A. Hughes (1997b), 'The changing anatomy of corporate control and the market for executives in the United Kingdom', *Journal of Law and Society*, **24**, 104–23.

Cowling, K. (1982), *Monopoly Capitalism*, London and Basingstoke: Macmillan Press.

Cowling, K. and R. Sugden (1998), 'The essence of the modern corporation: markets, strategic decision-making and the theory of the firm', *Manchester School*, **66**, 59–86.

Cox, J.C. and M. Rubenstein (1985), *Option Markets*, Englewood Cliffs, NJ: Prentice Hall.

Demsetz, H. and K. Lehn (1985), 'The structure of corporate ownership – causes and consequences', *Journal of Political Economy*, **93**, 1155–77.

Demsetz, H. and B. Villalonga (2001), 'Ownership structure and corporate performance', *Journal of Corporate Finance*, **7**, 209–33.

Ezzamel, M. and R. Watson (1998) 'Market comparison earnings and the bidding-up of executive cash compensation: evidence from the United Kingdom', *Academy of Management Journal*, **41**, 221–31.

Finkelstein, S. (1992), 'Power in top management teams – dimensions, measurement, and validation', *Academy of Management Journal*, **35**, 505–38.

Finkelstein, S. and D.C. Hambrick (1989), 'Chief executive compensation – a study of the intersection of markets and political processes', *Strategic Management Journal*, **10**, 121–34.

Hall, B.J. (2000), 'What you need to know about stock options', *Harvard Business Review*, **78**, 121–9.

Hall, B.J. and J.B. Liebman (1998), 'Are CEOs really paid like bureaucrats?', *Quarterly Journal of Economics*, **113**, 653–91.

Hall, B.J. and K.J. Murphy (2000), 'Optimal exercise prices for executive stock options', *American Economic Review*, **90**, 209–14.

Hall, B.J. and K.J. Murphy (2002), 'Stock options for undiversified executives', *Journal of Accounting and Economics*, **33**, 3–42.

Hallock, K.F. and K.J. Murphy (1999), *The Economics of Executive Compensation*, Cheltenham, UK and Northampton, MA: Edward Elgar Publishing.

Hambrick, D.C. and P.A. Mason (1984), 'Upper echelons – the organization as a reflection of its top managers', *Academy of Management Review*, **9**, 193–206.

Hampel, R. (1998), *Committee on Corporate Governance: Final Report*, London: Gee Publishing.

Holmstrom, B. (1982), 'Moral hazard in teams', *Bell Journal of Economics*, **13**, 324–40.

Holmstrom, B. and P. Milgrom (1987), 'Aggregation and linearity in the provision of intertemporal incentives', *Econometrica*, **55**, 303–28.

Jensen, M.C. and K.J. Murphy (1990a), 'CEO incentives – it's not how much you pay, but how', *Harvard Business Review*, **68**, 138–49.

Jensen, M.C. and K.J. Murphy (1990b), 'Performance pay and top-management incentives', *Journal of Political Economy*, **98**, 225–64.

Lambert, R.A. and D.F. Larcker (2001), 'How employees value (often incorrectly) their stock options', University of Pennsylvania, The Wharton School.

Lambert, R.A., D.F. Larcker and R.E. Verrecchia (1991), 'Portfolio considerations in valuing executive compensation', *Journal of Accounting Research*, **29**, 129–49.

Lambert, R.A., D.F. Larcker and K. Weigelt (1993), 'The structure of organizational incentives', *Administrative Science Quarterly*, **38**, 438–61.

Main, B.G.M. (1993), 'Pay in the boardroom – practices and procedures', *Personnel Review*, **22**, 3–14.

Main, B.G.M., A. Bruce and T. Buck (1996), 'Total board remuneration and company performance', *Economic Journal*, **106**, 1627–44.

Main, B.G.M., C.A. O'Reilly and J. Wade (1993), 'Top executive pay – tournament or teamwork', *Journal of Labor Economics*, **11**, 606–28.

McCahery, J.A., P. Moertland, T. Raaijmakers and L. Renneboog (2002), *Corporate Governance Regimes: Convergence and Diversity*, Oxford: Oxford University Press.

Milgrom, P. and J. Roberts (1992), *Economics, Organizations, and Management*, Englewood Cliffs, NJ: Prentice Hall.

Mirrlees, J.A. (1976), 'Optimal structure of incentives and authority within an organization', *Bell Journal of Economics*, **7**, 105–31.

Mirrlees, J.A. (1997), 'Information and incentives: the economics of carrots and sticks', *Economic Journal*, **107**, 1311–29.

Mirrlees, J.A. (1999), 'The theory of moral hazard and unobservable behaviour: Part I', *Review of Economic Studies*, **66**, 3–21.

Monks, R. and N. Minow (2000), *Corporate Governance*, 2nd Edition, Oxford: Basil Blackwell.

Murphy, K.J. (1985), 'Corporate performance and managerial remuneration – an empirical analysis', *Journal of Accounting and Economics*, **7**, 11–42.

Murphy, K.J. (1999), 'Executive Compensation', in O. Ashenfelter and D. Card (eds), *Handbook of Labor Economics*, Amsterdam and New York: North-Holland.

Murphy, K.J. (2002), 'Explaining executive compensation: managerial power versus the perceived cost of stock options', *University of Chicago Law Review*, **69**, 847–69.

O'Reilly, C.A., B.G. Main and G.S. Crystal (1988), 'CEO compensation as tournament and social comparison – a tale of 2 theories', *Administrative Science Quarterly*, **33**, 257–74.

Pfeffer, J. (1981), *Power in Organizations*, Boston, MA: Pitman.

Rajan, R.G. and L. Zingales (1998), 'Power in a theory of the firm', *Quarterly Journal of Economics*, **113**, 387–432.

Rajan, R.G. and L. Zingales (2001a), 'The firm as a dedicated hierarchy: a theory of the origins and growth of firms', *Quarterly Journal of Economics*, **116**, 805–51.

Rajan, R.G. and L. Zingales (2001b), 'The influence of the financial revolution on the nature of firms', *American Economic Review*, **91**, 206–11.

Schaefer, S. (1998), 'The dependence of pay-performance sensitivity on the size of the firm', *Review of Economics and Statistics*, **80**, 436–43.

Shleifer, A. and R.W. Vishny (1997), 'A survey of corporate governance', *Journal of Finance*, **52**, 737–83.

Smith, C.W. and R.M. Stulz (1985), 'The determinants of firms hedging policies', *Journal of Financial and Quantitative Analysis*, **20**, 391–405.

Smith, C.W. and R.L. Watts (1992), 'The investment opportunity set and corporate financing, dividend, and compensation policies', *Journal of Financial Economics*, **32**, 263–92.

Tirole, J. (2001), 'Corporate governance', *Econometrica*, **69**, 1–35.

Useem, M. (1984), *The Inner Circle*, Oxford: Oxford University Press.

Vives, X. (ed.) (2000), *Corporate Governance: Theoretical and Empirical Perspectives*, Cambridge: Cambridge University Press.

Yermack, D. (1995), 'Do corporations award CEO stock-options effectively?', *Journal of Financial Economics*, **39**, 237–269.

Zajac, E.J. and J.D. Westphal (1994), 'The costs and benefits of managerial incentives and monitoring in large US corporations – when is more not better?', *Strategic Management Journal*, **15**, 121–42.

Zingales, L. (2000), 'In search of new foundations', *Journal of Finance*, **55**, 1623–53.

12. Advertising and the evolution of market structure in the US car industry[1]

Paul A. Geroski and M. Mazzucato

1. INTRODUCTION[2]

It is widely believed that an industry with high levels of sunk costs is likely to be more highly concentrated than one with lower levels of sunk cost (Sutton, 1991). This proposition is sometimes taken to suggest that an increase in sunk costs will lead to a rise in concentration. When expressed in this form, this proposition would, for example, lead one to expect that the escalation of advertising which occurred at the end of the 1970s in the US car industry – an increase of more than eightfold (in nominal terms) from the early-middle 1970s through to the late-middle 1990s – would have increased the level of concentration in the industry. In fact, concentration actually fell during that period.

To understand what might underlie this puzzle, one needs to recognise that advertising can have two rather different effects on competition. On the one hand, advertising expenditures are both fixed and (usually) sunk, and this can serve to limit entry and reduce the number of firms that can profitably operate in a market. On the other hand, firms can use advertising to attract attention to their products and induce switching behaviour by consumers. It is, therefore, possible that advertising can also facilitate entry, and that entrants who attempt to advertise their way into a market may partially or even totally displace incumbents, gaining enough sales revenue to cover their fixed costs even in a stagnant market. If this happens, one will observe both an increase in total industry advertising (particularly if incumbents respond to advertising-led entry by increasing their own advertising) and a fall in market concentration. Roughly speaking, this is what seems to have happened in the US car industry in the post-war period.

To understand what produced this apparently perverse outcome in the US car industry, we need to understand how advertising affects consumer demand. This raises some tricky issues, since simply putting advertising in the consumer's utility function is not a satisfactory way forward. In this chapter, we outline a simple model of competition where advertising can, in principle, facilitate entry (at least temporarily). Although the model has some special assumptions, it is not a wholly implausible description of what happens in the car market. Product quality is the key driver of consumer choice in this model, while advertising plays a role in directing consumers to alternatives should they choose to switch from low to high quality products. Although it has no effect on preferences or on demand in the long run, advertising does, in this model, create an opportunity for entrants to attract buyers in the short run and, if their products are of high enough quality, to keep them in the market in the long run. The outcome of the model is a relationship between market and advertising shares and, therefore, it effectively provides the link between advertising activity and movements in industry concentration which we are seeking.

In Section 2 below, we spell out the model of the relationship between market and advertising shares that we will use in the empirical analysis, and in Section 3, we apply it to a very thin data set describing the US car industry in the post-war period. Since most of the entrants involved in these events were foreign-owned producers, the simplest level at which one can observe this competitive process in this industry is by aggregating the data into two 'players': all domestic producers and all foreign producers. We report results at this level of aggregation, and then show that they are also observable at the firm level by applying the model to seven leading firms in the market (three domestic and four foreign-owned). In Section 4, we pursue two further issues which arise from using the model to interpret the data: the dynamics of the escalation of advertising which occurred with entry, and the timing of the entry challenge itself. Section 5 summarises the results and notes a number of caveats.

2.   MARKET SHARES AND ADVERTISING

To understand how an advertising war might lead to changes in market structure, we need to understand how advertising affects demand.

2.1 Advertising Shares and Market Shares

Consider the following stylisation of consumer choice. Cars are an experience good, but the characteristics of particular models change more often than particular consumers purchase them. As a consequence, there is only a limited amount of relevant (that is, experiential) information about particular models available to consumers prior to purchase. Further, the information that a user accumulates about a particular car through own use is always incomplete. Accurately measuring the user value of some pertinent characteristic (for example durability, or how it performs in adverse circumstances) requires extensive usage, and changes in characteristics over time means that this year's new car is not exactly comparable to last year's version of the same car. The implication is that dissatisfaction with last year's car will not necessarily lead to switching behaviour when the consumer purchases a new car this year; nor, for that matter, will satisfaction necessarily guarantee repeat purchasing.

Some notation will help us to express this more precisely. Suppose that car j has a level of 'quality' $\lambda_j (>1)$. By construction, λ_j measures 'quality' in terms of repeat purchase: a 'high quality' car will generate a higher level of repeat purchasing than a 'low quality' car. A consumer who purchases j in t will, by period $t+1$, have formed a view about whether s/he is satisfied or not. Suppose that if s/he is satisfied, s/he will repeat the purchase again in t with probability $(1 - 1/\lambda_j)$; otherwise s/he will switch to another car with probability $1/\lambda_j$. The key question is what determines the choice of a new car if the consumer elects to switch in period $t+1$. If firms do not compete on price and if quality is difficult to observe with any accuracy, then it is hard to see a 'rational' basis for choosing between different brands.[3] In these circumstances, consumers may turn first to the alternatives which they are most aware of. There are many ways to measure 'awareness', but one obvious possibility is in terms of relative advertising intensity. If the level of advertising of car k, A_k, is high relative to total market advertising, then many consumers are likely to be aware of car k and some number of them will opt for k if they become dissatisfied with car j (and more will do so than for some other car i which is advertised less intensively than car k).[4] If all consumers behave in this way, it turns out that in the long-run market shares will be proportional to advertising shares,

$$Q_j/Q = \theta_j A_j/A, \qquad (12.1)$$

where Q_j is the output of firm j, A_j is total advertising by firm j, Q is total industry output, A is total industry advertising and $\theta_j \equiv \lambda_j / \Sigma \lambda_j (A_j/A)$ is a measure of the relative 'quality' of car j.[5]

It is worth making three observations about (12.1). First, advertising has both a pro- and an anti-competitive effect in this model. On the one hand, an entrant who can come in with a large enough advertising share can claim a place in the market. However, as that entrant tries to do so (that is, as it advertises and as incumbents respond), the total volume of advertising in the market will rise, and this, in turn, increases the cost of 'acquiring' an advertising share of any given size. Clearly, this disadvantages entrants (because it raises the fixed and sunk costs of entry), and closes the window of opportunity which had originally facilitated their entry. In other words, the dynamics of entry competition may mean that the pro-competitive effect of advertising is likely to be transitory; that is that the advertising directly and indirectly caused by the arrival of entrants (and the advertising war it sparks off) may lead to a deterioration in the initially favourable market conditions which discourages or deters subsequent entrants.

The second observation is that advertising does not work in a vacuum. In this model, advertising attracts buyers who are dissatisfied with their existing choice: the driver of switching is product quality, not advertising. A firm that advertises (relatively) heavily but sells a poor quality product will attract many new buyers (who are dissatisfied with other low quality products) but will also lose many existing buyers (who become dissatisfied with the low quality of the product). By contrast, a high quality firm that does not advertise will retain most of its existing customers but will not attract many new ones, and its market share may be higher or lower than a low quality/high advertising firm (its customer churn will, however, be lower). The model predicts that two firms with the same market share but different levels of quality will, of necessity, display different levels of advertising, and that the low quality/high advertising firm will experience more churn amongst its consumers than the higher quality firm will.

Third, it is clear from (12.1) that there are, in principle, many different vectors of advertising across firms which sustain the same vector of market shares: if the levels of advertising by all firms in any particular equilibrium were multiplied by the same amount, market shares would remain unchanged. This means that the profits of all firms at any particular equilibrium could be improved if the advertising of each fell by the same proportional amount (since this would have no effect other than reducing the fixed costs of each firm). It is not entirely clear how firms might bring about this reduction, although it is at least conceivable that a formal agreement might work. More likely is some kind of tacit understanding. Suppose that an industry is composed of a group of incumbents who are undisturbed by entry and display relatively constant market shares over a long period of time. In such a setting, mutual awareness and a common interest in keeping advertising expenditures under control might yield an outcome like (12.1) in which relatively modest levels of advertising support market shares for each incumbent firm. The interesting thing about this outcome is that it is liable to be rather unstable. The more successful such a tacit (or, perhaps, formal) understanding is in reducing total industry advertising, the more likely it is (ceteris paribus) that entrants will be attracted to the market: after all, the lower is total industry advertising, the less expensive it is to 'purchase' market share through advertising. This, of course, may set off an advertising war as incumbents respond to the encroachments of entrants, driving the industry to a new, high advertising equilibrium.

Our final task is to translate (12.1) into an empirical model. Consumer behaviour of the type discussed above only generates (12.1) as a long-run relationship, and it is easy to believe that (12.1) might not literally hold at every data point even if the model is correct. One easy way to generalise (12.1) to allow for this is to write it in an error correction framework,

$$\Delta MS_j(t) = \varphi_0 MSj(t-1) + \varphi_1 ASj(t-1) + \varphi_2 \Delta MS_j(t-1)$$
$$+ \varphi_3 \Delta AS_j(t-1) + \mu_j(t), \tag{12.2}$$

where $MS_j \equiv Q_j/Q$, $AS_j \equiv A_j/A$ and $\mu_j(t)$ is a white noise error. Since, in equilibrium, all of the first difference terms are zero, (12.2) yields an estimate of $\theta = -\varphi_1/\varphi_0$. However, it may be unwise to assume as a matter of course that θ is a constant: for example, very large shifts in advertising shares between firms with very different quality levels (or changes in any number of pertinent exogenous variables) may cause θ to drift over time. In the absence of any observed measures of 'quality', the simplest extension of the model that allows one to control for this would be to let the parameter φ_1 evolve over time. If, for example, φ_1 were a linear function of a deterministic time trend, then (12.2) would include an additional term in $AS_j(t-1)*T$, where T is the time trend.

There are several useful things that one can learn from estimating (12.2), but the main one centres on establishing whether or not $\theta = 0$. Since the left-hand side of (12.2) describes movements in market structure over time, $\theta = 0$ corresponds to a situation where advertising has no effect on market concentration (the null hypothesis being that market shares and, therefore, levels of market concentration, evolve randomly). Going to the other extreme of the parameter space, if all firms enjoy the same repeat probability (and, therefore, 'quality' in this model), $\theta = 1$ and market shares and advertising shares are identical, which effectively means that movements in the level of market concentration are completely determined by advertising decisions.

3. THE US CAR INDUSTRY IN THE POST-WAR PERIOD

The data set that we will be using describes the evolution of market shares in the post-war US car industry. It basically consists of information on output and advertising for almost all firms active in this industry for just over 40 years. This provides information on market and advertising shares, but, as will become clear, the data set lacks the kinds of exogenous variables which one would need to track movements in 'quality' with accuracy. The data enable us to infer some useful things about the properties of the θ_j across firms and over time, but that is about all.

Our first step is to discuss the data and provide an overview of events. Then we look at the relationship between market shares and advertising shares using (12.1) and (12.2), aggregating the data into a particularly simple form that reduces the industry to two players: domestic and foreign firms. Not only is this a roughly accurate characterisation of the different groups of firms apparently responsible for the events we observe, but using a two player model makes it much easier to understand the dynamics of the market. We then disaggregate the data, and re-estimate the model on firm-specific data for seven of the largest firms in the market (three domestic firms and four foreign firms). This enables us to enrich our account of the dynamics that unfolded after entry into this market, but it also shows just how robust the two-player characterisation is.

3.1   The Data[6]

The two features of the post-war evolution of the car market over the period 1954–96 that we are most interested in here are displayed in Figure 12.1. The first is that during the first 15 or so years of the sample period total industry advertising intensity was stable at relatively low levels. It crept up gently through to the middle 1970s before escalating very rapidly through the 1980s and into the 1990s: the level of nominal advertising expenditures rose by a factor of 8.73 between 1976 and 1996; real advertising expenditures (that is, nominal advertising expenditures divided by the consumer price index) rose by a factor of 3.52. The second interesting feature of the data is that total industry advertising and industry advertising intensity (that is, total advertising divided by sales) and the three firm concentration ratio (defined here as the sum of the shares of Ford, GM and Chrysler) are negatively correlated over the period. Much the same correlation applies between total industry advertising and industry advertising intensity and the Herfindahl. The correlation between total industry advertising levels and these two concentration measures is: -0.8622 for the three firm concentration ratio, and -0.7529 for the Herfindahl, while that between each concentration measure and industry advertising intensity is: -0.7212 and -0.8882 respectively.

It is, of course, possible that the apparent correlation between concentration and advertising shown in Figure 12.1 is spurious. One obvious possibility is that market size might have increased during the period, making increases in advertising profitable for firms and, at the same time but for

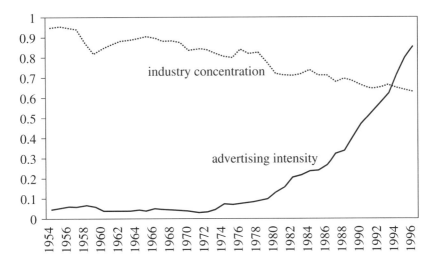

Figure 12.1 Industry advertising intensity and the three firm concentration ratio

entirely different reasons, deconcentrating the market by creating new market segments for fringe or entrant firms to colonize. However, there is no easily discernible upward or downward trend in total industry sales from the mid-1970s until the end of the period (although there are very substantial cyclical fluctuations). The correlations between market size and the two measures of concentration are: -0.4931 and -0.3367 (which is what one expects), while the correlation between total sales and total advertising is only 0.1703.

In fact, it is more likely that the events described on Figure 12.1 were caused by entry. As is well known, this period saw foreign-owned carmakers enter the US market on a fairly large scale and make serious inroads into the share of the top three US firms. To see the role played by these entrants, it is necessary to disaggregate the data. We focus on two groups: the three US producers (GM, Ford and Chrysler, collectively labelled *domestic* producers) and the major non-US- (that is *foreign-*) owned players (specifically: Honda, Volkswagen, Nissan and Toyota). These two groups do not entirely exhaust the population of US car producers and, as a consequence, the sum of their market and/or advertising shares do not sum to unity (although they average 0.97 and 0.95 respectively throughout the period).[7] At the beginning of the period, the collective market share of domestic firms was above 0.95, but by the end of the period it had fallen below 0.65. Foreign producers began making inroads into the collective share of domestic players in the 1960s. By 1970, their share of the market was 14 per cent, and it rose steadily to about

35 per cent at the end of the sample period. This invasion was led by Volkswagen, who established themselves in the US more quickly than the others, and was (jointly with Honda) the leading foreign player (from amongst the group under consideration) at the end of the period. The last two substantial entrants in our sample period were Mazda and Mitsubishi, whose presence in the market was felt from the mid-1980s on.

As it happens, the sharp escalation in industry advertising also dates from the early to middle 1970s, and it occurred because both domestic and foreign-owned firms increased their advertising (the correlation between the advertising of these two groups of firms is 0.9862). Figure 12.2 tells the basic story. Both foreign and domestic firms had similar advertising intensities in 1970, but by 1973 foreign firms were advertising noticeably more intensively. Domestic firms responded and both had similar advertising intensities in 1981 and again in 1985, but after 1981 and again after 1985 foreign firms raised their advertising intensities above those of domestic rivals. Domestic firms finally caught up in 1995 and 1996, and advertised more intensively than their foreign rivals in the last two years of the sample period. The interesting thing about this escalation in advertising is that the advertising of foreign based firms rose with their total sales (the correlation is 0.8156) while that of domestic based producers also rose despite a fall in their sales (the correlation is -0.3976). It is difficult to be absolutely sure, but this pattern is certainly consistent with the view that the advertising war which developed was initiated and sustained mainly by the aggressive market penetration goals of foreign firms.

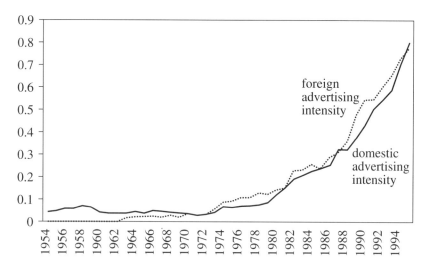

Figure 12.2   Domestic and foreign advertising intensity

3.2 Market and Advertising Shares for Domestic and Foreign Firms

The model outlined in Section 2 above suggests that the movements in concentration and advertising shown on Figure 12.1 were causally related, with the key relationship being a simple linear relation between market shares and advertising shares. When applied to aggregated data on the top three US producers, this market share equation is, of course, a concentration equation.

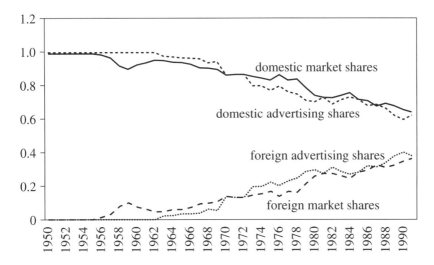

Figure 12.3   Foreign and domestic market and advertising shares

The basic features of the story told in Section 2 are very clearly evident in the data, as can be seen in Figure 12.3. The simple correlation between advertising and market shares for both domestic and foreign firms is 0.9159 and 0.9590.[8] Both series fell over time for domestic firms and both rose for foreign firms. A naive exploration of the model developed in Section 2 might start from equation (12.1). Simple linear regressions of market shares on advertising shares for domestic firms and foreign firms yield high R^2s (0.84 and 0.92), and the estimates of the coefficient on advertising shares (which are naive estimates of θ) that these regressions produce are 0.76 and 0.79 for domestic and foreign firms respectively (the *t*-values are 14.6 and 21.7). Including time trends in these regressions causes the coefficients on advertising share to fall to 0.17 and 0.11 respectively, but both of the coefficients are positive and significantly different from zero, and the time trends are very significant. Further, the coefficient on the domestic (foreign) trend is negative (positive), which is consistent with the view that the quality of foreign cars rose steadily throughout the period.[9] Given the fact that both series trend, this is not a surprise. The implication is that at this level of aggregation, it may be easy to confound the effect of advertising share on market share with any kind of secular change (such as a change in 'quality') which might be accurately described using a linear time trend.

One of the more serious problems with the naive regression is a concern that advertising shares might be correlated with the residual (for example because of simultaneity bias), leading to biased estimates of θ. We explored several different empirical models of advertising shares, using each to develop instruments for advertising shares. The best model that we developed included two lagged dependent variables plus the growth in US GDP, total car production and total industry advertising. Aside from the lagged dependent variables, the lagged growth of domestic and foreign advertising were the most notably significant variables. Almost all of the equations of this type that we ran provided pretty good fits. Using these equations to generate instruments yielded estimates of θ which were very close to those generated by OLS regressions on the naive model (12.1): $\theta = 0.731$ (rather than 0.763) for domestic firms, and 0.840 (rather than 0.786) for foreign firms. Much the same results were observed in all the experiments of this type that we conducted, and we conclude that the several shortcomings of the naive estimates of θ probably do not include the problem of simultaneity bias.

As noted in Section 2, there is an implicit assumption in (12.1) and (12.2) that the returns to advertising are constant. Since domestic firms are much larger and advertise much more than foreign firms, it is possible that at least some of the movements in market share that we observe are driven by diminishing returns (for domestic firms) or increasing returns (for foreign firms). An easy way to explore this possibility is to regress the log of market shares on the log of advertising shares. This yields naive but statistically significant estimates of 0.966 and 0.916 respectively on the returns to scale parameter (denoted e in footnote 5), which is difficult to distinguish from constant returns. When a time trend is included, both coefficients fell but remained significant. As before, the time trend has a positive slope for foreign firms and a negative slope for domestic firms. At the very least, these regressions suggest that the effects of advertising on market shares does not display increasing returns.

Since (12.1) is most reasonably thought of as a long-run relationship, the error correction representation (12.2) may be more appropriate than naive regressions of current period advertising shares on current market shares. Table 12.1 displays estimates of two versions of (12.2). Recall that, in equilibrium, market shares and advertising shares are linked by a factor of proportionality, $\theta = -\varphi_1/\varphi_0$. In regressions (i) and (iii), this factor of proportionality is assumed to be constant; in (ii) and (iv), it is allowed to follow a deterministic trend (which gives rise to a term which is the product of advertising share and a time dummy). Since θ is a measure of 'relative quality', this slight generalisation allows for quality differences between firms to vary over time. Focusing first on (i) and (iii), both of the lagged market and advertising shares variables are significant, and together imply estimated values of $\theta = 0.723$ and 0.779 for domestic and foreign firms respectively. These estimates are very close to those obtained from the naive regressions based on (12.1) discussed above. Regression (iii) displays mild signs of misspecification and suggests that the specification shown in (ii) and (iv) might be more appropriate. Unsurprisingly, the inclusion of the interactive variable reduces the t-value on lagged advertising shares, but it is clear that (iv) in particular cannot be simplified to (iii). Regressions (ii) and (iv) imply that: $\theta = 0.442 - 0.00689*T$ for domestic firms, and $\theta = 0.292 + 0.0118*T$ for foreign firms (where T is a linear time trend). The implication of these estimates is that domestic firms were initially perceived to be of higher quality, but that after 1960 the relative quality ranking reversed.

Table 12.1   Regression estimates of equation (12.2) by groups

	Domestic		Foreign	
	(i)	(ii)	(iii)	(iv)
CNST	0.047	0.156	0.019	0.030
	(1.52)	(2.17)	(2.89)	(3.45)
$MS(-1)$	−0.231	−0.292	−0.267	−0.425
	(2.13)	(2.68)	(2.25)	(3.02)
$AS(-1)$	0.167	0.129	0.208	0.124
	(1.89)	(1.50)	(2.19)	(1.23)
$\Delta MS(-1)$	0.276	0.325	0.158	0.224
	(1.49)	(1.70)	(1.04)	(1.45)
$\Delta AS(-1)$	−0.175	−0.162	−0.163	−0.134
	(1.19)	(1.04)	(1.34)	(1.34)
$AS(-1)*t$	–	−0.002	–	0.005
	–	(1.51)	–	(2.07)
R^2	0.146	0.1822	0.158	0.225
RESET	$F(3,33) - 0.14$	$F(3,32) = 0.01$	$F(3,33) = 2.48$	$F(3,32) = 0.82$
LLH	100.186	101.067	108.226	109.944

Note: *The dependent variable to the first difference of market shares (absolute values) of statistics are given in the brackets below the estimated coefficients: all estimates of standard errors are heteroskedastic-robust; RESET is the Ramsey RE-Set Test; LLH is the log of the likelihood.

To assess the power of this particular empirical specification, it is important to compare it to something reasonably meaningful. In the case of (12.1) and (12.2), this could be the null that changes in market shares are random, meaning that market shares follow a random walk. It is easy to reject this particular null. However, market shares are bounded between zero and unity, and a more reasonable alternative null hypothesis is that all of the coefficients in (12.2) save that on lagged market share are zero (this is observationally equivalent to assuming that market shares follow an AR(1) process). Here the decision is more marginal, but still reasonably clear. One way or the other, using advertising shares to explain market shares is a noticeable improvement on just presuming that market shares vary randomly or follow a simple auto-regression.

Another way to assess the model is to explore a range of extensions to it. We did this in two ways. First, we experimented by adding a range of other variables in (i)–(iv), including: the rate of growth of US GDP, the rate of growth of the consumer price index and the producers price index, the rate of growth of industry output and of total industry advertising, the log of market size and dummy variables identifying the arrival of the first major foreign entrant (Volkswagen) and the last two (Mitsubishi and Mazda). Although several of these variables had a statistically significant impact on market shares, in no case did the inclusion of one or more of them lead to any qualitative differences in the inferences drawn from Table 12.1. However one specifies (12.2), there seems to be a fairly close and fairly robust linear association between market shares and advertising shares for domestic and foreign firms.[10] Working in the other direction yields much the same conclusion: namely, that the estimates shown in (i)–(iv) are fairly robust. Amongst other things, we dropped $\Delta AS(t-1)$ without having much effect on the estimates. Both $\Delta AS(t-1)$ and $\Delta MS(t-1)$ can also be dropped without much affecting estimates of the θ, and adding further lags in $\Delta AS(t)$ and $\Delta MS(t)$ has no substantive impact either. As before, however, including a time trend has a big effect: estimates of the θ drop noticeably, and the time trend is negative (positive) and significant for domestic (foreign) firms.

The second way that we generalised (12.1) is to rewrite it in a form which makes it look more obviously like a demand curve, namely

$$\log Q_j(t) = \varphi_0 + \varphi_1 \log Q(t) + \varphi_2 \log A_j(t) + \varphi_3 \log A(t) + \xi_j(t), \quad (12.3)$$

where $Q_j(t)$ is the output of firm j, $A_j(t)$ is its advertising, and Q and A are total industry output and advertising respectively. Equation (12.3) reduces to (12.1) if $\varphi_1 = 1$ and $\varphi_2 = -\varphi_3$. Judged on normal statistical grounds, these restrictions cannot quite be accepted when (12.3) is applied to domestic or to foreign firms, but the estimates of these three parameters are not very different from the restrictions: for domestic firms, the estimates of (12.3) are: $\varphi_1 = 1.03$, $\varphi_2 = 0.401$ and $\varphi_3 = -0.470$; for foreign firms, $\varphi_1 = 0.789$, $\varphi_2 = 0.441$ and $\varphi_3 = -0.230$. In both cases, it seems plain that market and advertising shares are positively correlated. Since (12.3) looks rather like a demand curve, we also included the log of the producers' price index as an additional explanatory variable. For domestic firms, this recorded a statistically significant coefficient $= -3$; the producer price index was not significant in the foreign output equation.[11] We also included other variables (time trends, the growth of GDP, and so on), all without changing the qualitative features of the results; that is, that estimates of (12.3) come close to satisfying the restrictions needed to simplify it to (12.1).

3.3 Market and Advertising Shares for Seven Firms

Broadly speaking, the results are very similar when (12.1) or (12.2) are applied to the seven individual firms who compose the two groups that we have been looking at. In the naive regressions based on (12.1), all the co-efficients on $AS(t)$ are positive and significant; with the exception of Volkswagen, naive estimates of θ for domestic firms are much lower (0.458, 0.543 and 0.532 for General Motors, Ford and Chrysler respectively) than those for foreign firms (0.964, 0.361, 0.760 and 0.834 for Honda, Volkswagen, Nissan and Toyota respectively). Adding in a time trend has (as before) the effect of substantially reducing the estimated coefficient on $AS(t)$ in all regressions. All of the trend terms are significant; those for domestic firms are negative, while those for foreign firms are positive. More interesting are estimates of log $MS(t)$ on log $AS(t)$ (recall that these provide estimates of the returns to scale in advertising). All of these estimates (of the parameter e identified in footnote 5) are statistically significant, and those on three of the four foreign firms are very close to unity (the coefficient on Volkswagen is 0.750, a little lower than the others). The three domestic firms, however, show clear signs of diminishing returns (with coefficients of 0.400, 0.449 and 0.665), something that was not evident in the aggregated regressions. The implications of diminishing returns to advertising is, of course, that their advertising expenditures are less effective in generating increases in market share than the much smaller level of expenditures made by foreign firms.

Since none of the four foreign firms operated throughout the period (Volkswagen was present for 32 years, Honda for 26, Nissan for 32 and Toyota for 21), there is some possibility that sample selection bias might lead us to make erroneous inferences about the size of θ estimated from them. (The regressions just discussed were run only for those years when the firms were actually present in the market). We therefore reran all of these regressions (and those reported below) on the full sample period (including the sample years when these firms were not operating) and on the sub-sample of years when the firms were present, but including an inverse Mills ratio derived from a probit regression describing market presence. Although there were some differences in the estimates of θ between the full sample and the censored sample, they do not seem to be qualitatively important (θ = 0.51 for the full sample for Volkswagen, and 0.36 for the censored sample; for Honda, the estimates were 1.02 and 0.964; for Nissan, they were 0.83 and 0.76; and for Toyota, they were 0.79 and 0.83 respectively). Similar observations apply for the regressions with an explicit sample selection correction.

The analogues of regressions (i) and (iii) in Table 12.1 yield estimates of θ = 0.737, 0.231, 0.606, 0.981, 0.891, 0.924, and 0.742 respectively when applied to the seven firms. These estimates do not seem to be as closely related to the naive estimates of θ as was the case with the estimates using more aggregated data displayed in Table 12.1. Nonetheless, it seems clear that the disaggregated estimates have the same feature as was evident in Table 12.1, namely that the estimated values of θ are rather lower for the three domestic firms than they are for the four firms (in fact, the estimate for Ford seems to be implausibly low). Further (and as with the aggregate estimates), the estimates of θ for the three domestic firms appear to fall over time, while those of (three out of four) of the foreign firms rise over time.

The regressions in Table 12.2 show estimates generated from regressions that apply the specification used in (ii) and (iv) to General Motors, Ford, Chrysler, Honda, Volkswagen, Nissan and Toyota respectively. It is clear that, as before, including the interaction time trend tends to reduce both the size and significance of the estimated coefficient on $AS(t-1)$. Regressions (v)–(xi) yield estimates of θ = 0.243 − 0.012*T, −0.663 − 0.007*T, and 0.450 − 0.004*T for the three domestic firms (the Ford estimates are still rather implausible), and −0.030 + 0.026*T, 0.913 − 0.046*T, −0.190 + 0.028*T and 0.003 + 0.017*T for the foreign firms (note that Nissan has an estimated value of θ < 0 for the first years of the sample, while Volkswagen's θ falls throughout the period). As before, these estimates are robust to dropping $\Delta AS(t-1)$ and/or $\Delta MS(t-1)$, or including more lagged values of each.

4.   TWO FURTHER ISSUES

It is difficult to resist the conclusion that market and advertising shares are closely correlated in this market, and hard to argue that this correlation is spurious. Our puzzle – the observation that industry concentration fell

Table 12.2   Regression estimates of equation (12.2) by firm*

	(v) GM	(vi) Ford	(vii) Chrysler	(viii) Honda	(ix) Volkswagen	(x) Nissan	(xi) Toyota
CNST	0.098	0.114	0.040	0.004	0.030	0.006	0.006
	(0.965)	(1.98)	(1.54)	(1.93)	(7.85)	(2.18)	(1.36)
$MS(-1)$	-0.247	-0.258	-0.615	-0.307	-0.587	-0.320	-0.351
	(1.65)	(1.97)	(3.19)	(1.70)	(6.21)	(2.29)	(2.03)
$AS(-1)$	0.060	-0.171	0.277	-0.010	0.536	-0.061	0.001
	(0.559)	(1.08)	(1.82)	(0.050)	(4.54)	(0.407)	(0.008)
$\Delta MS(-1)$	-0.263	-0.284	-0.009	0.338	-0.011	-0.246	0.191
	(1.56)	(1.84)	(0.055)	(1.404)	(0.093)	(1.41)	(0.968)
$\Delta AS(-1)$	-0.073	-0.029	0.010	-0.066	0.137	-0.010	0.072
	(0.453)	(0.160)	(0.075)	(0.363)	(1.18)	(0.073)	(0.616)
$\Delta AS(-1)^{xt}$	0.003	-0.002	-0.003	0.008	-0.027	0.009	0.006
	(0.720)	(1.76)	(1.54)	(0.972)	(6.83)	(1.59)	(1.20)
R^2	0.227	0.297	0.322	0.215	0.742	0.345	0.249
RESET	$F(3,32)=1.79$	$F(3,32)=1.28$	$F(3,32)=0.98$	$F(3,17)=0.98$	$F(3,23)=3.40$	$F(3,23)=44$	$F(3,22)=1.55$
LLH	87.678	99.281	117.28	103.41	128.09	118.17	105.50

Note: * As for Table 12.1; regressions (viii)–(xi) were estimated only for those time periods where they produced positive output: $N = 26$, 32, and 31, respectively.

during a period when industry advertising rose substantially – helps us understand how a rise in advertising accompanied by a change in advertising shares that is sparked by entry could induce a fall in concentration, but it leaves at least two questions in the air: what sparked the advertising war?; and what were the dynamics which drove advertising to such heights? We briefly consider each in turn.

4.1   The Timing of Entry

Roughly speaking, the simple model that we have been exploring suggests that entry will occur when advertising share is 'inexpensive' to acquire (and, indeed, that entry will stop when the cost of acquiring advertising share rises). If, for some reason, an industry has fallen into an equilibrium with low levels of advertising, then it is likely to be vulnerable to entry. A quick glance at Figure 12.1, however, suggests that this story is incomplete. The US car industry apparently spent virtually all of the 1950s and 1960s in such a low-level equilibrium without, however, attracting entry or allowing a substantial penetration into the market by entrants. Further, the 1950s and 1960s were a period of very rapid market growth, a condition which is generally thought to facilitate entry. By the early 1970s, the market was showing some signs of levelling off, and throughout the rest of the period it certainly did not display growth rates anything like those recorded earlier in the period. Thus, the conditions were right for entry – 'right' in the sense of being a good time to enter and achieve a substantial market presence – in the late 1960s and early 1970s when entry actually occurred, but, equally, the conditions seem to have been right for possibly about 15–20 years before entry actually occurred.

There are at least two possible resolutions to this little puzzle. The first is to note that the time of entry into a market by a new firm often precedes the time when it begins to seriously steal share from incumbents by a considerable number of years. There are all kinds of teething troubles that new entrants face, particularly when they must design cars that will suit a new market, construct production facilities to produce these cars economically and establish their own distribution network. Our discussion of 'entry' in Section 3 and immediately above has effectively been in terms of the timing of market share penetration (which is what our data record), and it may well be that entry in terms of presence actually occurred when the data suggests that it ought to have done. However, since our data does not record the timing of entry in terms of presence, this can only be a conjecture. A second consideration is complementary to this, which is that entry penetration may occur when exogenous events alter cost or demand in a way that suits the entrant. Expressed in the terms of (12.1), this argument says that something may have occurred (the obvious candidate in this respect was the oil price shock in 1973 and the consequent rise in petrol prices) which raised the θ value of entrants (especially those who produce small, fuel-efficient cars). Increases in θ make advertising more attractive (each new buyer converted through advertising stays loyal longer the larger is θ), and that might have been enough to encourage entrants to increase their advertising and try to penetrate more deeply into the market. However, since we have no direct observations of 'quality' (either), this too must remain just a conjecture.

4.2 Advertising Wars

The sharp rise in industry advertising shown in Figure 12.1 looks rather like an advertising war. This observation begs two further questions: how does one identify an advertising war? and what is it that drives the levels of advertising up so steeply during such a war? To answer these questions, one must have a reference point, and the most natural place to start is to examine advertising choices in 'normal' circumstances.

The relationship captured in (12.1) is behavioural: it is a consequence of the fact that consumers behave in certain way and does not result from decisions by firms. In a sense, it is analogous to a conventional demand curve, and profit-maximising firms will accept it as a constraint when they choose optimum levels of advertising.[12] The Dorfman–Steiner condition suggests that the optimal choice of advertising will set the level of advertising to be some proportion of sales, the particular proportion depending on the price and advertising elasticities of demand. This turns out to be the case even when the kind of consumer behaviour that underlies (12.1) occurs. Schmalensee (1976 and 1978) has shown that in this case a Nash equilibrium in advertising yields a vector of optimal levels of advertising, A^*_j, which are proportional to output choices, Q_j (the factor of proportionality depends in this case on λ_j and on the costs of producing higher quality products). If, as before, we do not assume that all of the data reflect optimum choices or equilibrium outcomes, then a natural way to express this first order condition is as

$$\Delta Z_j(t) = \alpha_0 + \alpha_1 Z_j(t-1) + \varepsilon_j(t), \tag{12.4}$$

where $Z_j \equiv (A_j/Q_j)$, the ratio of advertising to sales and $\varepsilon_j(t)$ is a white noise error. Equation (12.4) allows actual advertising choices to (temporarily) depart from optimal choices (as might occur, for example, if there were adjustment costs associated with scaling an advertising campaign up or down). The quantity $(-\alpha_0/\alpha_1)$ is an estimate of the equilibrium advertising sales ratio for firm j, and, as before, it is not necessary to assume that it is constant over time: α_0 could be modelled as depending on a vector of observables, or a time trend.

Equation (12.4) is built on relatively simple and static foundations, and it is unlikely to be an accurate description of decisions that firms make about advertising spending when entrants are challenging incumbents and the total volume of advertising in the market is rising rapidly. It is difficult to develop a model describing how firms make decisions during an advertising war, for, in these circumstances, firms are liable to be heavily influenced by expectations about the actions of their rivals and these are not always well grounded in the fundamentals. However, there are liable to be two distinguishing features of an advertising war: first, it is possible that the advertising expenditures of particular firms will rise even when their sales fall (a clear violation of the Dorfman–Steiner conditions), and, second, it is likely that one will observe firms to change their advertising spending directly in response to the actions of their rivals.

The first distinguishing feature of an advertising war can be explored by generating estimates of the quantity $(-\alpha_0/\alpha_1)$: if these are negative, then it is almost sure that a sustained departure from the 'normal' conditions described by Dorfman–Steiner has occurred. The second distinguishing feature can be built into (12.4) by generalising it to allow firm j to respond directly to the advertising of its rivals. This suggests a formulation such as

$$\Delta Z_j(t) = \alpha_0 + \alpha_1 Z_j(t-1) + \alpha_2 \Delta R_j(t-1) + \varepsilon_j(t), \tag{12.5}$$

where $\Delta R_j(t-1)$ is the change in the advertising activities of j's rivals. Note that we assume it takes one period for firms to respond to the actions of rivals.[13] In essence, this specification allows for a much longer, much more systematic departure from equilibrium than (12.4) allows, and, more important, associates it with the observed actions of particular rivals. At equilibrium, $\Delta Z_j(t) = \Delta R_j(t-1) = 0$, and so $A_j = (-\alpha_0/\alpha_1) Q_j$, which is consistent with the first order conditions describing the optimal choice of advertising in 'normal' (that is non-war) conditions.

To give this extension of (12.4) some substance, one must specify $R_j(t)$. Possibly the simplest specification is to write $\Delta R_j(t-1) = \Sigma \omega_k \Delta A_k(t-1)$, where the ω_k are weights reflecting the degree to which each rival k presents a substantive competitive challenge to j, and would be the object of econometric estimation. This specification supposes that firm j responds directly to any change in the advertising of its various rivals k, a course of action which seems rather naive. A more sophisticated firm might try to predict what its rivals are likely to do, and then respond only to departures from that prediction; that is it may respond only to 'surprise' changes in the advertising of its rivals. The thinking here is that firm j will understand (and, therefore, incorporate) the equilibrium behaviour of its rivals j in its own (equilibrium) advertising choices, but systematic departures from equilibrium behaviour by rivals is taken to indicate the existence of a 'new regime' in which advertising is being chosen strategically by rivals to increase their market shares. One way to capture this is to imagine that firm j uses (12.4) to generate a predicted value of Z_k – call it $Z_k^*(t)$ – for each rival k, and then let $\Delta R_j(t) = \Sigma \omega_k [Z_k(t) - Z_k^*(t)]$. In this specification, equilibrium requires two conditions: $A_j = (-\alpha_0/\alpha_1) Q_j$ and $Z_k(t) = Z_k^*(t)$; that is no firm is surprised about the behaviour of its rivals.

It turns out that the data are clearly consistent with the view that what we observe in the post-1970 sub-period is an advertising war, but it is very difficult to get clean estimates of the parameters describing the dynamics of that war. Figure 12.2 shows that advertising by both domestic and foreign firms rose almost exponentially over time and this basic pattern is evident throughout the data no matter how much one disaggregates it. Amongst other things, this means that the advertising of different firms is very highly correlated over time, and this is even true when one compares first differences between firms. The simple correlation between the advertising of domestic and foreign firms is 0.9860; the correlation between the first difference in domestic and foreign advertising is 0.5081, while that between domestic and foreign advertising intensity is 0.9734. Regressing domestic advertising on foreign advertising yields an estimated coefficient of 1.68 ($t = 22.02$) and $R^2 = 0.976$. A regression in first differences yields a coefficient of 0.852 ($t = 3.75$) and $R^2 = 0.26$.

The really interesting feature of the data is that advertising by domestic firms is negatively correlated with their sales -0.3941. A simple regression of domestic advertising on the sales of domestic firms for the whole sample period yields a coefficient of -0.278 (2.21) with an $R^2 = 0.104$. However, repeating the levels regressions for the period before 1974 for domestic firms yields an estimated coefficient of 0.016 (2.42) with $R^2 = 0.252$. It seems, then, that there is a correlation between domestic advertising and sales, but only in the pre-1970s. After that advertising seems to rise while sales fall, and this generates a full sample correlation between the two which is negative. For foreign firms, the pattern is rather different. The partial correlation between sales and advertising is 0.8156, while a regression of advertising on sales for foreign firms over the whole period gives an estimated coefficient of 0.545 (8.131) with $R^2 = 0.665$. There is some evidence that the correlation between advertising and sales is weaker before 1974 than for the period as a whole, but it is hard to be sure (most of the foreign producers did not operate on any scale before 1970, and, as a consequence, there are relatively few observations on their sales and advertising in this early period). Post-1974, foreign sales and foreign advertising rose, but the latter rose more (363 per cent between 1974 and 1996, as compared to the 134 per cent rise in sales over the period).[14]

It is very difficult to generate acceptable regressions describing the inter-action between the advertising intensity (or total advertising expenditures) of domestic and foreign firms because the advertising of both sets of firms is so highly correlated. Table 12.3 shows two regressions based on (12.4) for domestic firms and two for foreign firms which explain advertising inten-sity. In the first (regressions (xii) and (xiv)), lagged changes in rivals' adver-tising are included; in the second (regressions (xiii) and (xv)), lagged changes in rivals' advertising intensity are included. Two features stand out. First, it appears that domestic advertising responds to foreign advertising but not the reverse, and, second, it appears that the foreign advertising equations fit relatively poorly. We experimented with several 'surprise' terms, and generally speaking they had a larger and more significant impact in the domestic advertising than in the foreign advertising equation. They were not significant in either case, however.[15] We also replicated the regres-sions on Table 12.3 using more lagged dependent variables, or more lagged

Table 12.3   Regression estimates of equation (12.5)

	Domestic		Foreign	
	(xii)	(xiii)	(xiv)	(xv)
CNST	−0.005	−0.005	0.008	0.008
	(−1.73)	(1.405)	(1.97)	(1.29)
$(A/Q)_{t-1}$	0.128	0.130	0.054	0.097
	(5.513)	(7.451)	(1.02)	(2.45)
$R^{(1)}$	6.31^{-08}	–	-1.0^{-08}	-1.423
	(1.96)	–	(0.241)	(1.421)
$R^{(2)}$	–	0.184	–	
	–	(1.49)		
	–	–		
R^2	0.759	0.765	0.125	0.168
RESET	F(3.35) = 1.44	F(3.35) = 1.04	F(3.35) = 1.059	F(3/35) = 0.38
LLH	109.08	109.89	86.96	87.99

Notes:
The dependent variable is the first difference in the advertising industry. Absolute values of *t*-statistics are given in brackets below the estimated coefficients: all estimates are heteroskedastic – robust. RESET is the Ramsey Re-Set Test; LLH is the log of the likelihood.
$R^{(1)}$ = the change in rivals advertising lagged and $R^{(2)}$ = the change in rivals advertising intensity lagged.

terms in rivals' advertising. There are some signs that second and third lagged terms in domestic advertising have a bigger and more precisely determined impact on foreign advertising intensity than domestic advertising once lagged, suggesting that foreign firms may be rather slower than domestic firms to respond to rival's advertising. Finally, we replicated all of these regressions using total nominal advertising expenditures rather than advertising intensity. Although this generated numerous small differences in the regressions shown in Table 12.3, the basic bottom line is the same: there is at least some evidence that both domestic and foreign firms respond to changes (surprise or otherwise) in their rivals' advertising. Further, in the case of domestic firms, these responses clearly lead to an escalation in advertising intensity, and to a rise in total advertising notwithstanding a modest decline in sales.

Replicating the regressions shown in Table 12.3 (plus the others alluded to above) at the level of the seven individual firms that we have focused on is complicated by the need to specify which rivals in particular each firm responds to. This creates a major problem since advertising and advertising intensity is very highly correlated across firms (none of the partial correlations of advertising or advertising intensity between the seven firms is below 0.80). Unsurprisingly, many of the regressions produced rather unstable coefficients when terms in the advertising of different rivals were included, and most of them produced very low *t*-statistics. It is, however, true that all seven firms responded to the advertising of one or more of their rivals, and, further, the three domestic firms appeared to respond more to the advertising of their foreign rivals than the latter did to advertising by the three big domestic market leaders.

5.   CONCLUSIONS

Our exploration of the post-war history of the US car industry has focused on the stylised fact displayed in Figure 12.1, namely that there was a very sharp escalation of industry advertising which occurred at the same time as industry concentration fell. To help account for this phenomenon, we outlined a model whose prime distinguishing feature is an equilibrium relationship between market and advertising shares. One interesting feature of this particular relationship is that it is consistent with many different equilibrium levels of advertising by firms in the market. As a consequence, it is not hard to believe that the arrival of new competitors would increase the advertising of all firms operating in the market. If, in addition, these entrants are able to seize a sizeable share of the market post-entry, then one would expect to observe higher levels of industry advertising and lower levels of concentration as compared with the situation pre-entry. This story seems to be at least roughly consistent with the data, as Figures 12.2 and 12.3 show. There is almost no question that there exists a strong and pretty robust relationship between market shares and advertising in the data that we have examined. Further, there are fairly good reasons for thinking that the escalation of advertising we have observed in this industry was initiated by foreign firms, and the data provide some support for the view that total industry advertising rose sharply because firms departed from normal advertising decision rules and began to respond directly to previous increases in advertising by their rivals.

Just how plausible is this story? The entry dynamics that we have focused on here are not peculiar to the US car industry. Entry has been observed to provoke an advertising war in other sectors,[16] an observation which is not inconsistent with survey evidence which suggests that the response to entry by incumbent firms (when they do, in fact, respond) is primarily by using marketing tools more extensively.[17] When this happens, it seems clear that there is no obvious reason to expect that the resulting escalation in sunk costs will necessarily be associated with an increase in industry concentration.[18] Although it is hard to dispute the proposition that higher levels of sunk costs are likely to be associated with higher levels of concentration across industries, the results reported in this chapter suggest that increases in sunk costs in a particular sector may not induce a rise in concentration in that sector over time. In particular, the particular process by which sunk costs escalate may be an important determinant of whether concentration goes up as well; that is it may matter who initiates the escalation in sunk costs, and why. To put this point a different way, symmetric models of sunk cost competition may give a misleading guide to outcomes in markets where already established firms have to compete with later arriving entrants.[19]

There are, of course, a number of caveats about the work that we have reported which need to be registered. Most of what we have observed is more clearly discernible in aggregated data than at the individual firm level. This is probably to be expected, and our feeling is that the kind of simple models and data we have been using do not make enough allowances for heterogeneities between firms. This is, perhaps, most apparent in the regressions which try to trace which (if any) of its rivals each firm responds most to when choosing its advertising expenditures. We have also made limited progress in describing the mechanics of the interdependence in advertising decisions between different firms simply because the data is so collinear. This, of course, is consistent with the view that firms match each others' advertising decisions very closely, but it does make it difficult to generate precise, reliable estimates of the relevant coefficients. The other caveat worth recording is that we have not been able to measure what is probably the most important feature of the relationship between advertising and market shares, namely those features of the product which induce switching by consumers. We have included time trends where appropriate to try to allow for the effect of changes in quality over time, but this is hardly satisfactory, not least because both market and advertising shares trend over time in our data.

One final observation is worth making. Notwithstanding its several shortcomings, our examination of the recent history of the US car industry suggests quite clearly that advertising can facilitate entry, and is not, therefore, necessarily a barrier to entry.[20] Certainly, it seems to be the case that foreign firms blasted their way into the US market using advertising (and perhaps by selling higher quality products). However, it is also important to resist the conclusion that advertising is necessarily pro-competitive for at least two reasons. First, the opportunity for entrants to 'acquire' market share disappeared as more and more entrants took advantage of it, and as incumbents responded by increasing their own advertising. As a consequence, the burst of entry facilitated by entry was of finite length – in other words, advertising provided only transitory assistance to entrants. Second, the model we have been using to interpret the data suggests that the key to the success of entrants was probably product quality and not advertising. What induces consumer switching in this model is product quality; advertising only affects the decision of what other product to switch to. Put another way, advertising has only a short-run effect on behaviour in this model: the long-run demand for a particular car depends on its quality and not on how much it is advertised.

NOTES

1. The views expressed in this chapter are ours alone and not necessarily those of the Competition Commission or anyone connected with it. We are obliged to the ESRC for financial support, and to Mike Scherer, Dick Schmalensee, John Scott, Steve Martin and seminar participants at the IFS, WIFO, University of Essex, Nova University in Lisbon and Bocconi University for helpful comments on an early draft. The usual disclaimer applies.
2. *A personal note:* I arrived as a graduate student at the University of Warwick in the mid-1970s, just as two separate strands of Keith Cowling's research – the work on advertising and the work on the UK car industry – was coming to a conclusion. My own interest in these two areas did not get aroused for another decade or so (and then mainly through joint work with another Warwick graduate, Andy Murfin), and I have never been able to work out where the ideas that I was exposed to by Keith and others at Warwick ended and my own (more modest) ideas started. Actually, to be perfectly honest, I have never tried very hard to work it out – it is easier and more sensible just to acknowledge what has long been obvious to me, namely that my debt to Keith in this area – as in many, many others – is enormous. It is more than a pleasure to contribute a chapter full of what

may well have been his ideas originally to a volume designed to honour his contributions to economics. *PAG*

3. The assumption that firms do not compete on price is not as restrictive as it appears at first sight: much the same substantive effects occur if price matching between firms occurs and eliminates all apparent quality adjusted price differences between their different brands.

4. Rationales for this specification include the following: consumers might, for example, take advertising to be a signal of quality on the grounds that only high quality producers will be willing to advertise; see Nelson (1974) or, following Sutton (1991), it may be that advertising somehow raises consumers willingness to pay (for example by enhancing the product's brand image).

5. This model is set out in Smallwood and Conlisk (1979) and explored in Schmalensee (1976, 1978 and 1992). These authors consider a slightly more general version of the model which yields an equilibrium relationship: $Q_j/Q = \lambda_j(A_j^e/(\Sigma\beta_j A_j^e))$, which allows for random choices by consumers ($e = 0$), diminishing returns to advertising ($e < 1$) and increasing returns ($e > 1$). Defining $\theta_j \equiv \lambda_j/\Sigma\lambda_j(A_j/A)^e$, it follows that $Q_j/Q = \theta_j(A_j/A)^e$. This more general model is a simple extension of (12.1) that is most easily explored by regressing the log of Q_j/Q on log A_j/A, and testing whether the coefficient on the latter differs from unity.

6. The data that we have used comes from the following sources: *new car sales* data for domestic firms are from annual editions of *Moody's Industrial Manual* (1954–98) and from *Wards Automotive Yearbook* (1965–98). Net sales are defined as sales minus excise taxes, sales taxes, discounts, returns and allowances. Data for the foreign firms are from *Ward's Automotive Yearbook* (1965–98). Figures for domestic car sales coincide in *Moody's Industrial Manual* and in *Ward's Automotive Yearbook*; *advertising* data for the period 1954–1998 have been provided by *Ad-Age*, an agency of Crain Communications Inc. These figures are total advertising expenditures and are found in the annual list of the advertising expenses of the 100 top US advertisers studied annually by Ad-Age; and *GDP, CPI, and PPI (for motor vehicles)* data (1982 = 100) are from the web site of the Bureau of Labor Statistics. It is worth noting that our advertising data do not appear to correspond closely with that reported in the FTC Line of Business data for the relevant overlap years.

7. The other domestic US players during the period (and their average market shares from 1954 until their year of exit) were: American Motors (3.2 per cent, exit 1987), Hudson (0.26 per cent, exit 1958), Packard (0.34 per cent, exit 1959), Studebaker (1.36 per cent, exit 1965), Nash (0.54 per cent, exit 1958), Willy's (0.08 per cent, exit 1956) and Kaiser (0.05 per cent, exit 1956). Mitsubishi and Mazda entered the market too late to generate enough of a times series for serious estimation, and the other 'foreign' entrants registered too small a market share to warrant inclusion. In a sense, our sample of firms is subject to 'survivor bias', and this probably means that our estimates of θ for these survivors is higher than the true value of θ for all firms, successful or not, in the US car industry population.

8. It has been suggested that if firms use a simple rule of thumb to determine their advertising (say, devoting 5 per cent of sales revenue to advertising), then market and advertising shares will be correlated by construction. This is not quite right. For a start, it requires all firms to use the same rule of thumb (that is, the same 5 per cent). More fundamentally, it cannot be an explanation for the correlation that we have found simply because advertising sales ratios (as we have seen) rocketed during the period without disturbing the basic market shares/advertising shares correlations reported in the text.

9. This observation seems similar to (or at least not inconsistent with) that made by Mannering and Winston (1991), who argue that domestic US car producers lost 'brand loyalty' after 1980. They provide some evidence for this by examining repeat purchase behaviour, and the movements in repeat buying patterns over time which they observe are not difficult to reconcile with the movements in 'quality' that appear in our regressions.

10. The rate of growth of the domestic US car market had a significant positive (negative)

effect on domestic (foreign) market shares, while the growth of total advertising and the Mitsubishi/Mazda dummy had significant negative effects. Market size and the rate of growth of GDP had (surprisingly) no significant impact on the regressions. When an advertising share/time dummy interactive variable was included, the growth of advertising and the Mitsubishi/Mazda dummy became insignificant (not surprisingly).

11. This is not surprising as the index is dominated by domestic car prices and will not reflect the lower prices of many of the cars produced by foreign firms.

12. Note that if quality is taken to be exogenous, then advertising is the sole choice variable in this very simple model: prices are, by assumption, fixed (or firms are assumed to price match so that price is not a major basis for choice between them) and output is driven by the advertising choices of all firms at equilibrium. In fact, θ_j depends in principle on the choices made by firms which determine 'quality'. However, these (for example product design) are likely to be exogenous to short term output choices.

13. This is probably too strong. Firms will not always be taken by surprise when rivals or entrants raise/lower advertising by more than would otherwise be the case, and they may, therefore, begin to respond contemporaneously with (or even before) the surprise occurs. For simplicity, we neglect this possibility. It is worth noting, however, that this assumption does lead to a considerable simplification of the econometric model that we will ultimately be using.

14. A slightly different approach to this issue is reported in Elliot (2001) who undertakes a cointegration analysis of advertising in the US soft drinks industry. This study also suggests clear, systematic departures from 'normal' advertising behaviour.

15. In essence, we developed a range of models of domestic and foreign advertising (usually involving lagged dependent variables, lagged values of rivals advertising, lagged values of GDP and so on), and used these to generated 'predicted' values – the Z^*_k referred to at the end of Section 2 above. In most cases, the fits were pretty good, and the corresponding 'surprise' terms – the $[Z_k - Z^*_k]$ – generated positive coefficients, but the standard errors on these estimates were always very high.

16. For example, see Alemson (1970), who records the impact of entry into the Australian Tobacco industry, and Geroski and Murfin (1990 and 1991), who study the effect of entry competition on advertising in the UK car industry. Other recent studies of the effect of advertising on entrants in particular sectors includes Leffer (1981) and Rizzo and Zeckhauser (1990).

17. See Cubbin and Domberger (1988), Smiley (1988), and Singh et al. (1998).

18. Our advertising data probably understate the level of sunk costs, since expenditures on 'quality' are also liable to be sunk for the most part. Furthermore, if one believes that firms advertise mainly when they have a good reason to – for example, when the 'quality' of their product goes up – then observed expenditures on advertising will be positively correlated with unobserved (but equally sunk) expenditures on 'quality'.

19. Although the relationship between advertising and concentration that we have observed seems to be inconsistent with his arguments, in fact the main thrust of Sutton's work is on the relationship between concentration and market size, and nothing in our data is obviously inconsistent with his arguments about a lower bound to concentration in the US car industry. Further, the nature of his argument about how endogenous sunk costs increase market concentration suggests a process by which a fragmented market creates incentives for some firms to advertise and increase their market share, particularly when market size increases (1991, p. 48), and this too is not obviously inconsistent with our interpretation of the data. The difference is that the key actors in the US car industry were entrants, which is, of course, why concentration – measured as the shares of the leading (that is domestic and incumbent) players – fell.

20. Using a rather different approach to ours, Greuner et al. (2000) examine data on profits, sales and advertising in the US car industry from 1970 to 1994 and argue that advertising does not impede entrants, not least because it transmits information. This paper also contains numerous references to the literature on the effects of advertising on entry barriers and previous work on the US car industry.

REFERENCES

Alemson, M. (1970), 'Advertising and the nature of competition in oligopoly over time', *Economic Journal*, **80**, 282–306.

Cubbin, J. and S. Domberger (1988), 'Advertising and post-entry oligopoly behaviour', *Journal of Industrial Economics*, **37**, 123–40.

Elliot, C. (2001), 'A cointegration analysis of advertising and sales data', *Review of Industrial Organization*, **18**, 417–26.

Geroski, P. and A. Murfin (1990), 'Entry and industry evolution: the UK car industry, 1958–83', *Applied Economics*, **23**, 799–810.

Geroski, P. and A. Murfin (1991), 'Entry and intra-industry mobility in the UK car market', *Oxford Bulletin of Economics and Statistics*, **53**, 341–60.

Gruener, M., D. Kamerschen and P. Klein (2000), 'The competitive effects of advertising in the US automobile industry, 1970–94', *International Journal of the Economics of Business*, **7**, 245–61.

Leffer, K. (1981), 'Persuasion or information? The economics of prescriptive drug advertising', *Journal of Law and Economics*, **24**, 45–74.

Mannering, F. and C. Winston (1991), 'Brand loyalty and the decline of American automobile firms', *Brookings Papers on Economic Activity*, Microeconomics Supplement.

Nelson, P. (1974), 'Advertising as information', *Journal of Political Economy*, **81**, 729–54.

Rizzo, J. and R. Zeckhauser (1990), 'Advertising and entry: the case of physicians' services', *Journal of Political Economy*, **98**, 476–500.

Schmalensee, R. (1976), 'A model of promotional competition in oligopoly', *Review of Economic Studies*, **43**, 493–507.

Schmalensee, R. (1978), 'A model of advertising and product quality', *Journal of Political Economy*, **86**, 485–503.

Schmalensee, R. (1992), 'Sunk costs and market structure: a review article', *Journal of Industrial Economics*, **40**, 125–34.

Singh, S., M. Utton and M. Waterson (1998), 'Strategic behaviour of incumbent firms in the UK', *International Journal of Industrial Organisation*, **16**, 229–51.

Smallwood, D. and J. Conlisk (1979), 'Product quality in markets where consumers are imperfectly informed', *Quarterly Journal of Economics*, **93**, 1–23.

Smiley, R. (1988), 'Empirical evidence on strategic entry deterrence', *International Journal of Industrial Economics*, **6**, 167–80.

Sutton, J. (1991), *Sunk Costs and Market Structure*, Cambridge MA: MIT Press.

13. Keith Cowling and Warwick: the contribution to the University

Michael Shattock

Other chapters relate to Keith Cowling as an academic economist and his influence on the development of his subject but this chapter is intended to convey an aspect of his career which may perhaps surprise some of his international colleagues, his commitment to the University and its development. Nowadays this is rather an unfashionable way of expending one's energies: the impact of the Research Assessment Exercise (RAE) and of growing specialisation within disciplines have increasingly led UK academics, particularly younger academics, to concentrate their energies on their own work to the exclusion of wider responsibilities within their department or university, even though effective institutional governance and management demand (both legally and in best practice), a substantial contribution from the academic community. Keith's career represents a model of how to balance the demands of a research and teaching career with the responsibilities that go with a substantial input to the running of his department and the University. Keith was in fact much more than a 'good University citizen' and his contribution over 36 years is one of the reasons why the Economics Department and the University occupy the position that they do. Moreover, Keith's contribution spans a period of enormous change in universities and it is a tribute to his resilience that unlike so many of his contemporaries around the university system he retained this institutional commitment to the extent that for his last three years of full-time service as a Professor of Industrial Economics, carrying a significant academic load, he was chairman of the Faculty Board and a member of the Senate Steering Committee, the central policy and executive committee of the University.

In the UK higher education system, even though we have moved from elite to mass and increasingly to universal higher education (Trow, 1974), the professorial title still carries with it a range of institutional responsibilities which are different in kind from those that can reasonably be required, though they are often given, by non-professorial academic staff. These responsibilities are to the discipline, to the wider professional world of one's subject and to one's students, and particularly to graduate students (some of whom may follow their supervisor into university teaching), to one's department and to one's colleagues (perhaps particularly one's junior academic colleagues), and finally to the university itself. Keith has carried out all these responsibilities admirably and, while others have referred to them, I would especially mention in this context his involvement with European economic affairs and his care towards graduate supervision.

Keith was appointed senior lecturer at Warwick in 1966, only one year after the University's first intake of students. He had had a brief but spectacular career at Manchester: he was appointed to an assistant lectureship there in 1961 straight from completing his doctorate at Illinois, promoted to lecturer in 1963 and promoted again to senior lecturer in 1965. On appointment to Warwick he joined a group (it did not become a department till 1970) of six, including two professors. The further particulars, stated presciently:

> In the selection of staff the greatest weight will be attached to scholarship [which would nowadays be called 'research'] and to the capacity to contribute to the building up of a strong school of economics.

Keith fully met the criteria. Three years later the University was looking for a third professor to fill the Clarkson Chair of Industrial Economics. Keith had started academic life as an agricultural economist and it was his move to Warwick that had consolidated his transfer into the relatively new field of industrial economics. When referees were approached as to his suitability for a readership they reacted forthrightly one saying that Warwick had a reputation for avant-garde appointments and that he would place Cowling in that category.

Keith was appointed to the chair at the youthful age of 33 with the remit to develop the new specialism within the Department. He reacted with what was to become a customary vigour over staffing matters by demanding three or four new appointments from central University funds to support his field and, although in the end he had to be satisfied with only two, he could nevertheless claim to have made a good start.

Some interesting academic work has been done on the taxonomy of disciplines and their tendency to fragment into sub disciplines and into 'hard' and 'soft' dimensions (Becher and Kogan, 1992 and Becher and Trowler, 2001) and it would not be unfair to say that whether as a result of academic competition amongst the sub-specialisms, or personalities, or the disturbed atmosphere of student revolt within the University, the Department was not at this time a happy place. Keith, who at Manchester had a reputation for impatience with the old guard, rather emphasised internal divisions by leading one group of economists, including of course the industrial economists, off to the Students Union-run bar in the Sports Pavilion for 'beer and pie' lunches while another group frequented the (now defunct) senior common room. However, in 1971, just a year after being elected to the Clarkson Chair, Keith became a member of the Board of the Faculty of Social Studies, and was elected from the Board onto the Senate. In 1975 he became Chairman of the Department. He had by now moved into a much more central role in the Department and it was as Chairman and subsequently as 'professor responsible' (a role that needs some explanation) that he made his most considerable contribution to the standing of the Department.

Anyone wishing to read the debates that were taking place at that time in regard to the leadership of academic departments should refer to *Power and Authority in British Universities* (Moodie and Eustace, 1974) which was published in the period when the concept of the single permanent professorial head of department was giving way to electoral systems for departmental headships, rotation schemes among multi-professorial groups, and fixed terms for headships of three to five years. Warwick had anticipated this debate. When the first professors were appointed in 1964–65 it was not to departmental headships but to develop their subjects within a somewhat nebulous school structure. This structure rationalised itself initially into Schools of Studies to manage courses and Subject Schools to manage disciplines, that is staff, but in 1970 the Senate transmuted the latter into academic departments with three-year elected chairmen, and the Schools of Studies became sub-faculties which themselves were found to be otiose some years later. But the initial appointment of foundation professors to found 'subjects' and their later conversion into chairmen of departments for those subjects represented a critical contribution to Warwick's future success. Although all but one of the foundation professors chose not to continue as chairmen of departments after the 1970 decision, thus opening the way for the creation of an electoral system, elected chairmen felt a similar weight of responsibility for the subject or discipline which went beyond simply running a department in a reasonably consensual way.

By comparison, most of the wholly new university foundations of the 1960s (Sussex, East Anglia, Stirling, Ulster) opted for interdisciplinary schools where disciplines were dissipated in association with conjoint fields of interests. Schools of European Studies or Environmental Studies might have produced exciting undergraduate programmes but they did not have strongly defined research agendas, they appointed staff much more with a view to providing a broad spread of teaching options than to building up research groupings and they tended to promote leadership roles to manage teaching programmes rather than as at Warwick to develop a discipline. Warwick, while adopting an electoral basis for selecting its departmental chairs, qualified it by requiring the chairman to be of at least senior lecturer grade and in practice the majority were professors. When a non-professor was elected, a professor (the 'professor responsible') was appointed by the Professorial Board (only York amongst the new universities entrenched a professorial role in the governance of the university in this way) to be responsible for all staffing matters – promotions, study leave applications, and appointments. Obviously the role of the chairman or 'professor responsible' was especially important when it came to the appointment of professors, because of their presumed academic leadership role, and in internal promotion matters, because internal promotions to readerships and professorships tend to define the quality of departments. The chairman was, of course, ultimately responsible for making the necessary recommendations on all personal issues, but he or she was expected to work closely with other professors in the department. This ensured a consistency of view and a concentration on taking personnel decisions from a strongly academic and research-intensive standpoint. It was in these staffing areas that Keith excelled and set a pattern which the Department has followed to this day.

When Keith became chairman the other professors were Avinash Dixit, Alec Ford (who became a Pro-Vice-Chancellor and therefore did not play a large part in departmental matters), Alan Kirman and John Williamson. The first issue for Keith was the replacement of Graham Pyatt, who had gone to the World Bank. Keith immediately demonstrated the tenacity of purpose in netting the person the professorial group wanted which was to distinguish his six years as chairman and 'professor responsible'. The first appointment was to be Ken Wallis, then at LSE. Having established that there were particular reasons why an offer had to be placed in Wallis's hands by a certain date he persuaded the electoral board to hold an emergency meeting on a Saturday morning, and because Jim Mirrlees, one of the two external assessors, could not be present (the other was Rex Bergstrom) persuaded the Vice-Chancellor to agree that Sir John Hicks, who lived locally, should be drafted in at two days notice in his place to interview the candidate the Department wanted. (It was to be a critical appointment because Wallis was later himself to become a long-term and highly effective chairman of the Department.)

However, a single appointment at this level did not satisfy Keith because it left Pyatt's interests in development economics not covered and Keith not only persuaded the University that a second professorship had to be created but coupled with it that he had persuaded Nick Stern to leave Oxford to take it. There was determined resistance in the University's resource allocation body, the Estimates and Grants Committee, to allowing Economics to recruit yet another professor (it already had five). That Keith persuaded them is a tribute to his negotiating skills particularly as his economics colleague, Alec Ford, who chaired the committee, would have had to leave the room under the Committee's rules when the item was discussed. The minute that the new post be approved, was made:

> subject to the Department of Economics' acceptance of a worse staff student ratio in recognition of the high number of professors for one year and the deferral of the impending lecturer vacancy until September 1978. (Estimates and Grants Committee 8 March 1977)

and gives an indication of what Keith had to throw into the pot to get the post established. In the last year of his three-year chairmanship he recruited Marcus Miller in place of the departing John Williamson and, when he was 'professor responsible', Kevin Roberts. In the same month as the latter's appointment he was also on the electoral board which appointed Robert Skidelsky to a professorship in the Department of International Studies (he is now in the Economics Department). Keith was always anxious to have top-ranked economists as external assessors to electoral boards not only to give their views on paper but also to attend the interviews, and the names of Mirrlees, Hahn, Bergstrom and Goodhart recur. He was also keen to secure very strong internal membership of electoral boards: the board for Miller, already a professor at Manchester, comprised, for example, the Vice-Chancellor, as always in the chair, three economists – Cowling, Dixit and Wallis, and two professors from other departments, Hugh Clegg and Christopher Zeeman, both very eminent in their fields.

Another important characteristic of Keith's period as chairman/'professor responsible', and something which was continued under Wallis, was a toughness in regard to internal promotions; indeed in the period up to 1986 only two members of staff in the Department were promoted to Readerships: Norman Ireland and Paul Stoneman, and only one to a personal professorship: Jesus Seade. This was not necessarily an internally popular policy but laid down an important marker as to the kinds of people Warwick wanted to recruit at the most senior level. Good departments are not built overnight, which is why so many universities fail when they try to achieve quick fixes for the RAE, but rather by being selective in appointments over a long period, by ensuring that working conditions in the department and relationships between senior and junior colleagues encourage high quality performance and by strong intellectual leadership. Keith's period as chairman, coming after the departure of some senior figures and some political turmoil generally in the University, set an ambitious course from which the Department has not deviated, and his determination to attract the highest calibre professoriate (and his ruthless manipulation of the procedures to achieve it) laid the foundations of the Department as it is today.

Keith's contributions to the University were certainly not, however, limited to helping build a very successful Department: he was a member of

Senate for 21 of his 36 years service, serving from 1972–73 to 1977–78 and then, after a break, from 1985–98 to 2001–2. During all of this time he was a member of the Board of the Faculty of Social Studies (representing the Economics Department) and it was always from the Board constituency that he was elected to Senate; in his last three years he was chairman of the Board. He served on the key academic resource allocation body, the Estimates and Grants Committee, during part of his first period on Senate, a sure mark of the confidence in which his judgement was held by his colleagues, and again from 1989–90 to 1992–93 and from 1999–2000 to 2001–02. He would certainly have served for longer in the earlier period had not his economist colleague Alec Ford been appointed Pro-Vice-Chancellor and chairman of the Committee and the rules forbade two people from the same department serving. At various times he served on the Committee on Chairmen of Departments which watched over and occasionally intervened in the process of electing chairmen of departments, chaired the Higher Degrees Committee, sat on the University's Finance and General Purposes Committee, the Library Committee, the Academic Policy Committee and the Strategy Committee and, until its abolition in 1998, was a regular attender at the meetings of the Professorial Board.

As with the headship of departments, university governance and management has changed enormously over the period of Keith's involvement. Unlike the civic universities Warwick had never had a traditional senate on which all heads of departments and professors sat *ex-officio*, but from the beginning had had an elected senate with representation elected from the Professorial Board, the Faculty Boards and the Assembly (the body of all academic staff). And its numbers were restricted to around 35–40 rather than the 100 or so which could find itself brought together at say Leeds (Halsey and Trow, 1971; Moodie and Eustace op. cit). When Keith first joined the senate in 1971 it was still possible for Halsey and Trow to write of UK universities that: 'not too much must be made of formal constitutions. In practice the effective ruling body of all the modern universities is the senate' (Halsey and Trow, 1971, p. 111). This statement, however, ignored the role of the council, the formal governing body, which it regarded as irrelevant to the real running of the university.

The collapse of the quinquennial funding system and the end of the 'golden age' of state funding from 1945 to 1974 (Shattock, 2002) meant that university governance was coming under financial pressures it had not had to face since the 1920s and 1930s, long before Warwick had ever been dreamed of. The Jarratt Report (CVCP, 1985) sought under the post-Thatcher marketisation of higher education to re-balance key decision-making power away from senates and back to councils. In practice the effect of this was often to reinforce the powers of the executive, the vice-chancellor, designated by Jarratt as 'the chief executive' of the university. Jarratt implied that traditional senates were too protective of academic self interest to cope with conditions of financial stringency and argued that the legal powers of lay-dominated university councils had to be reinvoked. This argument was advanced on a false analogy comparing governing bodies with company boards; the analogy was reinforced by the Thatcher government in relation to the governance structure of the former polytechnics, created universities in 1992, and in the Report of the National Inquiry into Higher Education (the Dearing Report) (HMSO, 1997).

At Warwick one strand of the 1970s 'troubles' lay in a conflict between the council and the senate, which the senate effectively won, but one of the outcomes, initially designed to reinforce senate powers at the expense of the vice-chancellor's, was the Steering Committee, with its almost day-to-day involvement in overall institutional decision making. Another was the reinforcement of the standing of the Estimates and Grants Committee chaired by a pro-vice-chancellor, not the vice-chancellor, as the body accountable to the senate for the allocation of resources to academic departments, and charged to do so on the basis of senate policy rather, than was often the case in other institutions, on the hunch, whim or poor individual judgement of a powerful vice-chancellor. The effectiveness of these two bodies over the years have had a significant impact on the University's ability to weather financial storms, to continue to take new initiatives and to foster academic success. The council has never sought to establish the dominant role demanded by Jarratt (although its Finance and General Purposes Committee has always played a key role in the University's financial affairs) and the creation in the 1990s of a Strategy Committee as, effectively, a committee of the steering committee and the senior lay officers, has obviated any requirement for council itself to seek the kind of strategic role that the Dearing Report sought for governing bodies; it has also embedded the power of the academic community in the determination of the University's development. The creation of the Steering Committee itself has ensured that the executive powers of management, vested legally in the Vice-Chancellor (but effectively shared with other senior administrative officers), have been exercised in close consort with a powerful academic group. Burton Clark has identified as a key element in the successful modern university the creation of a 'central steering core' of senior academics and administrators, in place of the lone chief executive (Clark, 1998). Warwick's standing in the many league tables represents an endorsement of this ability to retain the academic community at the heart of its management while adapting its decision-making structures to the much more demanding financial and competitive climate of the 1990s.

Keith's involvement with these changes has been close and, as his membership of key institutional bodies indicates, he was himself part of a long process of institutional adaptation to the changing environment. From joining a senate which certainly saw itself as operating in the Trow/Halsey tradition, his last three years of full-time service was as a member of the University's inner cabinet, the Steering Committee, which effectively ran the University on behalf of the senate. In the modern era the sheer pressure of business, the repeated veiled diktats from government bodies, the competitive demands posed by the RAE and the research councils and the importance of regional involvement make it impossible to engage fully a senate of even only 35–40 members in the process of self government without leaving the operational choices to be taken by a smaller management group reporting to a governing body that is too distant from the action to exercise effective control. In most universities this management group has comprised either a vice-chancellor, acting on his or her own, or a management team answerable directly to the vice-chancellor. The Warwick Steering Committee, while it has sometimes seemed to some senate members to make the senate almost redundant, nevertheless represents the best route to ensuring that the academic community retains a form of engagement with the critical issues of university management. Clark (1998) called Warwick 'a model for universities in Europe' and his concept of the 'central steering core' was built around it.

Keith not only played a positive part in these changes but was also a distinctive voice. While always taking a 'university' view, he never lost sight of the fact that he was a representative of a Social Studies interest, and although supporting the need for effectiveness at the heart of the University's management he was a stern defender of senate's rights; he was always a good 'company man' but sometimes from an uncomfortably sceptical position. He was also interested in new initiatives: three perhaps stand out because they reflect different sides of his interests. The first was early in the 1980s when he found himself on an *ad hoc* strategy committee called together by the vice-chancellor in the wake of the 1981 cuts. Keith and the then Academic Registrar (myself) persuaded an unenthusiastic group that University decision making would be improved by the annual publication of a digest of statistics comparing the performance of departments against internal and national data. This proposal later crystallised into the *Academic Data Base*, published each November, which provides probably the most comprehensive data about an institution produced by any university in the UK. The value of the data is its transparency which both enables departments to compare their performance with other departments in the same institution and their league placing with their comparator departments nationally but also gives the University key data, impartially prepared, from which it can determine the University's strengths and weaknesses and overall performance. There is no doubt that the *Data Base* acts as a stimulus to better performance because it encourages the competitive spirit; perhaps more important it provides a trusted collection of data for the Estimates and Grants Committee and the Strategy Committee which removes much of the posturing and pretension which can be an inevitable concomitant to any internal bidding process for resources.

Keith's second initiative lay in a very different area. The sharp fall in the unit of resource of the state funding – some 45 per cent between 1985 and 2000 – was compensated for at Warwick by a decision to generate income from other sources. This programme has grown successfully, with the Economics Department, after a slow start, participating fully through its various postgraduate programmes. But in 1991 a small group of professors, Keith, George Bain (Business School), Kumar Bhattacharrya (Manufacturing Engineering) and Chris Thompson (French) took it upon themselves to push the University to try to fundraise in an American university sense. They persuaded the University, and a very reluctant vice-chancellor, to undertake a feasibility exercise by appointing a consultant to examine what steps needed to be taken. This was a valuable exercise because one of the findings was that while well known in Whitehall and within academic circles the University did not have a national profile with 'the man on the Clapham omnibus'. As a result the University established a Public Affairs Office, which led to a series of initiatives to raise the University's public image, and a Development Office, which through alumni funding alone has raised £1m to fund scholarships for students from disadvantaged backgrounds. Sadly, only now is the University finally taking major steps to mount a significant fundraising effort but the seeds of the current efforts lie in the work of the group referred to a decade ago.

My final example of Keith's positive role is his sponsoring of a proposal to set up an Institute of Advanced Studies in the Social Sciences at Warwick. In a way this is not a new idea for Keith because in 1971 he had been appointed Joint Director with Hugh Clegg of the Centre for Industrial, Economic and Business Research (CIEBR) which was a vehicle to encourage a collaboration between Business Studies (now the Warwick Business School) and Economics, a prototype of his present idea. However as Chairman of the Faculty Board and member of Strategy Committee he has made this project his own, and has put forward, undaunted by formidable opposition, not unlike that which opposed two professorial posts for the price of one a quarter of a century ago, a proposal for a £10m building to house the Institute. This is a fight he has yet to win but it is a tribute to his ambition for the University that he should still be looking forward not backwards, and tackling a new project of such magnitude.

In yet another way too Keith has perhaps returned to his roots. A trialist in his teens for Scunthorpe United FC, and a lifelong enthusiast for the beautiful game, he has found a link between his pastime and his academic life in some work on the economics of football which led to a paper 'Strategic Decisions and Public Interest: Modern Corporations and the Case of Football' (Branston et al., 1999). This paper argued for greater stakeholder involvement in the corporate governance of football clubs in order to protect the public interest (the particular example quoted was the possibility of BSkyB taking a major shareholding in Manchester United), an issue close to Keith's heart. But I suspect that the paper was also consistent with Keith's view of university governance and his role in it, even though, as a member of the Steering Committee, he finished up in the Directors' Box. One can only hope that his dissatisfaction with Coventry City FC's failures can be balanced with continued satisfaction in the progress of Warwick. Would he now like to play a stakeholder director role at Highfield Road?

Universities do not rise to the distinction Warwick has achieved without the contributions of a lot of people, and without good fortune and financial support. Warwick, in particular, has benefited from the contributions of its senior academics but few of them have devoted so much time and energy to the place as Keith. He has shown that it is possible to balance research, teaching and a major contribution to the interests of the institution in spite of the way these activities can compete with one another for time and energy; Warwick's future will depend on his successors showing a similar commitment. Too many universities have found ways to exclude senior academics from a significant voice in their institutions' future, and too many academics have acquiesced in their freedom from inconclusive meetings. No good university can survive for long without such an input and we should salute colleagues like Keith who have demonstrated that good teaching and good research are not incompatible with making a creative contribution to the management and governance of a university.

REFERENCES

Becher, T. and M. Kogan (1992), *Process and Structure in Higher Education*, London: Routledge, p. 149.

Becher, T. and P.R. Trowler (2001), *Academic Tribes and Territories*, SRHE/Open University Press, p. 186.

Branston, J.R., K. Cowling, J. Michie and R. Sugden (1999), 'Strategic Decisions and the Public Interest: Modern Corporations and the Case of Football', Paper given at EARIE, Torino, Italy.

Clark, B.R. (1998), *Creating Entrepreneurial Universities*, Pergamon.

Halsey, A.H. and M. Trow (1971), *The British Academics*, Faber and Faber.

Moodie, G.C. and R.B. Eustace (1974), *Power and Authority in British Universities*, London: Allen and Unwin.

Report of the National Committee (the Dearing Report) (1997), *Higher Education in the Learning Society*, HMSO, Chapter 15.

Report of the Steering Committee for Efficiency Studies in Universities (the Jarratt Report) (1985), CVCP, HMSO.

Shattock, M.L. (2002), 'Rebalancing modern concepts of university governance', *Higher Education Quarterly*, **56** (3), July.

Trow, M. (1974), 'Problems in the transition from elite to mass higher education', *Policies for Higher Education: General Report to the Conference on Future Structure in Post-Secondary Education*, Paris: OECD.

14. Keith Cowling's academic publications

BOOKS AND MONOGRAPHS

- *Industrial Policy in Europe: Theoretical Perspectives and Practical Proposals* (ed.), Routledge, 1999.
- *Europe's Economic Challenge: Analyses of Industrial Strategy and Agenda for the 90s* (ed. with P. Bianchi and R. Sugden), Routledge, 1994.
- *Beyond Capitalism: Towards a New World Economic Order* (with R. Sugden), Pinter, 1994.
- *Current Issues in Industrial Economic Strategy* (ed. with R. Sugden), Manchester University Press, 1992.
- *A New Economic Policy for Britain: Essays on the Development of Industry* (ed. with R. Sugden), Manchester University Press, 1990.
- *Industrial Policy after 1992: An Anglo-German Perspective* (ed. with H. Tomann), Anglo-German Foundation, 1990.
- *Transnational Monopoly Capitalism* (with R. Sugden), Wheatsheaf, 1987.
- *Out of Work: Perspectives on Mass Unemployment* (ed.), University of Warwick, 1984.
- *Monopoly Capitalism*, Macmillan, 1982. Revised Japanese edition, 1988.
- *Mergers and Economic Performance* (with others), Cambridge University Press, 1980.
- *Advertising and Economic Behaviour* (with J. Cable, M. Kelly and T. McGuiness), Macmillan, 1975.
- *Market Structure and Corporate Behaviour: Theory and Empirical Analysis of the Firm* (ed.), Gray-Mills, 1972.
- *Resource Structure of the Agricultural Industry: An Economic Analysis* (with D. Metcalf and A.J. Rayner), Pergamon, 1967.
- *Determinants of Wage Inflation in Ireland*, Economic Research Institute, Dublin, 1965.

ARTICLES AND PAPERS

- 'Revisiting the Roots of Japan's Economic Stagnation: The Role of the Japanese Corporation' (with Philip Tomlinson), *International Review of Applied Economics*, October 2002.
- 'The Problem of Regional "Hollowing Out" in Japan: Lessons for Industrial Policy', in R. Cheung et al. (eds), *Urban and Regional Prosperity in a Globalised New Economy* (with Philip Tomlinson), Edward Elgar, 2003.
- 'The Japanese Crisis: A Case of Strategic Failure' (with Philip Tomlinson), *Economic Journal*, June 2000, **110** (464) 358–81. (Selected as one of the top 25 articles in economics worldwide in the previous quarter and published in summary form as 'Japan's Hollowing Economy', *Economic Intuition*, Fall 2000. Also selected by Alan Wheatley (Reuters) for transmission from Tokyo (June 26) as *Exodus of Big Firms Blamed for Japan's Economic Woes*, 2000.)
- 'Declining Concentration in UK Manufacturing? A Problem of Measurement' (with Fahmi Mohd Yusof, and Guy Vernon), *International Review of Applied Economics*, **14** (1), January 2000.
- 'The Wealth of Localities, Regions and Nations: Developing Multinational Economies' (with Roger Sugden), *New Political Economy*, **4** (3), 1999, 361–78.
- 'A Reorientation of Industrial Policy: Horizontal Policies and Targeting', in Keith Cowling (ed.), *Industrial Policy in Europe* (with C. Oughton and R. Sugden), 1999, ibid.
- 'Modern Corporations and the Public Interest' (with R. Branston, N. Brown, J. Michie and R. Sugden), in S. Hamil, J. Michie and C. Oughton (eds), *The Business of Football: A Game of Two Halves*, Mainstream Publishing, Edinburgh, 1999.
- 'Technology Policy: Strategic Failures and the Need for a New Direction', in Jonathan Michie and John Grieve-Smith, *Globalization, Growth and Governance* (with Roger Sugden), Oxford University Press, 1998, pp. 239–62.
- 'The Essence of the Modern Corporation: Markets, Strategic Decision-Making and the Theory of the Firm' (with Roger Sugden), *The Manchester School*, **66** (1), January 1998.
- 'Strategic Trade Policy Reconsidered: National Rivalry vs Free Trade vs International Cooperation' (with Roger Sugden), *Kyklos*, **51** (1998), Fasc. 3, 339–57.
- 'Politicas Estructurales Proactivas para las "Regiones Menos Favourecidas"; Estrategia Industrial en la Union Europea y el

Mercosur' (with R. Sugden), *Contabilidad, Auditória e Impuestos*, Santiago-Chile, No. 63, July, 76–104, 1997.

- 'Capacity, Transnationals and Industrial Strategy (with R. Sugden), in J. Michie and J. Grieve Smith (eds), *Creating Industrial Capacity – Towards Full Employment*, Oxford University Press, 1996.
- 'Beyond Capitalism and State Socialism' (with R. Sugden), in J. Hölscher, A. Jacobsen, H. Tomann and H. Weisfeld (eds), *Economic Policy and Development Strategies in Central and Eastern Europe*, Metropolis, 1996.
- 'Productivity Growth, Product Quality and the Production Process' (with G. Vernon), in D. Mayes (ed.), *Sources of Productivity Growth*, Cambridge University Press, 1996.
- 'Reflections on the Privatisation Issue', in H.J. Chang and P. Nolan (eds), *The Transformation of the Communist Economics: Against the Mainstream*, Macmillan, 1995, pp. 162–76.
- 'Monopoly Capitalism and Stagnation', *Review of Political Economy*, **7** (4), 1995, 430–46.
- 'Structural Adjustment in Industry: The Roles of Government and Corporations within the Developed Countries: An Introduction', Trade and Development Board, UNCTAD, Geneva, March 1995.
- 'A more Creative Role for Industrial Policy', *Journal of Business Economics*, **1** (1), 1994, 15–17.
- 'Moving Away from Monopoly Capitalism: A New Focus for Industrial Policy', in D. Coates and J. Hillard, *Causes of UK Economic Under-Performance: The Key Texts*, Brighton, Harvester-Wheatsheaf, 1994.
- 'The Strategic Approach to Economic and Industrial Policy', in D. Coates and J. Hillard, *Causes of UK Economic Under-Performance: The Key Texts*, Brighton, Harvester-Wheatsheaf, 1994.
- 'The Limitations of the Transaction Approach to Organisation' (with R. Sugden), in C. Pitelis (ed.), *Transaction Costs, Market and Hierarchies*, Routledge, 1994.
- 'Human Resources and Industrial Development: New Social Roles' (with R. Sugden), *International Journal of Technology Management*, **9** (3/4), 1994, 287–96.
- 'Industrial Strategy: Guiding Principles and European Context' (with R. Sugden), in P. Bianchi, K. Cowling and R. Sugden (eds), *Human Factors in Organisational Design and Management – IV*, North Holland, 1994.
- 'Privatisieurrun, Demokratisierung und Effizienz', in J. Hölscher et al., *Bedingungen Ökonomischer Entwicklung in Zentralosteuropa*, Metropolis-Verlag, 1993, 252–72.

- 'Strategic Industrial Policy: Relevance and Form', in K. Hughes (ed.), *The Future of UK Competitiveness and the Role of Industrial Policy*, Policy Studies Institute, 1993.
- 'A Strategy for Industrial Development as a Basis for Regulation' (with R. Sugden), in R. Sugden (ed.), *Industrial Economic Regulation: A Framework and Exploration*, Routledge, 1993, 44–62.
- 'Industrial Strategy: a Missing Link in British Economic Policy' (with R. Sugden), *Oxford Review of Economic Policy*, **9** (3), Autumn 1993, 83–100.
- 'Short-termism, Transnationalism and the British Economy', submission to the Enquriy of the Employment Committee, House of Commons, January 1993.
- 'Professor Bianchi's Comment: A Rejoinder' (with R.A. Naylor), *Metroeconomica*, **43**, 1992, 327–8.
- 'Norms, Sovereignty and Regulation' (with R.A. Naylor), *Metroeconomica*, **43**, 1992, 177–204.
- 'An Autobiographical Sketch', in P. Arestis and M. Sawyer (eds), *A Biographical Dictionary of Dissenting Economists*, Edward Elgar, 1992, pp. 102–8 (2nd Edition, 2000).
- 'Industrial Integration, East and West. Planning the Market Economy', in J. Davis (ed.), *The Economic Surplus in Advanced Economies*, Edward Elgar, 1992, pp. 177–88.
- 'Monopoly Capitalism Revisited', in A. Del Monte (ed.), *Recent Developments in the Theory of Industrial Organization*, Macmillan, 1992, pp. 148–61.
- 'Industrial Policy and the Interaction between Large and Small Firms', in C. Tolomelli, *Le Politiche Industriali Regionali: Experienze, Sogatti, Modelli*, CLUEB, Bologna, 1992, pp. 141–4.
- 'Industrial Integration, East and West', *Kurswechsel*, special edition on Eastern Europe, Spring 1991, 1–11.
- 'The Modern European Corporation: Transnational and Decentralized?', in D. Sadowski (ed.), *Employers Associations in Europe – Policy and Organisation*, Kluwer, 1991, pp. 100–24.
- 'The Strategic Approach', in K. Cowling and R. Sugden (eds), *A New Economic Policy for Britain: Essays on the Development of Industry*, Manchester University Press, 1990.
- 'Merger and Monopoly Policy' (with M. Sawyer), in K. Cowling and R. Sugden (eds), *A New Economic Policy for Britain: Essays on the Development of Industry*, Manchester University Press, 1990.
- 'New Directions for Industrial Policy', in K. Cowling and H. Tomann (eds), *Industrial Policy after 1992: An Anglo-German Perspective*, Anglo-German Foundation, 1990.

- 'A New Industrial Strategy: Preparing Europe for the Turn of the Century', *International Journal of Industrial Organization*, June 1990, 165–84.
- 'Exchange Rate Adjustment and Oligopoly Pricing Behaviour' (with R. Sugden), *Cambridge Journal of Economics*, **13**, 1989, 373–93.
- 'A Policy for Nurturing a Small Firms Economy', *Review of Industrial Economics*, 1989/4, 67–72.
- 'Merger Policy and Industrial Policy', *Northwestern Journal of International Law and Business*, **9**, 1989, 599–604.
- 'Merger Policy, Industrial Strategy and Democracy', *British Review of Economic Issues*, Autumn 1987, 29–50.
- 'An Industrial Strategy for Britain: The Nature and Role of Planning', *International Review of Applied Economics*, January 1987, 1–22.
- 'Market Exchange and the Concept of a Transnational Corporation: Analysing the Nature of the Firm' (with R. Sugden), *British Review of Economic Issues*, Spring 1987, 57–68.
- 'Internationalisation of Production and Deindustrialisation', in A. Amin and J. Goddard (eds), *Technological Change, Industrial Restructuring and Regional Development*, Allen and Unwin, 1985, pp. 23–40.
- 'The Political Economy of Oligopoly', *Economics*, Winter 1985, 147–52.
- 'Planning the British Economy: Some Comments', *Economics of Planning*, **19** (3), 1985, 145–50.
- 'Economic Obstacles to Democracy', in R.C.O. Matthews (ed.), *Economy and Democracy*, Macmillan, August 1985.
- 'Advertising and the Economic System', *Economic Review*, May 1985, 2–6.
- 'Responses to Unemployment: An Alternative Economic Strategy', in *Out of Work: Perspectives of Mass Unemployment*, University of Warwick, 1984.
- 'Excess Capacity and the Degree of Collusion: Oligopoly Behaviour in the Slump', *Manchester School*, December 1983, 341–59.
- 'Advertising and Labour Supply: Work Week and Work Year in U.S. Manufacturing Industries, 1919–76' (with J. Brack), *Kyklos*, 1983, 285–303.
- 'Wage Share, Concentration and Unionism' (with I. Molho), *Manchester School*, June 1982, 99–115.
- 'Generalized Regression Estimation from Grouped Observations: A Generalization and an Application to the Relationship between Diet

and Mortality' (with D. Leech), *Journal of Royal Statistical Society*, Series A, 1982, 208–23.

- 'Monopolies and Mergers Policy: A New Perspective', *Socialist Economic Review*, Merlin Press, 1982.
- 'Nationalised Industries and Energy Policy', *Socialist Economic Review*, 1981, 287–9.
- 'Price Formation and Import Penetration in U.K. Manufacturing Industry' (with A. Murfin), *Recherches Economiques de Louvain*, September 1981, 307–33.
- 'Oligopoly, Distribution and the Rate of Profit', *European Economic Review*, 1981, 195–224. (Reprinted in M. Sawyer (ed.), *Post Keynesian Economics*, Edward Elgar, 1988.)
- 'The Social Costs of Monopoly Power Revisited' (with D. Mueller), *Economic Journal*, September 1981, 721–5.
- 'Advertising and the Aggregate Demand for Cigarettes: A Reply to Johnston' (with T. McGuiness), *European Economic Review*, 1980.
- 'Monopoly, Welfare and Distribution', in Artis and Nobay, *Contemporary Economic Analysis: A.U.T.E. Conference 1977*, Blackwell, 1978.
- 'The Social Costs of Monopoly Power' (with D. Mueller), *Economic Journal*, December 1978. Reprinted in J.M. Buchanan, R.D. Tollison and G. Tullock (eds), *Toward a Theory of the Rent-seeking Society*, 1980; *The Modern Corporation: Profits, Power, Growth and Performance*, D.M. Mueller (ed.), Wheatsheaf, 1986; and *Neoclassical Microeconomics*, R.E. Kuenne (ed.), Edward Elgar, 1988.
- 'Price–Cost Margins and Market Structure' (with M. Waterson), *Economica*, August 1976.
- 'On the Theoretical Specification of Industrial Structure–Performance Relationships', *European Economic Review*, July 1976.
- 'Advertising and the Aggregate Demand for Cigarettes' (with A.J. McGuiness), *European Economic Review*, July 1976.
- 'Optimality in Firms' Advertising Policies: An Empirical Analysis', in K. Cowling (ed.), *Market Structure and Corporate Behaviour: Theory and Empirical Analysis of the Firm*, Gray-Mills, 1972.
- 'Hedonic Price Indexes for U.K. Cars' (with J. Cubbin), *Economic Journal*, September 1972.
- 'Price, Quality and Advertising Competition: An Econometric Analysis of the U.K. Car Market' (with J. Cubbin), *Economica*, 1971.
- 'Price, Quality and Market Share' (with A.J. Rayner), *Journal of Political Economy*, **78** (5), November/December 1970.
- 'Demand for Farm Tractors: A Comparison of the U.S. and U.K.'

(with A.J. Rayner), *American Journal of Agricultural Economics*, November 1968.

- 'Labour Transfer from Agriculture: A Regional Analysis' (with D. Metcalf), *Manchester School*, March 1968.
- 'Wage Inflation in the U.K.: A Regional Analysis' (with D. Metcalf), *Bulletin of the Oxford Institute of Economics and Statistics*, March 1967.
- 'Demand for a Durable Input: the U.K. Market for Farm Tractors' (with A.J. Rayner), *Review of Economics and Statistics*, November 1967.
- 'Regional Wage Inflation in the U.K.' (with D. Metcalf), *District Bank Review*, June 1967.
- 'Demand for Fertilizer: U.K. 1949–65' (with D. Metcalf), *Journal of Agricultural Economics*, 1967.
- 'Determinants of Wage Inflation in Scottish Agriculture' (with D. Metcalf), *Manchester School*, June 1966.
- 'Exports, Imports and Consumption of Agricultural Products in a Rapidly Growing Economy: the Case of Libya' (with H. Zlitni), *Farm Economist*, December 1966.
- 'An Analysis of the Determinants of Wage Inflation in Agriculture', *Manchester School*, June 1965.
- 'Supply Responses on Dairy Farms in North-East Illinois' (with C.B. Baker and M.B. Langham), Research Bulletin, University of Illinois, 1965.
- 'Milk Supply Response: An Inter Breed Analysis' (with T.W. Gardner), *The Statistician*, **14** (3), 1964.
- 'Analytical Models for Estimating Supply Relationships in the Agricultural Sector: A Survey and Critique' (with T.W. Gardner), *Journal of Agricultural Economics*, **XV** (3), June 1963 (French translation in *Economie Rurale*, 1964).
- 'Labour Input in Milk Production: An Analysis of the Qualitative and Quantitative Determinants', *Farm Economist*, **4**, 1963.
- 'Producer Behaviour in the Choice of Sugar Beet Varieties: Comparisons of Game Theoretic Solutions with Actual Behaviour' (with R.J. Perkins), *Bulletin of the Oxford Institute of Statistics*, **25** (3), 1963.
- 'A Polyperiod Model for Estimating the Supply of Milk' (with C.B. Baker), *Agricultural Economics Research*, **XV** (1), January 1963.

Index